D1570257

# PRAISE FOR *WORLD WAR IN SYRIA*

"Impressive in its scholarship, pondered in its judgements, above all searing in its dissection of Western powers' war on Syria waged over many decades, the book is a must-have on the bookshelves of any serious fair-minded student of Syria."

> – Peter Ford, British Ambassador to Syria from 2003–2006.

"The most detailed history of the war in Syria so far, providing a richness of highly interesting details, as well as a critical analysis of its complex international and domestic dimensions, rarely encountered in other Western publications."

> – Nikolaos van Dam, former Special Envoy for Syria, 2015–16. Ambassador of the Netherlands to Iraq, Egypt, Turkey, Germany and Indonesia, 1988–2010. Author of *Destroying a Nation: The Civil War in Syria.*

"A. B. Abrams explores the widening scope of the Syrian conflict in his important book. Solving Syria's civil war will require a regional approach engaging stakeholders whose interests are fundamentally opposed."

> – David L. Phillips, Senior Adviser in the Clinton, Bush, and Obama State Departments. Former Senior Fellow at the Atlantic Council. Director of the Program on Peace-Building and Human Rights, Columbia University ISHR.

"Abrams is a meticulous guide to the labyrinth of Syria's modern political history."

> – Richard W. Murphy. U.S. Ambassador to Syria, 1974 to 1978. Consul in Aleppo, Syria, 1960–63.

"A. B. Abrams has written an extremely informative and illuminating account on the international dimension of the origins, outbreak and evolution of the Syrian conflict. His empirically rich analysis in this nuanced and comprehensive study make it one of the best books, if not the best book, written about the Syrian crisis. This book is a MUST read for anyone who wants to understand the Syrian conflict, the Middle East, and the role of the great powers in the region."

> – Jubin Goodarzi, Professor and Deputy Head of International Relations, Webster University, Geneva. Former consultant and political adviser on Middle Eastern affairs for the UNHCR. He formerly held posts at Chatham House, CSIS and the Ford Foundation.

"The countries intervening in Syria without approval of the Security Council under Chapter VII were consciously violating international law. Abrams' intensive, highly-documented work provides an excellent resource for understanding the historical and present dimensions of the conflict."

- Alfred De Zayas, Professor, Geneva School of Diplomacy. Former UN Independent Expert on the Promotion of a Democratic and Equitable International Order.

"A. B. Abrams has written a timely, balanced and insightful account of the Syrian war. The book is well-researched and provides both the necessary historic context but reveals also present-day drivers that resulted in Syria becoming a theater for regional and global competition for influence."

- Alex Vatanka, senior fellow in Middle East Studies at the U.S. Air Force Special Operations School. Senior fellow and director of the Iran program at the Middle East Institute, Washington D.C. Adjunct professor at Wright-Patterson Air Force Base.

"An impressive and comprehensive feat of in-depth research, most notably concerning developments in political and military strategy of international actors in the Syrian war. The author provides a unique and sophisticated chronological overview of pre-war socio-political and economic realities in Syria, a detailed description of the conflict over its entire duration, and an outline of possible post-war scenarios. An exceptional feature of the book lies in the author's profound understanding of how supplies of specific armaments on both sides influenced the course of the war. *World War in Syria* is an excellent work, highly beneficial for war and security studies professionals and students, as well as for historians, international relations scholars and the general public wishing to better understand the effects of external involvement on the development and outcome of the Syrian conflict."

- Daria Vorobyeva, Centre for Syrian Studies, University of St. Andrews. Co-Author of *The War for Syria: Regional and International Dimensions of the Syrian Uprising.*

"A superb narrative dealing with tactical, operational and strategic matters of that war, in as fine military history writing as any by the first rate military historian, and also shows a horrendous toll this war exerted on the people of Syria. It is a superb book which makes a great contribution to the field of study of the Middle East and of global politics and balance of forces."

- Andrei Martyanov, former naval officer. Frequent contributor to the U.S. Naval Institute Blog. Author of *The (Real) Revolution in Military Affairs.*

# WORLD WAR IN SYRIA

## A.B. ABRAMS

Clarity Press, Inc.

Clarity Press, Inc.
2625 Piedmont Rd. NE, Ste. 56
Atlanta, GA 30324, USA
https://www.claritypress.com

# TABLE OF CONTENTS

# ABBREVIATIONS

AKP – Adalet ve Kalkınma Partisi (Justice and Development Party) (Turkey)

APC – Armoured Personnel Carrier

ASPR – Arab Socialist Resurrectionist Party

CIA – Central Intelligence Agency

CONEFO – Conference of the New Emerging Forces

DPRK – Democratic People's Republic of Korea

FSA – Free Syrian Army

GANEFO – Games of New Emerging Forces

GNA – Government of National Accord (Libya)

GDP – Gross Domestic Product

IRGC – Iranian Revolutionary Guards Corps

IO – Information Operations

IS – Islamic State

ISI – Inter-Services Intelligence (Pakistan)

MaRV – Manoeuvring Re-Entry Vehicle

NATO – North Atlantic Treaty Organisation

NGO – Non-Government Organisation

NSyA – New Syrian Army

OPCW – Organisation for the Prohibition of Chemical Weapons

PKI – Partai Komunis Indonesia (Communist Party of Indonesia)

PKK – Partiya Karkerên Kurdistanê (Kurdistan Workers' Party)

PNAS – Proceedings of the National Academy of Sciences

PUK – Patriotic Union of Kurdistan

PYD – Partiya Yekîtiya Demokrat (Democratic Union Party) (Syria)

SAA – Syrian Arab Army

SANA – Syrian Arab News Agency

SDF – Syrian Democratic Forces

SMC – Supreme Military Council (Free Syrian Army)

TINO – Turkish National Intelligence Organization

UAE – United Arab Emirates

UAV – Unmanned Aerial Vehicle

UN – United Nations

UNESCO – United Nations Educational, Scientific and Cultural Organization

UNSC – United Nations Security Council

US – United States

USSR – Union of Soviet Socialist Republics

YPG – Yekîneyên Parastina Gel (People's Protection Units)

# TERMS

**Arab Middle East:** The Middle East excluding non-Arab states Turkey, Iran and Israel.

**Gulf States:** The countries of the Gulf Cooperation Council including Saudi Arabia, Oman, the United Arab Emirates, Bahrain, Qatar and Kuwait. In the context of the Syrian War it will refer primarily to the three parties which heavily involved themselves in the conflict – Saudi Arabia, Qatar and Kuwait.

**Islamist:** Referring to groups or individuals as Islamist or Islamic is based on their own self professed ideological affiliations, rather than a judgement passed on their adherence to Muslim teachings or Islamic law.

**Middle East:** Countries on and immediately surrounding the Arabian Peninsula in southwest Asia including Iran, Iraq, Syria, Turkey, Jordan, Israel and Palestine, Egypt, Saudi Arabia, Yemen, Oman, the United Arab Emirates, Bahrain, Qatar and Kuwait.

**Middle East and North Africa:** Region encompassing the Middle East, as well as the African states of Morocco, Algeria, Tunisia, Libya and Sudan.

**Soviet Bloc:** Soviet-led alliance of socialist states including Warsaw Pact members Bulgaria, Czechoslovakia, East Germany, Hungary, Poland and Romania as well as the USSR itself and the Mongolian People's Republic. All but the USSR had seen socialist parties initially placed in power by Moscow, received consider-able Soviet aid and would later collapse with the Cold War's end.

**Terrorist:** As this work is not written from the perspective of any particular country or region, only those groups or organisations classified as terrorist in nature by the United Nations will be referred to as such – as opposed to those termed terrorists uni-laterally by a particular state (the latter can be confusing – Iran for example unilaterally designates the U.S. Military and the Pentagon as terrorist groups, while the U.S. unilaterally designates branches of the Iranian armed forces and the Iranian-aligned Lebanese political party Hezbollah as terror groups).

**Western Bloc:** Alliance of leading Western powers established in the early Cold War and led by the United States. The founding members of the North Atlantic Treaty Organisation including Belgium, Britain, Canada, Denmark, France, Germany, Italy, Norway, the Netherlands, Luxembourg, Portugal and the United States, as well as Five Eyes members Australia and New Zealand. All but Canada, Australia, New Zealand, Luxemburg and Norway were major colonial powers – with these having spent extended periods incorporated into larger European empires.

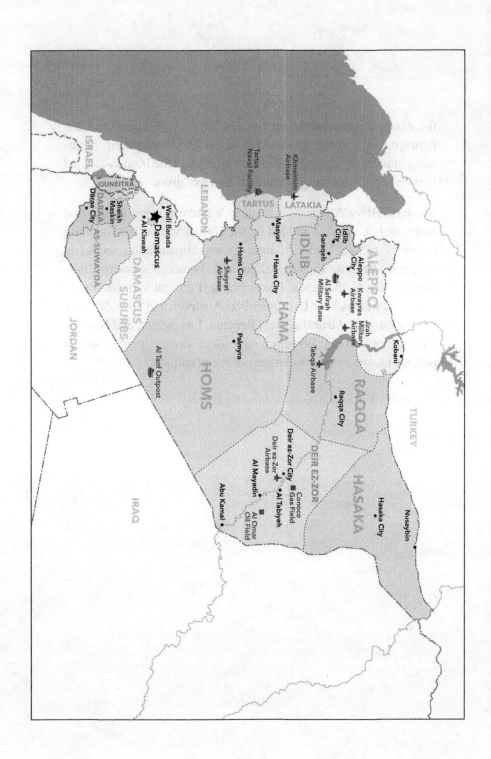

# Chapter 1

# Why Syria? How Conflict with the West and Israel Made Damascus a Target for Regime Change

## Origins of Syria's Conflict with the Western World

The purpose of this work is to offer an assessment of the Syrian War and the nature of international involvement therein. To this end background regarding Syria's place in both the Middle East and the wider world, the policies of its government, and the history of its foreign relations, all provide vital context.

Syria was one of the first French colonial possessions to gain independence under the immediate post–Second World War wave of decolonisation. A strong nationalist movement in the country staged widespread protests against the re-imposition of Paris' rule from May 1945, which in some instances saw French military personnel violently targeted. Protests were met with machine gun, mortar and heavy artillery fire and indiscriminate bombing raids targeting three of Syria's main cities – Damascus, Homs and Hama.[1] This closely resembled the way France would also respond to demands for independence in Algeria[2] and Indochina,[3] where French misconduct was if anything far more severe. Widespread massacres of the civilian population continued for several days, and in Damascus alone the death toll within three days had surpassed 800 residents, with many mutilated by French soldiers and buried in mass graves.[4] The severity of the attacks, carried out to teach the Syrians "a good lesson" according the French commanding general,[5] was widely attested to by foreign observers. A Soviet citizen who had taken shelter at Damascus' Orient Palace Hotel, who had lived through the battle of Stalingrad, remarked that he had "never been through such an experience as this."[6] British observers painted a very similar picture,[7] with Minister to the Levant Terence Shone reporting "indiscriminate shelling" and soldiers "behaving like madmen, spraying the streets with machine-gun fire from vehicles and buildings." "The French have instituted nothing short of a reign of terror in Damascus," he concluded.[8] British intervention to prevent further massacres, which risked turning public opinion across the Arab world decisively against the European colonial powers, was paired by considerable pressure from Syrian nationalist groups, forcing Paris to eventually cede its mandate over the country. The last French forces left in April 1946, a date celebrated to this day as the beginning of Syria's practical independence.

Syria experienced a volatile early history as an independent state, including a brief but disastrous war with European Jewish settlers in neighbouring Palestine, which Syria entered alongside Egypt, Jordan and Iraq in 1948. The war resulted in the creation of the State of Israel as a Jewish and demographically overwhelmingly European country on Syria's western border, part of which was on territory which was historically considered part of Syria itself in pre-colonial times.[9] Calls within the early Israeli leadership to expand the state and eventually create a 'greater Israel,' which would encompass all of Syrian territory and those of many if its neighbours, led the new Western-aligned state to be perceived as a major long term threat.[10] Israel would thus emerge as a leading adversary for Damascus over the coming decades.

Multiple subsequent coups and countercoups were launched in Syria over the next 22 years, with three occurring in March, August and December 1949 followed by further coups in 1954, 1961, 1963 and 1970. The first was engineered by the U.S. Central Intelligence Agency (CIA) against the government of President Shukri Al Quwatli.[11] The administration was targeted primarily due to its lack of enthusiasm for a major American project, the Trans-Arabian Pipeline, which was intended to transport Saudi Arabian oil to Europe through Syrian territory. Quwatli's replacement, a general with a "strong pro-French orientation" named Husni Al Zaim, ran what Pentagon cables described as an "army supported dictatorship" with a "strong anti-Soviet attitude."[12] His government approved the pipeline in its first week in power, but was overthrown five months later by colonel Sami Al Hinnawi whose short-lived administration was itself toppled by another colonel, Adib Shishakli, in December. Shishakli's pro-Western government lasted four years before a coup deposed it and restored national elections. Al Quwatli was then re-elected in 1955, and his administration distanced itself from the West as a result of the CIA's involvement in the original March 1949 coup. Officially, however, the Syrian government positioned itself as a neutral party in the Cold War.

Tensions with Israel remained high following the war of 1948, with Syrian forces poorly equipped to guard against potential future threats. The new Jewish state quickly emerged as a major regional power, receiving not only large quantities of arms from France[13] but also considerable financial and technical support from across the Western world.[14] While Israeli activities were seen as a persistent danger to Syrian security, the most serious threat came from the Western Bloc nations led by the United States. Western powers had the capabilities needed to conduct heavy-handed interventions overseas, and widely targeted governments across the world deemed insufficiently anti-Soviet or otherwise unfavourable to Western interests. A wide range of means from assassination, destabilisation and economic warfare to outright invasion were employed to achieve Western ends. Pressure faced by Syria from the U.S. and its allies was thus far from atypical, with states stepping out of line with the Western-led order from Cuba[15] and North Korea to Indonesia,[16] Ghana[17] and North Vietnam among many others all placed under immense pressure by the Western Bloc.

U.S. Secretary of State John Foster Dulles proclaimed in 1956: "neutrality has increasingly become an obsolete conception, and, except under very exceptional circumstances, it is an immoral and short-sighted conception."[18] The message was clear – America and its allies would not tolerate those states which did not firmly align themselves against the Soviet Union and with the Western world. While the Soviet Union showed no such intolerance towards neutral states in the third world, the contrast between this and the absolutism of Western policy led neutral states to consistently be forced to align themselves with Moscow for protection against Western threats. Thus of the five founding members of the Non-Aligned Movement – Indonesia, Yugoslavia, India, Egypt and Ghana – none were ever attacked by the USSR but all without exception came under attack by the Western Bloc. This came either through extensive support for coups by the CIA (Ghana,[19] Indonesia[20]), by direct Western military intervention (Yugoslavia, Egypt, Indonesia), or by assassination attempts against their leaders (India in 1955, Indonesia in the 1950s and 1962, Egypt in 1957).[21] Syria's unwillingness under multiple successive governments to become a Western client state and abandon its independence in foreign policymaking made a close security partnership between Moscow and Damascus inevitable – as was also the case for Jakarta, Delhi, Cairo and most others which resisted assimilation into the Western sphere of influence.

Syria stood out among the Middle Eastern states and more generally in the Arab world as one of the very few which refused U.S. military aid. Such aid generally came with multiple strings attached including obligations to contribute to the 'defence of the free world,' shun ties to the Soviet Bloc countries and accept the presence of Western military advisors on one's soil. Damascus, much like other non-aligned nations such as Indonesia,[22] was sharply criticised in the West for allowing leftist elements to take part in its political process. This contrasted strongly with practices in the countries of the self-proclaimed 'free world' such as the Philippines[23] and South Korea. The latter saw suspected leftists placed in concentration camps, executed alongside their families and children, and buried in mass graves, often under Western supervision.[24] Such conduct was looked upon favourably in the U.S., with the American-installed government in Seoul killing 2% of its population at a conservative estimate from 1946–1949 when purging leftist and anti-American elements.[25] Similar mass killings were carried out in a number of countries targeting those whose political affiliations were deemed unfavourable for Western interests. The most extreme case was Indonesia, where a coup was engineered to bring a pro-Western government to power in 1965 after which U.S., Dutch, British and Australian intelligence supported the killings of an estimated 500,000–3 million suspected leftists, leftist sympathisers and their families.[26] Such countries were repeatedly held up in the West as dependable members of the 'free world' and referred to as democratic. While these were more extreme examples, 'free' nations in the Western sphere of influence were expected to take a hard line against leftist or pro-Soviet political activities within their borders, and Damascus became a target for its refusal to do so.

Strongly anti-communist sentiments and a McCarthyist atmosphere in the United States made any measure against communism widely acceptable particularly in the early Cold War years. This provided an effective pretext for hostile policies towards nationalist governments across the world which were outside the Western sphere of influence under the pretext that they were at risk of coming under communist influence, although most had simply rejected Western interference in their internal affairs but showed few real signs of possible communist takeover. Examples of non-communist nationalist governments targeted using such pretexts ranged from Indonesia[27] and Iran[28] to Congo[29] and Guatemala[30] among many others. It was thus consistent with this global trend for American reports to portray Syria, which stood out in the Middle East for its neutrality, its independence, and the absence of Western military personnel on its soil, as under a growing communist influence despite the fact that the communist party was never a leading political force in the country.

Reports from the U.S. National Security Council from 1955–56 warned regarding political trends in Syria: "If the popular leftward trend in Syria continues over any considerable period, there is a real danger that Syria will fall completely under left-wing control either by coup or usurpation of authority" … "the fundamental anti-U.S. and anti-West orientation of the Syrians is stimulated by inevitable political histrionics about the Palestine problem" … "Four successive short-lived governments in Syria have permitted continuous and increasing Communist activities" … "the Communists support the leftist cliques [in] the army" … "apathy

towards Communism on the part of politicians and army officers"
is a threat to security ... "the Arab Socialist Resurrectionist Party
(ASRP)" and "the Communist Party of Syria are capable of bringing about further deterioration of Syrian internal security" ... danger of ASRP "coup d'etat" and "increased Communist penetration
of government and army" ... "Of all the Arab states Syria is at the
present time the most wholeheartedly devoted to a neutralist policy
with strong anti-Western overtones" ... "If the present trend continues there is a strong possibility that a Communist-dominated
Syria will result, threatening the peace and stability of the area and
endangering the achievement of our objectives in the Near East"
... we "should give priority consideration to developing courses
of action in the Near East designed to affect the situation in Syria
and to recommending specific steps to combat communist subversion."[31] Similar warnings were conveyed by U.S. ambassador
to Syria James Moose Jr.,[32] and these conditions were more than
sufficient to be seen to necessitate decisive Western intervention
to 'correct' Syria's political process, much as was done in Korea,
Guatemala, Ghana, the Philippines and other non-Western states
with strong leftist or neutralist movements.[i]

Where there was a growing consensus in the United States
intelligence community on the need for action against Syria,
Britain was if anything even more decided that forceful Western
intervention was necessary. The British had established a base of
operations in the neighbouring Western-aligned kingdom of Iraq,
and placed considerable pressure on the U.S. to join their plans to
overthrow the government in Damascus, to which the CIA readily
assented.[33] Both Western allies were emboldened by the seamless
success of the coup they had engineered in Iran less than three

---

i   It was highly common at the time for states outside the Western sphere of
    influence to be labelled in the West as 'communist' or else under the threat of
    communist influence in order to provide pretext for attacks to impose Western
    control. As Guatemalan Foreign Minister Guillermo Toriello lamented as his
    country came under U.S. attack in 1953–54, the U.S. categorised "every
    manifestation of nationalism or economic independence, any desire for social
    progress" as 'communism.' (Blum, William, *Killing Hope: U.S. Military and
    C.I.A. Interventions Since World War II*, London, Zed Books, 2003 (Chapter
    10: Guatemala 1953–1954)).

years prior in August 1953, which had toppled its developmentalist non-aligned government. Iran's democratic credentials had meant little since its non-aligned and developmentalist policies contravened Western interests, and the country's vehemently pro-Western monarchy was subsequently reinstated.[34] Archibald B. Roosevelt Jr., grandson of the former U.S. President Theodore Roosevelt and a high-ranking officer in the CIA, played a key role in overseeing both coup attempts, and in Syria made multiple contacts within the country's right wing opposition. American support was pledged and considerable funds were provided to them to ensure a new government could be brought to power which was more amenable to Western interests. The date of the Syrian coup was repeatedly postponed, however, before being called off entirely by Roosevelt's local conspirators after the outbreak of the Suez Crisis and the Israeli invasion of Egypt. The CIA was accused by its furious local partners, falsely as it turned out, of having sought to time the Syrian government's overthrow to coincide with Israeli military action.[35]

Syria strongly supported the Egyptian position against the joint British, French and Israeli invasion in June 1956. When Egypt closed the Suez Canal by sinking ships loaded with cement, Syrian saboteurs, with their government's authorisation, destroyed pumping stations for the Iraq Petroleum Company's oil pipelines in Syria. This complemented the effects of the canal's closure by causing serious oil shortages in Western Europe, and the Syrian government simultaneously severed diplomatic relations with Britain.[36] In response to the growing perceived threat of Western or Israeli attack, as Egypt had just endured, Syria sought to bolster its defences by becoming one of the first Arab states to form military relations with the Soviet Union. While the Western world had for decades held an effective monopoly on arms sales to the Middle East, the rapid industrialization of the USSR in the 1930s had seen it emerge as a leading arms manufacturer with weaponry equalling and in many cases surpassing the quality of its Western counterparts.[37] The emergence of a major non-Western industrial economy with a world leading arms industry seriously undermined the centuries-old world order based on Western dominance, with significant implications across six continents, as Moscow provided weaponry to multiple states outside the Western sphere of influence across the world.

The first Soviet-Syrian arms deal marked the beginning of a long political and defence partnership which would shape Syria's political and security interests for decades, and saw it become a bulwark against both Western hegemonic designs and Israeli interests on the Arabian Peninsula with Moscow's backing. The USSR also began to provide considerable aid and technical assistance for infrastructure projects such as the Euphrates Dam, which alongside low interest loans was critical to both raising living standards in Syria and allowing Damascus to resist Western pressure.[38] Moscow's strong stance against the invasion of Egypt had won it admiration across the Arab world, with reports from Baghdad and Jeddah indicating that, even among pro-Western businessmen, intellectuals, and government officials, there was widespread support for Soviet actions. Syrian prime minister Sabri Al Asali recalled to a U.S. diplomat on November 8th that he had been shocked to see "flocks and droves" of well-wishers converging on the Soviet embassy the day before to show their appreciation for its solidarity with the Arab nation.[39]

In January 1957 CIA director Allan Dulles submitted reports "that the new Syrian Cabinet was oriented to the left,"[40] and two months later he warned President Dwight D. Eisenhower of an "increasing trend toward a decidedly leftist, pro-Soviet government."[41] The State Department clarified the nature of U.S. and British objectives in Syria that same month, stating in a particularly insightful internal document: "The British are believed to favour active stimulation of a change in the present regime in Syria, in an effort to assure a pro-Western orientation on the part of future Syrian governments. ... The United States shares the concern of the British Government over the situation in Syria."[42] The Department of Defence published a memorandum two months later in June mentioning the possibility of a coup against "the leftist Syrian Government."[43]

The new CIA attempt to engineer the Syrian government's overthrow was headed by Howard Stone, a legend in the agency

with considerable experience in the field of coups and destabilisation. Stone worked closely with Kermit Roosevelt, Archibald's
cousin, who was also of high rank in the agency. The coup attempt
made use of Syrian dissidents based in neighbouring Lebanon,
one of the most firmly Western-aligned states in the Arab world
at the time, alongside the Syrian military attaché in Rome who
the CIA slipped into Lebanon and provided with false documents
to travel secretly. The CIA considered the exiled former president Adib Shishakli as a leading candidate to head the post-coup
government – a figure of ill repute described by the CIA station
chief in Damascus, Miles Copeland, as having "committed sac-
rilege, blasphemy, murder, adultery and theft."[44]   Considerable
investments were also made in arming and winning over Syria's
radical Islamist opposition group the Muslim Brotherhood.
The Brotherhood would support the coup and installation of
a pro-Western government, and it would later be called upon
to carry out assassinations of officials the CIA or Britain's MI6
wanted taken out.[45] Plans called for the assassination of Syria's
chief of intelligence, the chief of its General Staff and the chief
of the Communist Party, with Kermit Roosevelt forecasting that
the pro-Western government, once installed, would "rely first
upon repressive measures and arbitrary exercise of power." This
reflected a broader trend across the third world where Western
powers were engineering multiple similar coups.[46]

Unlike in other Western target states, Syria's internal opposition appeared less than willing to work with the Western powers
to bring down their own government, with the living memory
of a brutal French occupation likely having played a major role
in their persuasion. So it was that officers in the Syrian Army
who had been assigned key roles in the operation informed the
country's head of intelligence, Abdel Hamid Sarraj, of the plot.
The officers handed over their CIA bribe money, and named the
American conspirators who paid them – U.S. military attaché
Robert Molloy, Vice Consul at the U.S. embassy Francis Jeton,
and Second Secretary for Political Affairs Howard Stone. These
were all CIA officers who had been placed in the embassy for the
purpose of affecting political change, and all were subsequently

expelled from Syria bringing an end to Western hopes to quickly install a client government in power. When leaving the country and approaching the border the humiliated Col. Molloy made a point of running his Syrian motorcade off the road and shouting to the fallen riders "Colonel Sarraj and his commie friends" should be told that Molloy would "beat the shit out of them with one hand tied behind his back if they ever crossed his path again."[47]

As was consistently the case for states across the world which opposed Western designs, Syria was increasingly portrayed as being under some kind of malign communist influence – the only plausible explanation in the minds of the U.S. and its allies for any party to reject what the West perceived as its own benevolence. The *New York Times*, for one, wrote that a prominent theory for why Syria expelled the American embassy staff from its territory was that Damascus "acted at the instigation of the Soviet Union."[48] President Eisenhower would later recall regarding the incident that "the suspicion was strong that the Communists had taken control of the government," although there was little evidence to substantiate this with communist elements never coming close to seizing power in Syria.[49]

From South Korea and Indonesia to Burkina Faso and Ghana, unfounded allegations that the Soviet Union was the puppeteer behind all opposition to Western domination served both to rationalise resistance in Western minds – ever perceiving themselves as a force for ultimate good – and to discredit those parties in the third world which failed to act in accordance with Western wishes. The CIA's failure to overthrow the Syrian government in early 1957 would hardly mark its final attempt at doing so. Five years later the new president John F. Kennedy would meet with British Prime Minister Howard Macmillan and agree, according to a CIA report, on plans for "Penetration and cultivation of disruptive elements in the Syrian armed forces, particularly in the Syrian army, *so that Syria can be guided by the West*" [italics added].[50] These efforts, too, ultimately failed with Damascus remaining free from Western control.

Syria's position in the crosshairs of the Western Bloc was particularly dire given that it bordered one of the NATO alliance's most militarily powerful member states – the Republic of Turkey. Following Turkey's accession to NATO in 1952 and its significant military commitment to the U.S.-led war effort in Korea, where its forces were responsible for multiple serious war crimes,[51] Ankara moved to intervene militarily in Syria with full American support in 1957. This was done under the pretext of preventing the consolidation of power by a pro-Soviet government in Damascus, which was portrayed in the U.S. as a move against 'international communism' to forcibly restore Syria to the Western sphere of influence by installing a Western client government.

A Turkish invasion was forestalled by Soviet intervention, with Soviet forces staging major manoeuvres on Turkey's northern and western borders and Moscow announcing that it "would come to the aid of Syria militarily" if it was attacked.[52] Soviet Premier Nikita Khrushchev warned Washington regarding Moscow's commitment to protect Damascus: "If war breaks out we are near Turkey and you are not. When the guns begin to fire, the rockets can begin flying and then it will be too late to think about it." This came just six weeks after the USSR had successfully tested the world's first intercontinental range ballistic missile, and was taken very seriously by American officials who quickly called for Turkey to stand down.[53] "We restrained the aggressors... preventing the destruction of the Syrian republic, and we accomplished it without a war," Khrushchev later recalled.[54] Nevertheless the threat from Turkey, considered the region's second greatest military power only to Iran, persisted throughout the Cold War bringing the NATO threat directly to Syria's borders.

## Arab-Israeli Wars and the Trials of the Arab Nationalist Movement

In 1958 Syria entered a short-lived political union with the nationalist Nasserist government of Egypt under the United Arab Republic, which was expected at the time to form the basis for a larger Arab superstate that would encompass much of the Middle East and Africa under a Pan-Arabist vision.[55] Damascus' decision to enter this union resulted largely from the considerable pan-Arab sentiments both within the government and among its population, with the U.S. State Department describing Egyptian President Gamal Abdel Nasser that year as a figure who "continues to represent the answer to the prayers of many Arabs."[56] The security situation was another major factor motivating the decision, with Syria having almost suffered a Turkish invasion the year before and continuing to face a serious threat of Western subversion. The U.S. had notably agreed in early 1958 to support the Iraqi monarchy in its efforts to acquire parts of north eastern Syria, posing another immediate threat to Syrian sovereignty.[57]

Syria's union with Egypt would be short lived and the effective subordination of the former to governance from Cairo, while initially welcomed, proved unpopular in practice particularly for Syria's military and political elites who now had far less say in running the country. A coup in Damascus in 1961 led to the country's secession from the United Arab Republic,[ii] and was followed by a series of coups and counter coups by a divided officer corps which concluded in a Ba'athist coup in March 1963. This was followed by an internal coup within the Ba'ath Party in February 1966 which marked the beginning of much closer cooperation with the USSR and a greater focus on economic development.[58]

Ba'athism was a school of socialist Arab nationalist thought developed in the early 20th century, which stressed the need for rejuvenation (Ba'ath) of the Arab nation against threats and humiliations by Western imperial powers.[59] The adoption of Ba'athism placed Syria in a natural alliance with other Arab republics which opposed Western hegemony over the Arab world, which by the end of the decade included Iraq, Egypt, Libya and Algeria. Algeria had joined after the overthrow of its French colonial administration in 1962, followed by Iraq after a Ba'athist takeover in early

---

ii  Egypt had notably been the more reluctant partner to join the union to begin with, and Nasser's government had not welcomed the responsibility of managing Syria's internal affairs. Although the leading political force in the Syrian Military, the Ba'ath Party, had been the loudest advocate of a union with Egypt, attitudes within the party had quickly changed once the consequences of Cairo's rule over Syria was realised. (Seale, Patrick, *The Struggle for Syria: A Study of Post-War Arab Politics, 1945–1958,* London, Oxford University Press, 1965 (pp. 51–52, 54, 58–59).

1963 – which had been preceded five years prior by a coup against its own Western-aligned monarchy in 1958. Sudan could also be considered a partial member of the grouping after a coup in 1964. These states between them formed an Arab nationalist power bloc led by Nasserist Egypt, and would come to cooperate closely on matters of defence and foreign policy while gaining considerable Soviet political, economic and material support.

While Syria's domestic political situation would stabilise somewhat from 1966, its relations with neighbouring Israel became increasingly tense. Israeli cultivation of land in the demilitarised zone between the two countries led to multiple skirmishes in the air, and with Israel widely suspected of developing nuclear weapons, the perceived threat was further exacerbated. France had notably provided Israel with a large plutonium-producing reactor, natural uranium to fuel it, and a reprocessing plant – everything the country needed to produce plutonium for a nuclear arsenal other than heavy water. The sale was largely funded by donations from Jewish communities in the Western world, and remains today the only time such an extensive amount of the technology required to build a nuclear bomb was transferred from one state to another.[60]

The nuclear program in particular led to increased Soviet interest in the Israeli issue and to growing support for its Arab neighbours. An abundance of support from Egypt, which had access to more advanced Soviet built combat aircraft such as the MiG-21 and Il-28 and far superior armour and artillery, fuelled predictions at a time of escalating Syrian-Israeli tensions that the Arab side would win a major victory should total war break out. Among other factors, the state of the Syrian officer corps which had endured a decade of repeated purges due to political instability, the focus of much of the military leadership on internal struggles rather than inter-state warfare, and a chain of command divided by political affiliations, left it in a weak position to go to war with its much better prepared neighbour. The fact that the bulk of Egypt's more capable units were in Yemen engaging Western and Saudi-backed forces also seriously undermined its combat potential.[61]

The Six Day War which commenced on June 5, 1967, saw
Syrian and allied Egyptian forces overwhelmingly defeated, with
Israel compensating for the quantitative and qualitative disadvantages in armaments with superior training, organisation and
preparation.[62] Its victory allowed Israel to annex the Egyptian-
held Gaza strip and Sinai Peninsula and the strategically located
Syrian Golan Heights, the latter which remains under Israeli control to this day. Syrian participation in the war was limited, with
the country remaining out of the conflict for the first four days.
Losses were relatively light at around 3000 personnel, little over
half the total Israeli losses,[63] as Egypt endured the vast majority
of Israeli attacks. The key to Israel's victory was the neutralising
of Syrian airfields, which took the majority of its air units out of
action and left the Israeli Air Force with uncontested control of the
skies, much as had been done against Egypt.

One of the keys to the Arab nationalist states' defeat in the
conflict was their faith in the solidarity of the Western-aligned
Arab monarchies, which proved to be their undoing on multiple
occasions. Israeli military intelligence would later reveal that the
Moroccan monarchy of King Hassan II, a close Cold War ally of
Western Europe and the United States, had passed recordings of
highly sensitive meetings by the Arab nationalist leaders in which
war plans were discussed, to Israeli intelligence.[64] Saudi Arabia
and Israel had similarly seen the Arab nationalist movement
headed by Damascus and Cairo as a mutual adversary earlier in
the decade, with Riyadh bolstering Tel Aviv's position by opening
a second front against the United Arab Republic with support
from the American CIA, British MI6, the Israeli Air Force and
British mercenary organisations in Yemen.[65] The Jordanian monarchy's partnership with Israel had similarly been instrumental to
the latter's victory against Syria, Egypt and Iraq in 1948, as historians would later document in detail.[66] In 1970 Amman approved
and voiced support for a prospective Israeli military intervention
against Syria to restore a favourable balance of power,[67] and three
years later provided an early warning to Washington regarding
Egyptian and Syrian war plans against Israel.[68] Thus faith among
the leaders of the Arab nationalist states that Arab solidarity

overrode the global split between Western and Soviet-aligned states repeatedly proved to be misplaced. Western client states such as Saudi Arabia, Morocco and Jordan, ruled by kings who relied on Western patronage to retain power, were natural allies of pro-Western Israel and natural adversaries of Soviet-backed Syria and Egypt. Thus, there was arguably never an Arab-Israeli struggle so much as there was a struggle between those states which accepted Western hegemony, including Israel, the Arab monarchies and the republics of Lebanon[iii] and Tunisia, and those nationalist Arab states which rejected subjugation to Western interests.

Israel's wartime gains saw it control several times as much territory as it had previously, and it quickly cemented these by heavily fortifying the Syrian Golan Heights and the Sinai Peninsula and by deploying its first nuclear warheads, which were active by 1970.[69] While territorial losses were considerable, the main fallout from the Six Day War for Syria and its partners was the shattering of faith in the Arab nationalist vision with a humiliating and overwhelming military failure.[70] The leader of the United Arab Republic, Egyptian President Nasser, who was seen as figurehead for Arab nationalism and anti-imperialism across the Arab world, offered his resignation but was soon forced back into office by mass protests. While rebuilding of the Egyptian and Syrian military inventories commenced quickly with generous Soviet assistance, the momentum behind the Arab Nationalist Bloc was diminished with morale low. The Israeli Air Force made a point of flying fighter aircraft over Arab cities which ensured this remained the case – emphasising the helplessness of the defeated parties. While aircraft could be replaced, pilots would take considerably longer to train. Egypt's promising program to develop the ambitious HA-300 'Arab fighter,' which although very costly had the potential to become one of the world's leading

iii Traditionally Western-aligned Lebanese sects would years later in the 1980s seek to engineer an Israeli-Syrian war, with their militias actively attacking Syrian forces, in order to enlarge the Israeli sphere of influence in their country at the expense of Soviet-backed Syria. (Schiff, Zeev, 'Dealing With Syria,' *Foreign Policy*, no. 55, Summer, 1984 (p. 93).)

fighter jets and was designed by German aviation legend Wilhelm Messerschmitt, had to be terminated due to the economic fallout from the Arab defeat.[71] These developments all undermined the positions of Egypt's allies, foremost among which was Syria.

Worse still for the Arab nationalist states, Israel's victory against all odds had gained it a vital new patron, the United States, and this new partnership brought an end to the Arab qualitative advantage on the battlefield. While Israel had previously been permitted to make only very limited purchases of American defensive weaponry, this changed after it had demonstrated its ability to counter well-armed Soviet defence partners on the battlefield. When combined with the Richard Nixon administration's desire to win both the Jewish vote in upcoming elections and the support of pro-Israeli political factions, Israel's victory in the Six Day War led to a major turnaround in U.S. policy regarding arms exports. Not only were Israeli requests for lower end weapons systems such as A-4 attack jets accepted but, in an unexpected move, very high-end hardware such as F-4E Phantom fighter jets and AIM-7 Sparrow air-to-air missiles were also offered. This signified that Israel had effectively overnight gone from a near non-client to a top tier client for arms, alongside countries like Japan and West Germany. This major turning point in U.S.-Israeli military relations would have significant consequences for the balance of power in the Middle East for decades, with Israel's general advantages in training and tactics complemented by state-of-the-art American technologies. U.S. arms deliveries to Israel had begun by the beginning of 1968, and new weapons systems were at least ten years ahead technologically of any of the relatively backward French systems on which Israel had previously depended, with equal and in some cases superior capabilities to the arms supplied to the Arab states by the USSR. The implications for Syrian security were significant.

The year 1970 saw yet another change in government in Syria, again from within the ranks of the Ba'ath Party, following disagreements between the head of the party apparatus, Major Salah Jadid, and the head of the military, Captain Hafez Al Assad. The 'Corrective Revolution' in November that year saw Assad prevail and take the position of prime minister, followed by the position of president the following year in March. This ended over two decades of successive coups in Syria, with Assad forming lasting party, military and intelligence establishments to ensure continued stability throughout his rule and after his death. November 1970 is thus considered a major turning point in Syria's political history, after which a much stronger state was established and attempts at external interference in the country's affairs faced a much more unified resistance.[72]

The new government in Syria supported the emergence of a National Progressive Front to better integrate other political parties into the leadership alongside the Ba'ath, including the Arab Socialist Union – a primarily urban Nasserist group, the Communist Party of Syria, the Arab Socialist Party – which had more support among the rural population, and the Socialist Union Movement. Members of these groups were all given an unprecedented degree of legitimacy and allowed to appoint candidates to the National Assembly, providing a much wider support base and greater political stability. The government also oversaw the establishment of popular organisations to further widen political participation, as well as its own support base among the population, including the General Union of Peasants, the General Federation of Trade Unions, the General Women's Federation and the General Union of Students and Revolutionary Youth Organisation.[73] Furthermore, Hafez Al Assad's administration quickly moved to build institutions which both raised living standards and improved long-term stability. Ambitious infrastructure projects, including providing electricity to the rural population, all served to distinguish the new leadership from its predecessors and won it considerable public support.[74] The security forces were restructured into what would be termed in the West, much to the chagrin of Damascus' adversaries there, a 'coup proof' system under which various agencies were tasked with closely monitoring both the military and one another, thereby ensuring plots to engineer the government's overthrow would be difficult to conceal. The result was that while the country was previously seen as a 'prize' over which medium and large powers fought, after the Corrective Revolution Syria increasingly emerged as a major player in its own right in regional affairs.[75]

Syria's Corrective Revolution came just seven months after the strongly Western-aligned Libyan monarchy was overthrown by military officers led by Colonel Muammar Gaddafi, with the presence of Soviet warships in the vicinity playing a key role in deterring Western intervention on the side of the embattled King Idris.[76] The newly formed Libyan Arab Republic would become the latest of several states to join the Arab nationalist movement and shift away from the Western sphere of influence. Despite the military debacle in 1967, the balance of power within the Arab world was continuing to shift against Western interests. By the beginning of the new decade four strongly pro-Western governments had been overthrown in the preceding twelve years – Iraq in 1958, Sudan in 1964, Libya in 1969 and the French colonial government in Algeria in 1962. While Arabs had almost all lived either under direct Western rule or otherwise in the Western sphere of influence at the time the Second World War ended, by 1970 governments in the Arab world "guided by the West," as British Prime Minister Macmillan had referred to it,[77] had been relegated to a shrinking minority.

The Corrective Revolution in Syria occurred less than two months after the death of the leader of the Arab nationalist movement and President of the United Arab Republic Gamal Abdel Nasser, which marked a major turning point in the Arab nationalist movement and the beginning of the end for the power bloc. Nasser's charisma had combined with Egypt's considerable soft power, using assets from radio broadcasts to its booming popular media industries such as music[78] and film[79] to build rapport with and win crucial support from populations even in the Western-aligned Arab states. His death was particularly notable given that his successor was neither a Nasserist, a pan-Arabist nor an anti-imperialist. Nasser's Vice President, Anwar Sadat, was appointed to the presidency immediately after his death, and the Sadat government showed early signs of a major shift away from the country's previous position against Western domination of the Middle East under the Arab nationalist cause.

In 1971, within a year of taking power, the new administration abolished the United Arab Republic, ending prospects for
a superstate envisioned by Nasser. As part of a broader effort to
improve relations with the Western Bloc, Sadat subsequently personally ordered the expulsion of Soviet military personnel who
had been vital to shoring up the country's defences after the Six
Day War.[80] The Soviets had most notably done so by setting up
and operating an air defence network, considered the strongest
in the world outside the USSR itself by American intelligence,[81]
by performing valuable reconnaissance flights over Israeli held
territory using their all new MiG-25R aircraft,[82] and even by dispatching officers to lead ground operations against Israeli forces.[83]
The Soviet Navy's amphibious landings near the Suez Canal had
also played a key role in deterring Israeli forces, which were
facing little Egyptian resistance, from capturing the strategically
critical waterway.[84] The Egyptians themselves had no comparable
capabilities to those offered by Soviet forces, and even among
anti-Soviet factions in the military the new president's decision
was seen as brash and as potentially seriously detrimental to the
country's defence.[85] The reception in Syria was similarly stunned
and negative, and Sadat subsequently urged Damascus to also
expel the much smaller number of Soviet advisors that were on
its territory.[86] Egypt's new trajectory would come to seriously
compromise the interests of the wider Arab nationalist movement,
with dire consequences for Syrian security.

Egypt had begun to rebuild its military for a reconquest of
the Sinai Peninsula almost immediately after its defeat in the Six
Day War, and even with a new leader in power it was difficult
for the country to reverse the momentum built in the military
establishment for such action. Syria joined Egypt in initiating
the Yom Kippur War in October 1973 and was assisted on the
ground by Iraqi armoured and air units, North Korean pilots[87] and
Cuban ground troops[88] as well as advisors from the Soviet Union
itself. The Egyptian front saw support from Libya, Algeria[89] and
North Korea.[90] Israel meanwhile benefitted from massive supply
drops from the United States and the provision of some American
pilots to fly its new F-4E Phantom jets.[91] U.S. Air Force SR-71

surveillance aircraft also provided vital intelligence key to allowing Israeli ground troops to exploit weaknesses in their enemies'
lines.[92]

Despite considerable initial successes, both Egypt and Syria
were defeated overwhelmingly by Israel within 19 days, although
less overwhelmingly so than they had been six years prior.
According to Chief of Staff Saad Al Shazly, multiple 'political
interventions' by President Sadat in key aspects of military planning were key to Egypt's defeat. These ranged from dispatching
the country's valuable special forces into an obvious 'kill zone' in
Israeli held territory, to advancing ground units beyond the cover
of their air defences where they were, quite predictably, massacred
by Israeli air units. Indeed, Shazly strongly implied that Egypt's
routing may well have been the intention of the new president for
political reasons – although Sadat would claim, as the Egyptian
military does to this day, that the war ended in victory.[93]

On the Syrian front the Syrian Arab Army enjoyed multiple
advantages including superior armour, superior night fighting
capabilities and a much more sophisticated air defence network – although Israeli air power still proved overwhelming.
Unlike the Egyptians, however, Syrian ground forces did not
conduct near suicidal advances into Israeli kill zones and operated only under the cover of surface-to-air missile batteries, with
new missile systems such as the 2K12 KuB taking a heavy toll
on Israeli aircraft and limiting Israel's ability to use its air advantage.[94] Israeli forces were able to eventually gain the upper hand
on the ground and push Syrian forces out of the Golan Heights
before pushing deeper into Syrian territory. As the war neared its
end the SAA had prepared for a massive counteroffensive with
five fresh divisions fully replenished with Soviet armour, which
were deployed alongside long-awaited Iraqi reinforcements. The
offensive was expected at the very least to push Israeli forces
back to the Golan Heights, but ultimately was stalled when Egypt
and Israel both agreed to a ceasefire which was implemented on
October 23. While Syria was in a much stronger position to continue the war than Egypt had been, and appeared to have pursued
a much more sound strategy, the closure of the Egyptian front left

it unable to fight on its own and ensured the Golan would remain firmly in Israeli hands.

## Post-Arab Nationalism:
## Isolated Syria Confronts Israel and the U.S.

Syria's security situation for the remainder of the Cold War was dramatically affected by the drastic political shift which took place in neighbouring Egypt, ending the two states' longstanding partnership and leaving Damascus increasingly isolated in the face of multiple imminent security threats. With Egypt's Anwar Sadat government taking active steps after the Yom Kippur War to move into the Western sphere of influence, imprisoning or exiling Nasserist era officials, and downgrading ties to the USSR, Syria quickly emerged as the primary opponent of the imposition of Western hegemony in the Middle East. While Egypt had been prioritised for delivery of some of the most capable Soviet armaments, and was the first to employ systems such as the T-62 tank and 2K12 air defence system on a significant scale, the country's pivot westwards would force it to make do with third rate arms well below the standard required to engage a high end military power. Taking aerial warfare as an example, Egypt was not only denied access to advanced F-14 and F-15 fighter aircraft being marketed to higher priority Western allies such as Iran, Saudi Arabia and Israel, but even the much lighter and cheaper F-16s it was sold were strictly forbidden from carrying modern air-to-air or air-to-ground missiles and had heavy downgraded avionics. Egypt's fighters would thus come to be qualitatively outmatched by all its neighbours – from Sudan and Libya which acquired more advanced Soviet armaments to Israel, Saudi Arabia and Jordan which had superior calibres of Western weaponry.[95] This effectively neutralised the Arab world's leading military power and ensured that, should Cairo again leave the Western sphere of influence, it would have little capability to defend itself.

Egypt's ambitious domestic weapons programs, including those related to weapons of mass destruction, were closed down under the Sadat presidency, which ensured that Israel and the

Western powers would retain an indefinite advantage with their large nuclear, biological and chemical arsenals. Egypt's industrial economy meanwhile suffered, with major state companies producing products from cars to electronics closing down as protectionist measures for emerging industries were lifted and more established Western brands were allowed to flood its markets on favourable terms. The shift towards a highly import reliant economy and the rolling back of protections for Egypt's national industry reversed two decades of advances made under the Nasserist government. This relegated Egypt to an indefinite third world status, whereas its prior developmentalism had in many ways mirrored similar programs being pursued in Taiwan, South Korea and other successful military-run emerging economies.[96] The Anwar Sadat government thus neutralised Egypt not only as the political leader of the Arab Nationalist Bloc, with its separate peace agreement with Israel leading to its eviction from the Arab League, but also to its neutralisation as both an emerging economic powerhouse and a high-end military power. This had very serious consequences for the wider Arab world given Cairo's prior position of leadership.

Egypt's demise as a major power and its defection to partner with the Western Bloc marked the beginnings of major divisions in what remained of the Arab Nationalist Bloc. While Syria did receive some military aid from Libya in the form of MiG-23 fighters and T-62 tanks[97] in the mid-1970s, it received no Arab manpower contributions in its subsequent clashes with Israel or the United States. Indeed, Israeli Prime Minister Yitzhak Rabin alluded on more than one occasion to the fact that, in pursuing a separate peace deal with Egypt, a key Israeli goal had been to isolate Syria in this way.[98] Alongside further threats from Israel, which had been given high priority for delivery of the latest American arms due to its ongoing low-level hostilities with Soviet-aligned Syria, Damascus faced a further threat from a sizeable NATO military presence in the Middle East. This included NATO member state Turkey on its northwestern border, British military bases in Cyprus off its Western coast, and from 1982 the deployment of sizeable U.S., French and Italian troops in neighbouring Lebanon, later backed by British personnel. Although U.S. forces claimed to be neutral, American sources would later widely admit that this had been far from the case with an active role taken in combatting both anti-Western Lebanese factions and in attacking Syrian military positions.[99]

Syria faced threats to its sovereignty on a third front from the Muslim Brotherhood, which came as part of a much broader trend under which Islamist militants came to target Western adversaries across the world in the late Cold War years (see Chapter 2). The Muslim Brotherhood and ideologically related Islamist groups, advocating holy wars against secular governments and seeking to impose their own rule, had been close partners of the Western Bloc throughout the Cold War.[iv] They received considerable support from NATO member states, enabling them to more effectively target a number of Soviet-aligned and neutral governments. In Syria Islamist elements posed a persistent threat to state security and carried out terror attacks and targeted killings across much of the country. The Muslim Brotherhood notably staged a major armed uprising lasting almost three years from 1979 with the intention of toppling the government in Damascus and imposing strict Sharia Law nationwide. Had it succeeded, close partnership with the Western Bloc, acquiescence to Western interests and adoption of a harshly anti-Soviet policy were expected.

The Islamist uprising is thought to have seen over 1000 Syrian military personnel killed,[100] and resulted in armed jihadist militants taking control of the city of Hama before themselves being routed and taking heavy losses. Damascus notably accused U.S. intelligence and Western-aligned Arab states Saudi Arabia

---

iv The conflict between the Ba'ath Party and the Muslim Brotherhood had been ongoing for decades, and in 1948 when Hafez Al Assad was just 18 he had been singled out for targeting by the Islamist party for his exceptional service to the Ba'ath, attacked in the street and stabbed in the back. The injury took weeks to heal, and was one of the more minor of several clashes between the two parties before the Ba'ath came to power. In April 1964 the brotherhood had violently targeted Ba'ath Party members, ransacked wine shops and killed and mutilated a member of the National Guard. The Islamists used a mosque to stash weapons before the military flushed them out by the end of the month. (Seale, Patrick, *The Struggle for Syria: A Study of Post-War Arab Politics, 1945–1958,* London, Oxford University Press, 1965 (pp. 36, 92, 93).)

and Egypt of having supported the jihadist groups, accusing Egyptian President Sadat specifically of having played a role in the massacre of cadets by jihadists in a surprise attack on the Aleppo Artillery School in June 1979.[101] The following decade Israeli and Western experts would notably highlight the presence of radical Islamist elements as an asset to undermine Damascus which "would not be difficult to operate again" and offered "increased U.S. opportunities for destabilization activities if this form of pressure proves necessary."[102]

Facing a Western military presence in Lebanon, Israeli threats on its southwestern border and ongoing jihadist activities domestically, Syria was also threatened with the potential of a fourth front opening from neighbouring Iraq – formerly a major ally which had been its leading Arab supporter in the Yom Kippur War. Baghdad and Damascus had been on the verge of a political union in 1979, under which Syrian President Hafez Al Assad would have become Vice President of the unified nation and Iraqi President Ahmed Hassan Al Bakr would have served as head of state. Ties notably soured after Iraq's own Vice President Saddam Hussein staged a coup within the Iraqi Ba'ath Party which brought him to power.[103] Hussein ended talks for political unity and went on to form close ties with the Western Bloc, initiating a war with a major emerging Western adversary, the Islamic Republic of Iran, less than a year into his first term in office with full U.S. and European support. This closely followed the overthrow of the Western-aligned Iranian monarchy a few months prior in 1979. Western influence over Baghdad was such that the United States had seen fit to "urge Iraq to take the war to Syria" in 1983. Despite the ongoing Iran-Iraq War, the U.S. sought to engineer a diversion of Iraqi forces to invade Syria from its eastern border, thus undermining Damascus' ability to resist pressure on its fronts from Israel, the U.S., and internally from Islamist insurgents. CIA reports noted that Iraq would have the support of "virtually every Arab state except Libya," highlighting Syria's isolation and its position as almost the sole remaining impediment to achieving Western regional designs.[104] Iraq refused to launch an attack on Syria, but the fact that such a course of action was even contemplated bore testament to how much had changed in the Arab world and the degree to which Syria was now embattled.

In the early 1980s the U.S. National Security Council notably published a paper titled 'The Destabilisation of Syria' in which a range of options to increase pressure on the Middle Eastern state and if possible to topple its government were explored. One prominent proposal put forward in 1983 and examined by prominent members of the U.S. intelligence community Donald Fortier and Philip Dur, was to encourage Turkey to support attacks on and otherwise seek to destabilise Syria from its northern border. Such escalation would have been risky, however, given the possibility of direct Soviet intervention to support Damascus.[105]

Not only was Syria embattled politically, but it also suffered from a highly unfavourable military balance as Israel continued to receive considerable quantities of state-of-the art U.S. arms – much of it as military aid. From the mid-1970s, following the Yom Kippur War, Israel was spending an average of 24% of its gross domestic product (GDP) on the military, by some estimates the highest figure in the world, which by 1985 had risen to 28% of GDP.[106] While this was unsustainable in the long term and was fuelling runaway inflation and a tremendous budget deficit,[107] it provided Israel with the resources needed to apply considerable military pressure against Syria which, with Egypt out of the picture, was now the near sole focus of its conventional military buildup. The Israeli invasion of Lebanon in 1982, after gaining a green light from Washington,[108] only worsened Syria's situation as it faced the possibility of encirclement and a permanent stationing of Israeli assets along its southwestern border.

The situation was made all the more serious by the actions of Egypt's Anwar Sadat government, which worked closely with the United States to compromise advanced Soviet weapons technologies it had previously been provided with – technologies Syria relied on heavily for its own defence. After the Yom Kippur War Egypt illegally supplied MiG-23 fighters, 2K12 air defence systems and a range of other sensitive Soviet armaments to America. Egypt and Syria had been the first two countries in the world to receive these new weapons systems, which would be extensively analysed by the Americans to develop viable tactics and electronic warfare countermeasures to neutralise them.[109] Awareness of the performance limitations of the sensors, weaponry, engines and other features would provide the Western Bloc with an overwhelming advantage when engaging these systems in future, undermining the security of Soviet defence clients including Vietnam, North Korea, East Germany and Algeria among many others. As Saad Al Shazly noted regarding the impact of Egyptian actions: "When he broke with the Soviets in 1974, Sadat put all the sophisticated Soviet weaponry Egypt's armed forces possessed at the disposal of America. The damage this did to the Arab cause was incalculable; its effects will be felt for years." He attributed subsequent difficulties the Syrians faced countering Israeli air power largely to these Egyptian actions.[110]

Threats posed by the Western Bloc, by Israel as a major Western client, and by jihadist forces, were all connected in that all were working to further the interests of Western hegemony over the Middle East. Although the Israelis and the Islamist militant groups certainly had their own separate agendas, the heavy reliance of both on Western patronage meant that they could to a large extent be directed to act in the interests of this broader goal. The subduing of states which remained outside the Western sphere of influence such as Syria was vital to this end.

Syria's position as a lone remaining impediment to Western and allied designs in the Arab Middle East became particularly clear in the 1980s, with Saad Al Shazly, then in exile, referring to it as "the rock stemming the tide of Israeli hegemony in the Middle East."[111] Damascus' position in the eyes of the U.S. State Department, following Egypt's pivot West in the mid-1970s, was referred to by former Reuters correspondent and prominent British expert on Syrian political history Patrick Seale as "the enemy, the most militant of Israel's neighbours, the closest to Moscow, the only substantial obstacle" to U.S. designs for the region. The following decade, Seale noted: "The Arab Israeli dispute... became essentially a contest between Israel and Syria" as "Assad had proven himself the greatest single obstacle to Israel's aims in the Levant. Only if he were removed, or at least scared off the scene, could Israel proceed unchallenged... from Israel's point of view, Assad was a far more important target than either [Palestinian leader Yasser] Arafat or [Libyan leader Muammar] Gaddafi.... With real deterrent power, Syria has become a country Israel must hesitate to attack. Moreover, in a whole series of bruising engagements in the 1980s Assad fought off Israeli encroachments into his Levant environment: he foiled attempts to bring Lebanon and Jordan into Israel's orbit.... He has proved strong enough to frustrate a solution on Israel's terms. In so doing, he has made Syria the only adversary Israel needs to take seriously." In the eyes of Israeli Prime Minister Menachem Begin, according to Seale, Syria was "the main regional enemy to be neutralised," and Assad was "the principal enemy who could put at risk everything he held dear."[112]

Prominent British defence specialist Jonathan Marcus observed at the end of the decade: "Syria alone remains in the front line of the anti-Israeli struggle," noting that the other members of the former Arab nationalist power bloc had been taken out of the picture.[113] While opposition to Israeli actions at least rhetorically remained widespread, with only Egypt having officially recognised the state and concluded a peace agreement, arguably far more importantly the former united front among the Arab republics against Western hegemonic ambitions had been lost. This had been achieved so quickly and successfully that by 1981 the U.S. State Department saw an opportunity to form the basis of a stronger Western-aligned anti–Soviet power bloc in the Middle East, which aligned Israel and the Westphilian ('guided by the West') Arab states such Saudi Arabia and Egypt against challengers to Western interests in the region. Secretary of State Alexander Haig Jr. visited the Middle East early in 1981 to push forward this agenda, and on the basis that Syria remained the prime holdout of Soviet influence he strongly endorsed Israeli military operations against the country.[114]

The Syrian Arab Army suffered an overwhelming defeat at the hands of the Israeli Air Force in 1982, when Syria deployed ground units to neighbouring Lebanon to block Israeli efforts to expand its military presence there. While Palestinian

militants had launched multiple provocative attacks on Israeli
territory from Lebanese soil, Damascus was among multiple
parties which feared Tel Aviv would use this as a pretext for a
disproportionate response to annex Lebanon permanently into
its sphere of influence. Three days after launching a full-scale
invasion of Lebanon, Israel launched Operation Mole Cricket 19
on June 9 to gain air superiority over the Syrian-held Lebanese
Beqaa Valley. The valley was protected by approximately 30
2K12 KuB surface-to-air missiles batteries supported by MiG-23
and MiG-21 third generation fighters. The Israeli advantage of
more modern and much heavier F-15 fighters, the most capable
fielded by any Western air force at the time, was compounded
by its extensive knowledge of the capabilities of the Syrian jets
and air defences and in particular the most effective way to jam
their sensors. Much of this intelligence came courtesy of Egypt.
The result was an overwhelming Israeli victory with almost all air
defence systems destroyed and several dozen fighters lost, with
reports on the exact numbers varying. Israeli losses were confined
to two damaged F-15s and the loss of supporting drones. The fact
that the vast majority of participating Syrian fighters were configured for ground attack rather than air-to-air combat only worsened
its odds.

Israel's victory at Beqqa Valley – the most one-sided large-
scale battle between jet fighters in history – was effectively overseen by Defence Minister Ariel Sharon, who had led Israeli ground
forces on his own initiative to break Egyptian lines in the Yom
Kippur War. Sharon oversaw the Israeli occupation of Lebanon
and counterinsurgency operations there and would become one
of the most celebrated military officers in Israeli history. Syria's
plight following its defeat, however, would not go unheeded, and
while now isolated in the Arab world its strong stance against the
U.S. and its allies had won it considerable support elsewhere.
Under the new leadership of Yuri Andropov, the Soviet Union
moved quickly to update Syria's military inventory with some of
the most capable weapons it had ever offered for export. When
told by the defence and foreign ministers that the USSR could not
spare advanced weapons for Syria, Andropov retorted in a reflec-
tion of Damascus' newfound importance: "Take the from Red

Army stocks. I will not allow any power in the world to threaten Syria."[115] Saad Al Shazly noted regarding the massive ensuing Soviet aid package that Moscow:

> increased supplies of weaponry to Syria, sufficient in quantity and quality to sustain Syria's position in Lebanon against any American or Israeli threat. The re-equipment of Syria, in fact, was little short of awesome in its speed and scale. In June 1982, Syrian forces in Lebanon had suffered heavily in their confrontation with Israel. Syrian losses were put at 400 tanks, 100 aircraft and helicopters, and 18 battalions of SAMs [surface to air missiles]. The Soviet Union promptly replaced them all – with more modern equipment. On top of that the Soviet Union then gave the Syrians an extra 200 T-72 tanks; a battalion of the SS-21 [Tochka] battlefield missiles; strengthened Syria's air defences with a further 68 battalions of SAMs – including eight battalions of the long-range SAM-5 [S-200]; and gave its air force another 54 combat helicopters, 25 MiG-23s, and 25 MiG-25s.[116]

Syria was the first foreign client for the T-72 tank – which provided a considerable advantage against Israeli armour, the first client outside the Warsaw Pact for the OTR-21 Tochka precision guided ballistic missile – which placed targets across much of Israel within range, and one of the first two for the MiG-25 Foxbat interceptor. The MiG-25 remains today the world's fastest and highest flying combat jet ever to enter service, with capabilities far superior to those of the jets lost at Beqqa Valley, and was one of just two export-available Soviet jets capable of challenging Israel's F-15.[117] The number of Soviet military advisors in Syria more than doubled in the 3–4 years from 1982, while the number of combat aircraft, tanks, artillery pieces and air defence sites increased respectively from 440, 3,200, 2,600 and 100 to 650, 4,400, 4000 and 180.[118]

The result of Soviet assistance was a far more balanced distribution of power in the Lebanon War, allowing the SAA to hold its positions even after the Western powers had deployed to the theatre. Syrian S-200s were reportedly successful in downing three U.S. Navy combat jets in a single day on December 4, 1983, which was the first time an Arab state had directly confronted the U.S. militarily.[119] One U.S. pilot was captured and interrogated by Syrian forces, and American operations were widely considered a disaster with U.S. airstrikes on Syrian positions failing to cause significant damage.[120] Post-1982 military operations in Lebanon would mark the most successful operations against enemy state actors in Syria's modern history. According to multiple Western sources, Damascus at the time could rely not only on vast Soviet material support to effectively hold its own in an arms race with Israel, but was also protected by a Soviet promise to intervene directly should Israel attack Syrian territory. This ensured Syrian-Israeli clashes were relegated to Lebanese soil.[121]

Operations during the Lebanon War marked the solidifying of two of Syria's major defence partnerships and the beginning of two new partnerships, with support from actors other than Arab nationalist states increasingly relied on after the Arab Nationalist Bloc had all but disintegrated. Alongside its position as a priority client for high end Soviet arms and military aid, Syria received more direct assistance from North Korea, which had contributed air units to prior conflicts, but in this case deployed personnel on the ground to support the Syrian Arab Army. The Koreans provided not only pilots, but tank operators, missile technicians and officers for both training and frontline combat operations. According to Israeli reports, Korean operators of some 122mm rocket artillery batteries were killed and one of the Korean-made launchers captured during the conflict.[122]

More locally, the Lebanon War cemented Syria's emerging partnership with the Islamic Republic of Iran, and although ideologically very distant the two shared several common enemies and remained the only major actors in the region outside the Western sphere of influence. Syria not only provided armaments to support Iran's war effort against an Iraqi invasion,[123] countering considerable support the West, Egypt and the Gulf States gave Baghdad,[124] but it also cooperated with Iranian-aligned elements in Lebanon. Ties were also formed with the Iranian Revolutionary Guard Corps (IRGC) Quds Force, which had established a presence in Lebanon with the primary goal of countering Israel.[125] The Lebanon War also saw the rise to power of the Lebanese political party and paramilitary group Hezbollah, which carried out multiple attacks on Israeli forces in Lebanon and allegedly against U.S. and European forces as well. Although there were initially tensions between Damascus and Hezbollah, the two emerged as allies of convenience against a perceived common threat and would go on to form close defence ties. Approximately 500 Iranian infantry were deployed in a supporting role alongside Syrian forces during the Lebanon War, while Syria provided extensive assistance to many Iranian-affiliated insurgent groups combatting the Israeli presence in the south of the country.[126] Direct Soviet and Korean support, and the emergence of Iran and Hezbollah as parties Syria could work with, came to characterise Damascus' security relations long after the Lebanon War ended.

## A New Partnership:
## Syria and the Heart of the Axis of Resistance

Syria's strategic position declined considerably following the end of the Cold War in 1989, as the Soviet Union began to retreat from its overseas commitments to allied states including withdrawing from Eastern Europe and allowing the Warsaw Pact to collapse. The Soviet administration of Mikhail Gorbachev would notably place stricter restrictions on the export of advanced weapons systems to Syria, although no similar restrictions were placed by the Western powers on sales to Israel which resulted in a growing military disparity between the two rival Middle Eastern powers. Soviet recognition of Israel in January 1991 and the opening of mass migration of Soviet Jews to the country furthered Damascus' isolation and weakened its position considerably, while also providing a significant and much needed boost to the Israeli economy which brought it out of a hard recession and stimulated rapid GDP growth.[127] While the Soviets withdrew from the Middle East, Western involvement only grew and military support for Israel, including considerable military aid, remained consistent.

Seeking to improve relations with otherArab states in light of its growing isolation, and to take a firm stance against Iraqi expansionism which was a mutual threat to both the Arab Gulf States and to Syria itself, Damascus provided a token force of 14,500 troops to the U.S.-led coalition in 1990 during the First Gulf War. This represented around 1.5% of the coalition's overall personnel, over 70% of which were American.[128] This move was initially met with considerable criticism domestically, as despite Iraqi threats to Syria, the SAA's participation placed Damascus on the same side as the hostile Western powers and indirectly on the same side as Israel while breaking with the principle of Arab solidarity. Nevertheless, it would prove an excellent strategic decision. With the Soviet Union itself leading calls for action against Iraq, and offering to participate in the conflict, Syria would have only furthered its isolation in the post–Cold War world had it either sided with Iraq or remained neutral. Joining the coalition was hardly going to seal Iraq's fate, but it would keep Damascus off the Western Bloc's radar as the United States moved to declare a New World Order of unchallenged Western hegemony[129] – placing Syria lower on the list of targets than it would have otherwise been.

Damascus' participation in the Gulf War at negligible cost would pay considerable dividends, and aside from the significant political benefits it would receive $2.5 billion from the Gulf States and Japan in recognition of its contribution.[130] It would nevertheless face an increasingly unfavourable balance of power with the loss of trade and considerable aid from the Soviet Union after the superpower collapsed in 1991. By 2000, Tel Aviv University's Jaffe Center of Strategic Studies reportedly concluded regarding the military balance between the former peer powers "that the strategic balance between Israel and Syria has never been so tilted in Israel's favor, and that Damascus has no real military option."[131] Syria would move to cement defence ties with North Korea, Iran and Hezbollah – the latter two despite very considerable ideological differences – to strengthen its position. With the deterioration of its conventional forces in the 1990s, Korean support in particular was key to providing some form of deterrent against the massive Western, Israeli and Turkish forces situated near its borders through asymmetric means.[132]

The 1990s saw Syria's ballistic missile program accelerate rapidly, providing a cost effective and reliable deterrent and enabling it to threaten Israeli and Western targets to compensate for its conventional disadvantages. Syria began to acquire Hwasong-6 missiles from North Korea from 1991 to 1995, with the Koreans also providing training for Syrian technicians[133] and setting up associated construction facilities near Aleppo and Hama. The missiles' formidable ranges allowed them to threaten a wide range of Western military bases as well as targets across Israel and Turkey and could strike both countries even if fired from Syria's far east. Missiles were deployed from mobile launch vehicles, making them highly survivable. Syria would subsequently acquire Korean Toksa and Hwasong-9 missiles, the first of which had a short launch time and GPS guidance for high precision[134] and the latter which had double the range of the Hwasong-6 at 1000km. The sale of Patriot anti-missile systems to Israel by the United States[135] led the Koreans to equip Syria's Hwasong-9 arsenal with manoeuvring re-entry vehicles (MaRV), which made the missiles extremely difficult to intercept and largely negated the Patriot's deployment.[136] This kind of Korean support and provision of fundamentally new asymmetric capabilities played an increasingly essential role in guaranteeing Syria's security, with the country's conventional armed forces otherwise deteriorating and its formerly large and modern air force seeing training hours decline drastically and plans for new acquisitions terminated. Conservative upgrades to Syria's Soviet-era conventional forces, such as equipping older T-55 tanks with laser rangefinders and improving electronic warfare countermeasures on air defence systems, were also provided by North Korean experts.

Syrian President Hafez Al Assad passed away in June 2000 at 69 years of age, and the military and intelligence establishments he had set up soon afterwards approved his son Bashar as his successor. Hafez's first son, Bassel Al Assad, who held a doctorate in military sciences and was a commander of a Republican Guard brigade, was initially considered first choice for the presidency until his death in a car accident in 1994. The more mild-mannered younger son, who had previously worked as an ophthalmologist in London, had returned to Syria soon after his brother's death where his father oversaw the promotion of his image both among the public and in the military. While Hafez's Syria had hardly been a 'one man state,' appointing the charismatic leader's son to the presidency ensured a sense of continuity and avoided the potentially destabilizing effects of a struggle for power within the leadership of the country's military and intelligence communities or the Ba'ath Party. Appointing Bashar as leader, even if only as a figurehead, was seen as a way to ensure a smooth transition of power after Hafez's death.

While initially seen as only a face for the military and party establishments, Bashar Al Assad began to assert considerable influence over Syria's development in his first decade in power. With a British born wife and Western education, the influences of Western political and economic thought became increasingly evident, leading some to label the new president the 'Syrian Gorbachev.' Before his father's death Bashar had played a leading role in establishing internet connectivity in the country, and in his first years as president he was credited with moving the country away from the Ba'athist state-centered economic system and adopting a neoliberal reform agenda.[137] Underlining this shift just one year after taking power, the new president replaced nearly every economic official in cabinet, many of whom were ministers who had served under his father for decades.[138] Major reforms included privatization of universities, banks and media, reducing subsidies on a number of basic goods, reducing tariff protections for domestic industries and the breaking the state monopoly on education which the party had maintained since 1963. Government funding for education was cut, and the influence of the party was undermined with party flags featured much less prominently at state events – often not at all – and non-party officials promoted to senior positions in government.[139] Had it not been for the more conservative influence of the party leadership and the military and intelligence establishments, the Western-influenced reform process could very likely have been far more radical.

As has been widely observed since 2011, popular discontent in Syria was largely fuelled by opposition to its Western-style neo-liberal reforms moving Syria away from a state centred economy and towards privatisation. Former chair of the British Helsinki Human Rights Group and Oxford University lecturer in modern history, Dr. Mark Almond, was one of many to observe to this effect: "One of the big causes of discontent in Syria is precisely the transfer of the state assets into private hands." This contrasted strongly with Western portrayals of discontent motivated primarily by calls for greater Westernisation of the country's political system.[140]

The new president's plans for reform reportedly extended beyond domestic affairs and included a potential realignment away from Syria's traditional partners such as North Korea and Russia and towards a closer partnership with the Western world. A retired British lieutenant general told the writer in 2018 that Assad was widely known to have been personally seeking a closer defense partnership with the West to displace Syria's traditional allies – with the general blaming Western inaction for failing to support this initiative against the influence of the Ba'ath Party and military establishment. He was far from alone in expressing this opinion. Senate Foreign Relations Committee chairman John Kerry, the future U.S. Secretary of State, was among many in the West who saw the new president as a potential asset for expanding the Western sphere of influence. Kerry had predicted in 2009 regarding the impact of the new leadership in Damascus: "My judgment is that Syria will move; Syria will change, as it embraces a legitimate relationship with the United States and the West and the economic opportunity that comes with it."[141] Pulitzer Prize winning *Washington Post* reporter Joby Warrick notably described Western officials as "sensing potential in the young Western-educated leader" to pivot his country towards a pro-Western foreign policy alignment and adopt Western-style political and economic reforms. "Syria's first family cultivated a public image that suggested a desire for closer ties to the West," he highlighted, contrasting this to the period of Hafez Al Assad. Warrick further noted, as a promising sign from the Western perspective, that the new President Assad had enacted particularly aggressive Western-style reforms in his first months in office.[142] Syria to some extent came to resemble the Soviet Union under the Gorbachev administration, with a Westphilian reformist line taken by the president leading the military and intelligence establishments to conduct key aspects of foreign policy related to security independently, which often appeared contradictory to the presidential line.[143]

The military establishment placed a growing emphasis on ties to Iran and the increasingly powerful Hezbollah militia to form what would come to be known as the 'Axis of Resistance' against Western and Israeli influence. The military was also widely accused of providing refuge to members of Saddam Hussein's Ba'athist government after the U.S. invasion of the country in 2003, of turning a blind eye to operations by anti-U.S. Iraqi insurgents in the border regions, and of failing to sufficiently support America in neutralizing them. A further point of contention with the U.S. was ongoing Syrian military support for Palestinian jihadist groups such as Hamas which, unlike Hezbollah, used tactics that were widely considered acts of terrorism. This came as part of a broader policy of supporting all manner of Palestinian political groups from secular nationalists to Islamists to balance against Israeli power, and since Hamas was not recognized as a terrorist group by the United Nations or the vast majority of countries, support for it was legal although still controversial. By contrast the Syrian government, seeking to gain favor in Washington, would allow the extraordinary rendition of Al Qaeda suspects by the United States for interrogation in Syrian prisons. There, as was the norm for Middle Eastern states and increasingly for the United States itself,[144] several often brutal enhanced interrogation techniques were known to be practiced. It is uncertain whether these contradictory policies were signs of a divided Syrian foreign policy establishment or indicated that Damascus intended to somehow support resistance to Western hegemony while at the same time remaining in the United States' good graces with token conciliatory actions.

Syria's security situation deteriorated considerably from 2003 when the U.S.-led invasion of Iraq in March placed tens of thousands of NATO personnel on its eastern border. This complemented the Western alliance's already vast presences on Syria's northern and western borders and the presence to its south of both U.S. bases in Jordan and of Israel. Where Iraq, North Korea and Iran were labeled as targets for American attack under the 'Axis of Evil' by the George W. Bush administration in 2002, U.S. Undersecretary of State John Bolton would soon afterwards name Syria as part of 'Beyond the Axis of Evil' alongside Cuba and Libya, citing the threat posed by Damascus' alleged pursuit of weapons of mass destruction.[145] Not only was Syria criticised for its acceptance of high level members of Saddam Hussein's government as political refugees, but the demonstration of American military might in Iraq was also widely cited in Western media as a warning to Damascus. Shortly after Baghdad's capture President Bush's chief spokesman, Ari Fleischer, referred to Syria as a "terrorist nation" and a "rogue nation," with other U.S. officials and their British counterparts warning that Damascus needed to revise its behaviour or would face consequences. It was strongly implied by both media and officials in the West that, with the U.S. now deploying troops right across the border, Syria could be the "next Iraq."[146]

With threats against the country continuing to escalate, and the U.S. preventing President Assad from attending the United Nations General Assembly in 2005, the *New York Times* noted:

> Bush administration officials say their goal... toward Syria [is], to 'continue trying to isolate it.' Many in Washington argue that Syria is the 'low-hanging fruit' in the Mideast, and that the United States should send it down the path to 'creative instability'... Washington seems to be pursuing a policy of regime change on the cheap in Syria. The United States has halved Syria's economic growth by stopping Iraqi oil exports through

Syria's pipeline, imposing strict economic sanctions
and blocking European trade agreements. Regular
reports that the United States is considering bombing
Syria and freezing transactions by the central bank have
driven investors away.[147]

Despite the considerable threat, a number of factors played
into Syria's favour. American threats were likely bluster from the
very beginning, as Pyongyang and Tehran rather than Damascus
appeared next on Washington's target list. Considerable preparations were being made for a possible war with the former, and tensions on the Korean Peninsula began rising sharply from April.[148]
When the wars in Iraq and to a lesser extent Afghanistan took
turns for the worse, with insurgencies escalating, Syria fell further
down the list of American priorities. Perhaps most importantly,
Syria's North Korean-sourced ballistic missile arsenal was highlighted by a number of analysts as an important factor deterring
potential U.S. attacks in the aftermath of the invasion of Iraq in
2003 despite high tensions between Damascus and Washington.[149]
Syria's vast arsenal of chemical weapons, too, provided a vital
deterrent capability. As American journalist and foreign policy
expert Fred Kaplan noted in 2003, when U.S. military action
against Damascus was widely speculated, there was "one military
caveat... Syria really does have weapons of mass destruction,
probably more than Iraq ever had, and its whole military strategy
is geared to using them if necessary."[150] There was an irony to
the fact that the pretext for American military intervention against
Iraq, which proved to be entirely fabricated, was key to deterring
such intervention against Syria.[151]

As American and allied forces were increasingly bogged
down in Iraq by an insurgency which Damascus was at times
accused of aiding, Syria's security situation would improve
somewhat. The potential for a future flare in tensions on any
of its frontiers remained, however. While the new president
Assad continued to promote reforms from within, in the process
alienating significant portions of the population who saw the
privatisation agenda as fuelling further inequality, the defence

establishment continued to cement ties with its traditional partners. Damascus' ties to Pyongyang, Tehran and the increasingly
powerful Hezbollah, and its position as a conduit of arms and
other vital equipment to the Lebanese militia which was deployed
on the frontline of a potential conflict with Israel,[152] made it a
key pillar of the 'Axis of Resistance.' This Axis had effectively
replaced the Arab Nationalist Bloc as the primary opposition force
against Western dominance of the Middle East. As a result, when
a month-long war broke out between Hezbollah and Israel in the
summer of 2006, the former operating with Iranian, Korean and
Syrian backing and the latter with Western support,[153] it would
have significant consequences for Syria's security situation.

A number of factors made Hezbollah's war with Israel a highly
consequential event. It was the first major incident of successful
armed resistance on a significant scale to the Western-led order
after the Cold War's end, and along with Russia's victory over
Western-aligned Georgia two years later in defiance of European
and American demands it marked the end of the unipolar world
order under which Western power had been unchallenged. The war
was also the first in Israel's history which did not end in its military
victory, and despite overwhelming Israeli numerical and material
advantages Hezbollah proved to be better trained and organised
and to have better morale than any of the Arab nationalist forces
had ever had. A key material facilitator of the Lebanese militia's
victory was its heavily fortified and extremely large network of
tunnels and bunkers, which were constructed by North Korean
experts[154] based on their own extensive experience in the field.
Another was its access to advanced anti-tank munitions including
the Syrian-supplied Russian Kornet. Using the Kornet and other
lighter missiles Hezbollah was able to neutralise multiple Israeli
tanks, including the new Merkava IV which had joined the Israeli
Army just two years prior and was considered in Israel to be the
best in the world. Heavy losses to the militia shook the country's
faith in its capabilities.[155] Subsequent Israeli pressure on Russia
to place stricter controls on the export of the missiles led Syria to
send the Kornet to North Korea, where the design was studied and
improved to develop the Bulsae-3. This in turn would be provided

to both the SAA and to Hezbollah itself. [156] The Syrian Arab Army, for its part, within a year showed clear signs of attempting to emulate Hezbollah, from the forming of frontline anti-tank units trained to merge guerilla and conventional tactics to the construction of underground fortifications bordering the Israeli-held Golan Heights. These were based on those of Hezbollah, which in turn had based its tactics and fortifications on those of the North Korean military.

Hezbollah's effective performance in 2006 came as a major surprise and would highlight the threat posed to Western and Israeli interests by the growing Iranian-led axis. The *New York Times* would refer to it as "a militia trained like an army and equipped like a state," and was among several Western publications which stressed the shock its training and capabilities induced in Israel.[157] The conflict's outcome led to Syria's designation as a priority target due to its importance to the Lebanese militia's survival. Taking Syria out of the picture was increasingly highlighted by Western and Israeli sources as a way to cripple Hezbollah and cut its supply lines without having to confront the increasingly heavily armed and demonstrably lethal militia directly.[158]

In September 2007, thirteen months after Hezbollah's victory, the Israeli Air Force carried out a strike deep into Syrian territory to neutralise what was allegedly a North Korean built and staffed nuclear facility. The veracity of such reports regarding the nature of the target remains uncertain, with a number of nuclear experts and intelligence officials, including the Director General of the International Atomic Energy Agency, indicating that they were highly questionable. They highlighted that not only was there no evidence of a plutonium reprocessing plant, or of defences which would be expected at such a facility, but also no sign of any facility to produce nuclear fuel in Syria.[159] To fill this hole in the narrative, it was subsequently claimed that the alleged Korean built reactor was part of a wider plutonium program which Iran had partially outsourced to Syrian territory.[160] Why Tehran would do so given a reactor's far greater vulnerability and proximity to both Israel and U.S. forces based in Iraq is hard to fathom, however, as is the construction of an unconcealed reactor for over five years in plain sight and just 50km from the Iraqi border without alerting U.S. intelligence. Other Israeli sources claimed the reactor used uranium fuel which was delivered by ship from the North Korean capital Pyongyang itself. This too seemed very unusual given both the lack of major ports or nuclear facilities in Pyongyang and the very questionable viability of a Syrian nuclear program which would require fuel shipments from so far away.[161] It was noted by a number of reporters that alleged development of weapons of mass destruction, often fabricated, was frequently used as a pretext for hostile and illegal actions by the U.S. and its allies in the 2000s.[162] It remains possible that the attack, successfully portrayed as a daring raid evoking one of the Israeli Air Force's finest hours when a similar strike took out Iraqi nuclear facilities in 1981, was intended to boost the then poor morale in Israel which had suffered the shock of the country's first ever military defeat a year prior.[163] The true nature of the Israeli target can only be speculated.

Syria's attempts to modernise its conventional military forces was limited by a more constrained post–Cold War budget and by a lack of Russian support, the latter due largely to improvements in the Russian-Israeli relationship. In response to Israeli acquisitions of sophisticated new variants of the F-16 and F-15 fighters, Syria reportedly attempted to purchase eight MiG-31 advanced interceptors from Russia. Although terribly outnumbered, these had the potential to be a game changer and enjoyed many very significant performance advantages over Israeli fighters.[164] The deal was reportedly cancelled due to Israeli pressure on Moscow. Later Syrian attempts to purchase S-300PMU-2 air defence systems, which threatened to seriously undermine Israeli jets' ability to operate offensively, would also be blocked by Russia due to an Israeli request.[165] Syria's options to improve its air defences following the Israeli strike were thus limited, and were restricted primarily to upgrading the electronic warfare countermeasures of its Soviet-era arsenal with Korean assistance and to buying new missiles for its ageing Cold War era fighters.

Syria lacked the capabilities needed to prevent one-off airstrikes by Israel without risking serious escalation but retained sufficient strategic missile and chemical deterrents to prevent a full-scale enemy attack. Following Hezbollah's 2006 victory, the urgent need to weaken the 'Axis of Resistance' by targeting Syria scuppered Western plans to wait for a gradual Gorbachev-style shift in Syria under the new Assad government. The divisive nature of domestic economic reforms, however, and the growing penetration of pro-Western media both from Western countries and from Western-aligned Arab states, notably contributed to weakening the state on the home front. Given Syria's position as a high priority target, this had particularly significant consequences. The result from 2011, under a leading initiative by the Barack Obama administration to use both information warfare and non-state proxies to expand the Western Bloc's sphere of influence, would be a major war for the state's survival that would come to involve many of the world's major powers.

# Notes

1    Stirling, W. F., *Safety Last*, London, Hollis and Carter, 1953 (p. 231).
     Barr, James, *A Line in the Sand: Britain, France and the Struggle for the Mastery of the Middle East*, London, Simon & Schuster, 2011 (Chapter 25: Time to Call the Shots).
2    McDougall, James, *A History of Algeria*, Cambridge, Cambridge University Press, 2017 (pp. 179–181).
3    Rydstrom, Helle, 'Politics of colonial violence: Gendered atrocities in French occupied Vietnam,' *European Journal of Women's Studies*, vol. 22 (pp. 191–207).
     Information on the Memorial Stele, Official Website of Quảng Bình Provincial Government (https://dukhach.quangbinh.gov.vn/3cms/vu-tham-sat-lang-my-trach.htm).
     Barnet, Richard J., *Intervention and Revolution: The United States in the Third World*, New York, World Publishing, 1968 (p. 185).
4    'Who Walks in Damascus?,' *Time*, June 18, 1945.
     Barr, James, *A Line in the Sand: Britain, France and the Struggle for the Mastery of the Middle East*, London, Simon & Schuster, 2011 (Chapter 25: Time to Call the Shots).
5    'Déclarations du Général de l'Armée Beynet, Délégué Général et Plénipotentiaire de France du Levant aux Représentants de la Presse Etrangère sur les affaires de Syrie' [Statements by General of the Army Beynet, General Delegate and Plenipotentiary of France from the Levant to Representatives of the Foreign Press on Syrian affairs], June 9, 1945.

6    Stirling, W. F., *Safety Last*, London, Hollis and Carter, 1953 (p. 232).
7    Ibid (p. 232).
8    Roshwald, Aviel, *Estranged Bedfellows: Britain and France in the Middle East during the Second World War*, Oxford, Oxford University Press, 1990 (p. 204).
9    Galvani, John, 'Syria and the Baath Party,' *MERIP Reports*, no. 25, February 1974 (p. 3).
10   Greenberg, Joel, 'The World: Pursuing Peace; Netanyahu and His Party Turn Away from "Greater Israel",' *New York Times,* November 22, 1998.
11   Copeland, Miles, *The Game of Nations,* London, Weidenfeld and Nicolson, 1969 (p. 42).
     Little, Douglas , 'Cold War and Covert Action: The United States and Syria, 1945–1958,' *Middle East Journal,* vol. 44, Winter 1990 (pp. 51–75).
12   Weiner, Tim, *Legacy of Ashes: The History of the CIA,* New York, Anchor Books, 2007 (Notes: Chapter Nine).
     Little, Douglas, 'Cold War and Covert Action: The United States and Syria, 1945–1958,' *Middle East Journal,* vol. 44, Winter 1990 (pp. 51–75).
     Wilford, Hugh, *America's Great Game: The CIA's Secret Arabists and the Making of the Modern Middle East,* New York, Basic Books, 2013 (pp. 94, 101–103).
     Shlaim, Avi, 'Husni Zaim and the Plan to Resettle Palestinian Refugees in Syria,' *Journal of Palestine Studies,* vol. 15, no. 4, Summer 1986 (pp. 68–80).
13   Ziv, Guy, 'Shimon Peres and the French-Israeli Alliance, 1954–9,' *Journal of Contemporary History*, vol. 45, no. 2, April 2010 (pp. 406–429).
     Bass, Garry J., 'When Israel and France Broke Up,' *New York Times,* March 31, 2010.
14   Lewan, Kenneth M., 'How West Germany Helped to Build Israel,' *Journal of Palestine Studies*, vol. 4, no. 4, Summer 1975 (pp. 41–64).
     'German Reparations to Israel: The 1952 Treaty and Its Effects,' *The World Today*, vol. 10, no. 6, June 1954 (pp. 258–274).
     Lewis, Samuel L., 'The United States and Israel: Evolution of an Unwritten Alliance,' *Middle East Journal*, vol. 53, no. 3, Summer 1999 (p. 366).
15   Blum, William, *Killing Hope: U.S. Military and C.I.A. Interventions Since World War II*, London, Zed Books, 2003 (Chapter 30: Cuba 1959–1980s: The unforgivable revolution).
16   Abrams, A. B., *Power and Primacy: The History of Western Intervention in the Asia-Pacific*, Oxford, Peter Lang, 2019 (Chapter 4: Sukarnoism and the Rise and Fall of an Independent Indonesia: Wars both Overt and Covert to Return an Asian Power to Western Clienthood).
     Blum, William, *Killing Hope: U.S. Military and C.I.A. Interventions Since World War II*, London, Zed Books, 2003 (Chapter 14: Indonesia 1957–1958: War and pornography).
17   Stockwell, John, *In Search of Enemies: A CIA Story*, New York, W. W. Norton & Company, 1978 (p. 201).
     Prados, John, *Safe For Democracy: The Secret Wars of the CIA*, Chicago, Ivan R. Dee, 2006 (p. 329).

Hersh, Seymour, 'CIA Said to Have Aided Plotters Who Overthrew Nkrumah in Ghana,' *New York Times*, May 9, 1978.

18   Gabriel, Jürg Martin, *The American Conception of Neutrality After 1941*, London, Palgrave MacMillan, 2002 (p. 175).
Nashel, Jonathan, *Edward Lansdale's Cold War*, Boston, University of Massachusetts Press, 2005 (p. 96).

19   Stockwell, John, *In Search of Enemies: A CIA Story*, New York, W. W. Norton & Company, 1978 (p. 201).
Prados, John, *Safe For Democracy: The Secret Wars of the CIA*, Chicago, Ivan R. Dee, 2006 (p. 329).
Hersh, Seymour, 'CIA Said to Have Aided Plotters Who Overthrew Nkrumah in Ghana,' *New York Times*, May 9, 1978.

20   Abrams, A. B. *Power and Primacy: A History of Western Intervention in the Asia-Pacific,* Oxford, Peter Lang, 2019 (Chapter 4: Sukarnoism and the Rise and Fall of an Independent Indonesia: Wars both Overt and Covert to Return an Asian Power to Western Clienthood).

21   Cockburn, Andrew, *Kill Chain, Drones and the Rise of High-Tech Assassins*, London, Picador, 2016 (p. 84).
Blum, William, *Killing Hope: U.S. Military and C.I.A. Interventions Since World War II*, London, Zed Books, 2003 (Appendix III).

22   Abrams, A. B. *Power and Primacy: A History of Western Intervention in the Asia-Pacific,* Oxford, Peter Lang, 2019 (Chapter 4: Sukarnoism and the Rise and Fall of an Independent Indonesia: Wars both Overt and Covert to Return an Asian Power to Western Clienthood).

23   Ibid (Chapter 5: America in the Philippines: How the United States Established a Colony and Later Neo-Colony in the Pacific).

24   *The Times* (UK), December 18, 21 and 22, 1950.
Cumings, Bruce, *The Korean War: A History*, Modern Library Edition, 2010 (pp. 168, 181).
Nichols, Donald, *How Many Times Can I Die?* Brooksville, FL, Brownsville Printing Co., 1981.
Spencer, Richard, 'More than 100,000 massacred by allies during Korean War,' *The Telegraph*, December 29, 2008.
Shaines, Robert A., *Command Influence: A story of Korea and the politics of injustice*, Denver, CO, Outskirts Press, 2010 (p. 54).

25   Cumings, Bruce, *The Korean War: A History*, New York, Modern Library, 2010 (pp. 70, 133).
McCann, David R. and Strauss, Barry S., *War and Democracy: A Comparative Study of the Korean War and the Peloponnesian War,* Abingdon, Routledge, 2015 (p. 59).

26   Abrams, A. B. *Power and Primacy: A History of Western Intervention in the Asia-Pacific,* Oxford, Peter Lang, 2019 (Chapter 4: Sukarnoism and the Rise and Fall of an Independent Indonesia: Wars both Overt and Covert to Return an Asian Power to Western Clienthood).

27   Ibid (Chapter 4: Sukarnoism and the Rise and Fall of an Independent Indonesia: Wars both Overt and Covert to Return an Asian Power to Western Clienthood).

28  Blum, William, *Killing Hope: U.S. Military and C.I.A. Interventions Since World War II*, London, Zed Books, 2003 (Chapter 9: Iran 1953).

29  Ibid (Chapter 26: Congo 1960–1964).

30  Schlesinger, Stephen and Kinzer, Stephen, *Bitter Fruit: The Untold Story of the American Coup in Guatemala*, New York, Doubleday & Co., 1982 (pp. 143–144).
    Blum, William, *Killing Hope: U.S. Military and C.I.A. Interventions Since World War II*, London, Zed Books, 2003 (Chapter 10: Guatemala 1953–1954).

31  Blum, William, *Killing Hope: U.S. Military and C.I.A. Interventions Since World War II*, London, Zed Books, 2003 (Chapter 12: Syria 1956–1957).
    Declassified Documents Reference System:
    1992 volume: document no. 2326, 10 May 1955; no. 2663, 21 September 1955; no. 2973, 9 January 1956; no. 2974, 16 January 1956.
    1993 volume: document no. 2953, 14 December 1955; no. 2954, 26 January 1956; no. 2955, 27 January 1956.

32  Eveland, Wilbur Crane, *Ropes of Sand: America's Failure in the Middle East*, New York, W. W. Norton & Company, 1980 (p. 122).

33  Seale, Patrick, *The Struggle for Syria: A Study of Post-War Arab Politics, 1945–1958*, London, Oxford University Press, 1965 (pp. 283–306).
    Eveland, Wilbur Crane, *Ropes of Sand: America's Failure in the Middle East*, New York, W. W. Norton & Company, 1980 (pp. 135, 169–73, 182).

34  Bryne, Malcolm 'CIA Admits It Was Behind Iran's Coup,' *Foreign Policy*, August 18, 2013.

35  Eveland, Wilbur Crane, *Ropes of Sand: America's Failure in the Middle East*, New York, W. W. Norton & Company, 1980 (Chapters 11–20).
    *New York Times,* April 10, 1956.
    *New York Times,* October 17, 1956.

36  Yaqub, Salim, *Containing Arab Nationalism*, Chapel Hill, University of North Carolina Press, 2004 (pp. 52–53).

37  *The Indianapolis Star,* January 9, 1952 (p. 15).
    Stone, I. F., *Hidden History of the Korean War*, Amazon Media, 2014 (Chapter 47: 'Six Months of Futile Slaughter').
    Joiner, Stephen, 'The Jet that Shocked the West, How the MiG-15 grounded the U.S. bomber fleet in Korea,' *Air & Space Magazine*, December 2013.

38  Galvani, John, 'Syria and the Baath Party,' *MERIP Reports*, no. 25, February 1974 (p. 13).
    Petran, Tabitha, *Syria*, London, Ernest Benn, 1972 (p. 168).

39  Yaqub, Salim, *Containing Arab Nationalism*, Chapel Hill, University of North Carolina Press, 2004 (pp. 63–64).
    U.S. Embassy, Damascus, to Department of State (DOS), tel #1106, 8 November 1956. U.S. Consulate, Basra, to DOS, desp #24, 8 November 1956; and U.S. Embassy, Jidda, to DOS, tel #257, 10 November 1956, reel 11, *Confidential U.S. State Department Central Files, Palestine-Israel: Foreign Affairs*.
    U.S. Embassy, Amman, to DOS, tel #457, 6 November 1956, reel 10, and U.S. Embassy, Cairo, to DOS, tel #1389, 7 November 1956, reel 11,

ibid.; U.S. Embassy, Amman, to DOS, tel #464, 7 November 1956, reel 1, *Confidential U.S. State Department Central Files, Jordan.*
40   Eisenhower, Dwight D., *The White House Years: Waging Peace, 1956–1961,* New York, Doubleday & Company, 1965 (p. 196).
41   Declassified Documents Reference System, 1981 volume, document no. 26E, 22 March 1957.
     Blum, William, *Killing Hope: U.S. Military and C.I.A. Interventions Since World War II,* London, Zed Books, 2003 (Chapter 12: Syria 1956–1957).
42   Declassified Documents Reference System, 1981 volume, document no. 283, March 1957.
     Blum, William, *Killing Hope: U.S. Military and C.I.A. Interventions Since World War II,* London, Zed Books, 2003 (Chapter 12: Syria 1956–1957).
43   Declassified Documents Reference System, 1981 volume, document no. 471B, 17 June 1957.
     Blum, William, *Killing Hope: U.S. Military and C.I.A. Interventions Since World War II,* London, Zed Books, 2003 (Chapter 12: Syria 1956–1957).
44   Weiner, Tim, *Legacy of Ashes: The History of the CIA,* New York, Anchor Books, 2007 (Chapter 14: Ham-Handed Operations of All Kinds).
     Wilford, Hugh, *America's Great Game: The CIA's Secret Arabists and the Shaping of the Modern Middle East,* New York, Basic Books, 2012 (Chapter 18: Archie's Turn: Syria, 1956).
45   Kennedy, Robert F., Jr., 'Why the Arabs Don't Want Us in Syria,' *Politico,* February 22, 2016.
46   Fenton, Ben, 'Macmillan backed Syria assassination plot,' *The Guardian,* September 27, 2003.
     Kennedy, Robert F., Jr., 'Why the Arabs Don't Want Us in Syria,' *Politico,* February 22, 2016.
47   Blum, William, *Killing Hope: U.S. Military and C.I.A. Interventions Since World War II,* London, Zed Books, 2003 (Chapter 12: Syria 1956–1957).
48   *New York Times,* August 17, 1957 (p. 3).
49   Eisenhower, Dwight D., *The White House Years: Waging Peace, 1956–1961,* New York, Doubleday & Company, 1965 (p. 196).
50   CIA internal report, author's name deleted, 18 June 1962, the result of conversations with "Western diplomats" concerning the Kennedy-Macmillan meeting, in: Declassified Documents Reference System, 1975 volume, document no. 240A.
     Blum, William, *Killing Hope: U.S. Military and C.I.A. Interventions Since World War II,* London, Zed Books, 2003 (Chapter 12: Syria 1956–1957).
51   Appleman, Roy E, *Disaster in Korea: The Chinese Confront MacArthur,* College Station, Texas A&M University Press, 1989 (p.89)
     Levine, Alan J., *Stalin's Last War; Korea and the Approach to World War III,* Jefferson, McFarland & Company, 2005 (Chapter 10: Nadir and Recovery).
52   Khrushchev, Nikita, *Memoirs of Nikita Khrushchev, Volume 3: Statesman, 1953–1964,* University Park, Pennsylvania State University Press, 2007 (p. 869).
     Lesch, David, *Syria and the United States: Eisenhower's Cold War in the Middle East,* Boulder, CO, Westview Press, 1992 (p. 199).

U.S. National Archives at College Park, Maryland, Record Group 59, State Department, Central Decimal Files, 1955–59, Box 2682, Telegram 1105, Ankara to State Department, 16 October, 1957.

53 Yaqub, Salim, *Containing Arab Nationalism: The Eisenhower Doctrine and the Middle East,* Chapel Hill, University of North Carolina Press, 2004 (p. 170).

54 Khrushchev, Nikita, *Memoirs of Nikita Khrushchev, Volume 3: Statesman, 1953–1964,* University Park, Pennsylvania State University Press, 2007 (p. 870).
Easter, David, 'Soviet intelligence and the 1957 Syrian crisis,' *National Security,* vol. 33, no. 2 (pp. 227–240).

55 Hayoun, Massoud, 'The Coming Arab Identity Crisis,' *The Atlantic,* March 8, 2012.

56 Yaqub, Salim, *Containing Arab Nationalism: The Eisenhower Doctrine and the Middle East,* Chapel Hill, University of North Carolina Press, 2004 (p. 21).

57 Ibid (p. 7).

58 Seale, Patrick, *The Struggle for Syria: A Study of Post-War Arab Politics, 1945–1958,* London, Oxford University Press, 1965 (p. 108).

59 Galvani, John, 'Syria and the Baath Party,' *MERIP Reports,* no. 25, February 1974 (p. 5).

60 Keck, Zachary, 'The Story of How American Jews and France Built Israel's Nuclear Weapons,' *National Interest,* March 7, 2021.
Karpin, Michael, *The Bomb in the Basement: How Israel Went Nuclear and What That Means for the World,* New York, Simon & Schuster, 2007 (Chapter 3: A French Window Opens and Chapter 4: An Unprecedented Deal.)

61 Seale, Patrick, *The Struggle for Syria: A Study of Post-War Arab Politics, 1945–1958,* London, Oxford University Press, 1965 (pp. 113, 117).

62 Pollack, Kenneth M, 'Air Power in the Six-Day War,' *Journal of Strategic Studies,* vol. 28, no. 3 (pp. 471–503).
Peck, Michael, 'How Israel's Air Force Won the Six-Day War in Six Hours,' *National Interest,* June 2, 2017.

63 Gawrych, George W, *The Albatross of Decisive Victory: War and Policy Between Egypt and Israel in the 1967 and 1973 Arab-Israeli Wars,* Santa Barbara, CA, Greenwood Press, 2000 (p. 3).

64 Surkes, Sue, 'Morocco tipped off Israeli intelligence, "helped Israel win Six Day War",' *Times of Israel,* October 16, 2016.

65 Dorriil, Stephen, *MI6: Inside the Covert World of Her Majesty's Secret Intelligence Service,* New York, Simon and Schuster, 2002 (pp. 690–691).
Petersen, Tore T., *Challenging Retrenchment: The United States, Great Britain and the Middle East, 1950–1980,* Trondheim, Tapir Academic Press, 2010 (pp. 155–157).

66 Shlaim, Avi, *Collusion Across the Jordan: King Abdullah, the Zionist Movement and the Partition of Palestine,* Oxford, Clarendon Press, 1988.
Shlaim, Avi, 'The Debate about 1948,' *International Journal of Middle East Studies,* vol. 27, no. 3, August 1995 (pp. 287–304).

67   Seale, Patrick, *The Struggle for Syria: A Study of Post-War Arab Politics,*
     *1945–1958,* London, Oxford University Press, 1965 (pp. 159–162).
68   Kissinger, Henry, *Years of Upheaval,* London, Little Brown & Co., 1982 (p.
     461).
     Seale, Patrick, *The Struggle for Syria: A Study of Post-War Arab Politics,*
     *1945–1958,* London, Oxford University Press, 1965 (p. 186).
69   Jeremy Bob, Yonah, 'Was the Six Day War fought in part over Israel's
     nuclear program?,' *Jerusalem Post,* June 6, 2017.
70   Samuel, Sigal, 'How the Six-Day War Transformed Religion,' *The Atlantic,*
     June 5, 2017.
     Machairas, Dimitrios, 'The strategic and political consequences of the June
     1967 war,' *Cogent Social Sciences,* vol. 3, 2017.
71   'Helwan HA-300: Egypt's Indigenous Jet Fighter Program Under a Former
     Nazi German Scientist,' *Military Watch Magazine,* January 6, 2019.
72   Phillips, Christopher, *The Battle for Syria: International Rivalry in the New*
     *Middle East,* New Haven, Yale University Press, 2016 (pp. 5, 13).
     Ayubi, Nazih, *Overstating the Arab State, Politics and Society in the Middle*
     *East,* London, I.B. Tauris, 1995.
73   Galvani, John, 'Syria and the Baath Party,' *MERIP Reports,* no. 25, February
     1974 (pp. 3, 10, 13).
     Seale, Patrick, *The Struggle for Syria: A Study of Post-War Arab Politics,*
     *1945–1958,* London, Oxford University Press, 1965 (pp. 175–176).
74   Abboud, Samer N., *Syria,* New York, Polity, 2015 (p. 761).
75   Phillips, Christopher, *The Battle for Syria: International Rivalry in the New*
     *Middle East,* New Haven, Yale University Press, 2016 (pp. 12–13).
     Ayubi, Nazih, *Overstating the Arab State, Politics and Society in the Middle*
     *East,* London, I.B. Tauris, 1995.
76   Goldstein, Lyle J. and Zhukov, Yuri M., 'A Tale of Two Fleets – A Russian
     Perspective on the 1973 Naval Standoff in the Mediterranean,' *Naval War*
     *College Review,* vol. 57, no. 2, Spring 2004 (pp. 12–14).
77   CIA internal report, author's name deleted, 18 June 1962, the result
     of conversations with "Western diplomats" concerning the Kennedy-
     Macmillan meeting, in: Declassified Documents Reference System, 1975
     volume, document no. 240A.
     Blum, William, *Killing Hope: U.S. Military and C.I.A. Interventions Since*
     *World War II,* London, Zed Books, 2003 (Chapter 12: Syria 1956–1957).
78   Frishkopf, Michael, 'Nationalism, Nationalization, and the Egyptian Music
     Industry: Muhammad Fawzy, Misrphon, and Sawt al-Qahira (SonoCairo),'
     *Asian Music,* vol. 39, no. 2, Summer-Fall 2008 (pp. 28–58).
79   Samak, Qussai, 'The Politics of Egyptian Cinema,' *MERIP Reports,* no. 56,
     April 1977 (pp. 12–15).
     Al-Mahdy, Dina, 'The golden age of Egyptian cinema,' *Al Ahram,* April 7,
     2020.
     Messnaoui, Mostafa, 'History of Arab cinema (introduction to understanding
     and interpretation),' *Contemporary Arab Affairs,* vol. 7, 2014.
80   Daigle, Craig A., 'The Russians are Going: Sadat, Nixon and the Soviet
     Presence in Egypt, 1970–1971,' *Middle East Review of International*
     *Affairs,* vol. 8, no. 1, 2004 (pp. 1–15).

Seale, Patrick, *The Struggle for Syria: A Study of Post-War Arab Politics, 1945–1958,* London, Oxford University Press, 1965 (pp. 191, 195).

81    Recording of a conversation between Richard Nixon and William P. Rogers, April 22, 1971, 3:41 pm–4:35 pm, Oval Office, Conversation No. 486–7, National Archives, Nixon Presidential Materials, White House Tapes.

82    Gordon, Yefim, *MiG-25 "Foxbat" and MiG-31 "Foxhound": Russia's Defensive Front Line,* Leciester, Aeropax, 1997 (pp. 46–51).

83    Ginor, Isabella, 'Under the Yellow Arab Helmet Gleamed Blue Russian Eyes: Operation Kavkaz and the War of Attrition, 1969–1970,' *Cold War History*, vol. 3, no. 1, October 2002 (pp. 127–156).

84    Popov, V. I. 'Desantnye korabli osvaivayut Sredizemnoye more' [Landing ships are mastering the Mediterranean Sea], *Taifun,* February 2002 (p. 45).

85    El-Shazly, Saad, *The Crossing of the Suez,* American Mideast Research, 2003 (pp. 159–184).

86    Seale, Patrick, *The Struggle for Syria: A Study of Post-War Arab Politics, 1945–1958,* London, Oxford University Press, 1965 (p. 192).

87    Bechtol, Bruce and Maxwell, David, 'North Korean Military Proliferation in the Middle East and Africa: A Book Launch,' Presentation at the Korea Economic Institute of America, September 25, 2018.
      McCarthy, David, *The Sword of David: The Israeli Air Force at War,* New York, Skyhorse, 2014 (p. 9).

88    Metz, Allan, 'Cuban-Israeli Relations: From the Cuban Revolution to the New World Order,' *Cuban Studies,* vol. 23, 1993 (pp. 113–134).

89    Abadi, Jacob, 'Algeria's Policy toward Israel: Pragmatism and Rhetoric,' *Middle East Journal*, vol. 56, no. 4, Autumn, 2002 (p. 627).

90    El-Shazly, Saad, *The Crossing of the Suez,* American Mideast Research, 2003 (pp. 81–83).
      Leone, Dario, 'An unknown story from the Yom Kippur war: Israeli F-4s vs North Korean MiG-21s,' *The Aviationist,* June 24, 2013.

91    El Shazly, Saad, *The Arab Military Option,* London, Mansel, 1986 (pp. 84–85, 124).
      Cenciotti, David, 'Declassified Top Secret: SR-71 Blackbird Mission Over the Middle East,' *The Aviationist,* September 1, 2013.

92    El Shazly, Saad, *The Arab Military Option,* London, Mansel, 1986 (pp. 84–85, 124).
      Crickmor, Paul F., *Lockheed SR-71 Operations in Europe and the Middle East,* Oxford, Osprey, 2009 (pp. 7–13).
      Cenciotti, David, 'Declassified Top Secret: SR-71 Blackbird Mission Over the Middle East,' *The Aviationist,* September 1, 2013.

93    El-Shazly, Saad, *The Crossing of the Suez,* American Mideast Research, 2003.

94    Rabinovich, Abraham, *The Yom Kippur War: The Epic Encounter That Transformed the Middle East,* New York, Schocken Books, 2017 (p. 199).

95    'Can't Shoot Very Far; The Underwhelming Capabilities of Egypt's Massive F-16 Fleet and Why it is No Match for the Israel's Own Fighting Falcons,' *Military Watch Magazine,* October 13, 2018.
      'No F-15 For Egypt; How President Sadat Tricked His Generals Into a Bad Deal with the United States with Consequences Lasting to this Day,' *Military Watch Magazine,* June 24, 2018.

96  Yoo, Jung-ho, 'The Political Economy of Protection Structure in Korea,' in: Ito, Takatoshi and O. Krueger, Anne, *Trade and Protectionism, NBER-EASE Volume 2*, Chicago, University of Chicago Press, 1993 (pp. 361–385). Chaudhuri, Sudip, 'Government and Economic Development in South Korea, 1961–79,' *Social Scientist*, vol. 24, no. 11/12, November-December 1996 (pp. 18–35).

97  Stockholm International Peace Research Institute, Data on Libyan Arms Transfers to Syria (http://armstrade.sipri.org/armstrade/page/trade_register. php) (Accessed July 17, 2020).

98  'Cable – Tel Aviv to Washington – Rabin on Israeli Strategy and Negotiations with Egypt,' December 3, 1974, National Archives, Access to Archival Databases, U.S. State Department Central Foreign Policy Files. Rabin, Yitzhak in: Williams, Louis, *Military Aspects*, Abingdon, Routledge, 1975 (pp. 212, 216).

99  Zenko, Micah, 'When America Attacked Syria,' *Council on Foreign Relations*, February 13, 2012.
O'Sullivan, Christopher D., *Colin Powell: American Power and Intervention From Vietnam to Iraq*, Lanham, Rowman and Littlefield, 2009 (p. 28).

100 Conduit, Dara, 'The Syrian Muslim Brotherhood and the Spectacle of Hama,' *Middle East Journal*, vol. 70, no. 2, Spring 2016 (p. 212).

101 Van Dam, Nikolaos, *The Struggle for Power in Syria: Politics and Society under Asad and the Ba'th Party*, London, I. B. Tauris, 1996 (p. 93).

102 Schiff, Zeev, 'Dealing With Syria,' *Foreign Policy*, no. 55, Summer, 1984 (pp. 110–111).

103 Dawisha, Adeed, *Iraq: A Political History from Independence to Occupation*, Princeton, Princeton University Press, 2009 (p. 214). McDonald, Michelle, *The Kiss of Saddam*, Brisbane, University of Queensland Press, 2009 (p. 128).

104 Burrows, Thomas, 'Secret 1983 CIA intelligence report suggested America should encourage Saddam Hussein to attack Syria to secure oil pipeline to Med and Gulf,' *Daily Mail*, January 20, 2017.

105 Wills, David C., *The First War on Terrorism: Counter-terrorism Policy During the Reagan Administration*, Lanham, MD, Rowman & Littlefield, 2004 (pp. 71–72).

106 Golan, John W., *Lavi: The United States, Israel, and a Controversial Fighter Jet*, Potomac Books, 2016 (pp. 101–102).

107 Ibid (pp. 101–102).

108 Schiff, Zeev, 'The Green Light,' *Foreign Policy*, no. 50, Spring 1983.

109 Seale, Patrick, Interview with Dr. Ashraf Marwan, London, June 2, 1986.

110 El Shazly, Saad, *The Arab Military Option*, London, Mansel, 1986 (p. 115).

111 Ibid (pp. 189–190).

112 Seale, Patrick, *The Struggle for Syria: A Study of Post-War Arab Politics, 1945–1958*, London, Oxford University Press, 1965 (pp. 230, 361, 374, 473–475, 493).

113 Marcus, Jonathan, 'The Politics of Israel's Security,' *International Affairs*, vol. 65, no. 2, Spring 1989 (p. 233).

114 Schiff, Zeev, 'Dealing With Syria,' *Foreign Policy*, no. 55, Summer, 1984 (p. 101).

115 Patrick Seale Interview with General Mustafa Tlas, Damascus, May 14, 1984.

116 'Fighting America Through Syria; How the Soviet Union Armed its Middle Eastern Ally to Undermine the U.S. Position in Lebanon,' *Military Watch Magazine,* September 2, 2018.

117 'Soviet MiG-25 Foxbat vs. American F-15 Eagle: Which Was Better in Air to Air Combat?,' *Military Watch Magazine,* October 15, 2020.
'50 Years Flying Too Fast To Hit: MiG-25 Foxbat Marks Half Century as World's Fastest Combat Jet,' *Military Watch Magazine,* September 27, 2020.

118 Patrick Seale Interview with Qasim Ja'far, London, April 11, 1987.
Seale, Patrick, *The Struggle for Syria: A Study of Post-War Arab Politics, 1945–1958,* London, Oxford University Press, 1965 (pp. 398–399).

119 'Fighting America Through Syria; How the Soviet Union Armed its Middle Eastern Ally to Undermine the U.S. Position in Lebanon,' *Military Watch Magazine,* September 2, 2018.

120 Zenko, Micah, 'When America Attacked Syria,' *Council on Foreign Relations,* February 13, 2012.

121 Schiff, Zeev, 'Dealing With Syria,' *Foreign Policy*, no. 55, Summer, 1984 (p. 94).

122 Berger, Andrea, *Target Markets, North Korea's Military Customers in the Sanctions Era,* Abingdon, Routledge, 2017 (pp. 64–65).

123 Razoux, Pierre, *The Iran-Iraq War,* Cambridge, MA, Harvard University Press, 2015 (p. 553).
Milani, Mohsen, 'Why Tehran Won't Abandon Assad(ism),' *The Washington Quarterly,* vol. 36, no. 4, Fall 2013 (pp. 79–93).
Seale, Patrick, *The Struggle for Syria: A Study of Post-War Arab Politics, 1945–1958,* London, Oxford University Press, 1965 (p. 358).

124 Razoux, Pierre, *The Iran-Iraq War,* Cambridge, MA, Harvard University Press, 2015 (pp. 105–106).

125 Milani, Mohsen, 'Why Tehran Won't Abandon Assad(ism),' *The Washington Quarterly,* vol. 36, no. 4, Fall 2013 (pp. 79–93).
Geraghty, Timothy J., *Peacekeepers at War: Beirut 1983 – The Marine Commander Tells His Story,* Lincoln, NE, Potomac Books, 2009 (p. 165).
Ghoshani, Mohammad, 'Unity of Iranian and Lebanese Shi'as,' *Sharg,* July 27, 2006.

126 Seale, Patrick, *The Struggle for Syria: A Study of Post-War Arab Politics, 1945–1958,* London, Oxford University Press, 1965 (pp. 395–397).

127 'Aliya from the USSR / Commonwealth of Independent States,' *The Jewish Agency for Israel* (http://archive.jewishagency.org/historical-aliyah/content/28826).
Maital, Shilomo, 'The debilitating brain drain,' *Jerusalem Post,* February 6, 2013.
Aliyah, Da, 'Two Decades On, Wave of Russian Immigration to Israel Is an Outstanding Success,' *Haaretz,* April 10, 2018.

128 Leebaert, Derek, *Magic and Mayhem: The Delusions of American Foreign Policy From Korea to Afghanistan,* New York, Simon and Schuster, 2010 (p. 67).

129  *Foreign Affairs*, vol. 69. Issue 5, Winter 1990/91 (p. 23).
     Miller, Eric A. and Yetiv, Steve A., 'The New World Order in Theory and
     Practice: The Bush Administration's Worldview in Transition,' *Presidential
     Studies Quarterly*, vol. 31, no. 1, March 2001 (pp. 56–68).
     Bush, George H. W., Address Before a Joint Session of the Congress on the
     Persian Gulf Crisis and the Federal Budget Deficit, September 11, 1990.
     'George Bush Meet Woodrow Wilson,' *New York Times*, November 20,
     1990.
     *Foreign Affairs*, vol. 69. Issue 5, Winter 1990/91 (p. 23).
130  Moseley, Ray, 'Syria's. Support of U.S. in Gulf War Paying Dividends,'
     *Chicago* Tribune, March 12, 1991.
131  Kaplan, Fred, 'Assad's Situation; Syria's Military Machine May be
     Hollow – But it Isn't' Harmless,' *Slate*, April 15, 2003.
132  Ibid.
133  Berger, Andrea, *Target Markets, North Korea's Military Customers in the
     Sanctions Era*, Abingdon, Routledge, 2017 (p. 65).
134  Bechtol Jr., Bruce E., *North Korean Military Proliferation in the Middle
     East and Africa*, Lexington, University Press of Kentucky, 2018 (p. 20).
     KN-02 Short Range Ballistic Missile, Missiles, *Military Today* (http://www.
     militarytoday.com/missiles/kn_02.htm).
135  Borger, Julian and Arie, Sophie, 'US equips Israel with Patriot missile
     batteries,' *The Guardian*, January 17, 2003.
136  'Missile Technology Control Regime (MTCR): North Korea's Submitted
     Pursuant to Resolution 2050 (2012),' S/2013/337, 11 June 2013.
     Hughes, Robin, 'SSRC: Spectre at the Table,' *Jane's Defence Weekly*,
     January 22, 2014.
137  Amos, Deborah, 'Syrian Official Pushes for Economic Reform,' *NPR*,
     August 2, 2005.
     Amos, Deborah, 'Once-Socialist Damascus Displays New Wealth Glitz,'
     *NPR*, February 5, 2008.
138  'Middle East: Syria: Cabinet Shakeup Focuses on Economy,' *New York
     Times*, December 14, 2001.
139  Moubayed, Sami, 'Al Assad's Reform Balance Sheet,' *Carnegie Endowment
     for International Peace*, August 19, 2018.
140  'Democratic Syria could destabilize region – political analyst,' *RT*, May 7,
     2011.
141  'Why Washington is at a loss over Syria,' *BBC News*, April 2, 2011.
142  Warrick, Joby, *Black Flags: The Rise of ISIS*, New York, Doubleday, 2015
     (Chapter 17).
143  Jencks, Harlan W., *Some Political and Military Implications of Soviet
     Warplane Sales to the PRC*, Sun Yat Sen Centre for Policy Studies, National
     Sun Yat Sen University, Papers no. 6, April 1991 (p. 21).
     Joo, Sung Ho and Kwak, Tae Hwan, *Military Relations Between Russia
     and North Korea*, Journal of East Asian Affairs, vol. 15, no. 2, Institute for
     National Security Strategy, Fall/Winter 2001 (p. 301).
144  Matthews Dylan, '16 absolutely outrageous abuses detailed in the CIA
     torture report,' *Vox*, December 9, 2014.

Singer, Paul, 'Horrific details from the torture report,' *USA Today*, December 9, 2014.

145 Bolton, John, 'Beyond the Axis of Evil: Additional Threats from Weapons of Mass Destruction,' *Heritage Foundation,* May 6, 2002.

146 Gordon, Philip H., 'After Iraq: Is Syria Next?,' *Brookings Institute,* April 25, 2003.
Stout, David, 'U.S. Sharply Scolds Syria and Threatens Sanctions,' *New York Times,* April 14, 2003.
Schmitt, Eric and Weinraub, Bernard, 'A Nation at War: Military; Pentagon Asserts the Main Fighting is Finished in Iraq,' *New York Times,* April 15, 2003.

147 Landis, Joshua, 'Don't push Syria away,' *New York Times*, September 19, 2005.

148 Auster, Bruce B. and Whitelaw, Kevin, 'Upping the Ante for Kim Jong Il: Pentagon Plan 5030, A New Blueprint for Facing Down North Korea,' *U.S. News and World Report*, July 21, 2003.
'U.S. Repositioning Bombers Near North Korea,' *USA Today*, March 4, 2003.

149 Kaplan, Fred, 'Assad's Situation,' *Slate*, April 15, 2003.
Gordon, Philip H., 'After Iraq: Is Syria Next?,' *Brookings Institute,* April 25, 2003.

150 Kaplan, Fred, 'Assad's Situation,' *Slate*, April 15, 2003.

151 Schwarz, Jon, 'Lie After Lie: What Colin Powell Knew About Iraq 15 Years Ago and What He Told the U.N.,' *The Intercept,* February 6, 2018.
Matthews, Dylan, 'No, really, George W. Bush lied about WMDs,' *Vox*, July 9, 2016.

152 Hill, James, 'A Disciplined Hezbollah Surprises Israel With Its Training, Tactics and Weapons,' *New York Times,* August 7, 2006.

153 'U.S. Speeds Up Bomb Delivery for the Israelis,' *New York Times,* July 22, 2006.
'Israel to get U.S. "bunker buster" bombs – report,' *Reuters*, July 24, 2006.
Blumenthal, Sidney, 'The neocons' next war,' *Salon*, August 3, 2006.

154 Spyer, Jonathan, 'Behind the Axis: The North Korean Connection,' *Jerusalem Post*, May 22, 2010.
Dilegge, Dave and Bunker, Robert J. and Keshavarz, Alma, *Iranian and Hezbollah Hybrid Warfare Activities: A Small Wars Journal Anthology*, Amazon Media, 2016 (p. 261).
'Iranian officer: Hezbollah has commando naval unit,' *Sharq al-Awsat*, July 29, 2006.

155 Greenberg, Hanan, 'Why did Armored Corps fail in Lebanon?,' *Ynet News,* August 30, 2006.
Blomfield, Adrian, 'Israel humbled by arms from Iran,' *The Daily Telegraph*, August 15, 2006.

156 'Bulsae-3 in South Lebanon: How Hezbollah Upgraded its Anti-Armour Capabilities with North Korean Assistance,' *Military Watch Magazine*, September 3, 2019.

157 Hill, James, 'A Disciplined Hezbollah Surprises Israel With Its Training, Tactics and Weapons,' *New York Times,* August 7, 2006.

Matthews, Matt M., *We Were Caught Unprepared: The 2006 Hezbollah-Israeli War,* Fort Leavenworth, Kansas, U.S. Army Combined Arms Center Combat Studies Institute Press, 2006.

158 'Preparing for a Post-Assad Middle East: Hezbollah's Syrian Dilemma,' *Jamestown Foundation,* June 14, 2012.

Winer, Stuart, 'Barak: Fall of Assad regime will seriously hurt Iran and Hezbollah,' *Times of Israel,* May 17, 2012.

Cambanis, Thanassis, 'Hezbollah Considers a Future Without Syria's Assad,' *The Atlantic,* September 22, 2011.

159 Reynolds, Paul, 'Will Syrian site mystery be solved?,' *BBC News,* June 23, 2008.

Broad, William J. 'Syria Rebuilds on Site Destroyed by Israeli Bombs,' *New York Times,* January 12, 2008.

160 Lovelace Jr., Douglas C., *Terrorism: Commentary on Security Documents, Volume 145, The North Korean Threat,* Oxford, Oxford University Press, 2017 (pp. 129–130).

161 Katz, Yaakov and Hendel, Yoaz, *Israel Vs. Iran: The Shadow War,* Dulles, Potmac Books, 2012 (Chapter Three: Operation Orchard).

162 Jonathan, Marcus, 'US Syria claims raise wider doubts,' *BBC News,* April 25, 2008.

163 Mahanaimi, Uzi, 'Humbling Of The Supertroops Shatters Israeli Army Morale,' *The Sunday Times,* August 27, 2006.

Heller, Aron, 'Lebanon Offensive Criticised in Israel,' *Washington Post,* July 26, 2006.

164 'How Syria Nearly Became the World's First Country to Import Combat Jets with Phased Array Radars,' *Military Watch Magazine,* June 4, 2021.

'MiG-31 Foxhounds Over Damascus: How Syria's Game Changing Air Force Modernisation Plan Would Have Shaken Turkey and Israel,' *Military Watch Magazine,* April 21, 2020.

Felgenhauer, Pavel, 'The Strange Story of MiG-31 Jets for Syria,' *Jamestown Foundation,* vol. 4, issue 120, June 20, 2007.

'Беспилотники столкнули израильские министерства' ('Fighter Contract Self Destructed'), Коммерсантъ (Kommersant), May 20, 2009.

Melikishvili, Alexander, 'Russia Scraps MiG-31 Sale to Syria in Exchange for Israeli UAVs,' *Jamestown Foundation,* June 5, 2009.

Note: The signing of a MiG-31 interceptor contract was not confirmed by official Russian or Syrian sources, with some sources from both sides having denied it ever existed..

165 'Syria Will Deploy the S-300 Within Two Weeks; Russian Defence Ministry Takes Response to Israeli Actions Into Its Own Hands,' *Military Watch Magazine,* September 24, 2018.

# Chapter 2

# Historical and Geopolitical Context of the Syrian War

## Radical Islamism and Western Geopolitical Interests

The nature of the Syrian War can best be understood not in isolation, but as part of broader trends in U.S. and European foreign policy towards the non-Western world, particularly in regard to the means used by Western powers to bring about the subjugation of targeted states. The Western Bloc countries have partnered with and provided considerable assistance to radical Islamist militant groups to destabilise those countries outside the Western sphere of influence, including both neutral and Soviet-aligned states, for decades. The most prominent and overt Western victories gained through such means prior to the Syrian War were in Indonesia in 1965, in Afghanistan in the 1980s and 90s, and in Yugoslavia and the post-Soviet states in the aftermath of the Cold War. These efforts have been paired with Western economic and information warfare, and often also with direct attacks by Western powers or Western-aligned state actors. These prior operations, centred around close partnerships between the West and jihadist militants to neutralise states which had in various ways resisted Western global hegemony, are summarised below to provide context vital to understanding the nature of the war in Syria.

## The Indonesian Precedent

Indonesia provides a key example where, much as would be the case in Syria, a Western partnership with radical Islamist groups was key to undermining a state which had opposed Western hegemonic ambitions. There are several key parallels between Western operations against Indonesia in the early Cold War years, and those against Syria five decades later, with many consistent trends in the way the U.S. and its partners targeted the two independent Muslim-majority countries for destabilisation. Indonesia had been a leading founding member of the Non-Aligned Movement and, like all five founding members, had been placed under considerable Western pressure which eventually forced it to rely on the Soviet Union for protection. The country was also a founding member of the Beijing-Pyongyang-Hanoi-Phnom Penh-Jakarta Axis, the Games of New Emerging Forces (GANEFO) and the Conference of the New Emerging Forces (CONEFO) – all organisations created to counter Western power. Although Indonesian leader Sukarno had crushed communist efforts to seize power in the country, he ran a developmentalist and largely centrally planned economy and resisted Western pressure to ban the Partai Komunis Indonesia (PKI - communist party) from running in elections. With the Western Bloc eradicating communist and socialist movements across the third world, from the Philippines, South Vietnam and South Korea to Latin America, the fact that the Indonesian government was allowing the world's largest communist opposition party to run for election and organise freely was seen as an unacceptable offense.[1]

The U.S. aligned itself closely with Islamist elements in Indonesia, inviting Islamist leaders from there and several other countries to America under a program run covertly by the U.S. Information Agency in 1953. There relations were cemented and cooperation was agreed on against the common enemies of communism and secular nationalism.[2] In 1955, before Indonesia's first national election, the CIA gave a million dollars to the Islamist Masjumi Party to aid its election campaign and thwart both Sukarno's nationalists and the PKI. Such efforts failed due largely to the Masjumi's dubious finances.[3] From 1957 Indonesia faced a large-scale CIA orchestrated military campaign to overthrow its government using bombing raids, submarine operations and a very large mercenary army, as well as multiple attempts on President Sukarno's life by Islamist groups and several Islamist rebellions. Although the campaign included the largest CIA military operation ever undertaken, these early efforts were ultimately thwarted by Indonesia's armed forces.[4]

Indonesia would continue to be targeted by Islamists from within and by the U.S. and its Western allies from outside, with Britain, Australia and New Zealand also going to great lengths to destabilize the country. This included provision of arms and funding to separatist groups, radio broadcasts advocating autonomy or independence for certain regions, and initiation of a major psychological warfare campaign intended to "aid and encourage dissident movements inside Indonesia." The goal was to undermine stability and potentially provoke the breakup of Indonesia as a viable unified state.[5] The U.S. carried out black operations in Indonesia throughout the early 1960s, which were conducted with the express intention of exacerbating tensions between the military and the PKI, and if possible, causing a direct conflict to facilitate a forceful move against Indonesia's communists – exactly the result which was achieved in 1965.[6]

The value of a partnership with Islamist groups would become clear in 1965, when a Western backed military coup saw Islamist militants play a major role in purging those suspected of being unsympathetic to the new pro-Western government in Jakarta. Targets included PKI members and their families and suspected supporters, the Chinese ethnic minority and Sukarno loyalists. American expert on the Indonesian conflict professor Geoffrey B. Robinson was one of many to conclude, following his extensive study of the coup and subsequent massacres: "We have here clear evidence that in the year before the purported coup of October 1965, U.S. officials were seriously contemplating – and indeed starting to implement – strategies designed to encourage the army and its civilian allies [Islamist groups in particular] to act against the PKI, without leaving U.S. or other foreign fingerprints."[7]

The *New York Times* referred to the mass killings perpetrated by Islamists and the military in tandem, very often working from 'kill lists' provided by the U.S. embassy,[8] as "one of the most savage mass slaughters of modern political history."[9] Islamists were spurred on by warnings from extremist religious leaders of the evils of the 'atheistic' communist menace, and Imams instructed their followers that it was an obligation to kill suspected communists. These were said to be the lowest order of infidels, "the shedding of whose blood is comparable to killing chicken."[10] *Time* magazine wrote in December 1965: "Armed with wide-bladed knives called *parangs*, Moslem bands crept at night into the homes of the communists, killing entire families... Travelers... tell of small rivers and streams that have been literally clogged with bodies. River transportation has at places been seriously impeded."[11] *Life* magazine described the violence as being "tinged not only with fanaticism but with blood-lust and something like witchcraft."[12] CIA officer Edward Masters sent a cable from the U.S. Embassy in 1966 noting the 'problem' the authorities faced in dealing with communist prisoners. He stated: "Both in the provinces and Djakarta, repression of the PKI continued, with the main problem being that of what to feed and where to house the prisoners. Many provinces appear to be successfully meeting this problem by executing their prisoners, or killing them before they are captured, a task in which Muslim youth groups are providing assistance."[13] Estimates of the number of Indonesian civilians killed in the purge range from 500,000 to over 3 million.[14]

Indonesia subsequently downgraded or cut entirely ties with its former partners such as China, the Soviet Union, North Vietnam, North Korea and Nasserist Egypt, and disbanded or left organisations such as CONEFO. Efforts for state-led industrialisation were ended, and lucrative contracts enabled Western firms to access the country's immense resource wealth for decades and on highly favourable terms. The details of Indonesia's fate after falling under Western influence are subject for another volume.

## The Central Asian and Yugoslav Precedents

The Western campaign to destabilise and eventually bring about the downfall of the Democratic Republic of Afghanistan, the Soviet Union's closest strategic partner in Central Asia, is the offensive campaign which most closely resembles that against the Syrian Arab Republic three decades later. Many of the same means were used in both cases, with both states singled out for targeting largely in order to harm their strategic partners.

The Afghan War had its origins in an Islamist insurgency against the socialist and Soviet-aligned Democratic Republic of Afghanistan, a country which had been receiving considerable aid in fields ranging from infrastructure to military modernisation from Moscow. In the face of a growing perceived threat from Western-aligned neighbours Pakistan and Iran, Afghan President Daud Khan had initiated a military buildup in 1978 with Soviet assistance and signed a treaty that year which allowed Kabul to call upon Moscow's support if under attack.[15] Soviet allegations of Western support for insurgents against the Afghan government were made as early as February 1979. While third party intervention and an escalation of the war in Afghanistan was for many years portrayed in the West as having begun when the Soviet Union first deployed its military to the country in force, documents since declassified show that overt Western support for Islamist insurgents began in July 1979 at the very latest – half a year before the Soviets had intervened.[16] Concealing this fact for many years, however, allowed Western media to depict support for insurgents as a response to Soviet aggression – in contrast to Moscow's claim that it intervened in response to the West's targeting of the Afghan government, which American documents would later prove correct. As the Carter administration's National Security Advisor Zbigniew Brzezinski stated: "We didn't push the Russians to intervene, but we knowingly increased the probability that they would." He referred to U.S. support for jihadist groups as "drawing the Russians into the Afghan trap."[17]

Western involvement in the war in Afghanistan had two primary facets, the first being provision of major material support including both funding and armaments to Islamist insurgents both directly and through third parties such as Pakistan and Saudi Arabia.[18] The second pertained to war propaganda and the use of the Western Bloc's major information warfare assets, from Hollywood to ABC News,[19] to present a narrative which glorified the insurgency, delegitimised the Soviet premise for intervention and demonised the Soviet military. Given the insurgency's heavy reliance on funding and recruits from other Muslim states, and the Arab world in particular, the West's use of its global media presence to put forward the narrative that the Afghan people were oppressed by a malicious Soviet empire served as an effective recruitment tool for potential jihadists.

Under Operation Cyclone, the CIA and Britain's MI6 had provided several billion dollars' worth of material aid to radical Islamist groups, rather than to more moderate factions opposed to the Kabul government.[20] War materials for the insurgents were purchased primarily from non-Western third parties such as China and Egypt to ensure the operation was deniable.[21] CIA Station Chief in Kabul Graham E. Fuller described the primary recipients of armaments and other material aid as "nasty" and "ideologically zealous,"[22] and it mattered little that many of these militant groups were themselves virulently anti-Western.[23] Western assistance thus not only strengthened the Islamist insurgency profoundly, but also shaped the country's future in a much more radical direction by strengthening extremist insurgent groups over moderate ones. This directly resulted in the rise of Al Qaeda and later the Taliban.[24]

The extent of Western support for the insurgency in Afghanistan went so far as to include infrastructure support, with the CIA organising and financing the construction of the "impregnable cave fortress" of Tora Bora for use by militant forces.[25] When Pakistan's Inter-Services Intelligence agency (ISI) informed the CIA in 1985 of plans to work with insurgents to assassinate high ranking Soviet officers, the CIA supplied sniper rifles and sophisticated sighting scopes. The CIA and ISI also collaborated from around the same time to supply training schools to prepare Islamist insurgents for guerrilla warfare, one of which focussed on urban sabotage techniques. These provided insurgents with key skills, including how to build and conceal makeshift bombs with C-4 plastic explosives, and trainees were also provided with over 1000 chemical and electronic-delay bomb timers by the CIA. These materials and skills were used to attack bridges, tunnels, pipelines and other key infrastructure, as well as to carry out car bombings in Afghan population centres.[26]

The most notable case of American material support for jihadist insurgents was the delivery from 1986 of over 1500[27] Stinger man-portable surface-to-air missiles with advanced 'fire and forget' capabilities, which were advocated as a means of quickly increasing the cost of the war for the Soviets.[28] This undermined Afghan and Soviet forces' ability to use air power to provide fire-support, reconnaissance, convoy security, tactical airlift, mining, ambushes, and dismounted operations.[29] Although the Stinger's success was later grossly exaggerated in the West,[30] it did force Soviet air units to fly more cautiously, expending more resources in the process,[31] while causing some losses which were extensively photographed by insurgents and sent on to the United States.[32] The provision of Stingers was described as "removing this last fig leaf from the American secret war," ending all pretence that the U.S. was not openly arming jihadists against the Afghan state.[33]

American groups such as the Federation for American-Afghan Action, Free the Eagle, the Committee for a Free Afghanistan, and the Freedom Research Foundation, many with close ties to U.S. intelligence, played a key role in lobbying Congress for more direct American action. They also took the lead in influencing media outlets in the West and the Muslim world to cover the insurgency sympathetically.[34] Indeed, National Intelligence Officer Arnold Horelick described support for jihadist insurgency against the Afghan state and the Soviet Union as intended to "inflame Moslem opinion against them in many countries."[35] U.S. media went to considerable lengths to lionise Islamist militants, and to depict their cause as part of a global struggle against evil itself. Western media, ranging from popular media to news channels, consistently presented the USSR as a faceless, technologized and atheistic empire being resisted by noble and very humanised tribal people committed to traditional values. Prominent documentaries portrayed jihadist fighters as "brave peasant men who believe they are fighting for Allah,"[36] juxtaposing close-up images of the insurgents praying and fighting with outdated handheld weapons with scenes of powerful Soviet tanks and helicopters – but never the faces of Soviet soldiers themselves. This was one of many visual techniques used to dehumanise the adversary and create sympathy for the scantily armed "soldiers of God."[37] Portrayals were no different in popular media, with the producers of the film Rambo III, which was released during the war and was the most expensive film ever made at the time, having specifically assigned "the task of casting two dozen vicious looking Russian troops" who "were supposed to make your blood run cold." The film depicted an American hero fighting with fearless jihadist warriors against overwhelming odds and was dedicated to the Afghan insurgency.[38]

As would be the case with Syria, the U.S. also worked closely with client states in the region to undermine the target state – in this case cooperating closely with Pakistan. Director of Intelligence for the U.S. National Security Council Vincent Cannistraro stated regarding relations with Pakistan and the Afghan insurgents: "the CIA believed they had to handle this as if they were wearing a condom" – the Americans and insurgents being the sexual partners in this analogy and the Pakistanis the contraceptive which would keep CIA hands clean.[39] Arms transfers, for example, were most often made through the ISI.[40] When the CIA sought to escalate the conflict with attacks on strategic targets, the U.S. provided demolition experts and detailed satellite intelligence to help the ISI plan offensive operations, with ISI officers accompanying Afghan militants on many of these raids.[41] Teams of ISI personnel dressed as Afghans not only frequently operated alongside Islamist insurgents, but also conducted their own independent operations on Afghan soil against Afghan and Soviet forces.[42] The importance of U.S.-supplied intelligence to offensive operations against the Afghan state was repeatedly stressed by the Pakistani military leadership.[43]

The U.S. also supplied the Pakistani Air Force with F-16 fighters, the third ever export client for fourth generation Western aircraft, which allowed the formerly obsolete service to harass Afghan strike and transport aircraft. The F-16s frequently violated Afghan airspace and attacked targets such as cargo planes and attack jets, which significantly complicated counterinsurgency efforts by giving insurgents a degree of air support.[44] Pakistan's role in Afghanistan would have close parallels in the Syrian War, where more modern variants of the F-16 used by Turkey and Israel similarly forayed into the target state's airspace to provide air support to Western-backed insurgents. Turkey would also embed special forces[45] with jihadist militants in Syria and was responsible for handling arms transfers to them[46] and providing them safe haven on its territory,[47] in close coordination with the U.S., almost exactly as Pakistan had in Afghanistan.[48]

Alongside Pakistan, other U.S.-aligned Muslim states such as Egypt[49] and Saudi Arabia[50] also provided significant material support to the Afghan insurgency, with Saudi soft power as the centre of Sunni Islam further used to legitimise the conflict, which resulted in several thousand Arab volunteers joining the Western-orchestrated war effort.[51] The extremism of these Arab militants and the brutality of the atrocities they committed were severe even by the standards of an already harsh jihad, and were widely considered counterproductive for alienating the populace from the insurgency.[52] Arab jihadists in Afghanistan would receive CIA support,[53] with the agency reportedly openly recruiting militants from Arab states in Africa as well as from Saudi Arabia itself for deployment to Afghanistan.[54]

A particularly notable feature of the Afghan War, which would closely mirror the case in Syria years later, was the importance of Western global media in shaping its outcome. This allowed the West to frame the insurgency to the world as a virtuous cause against evil, rather than as terrorism, and to discredit Soviet narratives regarding the nature of their intervention. It was only after the war that Western analysts would begin to give more sober assessments as to exactly what kind of parties the Western world and its partners had backed and empowered.[55] Had the U.S. and its allies not intervened to support the Afghan insurgency, there is a very significant possibility that the USSR would not have dispatched its armed forces to Afghanistan. The insurgency not only would have lacked the support of public opinion in much of the world, but it would also have lacked the funds, arms, intelligence or training needed[56] to conduct any meaningful operations or recruit sufficient numbers of personnel to challenge the heavily armed and well trained Afghan government forces[57] – let alone the Soviet military.

The U.S. continued to provide massive material support to jihadist groups after the Soviet withdrawal from Afghanistan in 1989, ensuring a victory for jihadist elements over the secular government which was achieved three years later in 1992.[58] The fate of the formerly progressive and fast modernising country after its defeat, from sharp declines in the status of women, drug abuse, life expectancy and economic output to peace and stability, can be observed until today.

The war against the Afghan state was far from the end of Western involvement with extremist jihadist groups, which would go on to serve the interests of the Western world by working against both the disintegrating state of Yugoslavia and the remnants of Russian power after the Soviet collapse. Many of the jihadist militants who had been trained and armed in Afghanistan were transferred to Yugoslavia, escalating the already high tensions between Muslim and non-Muslim groups and supporting offensives against Serbian forces which opposed Western designs for the country. America's chief Balkans peace negotiator, Richard Holbrooke, himself testified that deployment of jihadists from Afghanistan played a key role in ensuring the survival of Western-aligned local militias in that conflict.[59] These deployments were one of several aspects of a full spectrum war on the country, which included not only information warfare and aid for a range of extremist separatist groups, but also a relentless Western bombing campaign specifically targeting civilian infrastructure.[60] U.S. use of highly toxic depleted uranium weapons against population centres in particular would have a serious detrimental effect on public health for generations to come.[61] The fate of the Yugoslav population in defeat was dire, with a rise in human trafficking and American soldiers on the ground found to have taken teenage and pre-teen girls as sex slaves.[62] The formerly thriving industrial economy was brought to ruin as the country's position as an independent pole in the international community was ended permanently, with its successor states brought firmly into the Western sphere influence.

The use of jihadist forces in the aftermath of the West's success in Afghanistan also had a major impact on Russian security. CIA National Council on Intelligence's Deputy Director Graham E. Fuller, a key architect in the creation of the jihadist insurgency in Afghanistan, stated regarding the agency's strategy in the Russian Caucasus in the 1990s: "The policy of guiding the evolution of Islam and of helping them against our adversaries worked marvellously well in Afghanistan against the Red Army. The same doctrines can still be used to destabilize what remains of Russian power."[63] The U.S. Congressional Task Force on Terrorism and Unconventional Warfare's director, Yossef Bodansky, detailed the extent of the CIA's strategy to use jihadist proxies for destabilisation:

> A formal meeting in Azerbaijan in December 1999 in which specific programs for the training and equipping of Mujahideen from the Caucasus, Central/South Asia and the Arab world were discussed and agreed upon, culminating in Washington's tacit encouragement of both Muslim allies [Arab states and Turkey] and U.S. 'private security companies' ... to assist the Chechens and their Islamist allies to surge in the spring of 2000 and sustain the ensuing Jihad for a long time... [the U.S. saw] Islamist Jihad in the Caucasus as a way to deprive Russia of a viable pipeline route through spiralling violence and terrorism.[64]

Russia's government claimed to have evidence of contacts between Islamist fighters and Western intelligence groups.[65] Known as the Arab Mujahideen in Chechnya, the militants came from a variety of nationalities but were united by their Arab Wahabist ideology – the same as that of Al Qaeda, the Islamic State and other radical Islamist groups, which had its origins in

the Arabian peninsula.[i] According to leading members of Saudi
Arabia's royal family, this extremist ideology was spread through
overseas religious education by the Saudi state at the request of
the Western powers specifically to provide a means of undermining the Soviet Union and its sphere of influence.[66] This capitalised
on Saudi Arabia's considerable wealth and its authority at the
centre of Sunni Islam – an asset which would later fuel the Syrian
insurgency with Saudi supported preachers specifically advocating violence towards Syria's religious minorities and a holy
war against the state.[67] Partnership with Wahabist Islam proved
a highly successful and extremely cost effective strategy for the
West, requiring relatively little investment and causing immense
damage to countries which resisted Western hegemonic ambitions.

Russia failed to counter jihadist activities on its territory
throughout the 1990s, although decisive military action in the
early 2000s making extensive use of mines and special forces
managed to push these forces out of the Chechen autonomous
region, which had been placed entirely under their control. Russia
in the 1990s, like Afghanistan and Yugoslavia, risked descend-
ing into chaos, with the jihadist insurgency in Chechnya and the
country's severe economic crisis potentially representing only
the first stages. President Vladimir Putin, who assumed office in
2000, recalled that Russia was set to undergo the same scenario
as Yugoslavia – chaos, destabilization and eventual fragmentation – likely followed by imposition of a Western military presence on its soil. He recalled in 2014 regarding Western actions:
"The support of separatism in Russia from abroad, including
the informational, political and financial, through intelligence
services, was absolutely obvious. There is no doubt that they
would have loved to see the Yugoslavia scenario of collapse and
dismemberment for us with all the tragic consequences it would

---

i   The *New York Times* would years later describe the prevalence of this as a
    Saudi policy of "continuing to spend billions of dollars spreading Wahhabism,
    its ultraconservative brand of Islam – which in turn inspires ISIS, Al Qaeda
    and other Sunni extremists – through a network of imams and mosques in
    countries like Kosovo, Indonesia and Pakistan," highlighting that it fuelled
    jihadism around the world. ('Fighting, While Funding, Extremists,' *New
    York Times*, June 19, 2017.)

have for the peoples of Russia."[68] Putin stated the following year, to much the same effect: "At the end of the 1990s Russia was pretty close to following the Yugoslav scenario."[69] A number of factors including new leadership from the turn of the century, the effectiveness of the intelligence agencies, an awareness of the Western modus operandi after witnessing the fates of Yugoslavia and Afghanistan, and America's shift from 2001 towards preoccupation in the Middle East and Afghanistan which relieved pressure on Russia, ultimately meant that the former superpower did not endure the same fate.

The Western Bloc's means for destabilising and subjugating states with significant Muslim populations, either as minorities or majorities, would show significant consistencies over several decades. An understanding of the means used to destabilise Indonesia, Afghanistan, Yugoslavia and Russia, therefore, is vital to placing later efforts to effect similar change in Syria in the context of broader trends in U.S. and allied foreign policy. As director of the United States National Security Agency under Ronald Reagan who oversaw the escalation of the Afghan war by proxy, Lieutenant General William Odom, noted in 2007: "Because the United States itself has a long record of supporting terrorists and using terrorist tactics, the slogans of today's war on terrorism merely makes the United States look hypocritical to the rest of the world."[70] Odom separately recalled: "In '78–79 the Senate was trying to pass a law against international terrorism – in every version they produced, the lawyers said the U.S. would be in violation."[71] As a CIA memorandum from 2010 similarly observed: "Contrary to common belief, the American export of terrorism or terrorists is not a recent phenomenon." It warned that greater international awareness regarding both this and "U.S. double standards in international law" could considerably reduce other states' willingness to cooperate and share intelligence with America.[72] This trend towards support for terror groups had very significant implications for how the U.S. and its allies would seek to seek to overthrow the Syrian state – an operation which would in many ways closely resemble the destabilisation of Afghanistan three decades prior.

## The Growing Centrality of Information Warfare to Western Overseas Offensives

Although Syria had been a leading Western adversary for decades, multiple factors led to the targeting of the country for intensive attack economically, militarily and using information warfare from March 2011. The means used to undermine the Syrian state, including full spectrum support for radical Islamist militants on the ground, social engineering using tools such as social media, and the emphasis on economic sanctions and blanket demonisation of the state throughout Western and Western-aligned media outlets, were all far from unprecedented.

Information warfare came to the fore of U.S. and allied efforts to undermine states outside the Western sphere of influence under the Barak Obama administration from 2009. It was emphasized over other forms of warfare for a number of reasons, ranging from its much higher cost effectiveness to the war-weariness of the U.S. population after the heavy-handed military interventions of the George W. Bush years. For the purposes of this work, information warfare will be defined as the manipulation of information trusted by a target without the target's awareness, leading the target to make decisions against their own interest, but in the interest of the one conducting information warfare operations. In the context of inter-state relations, information warfare has often involved the manipulation of public opinion by an enemy state in line with that offending state's interest. A notable contemporary example is the widespread Western claims of the malign influence of Russian media, including social media accounts sponsored by Moscow, on public perceptions in the Western world. Russia has allegedly used obscurantist means to promote Russophilian narratives and undermine faith in the institutions, political systems and ideologies of the targeted Western countries with the end goal of subversion and the furthering of Moscow's interests.[73] While reports of Russian information warfare efforts have been prominent since 2016, it is notable that Western states have made effective use of media, including social media, for essentially identical ends since at least 2010, targeting a number of adversaries ranging from North Korea[74] and Iran to Syria itself.

Information warfare under Obama often succeeded where military options and economic warfare were not viable. This included a focus on active dissemination of obscurantist political narratives supporting Western objectives – most often by demonising target governments, delegitimising their institutions and political systems, and promoting narratives which were both pro-Western and favourable in their coverage of Western sponsored political actors. Social media emerged as a key tool to promote such narratives, and Western governments maintained close cooperation with internet and social media companies such as Google and Twitter, which often directly supported such efforts.[75] This was coupled with provision of funding and training for pro-Western and anti-state activists and organisations through Western non-government organisations, which maintained very close cooperation with the CIA and other Western intelligence agencies.[76]

As a prominent 2015 paper on information warfare from the NATO Cooperative Cyber Defence Centre of Excellence noted, citing Russian sources: "information can be used to disorganise governance, organise anti-government protests, delude adversaries, influence public opinion, and reduce an opponent's will to resist." This can be coupled with other forms of warfare, perhaps preceding a ground invasion, but it can equally prove effective on its own.[77] The results of Western information warfare efforts, which escalated significantly during the Obama years, were seen in Ukraine,[78] Hong Kong,[79] Libya[80] and much of the Middle East[81] – destabilizing and in many cases toppling governments outside the Western sphere of influence.

Western information warfare offensives in Syria must therefore be understood as part of a revolution in the Western way of war, capitalising on new technologies such as social media to find new ways of targeting adversary states by directly accessing their populations. Successes targeting Arab states in the early 2010s were intended to be followed by further operations against other more capable Western adversaries. Attesting to this, following the success of information warfare efforts against Syria and Libya,

U.S. Senator John McCain, who would soon afterwards become Chairman of Senate Joint House Services Committee, referred to the new information offensive as "a virus that will attack Moscow and Beijing."[82] President of the Joseon Institute and founder of Liberty in North Korea and Pegasus Strategies Adrian Hong, who later led a violent attack on the Korean embassy in Spain and worked in close cooperation with U.S. intelligence,[83] stated in much the same vein following successful operations to destabilise Libya and Syria that the offensives were "a dress rehearsal for North Korea."[84] The Obama administration's strategy against North Korea in its first six years relied extremely heavily on information warfare,[85] which the president personally endorsed and expressed considerable faith in.[86]

Iran, meanwhile, which the United States considered its fourth 'Great Power Adversary' alongside China, Russia and North Korea,[87] had seen Western information warfare efforts bear fruit within months of the Obama administration's inauguration. American social media companies played a pivotal role in fuelling anti-government sentiments in 2009 and in organising protests over the disputed outcome of the country's presidential election. Western social media giant Twitter notably delayed its scheduled maintenance to remain active for the specific purpose of helping to facilitate Iranian protests.[ii] Twitter had reportedly made this decision upon the advice of Google Ideas director Jared Cohen, who was also a senior fellow at the Council on Foreign Relations and a prominent foreign policy advisor.[88] Cohen had himself strongly advocated the use of social media by Western powers to achieve

ii   Dr. James Jay Carafano, vice president of the Kathryn and Shelby Cullom Davis Institute for National Security and Foreign Policy, stated at the time regarding the importance of emerging technologies as new mediums for information warfare: "The American government should pay close attention to the Iranian experience. Web 2.0 (Facebook, Twitter, Google, YouTube etc.) technologies have a potentially important role to play in a range of endeavors related to U.S. national security." He stressed the importance of close partnerships between the government and social media companies to pursue foreign policy objectives overseas, and was one of several analysts at the time to highlight the importance of this to achieving Western policy objectives. (Cafarno, James, 'All a Twitter: How Social Networking Shaped Iran's Election Protests,' *The Heritage Foundation,* July 20, 2009.)

foreign policy objectives, gaining him the name in some circles of "director of regime change."[89]

Cohen advocated use of information warfare to topple governments that the West labelled "undemocratic," expressing his belief in a global mandate for the Western world to intervene against, force change in, and remake them in the West's own ideological image. He stated to this effect:

> Democratic states that have built coalitions of their militaries have the capacity to do the same with their connection technologies.... They offer a new way to exercise the duty to protect citizens around the world who are abused by their governments or barred from voicing their opinions. Faced with these opportunities, democratic governments have an obligation to join together... to bring about change. They must listen to those on the frontlines and recognize that their citizens' use of technology can be an effective vehicle to promote the values of freedom, equality, and human rights globally.[90]

Promotion of Western values, and purported concern for the wellbeing of peoples living in states outside the Western sphere of influence, was very consistently used as a pretext for subversive activities against governments opposed to Western hegemonic designs. The aforementioned examples of Indonesia, Afghanistan and Yugoslavia, which by any account were better off before Western destabilisation efforts, were cases in point. Syria, Iran, North Korea, China and others were similarly made targets for Western subversion under the pretext of humanitarianism.

Cohen was notably in the Middle East in early 2011, and spearheaded ideologically driven Google Ideas projects targeting U.S. adversaries in the region which emphasized engaging local communities and engineering "social change."[91] Wikileaks founder Julian Assange, who interviewed Cohen at length and published an extensive analysis of Google's important role in U.S. foreign policy designs, observed: "Cohen's directorate appeared to cross over from public relations and 'corporate responsibility' work into active corporate intervention in foreign affairs at a level that is normally reserved for states... According to the emails, he was trying to plant his fingerprints on some of the major historical events in the contemporary Middle East." Under Cohen: "Google's geopolitical aspirations are firmly enmeshed within the foreign-policy agenda of the world's largest superpower. Its influence on the choices and behaviour of the totality of individual human beings translates to real power to influence the course of history." Assange compared Google's relationship with and role in U.S. foreign policy activities to that of the private military company Blackwater/Xe Services/Academi, with both having revolving doors with the public sector and employing unique capabilities to further American interests.[92] Google's power was such that, according to Assange's 2014 assessment, it would soon be able to "interpose itself, and hence the United States government, between the communications of every human being not in China" – a very major asset for any social engineering effort.[93]

Complementing Google's operations, the U.S. had long provided extensive funding to nurture political opposition against multiple governments in countries outside its sphere of influence – including that of Syria. Leaked cables showed that an early policy review under the Obama administration stressed the importance of ongoing efforts to pursue "civil society programming" and "behaviour reform" to effectively reshape Syrian thought and political culture in line with U.S. interests. A cable from April 28, 2009, emphasized that if these secret social engineering programs were made public, they could be viewed as "an attempt to undermine the Assad regime" and "tantamount to supporting regime change." An example of one such program, carried out by the State Department's U.S.-Middle East Partnership Initiative, involved funding the anti-government satellite television network Barada TV, with the American origin of the funds kept secret.[94]

Information warfare came to the fore of U.S. and Western foreign policy efforts at a time when a global economic shift away from Europe and the United States and towards East Asia had limited Western options to exert pressure through unilateral sanctions and other economic warfare means. It was also a time when Western targets such as China, Iran and North Korea had begun to field increasingly sophisticated deterrence capabilities, which combined with the American public's war weariness after the Iraq War served to limit options for Western coercion through military force. It was therefore logical that the Western world would only increase its emphasis on information warfare to open up a third front through which to exert pressure. Thus, while offensive actions under the Bush administration can be characterised by tens of thousands of boots on the ground and conventional large scale military invasions, Obama's was characterised by presidential kill lists,[iii] extrajudicial drone assassinations[95] and more significantly by major investments in information warfare. The Syrian War has been a prime example of this, and the trend towards a focus on information warfare would continue over the following decade.

## Syria's Vulnerability as a Target and the Organisation of Western Information Warfare Efforts

The beginning of the Syrian War marked the convergence of multiple geopolitical and domestic trends which portended conflict, as well as a convergence of multiple *casus belli* which made it imperative for the Western Bloc and its regional partners to target the country. The Western-centred global financial crisis in 2008 had adversely affected the Syrian economy and much of the Arab world, placing downward pressure on living standards which was only further exacerbated by the new privatisation drive pursued under President Bashar Al Assad. Syria's relative isolation from the Western economies, however, meant that although the fallout from the 2008 crisis was significant, it was still much smaller than that affecting Western client states such as the gulf

---

iii Obama notably took the unprecedented step of assassinating U.S. citizens including children without trial, which had significant implications for American political culture and the rule of law (Bauman, Nick, 'The American Teen Whose Death-by-Drone Obama Won't Explain,' *Mother Jones,* April 23, 2015.) (Silverglate, Harvey, 'Obama Crosses the Rubicon: The Killing of Anwar al-Awlaki,' *Forbes,* October 6, 2011.)

countries and Egypt.[96] More serious than the financial crisis was an environmental crisis which followed from 2007 to 2010 in the form of one of the most intense droughts recorded in Syria. The multiple crop failures which resulted meant rural communities were particularly hard hit,[97] leading not only to price hikes but also to large scale migration to cities. Tensions between the urban populations and rural migrants were high, with the more conservative farmers tending to wear Islamic dress and practice a much more traditional lifestyle. This led to a culture clash when exposed to the much more Westernised lifestyles in cities where customs and dress, particularly for women, were very different. By forcing these two contrasting segments of Syrian society to live closer together, economic circumstances did much to drive them further apart, leading to a growing sense of alienation among the poor 'have nots' from the countryside from the urban elite. Economic austerity has traditionally provided fertile ground for radical politics, a trend observable throughout history,[98] which combined with contrasting values between conservative and liberal social groups meant that, when signs of an Islamist uprising emerged three years after the financial crisis, it was well timed to win over a significant segment of the population.

The U.S. foreign policy community was well aware of these trends, and alongside its allies was able to both exploit and in many cases exacerbate them to great effect. One of the first signs of more active U.S. efforts to destabilise Syria came in December 2006 in the form of a secret cable from the American embassy in Damascus titled 'Influencing the SARG [Syrian Arab Republic Government] in the End of 2006.' The cable's stated goal was to summarise assessments of potential vulnerabilities and how they could be exploited to this end. It highlighted that one "opportunity" was presented by a "potential threat to the regime from the increasing presence of transiting Islamist extremists" from Iraq in particular. It suggested that fuelling sectarian tensions among the country's Sunni majority could increase the Islamist threat to Syrian stability, which could be done in collaboration with Western-aligned Arab states as follows:

PLAY ON SUNNI FEARS OF IRANIAN INFLUENCE: There are fears in Syria that the Iranians are active in both Shia proselytizing and conversion of, mostly poor, Sunnis. Though often exaggerated, such fears reflect an element of the Sunni community in Syria that is increasingly upset by and focused on the spread of Iranian influence in their country through activities ranging from mosque construction to business. Both the local Egyptian and Saudi missions here (as well as prominent Syrian Sunni religious leaders) are giving increasing attention to the matter and we should coordinate more closely with their governments on ways to better publicize and focus regional attention on the issue.

The cable was written at the height of sectarian Sunni-Shia violence in Iraq, and it was impossible for anyone in the U.S. government to claim innocence regarding what such a policy in Syria could lead to. Moves to "publicize Syrian efforts against extremist groups in a way that suggests weakness" were also advocated, which had the potential to embolden jihadist groups to target the country. The cable further stressed efforts to present Syria's economic reforms as failing, to undermine the government's popular legitimacy, and to isolate Syria from the remainder of the Arab world while discouraging Gulf states from investing. It further advocated encouraging Western-aligned Arab governments to broadcast "the SARG's dirty laundry" on their television channels as a means to worsen relations and to influence Arab public opinion including within Syria itself.

A 2008 U.S. Army-funded report from the RAND Corporation think tank, *Unfolding the Future of the Long War*, presciently highlighted that Syria was among several "downstream countries that are becoming increasingly water scarce as their populations grow." It highlighted that this, combined with the effects of a rapidly rising population, a 'youth bulge' and internal economic inequalities, could lead to destabilisation. Also very presciently, the paper highlighted that the U.S. had several attractive options to manipulate the behaviour of increasingly powerful jihadist militant groups in the Middle East, including reliance on "covert action, information operations (IO), [and] unconventional warfare" to "use the nationalist jihadists to launch proxy IO campaigns." While the target of such proxy operations was officially listed as rival Islamist groups, what stood out was the paper's confidence in America's ability to manipulate radical jihadists to its own ends – a continuation from Afghanistan two decades prior. This was described as "Divide and Rule," and promised to strengthen the American position in the Middle East profoundly.[99] The primary target, however, would not be rival Islamists, but rather the government of Syria, capitalising on growing popular discontent in conservative and economically struggling communities to provide jihadist forces with a support base.

Perhaps more importantly than economic and social trends in Syria itself was the maturing of information warfare capabilities in the United States and an unprecedented emphasis on this type of warfare under the new Obama administration. The administration laid the ground for major investments in information warfare by the State Department, forming close public-private sector partnership with American tech giants to capitalise on their unique capabilities to manipulate public opinion globally. As the *New York Times* later reported, in an article titled 'US Groups Helped Nurture Arab Uprisings,' not only were uprisings against the Syrian state from March 2011 closely connected to Western NGOs, where the leaders of several anti-government groups had received extensive training, but the U.S. Congress and State Department had worked with tech giants to strengthen these operations. The *Times* reported: "A number of the groups and individuals directly involved in the revolts and reforms sweeping the region... received training and financing from groups like the International Republican Institute, the National Democratic Institute and Freedom House." Skills provided included using social networking and mobile technologies to promote calls for political change along Western lines. Among those sponsoring the meeting were Facebook, Google, MTV, Columbia Law School and the State Department.[100]

One of these conferences was attended by State Secretary Hillary Clinton, as well as staff from the State Department, Google and Facebook and members of leading U.S. media organizations. The tech giants' roles in preparing for these uprisings went beyond sponsoring training events, with the two companies organizing and hosting the events alongside the U.S. government, as made clear by the published event programme.[101] Secretary Clinton's emails, which were later leaked, further revealed the extent of cooperation between the U.S. government and leading tech giants to further foreign policy objectives against Syria. One of these leaks showed cooperation between Google and the State Department to undermine the Syrian government. Google Ideas director Jared Cohen, who formerly worked as an advisor to Hillary Clinton, wanted to encourage members of the Syrian military, then engaged in battles with U.S.-backed militants, to defect. Before Google launched a "defection tracker" Cohen consulted with the State Department.[102] This tracker, according to leaked emails from Secretary Clinton, was "designed to encourage more people to defect and give confidence to the rebel opposition."[103] Cohen had worked across the world to secure U.S. interests with groups ranging from Afghan companies, Islamic religious authorities and Indian film industries, among many others, to further the country's foreign policy agendas. His activities and statements were a strong indicator of the extent of the public-private partnership between the State Department, intelligence agencies and tech giants to pursue multiple often malign foreign policy agendas against those parties targeted for subjugation to Western interests.[104]

Google actively worked to closely support Western-backed anti-government militias in both Syria and Libya in 2011. Google Maps, for example, renamed various streets in government-controlled Damascus after jihadist leaders, wiping the internationally and UN recognised Syrian government off the map as a result. The application similarly renamed key sites in the Libyan capital in accordance with the names given by Western backed militant leaders. These actions reflected the company's political stances against both of the independent Arab governments and its close cooperation with U.S. foreign policy initiatives, including the overthrow of those governments non-compliant with Western hegemonic ambitions.[105]

Ulson Gunnar, a New York based geopolitical analyst specialising in Western foreign policy, noted regarding U.S. tech giants' close cooperation with the government to undermine the Syrian and Libyan states in 2011: "The purpose was clearly to create a unified network combining the U.S. State Department's direction, the tech-giants' technical capabilities, and influence of the U.S. media together to overwhelm the information space when finally the time came for the Arab Spring [uprisings] to unfold. And overwhelm it did."[106] Former State Department security official, and American intelligence company Stratfor's Vice President for Intelligence, Fred Burton, similarly noted regarding this public-private partnership to support U.S. offensives in the Middle East: "Google is getting WH [White House] and State Dept. support and air cover. In reality they are doing things the CIA cannot do."[107]

The value of American tech giants to the country's foreign policy designs had often been less directly assertive, but still played significant roles in undermining target states in other ways. Since 2009 and the partial success of information warfare operations in Iran, the CIA's Open Source Center used access to a massive database of information provided by American social media sites such as Facebook and Twitter to monitor public opinion in specific countries. The Associated Press reported regarding the importance of this to intelligence agencies:

> From Arabic to Mandarin Chinese, from an angry tweet to a thoughtful blog, the analysts gather the information, often in native tongue. They cross-reference it with the local newspaper or a clandestinely intercepted phone conversation. From there, they build a picture sought by the highest levels at the White House, giving a real-time peek, for example, at the mood of a region after the Navy SEAL raid that killed Osama bin Laden or perhaps a prediction of which Mideast nation seems ripe for revolt.[108]

Facebook has itself admitted to carrying out several social experiments on its users, often without their consent,[109] which have ranged from influencing voting patterns[110] to influencing the emotions of its users. A report by the Proceedings of the National Academy of Sciences of the United States (PNAS), titled *Experimental Evidence of Massive-Scale Emotional Contagion Through Social Networks*, stated: "Not only are the findings troubling – illustrating that Facebook possesses the ability to influence the emotions of its users unwittingly through careful manipulation of their news feeds – but the invasive, unethical methods by which Facebook conducted the experiment are troubling as well."[111] The potential applications of such techniques in states targeted by the West – for example to influence public opinion against their government and eventually to support a protest movement or insurgency – were manifold.

Western social media platforms have proven to be highly effective tools for social engineering to promote both Westphilian narratives portraying the West and Western-aligned parties positively, and narratives which demonize or otherwise undermine faith in political actors or ideologies targeted by the West. This has included the mass termination of accounts of parties spreading political messages seen as unfavorable to Western interests, ranging from North Korean video bloggers[112] to Myanmar's armed forces[113] and Chinese citizens critical of Western interference in their country[114] among many others[115] by Western social media giants such as Youtube, Twitter and Facebook. These companies have simultaneously provided an effective medium to spread Western favoured messages internationally. A notable example was the use of false 'sock puppet' social media accounts on a large scale by the U.S. Military for this purpose. The *Guardian* described one such program in early 2011 as using "software that will let it secretly manipulate social media sites by using fake online personas to influence internet conversations and spread pro-American propaganda." The system allowed multiple separate false identities based across the world to be controlled simultaneously by each U.S. Military personnel member with each identity having a convincing background, history and supporting details. According to the U.S. Central Command (CENTCOM), which oversaw the program, the system was designed exclusively to target foreign audiences and would post exclusively in foreign languages.[116]

The program was pursued under Operation Earnest Voice, which CENTCOM Commander General David Petraeus referred to as part of the U.S. Military's efforts to be "first with the truth" – namely to dominate the information space and counter political narratives abroad which were not favourable to U.S. interests.[117] Petraeus' successor, General James Mattis, described the goal of Operation Earnest Voice as "degrading the enemy narrative" – with multiple indications that the target would often be the population of the very country the U.S. considered the enemy.[118] This provided the U.S. with a highly potent tool[iv] for social engineering – whether to pose as dozens or hundreds of Iranian youths complaining of police brutality, as Cubans[119] praising the American political system or as Syrians describing issues in their country through sectarian paradigms and calling for reprisals or condemnation of other ethnic or religious groups. The potential applications of these kinds of highly potent Western social engineering tools were manifold, and multiple U.S. allies went on to invest heavily in such programs to control political narratives across the non-Western world. According to leaked documents from the British Foreign Office, such programs were prone to targeting younger generations in particular to spread pro-Western messages and shape identities and affiliations in ways that undermined Western adversaries.[120]

Beyond a wide range of information warfare tools which were able to target the Syrian population, Syria was also highly

---

iv  The use of social bots – artificial machine-run social media accounts able to post at higher rates than human operators – has been implemented to influence political narratives in favour of Western interests in the past. The 2009 protests in Iran and the aftermath of the 2019 coup in Bolivia are prominent examples where these were used to extensively shape narratives on social media to further Western interests. ('Bot campaign on Twitter fuels confusion about Bolivian unrest,' *The Verge*, November 18, 2019.) (Spencer, Keith A. and Karlis, Nicole, 'Who is behind the right-wing Bolivian botnet?,' *Salon*, November 20, 2019.)

vulnerable to Islamist insurgency due to the strength of the global jihadist movement at the time. The destabilisation of neighbouring Iraq under the George W. Bush administration had provided a major recruitment tool for jihadists in the Middle East region. This directly led to the establishment of Al Qaeda in Iraq as a new branch organisation which benefitted from considerable arms and expertise from former Ba'athist Iraqi military personnel in its ranks.[121] Although these groups were not directly aligned with the West, they were much stronger in 2011 than they had been 10 years prior and were well positioned to exploit chaos in neighbouring Syria to fill the power vacuum which quickly emerged and to carve out their own territory in the country. These groups were supported by other Islamist insurgent groups in Syria and by donations from Persian Gulf monarchies such as Saudi Arabia and Qatar. The Obama-era State Department was fully aware that the gulf was providing massive material support to the Iraqi Al Qaeda branch for operations in Syria, which suited Washington's interests well.[122] The U.S. Defence Intelligence Agency noted in the Syrian War's initial months that there was a significant "possibility of establishing a declared or undeclared Salafist [jihadist] principality in eastern Syria (Hasaka and Deir ez-Zor)," which was "exactly what the supporting powers in the opposition want, in order to isolate the Syrian regime." The Iraqi border regions were thus seen as ripe for conversion into some form of jihadist state long before this reality materialised on the ground, with the area initially occupied by other Al Qaeda affiliates and eventually by the Iraqi Al Qaeda branch, which renamed itself the Islamic State.[123]

Western capabilities to wage wars using militant Islamist groups as proxy forces had been refined over more than four decades and progressed considerably since the war in Afghanistan, with Syria's position in 2011 making it a promising target for such attacks. Multiple Islamist groups would receive significant support either directly from the Western powers, through Western-backed militias on the ground, or from Western-aligned states such as Israel, Turkey, Jordan and the Gulf states. Syria thus faced pressure not only from domestic conditions, but also from very mature and sophisticated information warfare operations and from a jihadist movement at the height of its power which the Western world was able to effectively manipulate.

## Casus Belli:
## Five Converging Rationales for Targeting Syria

While there were multiple converging *casus belli* which led the Syrian state to be targeted for destabilisation and eventual overthrow by the Western Bloc and its partners, one common factor underlying every rationale for targeting Syria was the country's position as an independent state under a single ruling party which was outside the Western sphere of influence. All states of this nature, from the Soviet Union and Ba'athist Iraq to Cuba, Afghanistan (pre-1992) and North Korea among many others, have been targeted for various economic, military and information warfare efforts. The final goal of these efforts has been to bring about their downfall, placing Western soldiers permanently on their soil and placing their territories and populations firmly within the Western sphere of influence. All reasons for targeting Syria are in some way consequences of this one single fact.

While 2011 was the opportune time to target Syria, in light of aforementioned factors such as growing social unrest after the 2008 economic crisis and a crisis in the agricultural sector, the Western decision to make war on the country was intended to yield five major benefits pertaining to Western and allied geopolitical interests. The first was the elimination of the final vestige of Ba'athism and Arab nationalism in the Middle East, much as neutralising Yugoslavia ensured permanent Western dominance over Eastern Europe by neutralising its last independent socialist state. Syria's party state represented the only remnant of an ideology and trans-national republican movement which had, at the height of its power in the late 1960s, appeared poised to permanently end Western hegemony in the Middle East. While Arab nationalism had sharply declined following the defection of Egypt to the Western Bloc in the mid 1970s, taking out the Syrian Ba'ath Party would put the final nail in its coffin and ensure Western dominance would have no secular challengers. Syria, by virtue of its ideology, party system, and refusal to conduct policy in line with Western interests, was a natural target for the Western world.

The second rationale for war was the need to isolate Iran and cripple Hezbollah, which was the primary *casus belli* involving the interests of Israel and the Gulf states as leading Western regional allies. The war in Syria notably began less than five years after Hezbollah's victory over the Israeli Defence Forces in southern Lebanon, the Jewish state's first ever defeat at the hands of an Arab military organisation and the first major loss for a Western-aligned force since the Cold War's end. Hezbollah had only demonstrated a fraction of its military capabilities, with its most capable weapons systems unused and its deepest bunkers and best fortified positions left wholly intact after the war's end. Its military capabilities and political clout had only continued grow in the aftermath.[124] Thus while it was imperative for Israeli and Western interests to neutralise the militia, no favourable military options for doing so existed. Hezbollah relied heavily on Iranian and North Korean material support, the bulk of which was channelled into Lebanon through neighbouring Syria, and it was hoped that forcing the overthrow of the government in Damascus would cripple the militia's ability to supply itself and isolate it from its leading sponsors. While Iran, Syria and Hezbollah were increasingly being referred to as an 'Axis of Resistance' against Western hegemony in the Middle East, taking Syria which was geographically central out of the picture had the potential to break this axis without direct military confrontation – destroying Hezbollah without the need for another war in Lebanon and leaving Iran almost totally isolated in the region.

This rationale for toppling the Syrian government was perhaps best expressed by U.S. presidential candidate Senator Mitt Romney in 2012, who stated: "Syria is Iran's only ally. It is the route for them to arm Hezbollah in Lebanon, which threatens Israel. Seeing Syria remove Assad is a very high priority for us. We need to coordinate our effort with our allies, particularly Israel. We need to make sure the insurgents there are armed."[125] The potential for a takeover of Syria by radical Sunni jihadists, who considered Shiites such as the people of southern Lebanon apostates and would carry out frequent sectarian massacres, also opened the possibility of creating a new front against Hezbollah from its Syrian border. This would be achieved at negligible cost to the Western powers or Israel. The fact that Western-backed Syrian militants were widely chanting violent anti-Hezbollah slogans and burning pictures of its leadership from the very outset of the unrest in the country, despite the Lebanese militia having had no major role in the country at that time, strongly indicated the potential for such a development from the outset.[126]

The third rationale for war was largely economic and pertained to Western intentions both to isolate Iran and to develop alternative sources of natural gas for Europe to that provided by Russia. This was the contest between two rival gas pipeline projects intended to supply the European market through Syrian territory – one from the Qatar's North Field across Saudi Arabia, Jordan, Syria and Turkey, and another from Iran's South Pars Field through Iraq and Syria. The Qatari project was strongly favoured[127] by the U.S. because it would allow its NATO allies to reduce dependence on Russian gas, potentially quite drastically in the long term, and instead be supplied by a dependable client state. Qatar had aligned its foreign policy very closely with Western interests ever since gaining independence from British rule in 1971 and was considered one of the West's most reliable regional partners, bearing a stark contrast to Iran's own relationship with the Western world. Damascus' choice of the Iran-Iraq-Syria pipeline and rejection of the Qatari deal in 2009 was described by analysts as a "direct slap in the face"[128] for the U.S.-approved Qatari plan.

Western news outlets subsequently widely claimed Damascus' decision was political in nature and intended to support the interests of two of its closest foreign partners, Moscow and Tehran. The potential overthrow of the Syrian government, however, opened up the possibility that a new government aligned with the West and the Gulf states would make a very different choice regarding pipelines on its territory, providing a major incentive for these parties to pursue this outcome.[129] As senior attorney for

America's Natural Resources Defense Council Robert F. Kennedy Jr. noted regarding the pipeline in a prominent article for *Politico*:

> Secret cables and reports by the U.S., Saudi and Israeli intelligence agencies indicate that the moment Assad rejected the Qatari pipeline, military and intelligence planners quickly arrived at the consensus that fomenting a Sunni uprising in Syria to overthrow the uncooperative Bashar Assad was a feasible path to achieving the shared objective of completing the Qatar/Turkey gas link...the CIA began funding opposition groups in Syria. It is important to note that this was well before the Arab Spring-engendered uprising against Assad.[130]

The fourth rationale for war was also largely geopolitical and pertained to the Western Bloc's efforts to isolate its four 'Great Power Adversaries,' foremost among which were China and Russia but including also North Korea and Iran. This would be achieved by targeting weaker states across the world which remained outside the Western sphere of influence with the intention of either imposing changes in government on or partitioning of the target states. This would result in new regimes closely aligned with the West on the international stage. After the toppling of Ba'athist Iraq and the absorption of communist South Yemen into the north, Syria remained the only state in the Arab Middle East outside the sphere of Western control. This made Syria a target alongside Libya, Venezuela,[131] Bolivia,[132] Sudan[133] and many other countries on which the Western powers would attempt to impose regime change, largely due their close ties to the higher-level Western adversaries. While major adversaries could not be targeted directly, the expansion of the Western sphere of influence globally and further isolation of these four high level target states from the international community could weaken them considerably. Syria's largest pre-war trading partner was China while its largest arms suppliers and oldest strategic partners were Russia and North Korea. Its fall would effectively ensure that these states would lose an important partner in the region.

The fifth and most controversial major benefit the Western Bloc looked to gain from the Syrian government's overthrow was the creation of a new launchpad for advances by jihadist groups against other Western adversaries. To understand the role a jihadist-controlled Syria would play, a key example was provided by the precedent set by Afghanistan where Western intervention significantly empowered such actors. After the overthrow of the Afghan People's Republic in 1992 with considerable Western support, Afghanistan would serve as a centre for Islamist power projection against Western adversaries for decades. Former Afghan President Hamid Karzai, having served 13 years in his post and worked closely with NATO powers, alluded to U.S. efforts to use Afghanistan as a hub for international jihadist operations by supporting transnational terror groups and the Islamic State (IS) group particular. He stated that the Western powers not only had failed to take any action against IS in Afghanistan, but also indicated that the terror group was receiving direct Western support. He recalled regarding IS in Afghanistan: "from the two years onwards to today, every day the local people, the local elders, government officials, media and others began to report that unmarked foreign helicopters, would go in and support extremists in all parts of the country... there's a lot of evidence, unfortunately, that shows that these extremist forces are supplied from the foreign bases within Afghanistan."[134] The only countries with 'foreign bases' in Afghanistan were the United States and its Western allies. It is notable that the same phenomenon, allegedly U.S. linked 'unmarked helicopters' supporting IS forces, was reported on numerous occasions in Syria,[135] where America would also establish a considerable military presence after large parts of the country were destabilised.

Regarding Afghanistan's role in Western designs for the wider Central Asian region, Karzai elaborated: "The support to Daesh [IS] in Afghanistan is not definitely meant for the purposes in Afghanistan. The U.S. has already established itself in Afghanistan. It doesn't need to have a reason to establish itself there. It must be for objectives beyond Afghanistan, to cause trouble in the region."[136] The former president's allegations would hardly be unthinkable considering both the numerous precedents set for the U.S. supporting Islamist forces in Afghanistan and other regions, as well as the formidable asset such a group's emergence in the country could provide. An Islamic State presence bordering Iran, China and the Russian sphere of influence in Muslim-majority Central Asia would have a severe destabilizing effect on all these U.S. adversaries. It could potentially spread a jihadist insurgency to China's Sunni Muslim majority Xinjiang Autonomous Region, as well as derailing the Chinese One Belt One Road initiative to integrate Central Asian economies and develop trade routes through the region.

A subjugated and jihadist dominated Syria, much like Afghanistan which had seen its government toppled twenty years earlier using many of the same methods, would serve as an effective hub for jihadist operations abroad – whether into Iraq to keep check on Iranian influence, into southern Lebanon targeting Hezbollah, or against Iran itself. Projection of jihadist power further afield, including against western China, Russia and Central Asian states, was also a significant possibility, should terror groups such as IS and Al Qaeda be able to operate freely from Syrian territory.[137] It was estimated that 9,000 fighters from Russia and Central Asia alone had joined jihadist groups in Syria and Iraq,[138] while an estimated 5000 from China's Uighur Turkic minority had also joined the frontlines in Syria alone.[139] The potential value of turning Syria into a well-positioned hub of operations against others which resisted Western hegemonic ambitions, much as Afghanistan had been, provided a fifth major incentive for the Western Bloc to undertake operations against the Syrian government.

# Notes

1   Wise, David and Ross, Thomas, *The Invisible Government*, New York, Random House, 1965 (p. 148).
    Blum, William, *Killing Hope: U.S. Military and C.I.A. Interventions Since World War II*, London, Zed Books, 2003 (p. 100).
2   Johnson, Ian, 'Washington's Secret History with the Muslim Brotherhood,' *The New York Review of Books*, February 5, 2011.
3   Burkholder Smith, Joseph, *Portrait of a Cold Warrior*, New York, Putnam, 1976 (p. 210–211).
4   Abrams, A. B., *Power and Primacy: The History of Western Intervention in the Asia-Pacific*, Oxford, Peter Lang, 2019 (Chapter 4: Sukarnoism and the Rise and Fall of an Independent Indonesia: Wars Both Overt and Covert to Return an Asian Power to Western Clienthood).
5   Easter, David, 'British and Malaysia Covert Support for Rebel Movements in Indonesia during the "Confrontation," 1963–1966,' *Intelligence and National Security*, vol. 14, no. 4, Winter 1999 (pp. 195–208).
    Robinson, Geoffrey B., *The Killing Season: A History of the Indonesian Massacres, 1965–66*, Princeton, NJ, Princeton University Press, 2018 (p. 107).
6   Robinson, Geoffrey B., *The Killing Season: A History of the Indonesian Massacres, 1965–66*, Princeton, NJ, Princeton University Press, 2018 (pp. 105).
7   'U.S. "actively supported" Indonesia mass killings in 1960s, documents reveal,' *RT*, October 19, 2017.
8   'U.S. Role in 1960s Indonesia Anti-Communist Massacre Revealed,' *Sputnik*, October 18, 2017.
    Martens, Robert, *The Indonesian Turning Point*, Amazon Digital Services, 2012 (Preface).
9   *New York Times*, March 12, 1966 (p. 6).
10  Henschke, Rebecca, 'Indonesia massacres: Declassified U.S. files shed new light,' *BBC News*, October 17, 2017.
11  *Time*, December 17, 1965.
12  *Life*, July 11, 1966.
13  Robinson, Geoffrey B., *The Killing Season: A History of the Indonesian Massacres, 1965–66*, Princeton, NJ, Princeton University Press, 2018 (pp. 106–107).
14  'Looking into the massacres of Indonesia's past,' *BBC News*, June 2, 2016. 'Indonesia's killing fields,' *Al Jazeera*, December 21, 2012.
15  The Russian General Staff, *The Soviet Afghan-War: How a Superpower Fought and Lost*, Lawrence, University Press of Kansas, 2002 (p. 10).
    Klose, Kevin, 'Soviets Sign Treaty With Afghanistan,' *Washington Post*, December 6, 1978.
16  Weiner, Tim, 'History to Trump: CIA was aiding Afghan rebels before the Soviets invaded in '79,' *Washington Post*, January 7, 2019.
17  Gibbs, David N., 'Afghanistan: The Soviet Invasion in Retrospect,' *International Politics*, vol. 37, June 2000 (pp. 241–242).
18  Crile, George, *Charlie Wilson's War: The Extraordinary Story of How the Wildest Man in Congress and a Rogue CIA Agent Changed the History of Our Times*, New York, Grove Press, 2003.

19    Atanasoski, Neda, *Humanitarian Violence: The U.S. Deployment of Diversity*, Minneapolis, University of Minnesota Press, 2013 (p. 115).
      *ABC News*, December 27, 1984.
      *ABC News*, September 10, 1985.
20    Bergen, Peter, *Holy War Inc.*, New York, The Free Press, 2001 (p.68).
      Coll, Steve, 'CIA in Afghanistan: In CIA's Covert War, Where to Draw the Line Was Key,' *Washington Post,* July 20, 1992.
21    Rubin, Barnett R., *The Fragmentation of Afghanistan: State Formation and Collapse in the International System,* New Haven, Yale University Press, 1995 (p. 197).
      Coll, Steve, 'CIA in Afghanistan: In CIA's Covert War, Where to Draw the Line Was Key,' *Washington Post,* July 20, 1992.
22    Bergen, Peter, *Holy War Inc.*, New York, The Free Press, 2001 (p. 69).
23    Ibid (pp.68–69).
24    Rashid, Ahmed, *Taliban: Militant Islam, Oil and Fundamentalism in Central Asia*, New Haven, CT, Yale University Press, 2001 (pp. 128–129).
      Cook, Robin, 'The struggle against terrorism cannot be won by military means,' *The Guardian*, June 8, 2005.
      'Al Qaeda's Origins and Links,' *BBC News*, July 20, 2004.
25    Weaver, Mary Anne, 'Lost at Tora Bora,' *New York Times,* September 11, 2005.
26    Coll, Steve, 'CIA in Afghanistan: In CIA's Covert War, Where to Draw the Line Was Key,' *Washington Post,* July 20, 1992.
27    Hoodbhoy, Pervez, 'Afghanistan and the Genesis of Global Jihad,' *Peace Research*, vol. 37, no. 1, May 2005 (p. 22).
28    Crile, George, *Charlie Wilson's War: The Extraordinary Story of How the Wildest Man in Congress and a Rogue CIA Agent Changed the History of Our Times,* New York, Grove Press, 2003 (Chapter 11: The Rebirth of Gust Avrakotos, Chapter 28: The Silver Bullet).
29    Alexiev, Alexander, *Inside the Soviet Army in Afghanistan*, prepared for the U.S. Army, Santa Monica, CA, RAND, 1988 (p. 33).
      McMichael, Scott R., *Stumbling Bear: Soviet Military Performance in Afghanistan*, London, Brassey's, 1991 (pp. 84, 89).
      Rais, Rasul Bakhsh, *War Without Winners*, Karachi, Oxford University Press, 1994 (p. 97).
      Crile, George, *Charlie Wilson's War: The Extraordinary Story of How the Wildest Man in Congress and a Rogue CIA Agent Changed the History of Our Times,* New York, Grove Press, 2003 (Chapter 29: The Other Silver Bullet).
30    Gady, Franz-Stefan, 'Afghanistan and The Stinger Myth,' *The Diplomat,* July 1, 2015.
31    The Russian General Staff, *The Soviet Afghan-War: How a Superpower Fought and Lost*, Lawrence, University Press of Kansas, 2002 (p. 312).
32    Crile, George, *Charlie Wilson's War: The Extraordinary Story of How the Wildest Man in Congress and a Rogue CIA Agent Changed the History of Our Times,* New York, Grove Press, 2003 (Chapter 28: The Silver Bullet).
33    Ibid (Chapter 28: The Silver Bullet).
34    Kuperman, Alan J., 'The Stinger Missile and U.S. Intervention in

Afghanistan,' *Political Science Quarterly*, vol. 114, no. 2, Summer, 1999 (p. 224).

35  Gates, Robert, *From the Shadows: The Ultimate Insider's Story of Five Presidents and How They Won the Cold War*, New York, Simon & Schuster, 2006 (p. 145).

36  Atanasoski, Neda, *Humanitarian Violence: The U.S. Deployment of Diversity*, Minneapolis, University of Minnesota Press, 2013 (p. 119).
Bryant, Hilda and Pauli, Richard, 'Afghanistan: Scenes from a Secret War,' 1984 (http://www.documentaryfree.com/watch/afghanistan-1984-scenes-from-a-secret-war).

37  Atanasoski, Neda, *Humanitarian Violence: The U.S. Deployment of Diversity*, Minneapolis, University of Minnesota Press, 2013 (p. 119).

38  '10 Things You Might Not Know About RAMBO III,' *Warped Factor*, September 5, 2019.

39  Coll, Steve, 'CIA in Afghanistan: In CIA's Covert War, Where to Draw the Line Was Key,' *Washington Post*, July 20, 1992.

40  Ibid.

41  Ibid.

42  Crile, George, *Charlie Wilson's War: The Extraordinary Story of How the Wildest Man in Congress and a Rogue CIA Agent Changed the History of Our Times*, New York, Grove Press, 2003 (Chapter 31: It's My War Goddamn It).

43  Coll, Steve, 'CIA in Afghanistan: In CIA's Covert War, Where to Draw the Line Was Key,' *Washington Post*, July 20, 1992.

44  Roblin, Sebastien, 'Pakistan's F-16s Battled Soviet Jets – and Shot Down the Future Vice President of Russia,' *National Interest*, March 16, 2019.

45  'Turkey and Syria trade fire as border skirmishes continue,' *France24*, October 7, 2012.
'Syrian Troops Arrest 4 Turkish Pilots in Aleppo: Report,' *Al Manar*, December 31, 2012.

46  Chivers, C. J. and Schmitt, Eric, 'Arms Airlift to Syria Rebels Expands, With Aid From CIA,' *New York Times*, March 25, 2013.
Taştekin, Fehim, 'Turkish Military Says MIT Shipped Weapons to al-Qaeda,' *Al-Monitor*, January 15, 2015.
Uslu, Emre, 'Has Turkey helped ISIS?,' *Today's Zaman*, August 31, 2014.

47  İpek, Yezdani, 'Syrian rebels: Too fragmented, unruly,' *Hürriyet Daily News*, September 1, 2012.
Yayla, Ahmet S. and Clarke, Colin P., 'Turkey's Double ISIS Standard,' *Foreign Policy*, April 12, 2018.

48  Sengupta, Kim, 'Turkey and Saudi Arabia alarm the West by backing Islamist extremists the Americans had bombed in Syria,' *The Independent*, May 12, 2015.
Bozkurt, Abdullah, 'US Defense Intelligence Agency says Turkey, Qatar supported al-Nusra Front,' *Nordic Monitor*, December 10, 2019.
Hersh, Seymour, 'Military to Military,' *London Review of Books*, vol. 38, no. 1, January 2016 (pp. 11–14).
Uslu, Emrullah, 'Jihadist Highway to Jihadist Haven: Turkey's Jihadi

Policies and Western Security,' *Studies in Conflict & Terrorism*, vol. 39, no. 9, 2016 (pp. 781–802).

Tanis, Tolga, 'Al-Assad in his last six months, US estimates,' *Hürriyet Daily News*, January 17, 2013.

49   Crile, George, *Charlie Wilson's War: The Extraordinary Story of How the Wildest Man in Congress and a Rogue CIA Agent Changed the History of Our Times,* New York, Grove Press, 2003 (Chapter 22: Mohammed's Arms Bazzaar).

Coll, Steve, 'CIA in Afghanistan: In CIA's Covert War, Where to Draw the Line Was Key,' *Washington Post,* July 20, 1992.

50   Bruno, Greg, 'Saudi Arabia and the Future of Afghanistan,' *Council on Foreign Relations*, December 10, 2008.

Rubin, Barnett, *Fragmentation of Afghanistan: State Formation and Collapse in the International System*, New Haven, Yale University Press, 1995 (pp. 100–101).

51   Sageman, Marc, *Understanding Terror Networks*, Philadelphia, University of Pennsylvania Press, 2004 (pp. 5–8).

Marshall, Andrew, 'Terror "blowback" burns CIA,' *The Independent*, November 1, 1998.

52   Sageman, Marc, *Understanding Terror Networks*, Philadelphia, University of Pennsylvania Press, 2004 (pp.58–59).

Akram, Assen, *Histoire de la Guerre d'Afghanistan* [*History of the Afghan War*], Paris, Editions Balland, 1996 (pp. 227–277).

53   Kepel, Gilles, *Jihad: The Trail of Political Islam*, Cambridge, Harvard University Press, 2002 (pp. 300–304).

54   Hoodbhoy, Pervez, 'Afghanistan and the Genesis of Global Jihad,' *Peace Research*, vol. 37, no. 1, May 2005 (pp. 15–30).

55   Burke, Jason, 'Frankenstein the CIA created,' *The Guardian,* January 17, 1999.

Fisher Max, 'Blowback: In Aiding Iranian Terrorists, the U.S. Repeats a Dangerous Mistake,' *The Atlantic,* April 6, 2012.

Bergen, Peter and Reynolds, Alec, 'Blowback Revisited,' *Foreign Affairs,* November/December 2005.

Weiner, Tim, 'Blowback From the Afghan Battlefield,' *New York Times,* March 13, 1994.

Boldak, Spin, 'The "blowback" from Afghanistan "Monster",' *The Baltimore Sun,* August 6, 1996.

56   Coll, Steve, 'CIA in Afghanistan: In CIA's Covert War, Where to Draw the Line Was Key,' *Washington Post,* July 20, 1992.

57   Marion, Forrest L., 'The Destruction and Rebuilding of the Afghan Air Force, 1989–2009,' *Air Power History*, vol. 57, no. 2, Summer 2010 (pp. 22–31).

58   Crile, George, *Charlie Wilson's War: The Extraordinary Story of How the Wildest Man in Congress and a Rogue CIA Agent Changed the History of Our Times,* New York, Grove Press, 2003 (p. 519).

59   O'Neil, Brandon, 'How We Trained Al Qaeda,' *Spectator*, September 13, 2003.

60 Dobbs, Michael, 'NATO's Latest Target: Yugoslavia's Economy,' *Washington Post*, April 25, 1999.
61 '"Up to 15 tons of depleted uranium used in 1999 Serbia bombing" – lead lawyer in suit against NATO,' *RT*, June 13, 2017.
62 Vine, David, *Base Nation, How U.S. Military Bases Abroad Harm America and the World*, New York, Henry Holt and Company, 2015 (Chapter 9: Sex for Sale, Section 5: Sold Hourly, Nightly or Permanently).
O'Meara, Kelly Patricia, 'US: DynCorp Disgrace,' *Insight Magazine*, January 14, 2002.
63 Congressional Record, Volume 151, Part 17, 109th Congress, 1st Session, October 7 to 26, 2005, U.S. Congress.
64 'American political scientist: Western Intelligence used Azerbaijan to export terrorism into Russia,' *Panorama*, May 30, 2015.
65 'Putin accuses U.S. of directly supporting Chechen militants,' *Press TV*, April 26, 2015.
66 'Spread of Wahhabism was done at request of West during Cold War – Saudi crown prince,' *RT*, April 18, 2018.
67 Lacroix, Stephane, *Saudi Islamists and the Arab Spring*, Kuwait Programme on Development, Governance and Globalisation in the Gulf States, Research Paper 36, May 2014.
Adaki, Oren, 'Preaching Hate and Sectarianism in the Gulf,' *Foreign Policy*, May 5, 2015.
Bunzel, Cole, 'The Kingdom and the Caliphate: Duel of the Islamic States,' *Carnegie Endowment for International Peace,* February 1, 2016.
68 Kremlin, President of Russia, *Presidential Address to the Federal Assembly*, December 4, 2014.
69 Bechev, Dimitar, *Rival Power: Russia's Influence in Southeast Europe*, New Haven, CT, Yale University Press, 2017 (Chapter 1).
70 Richards, Anthony, *Conceptualizing Terrorism*, Oxford, Oxford University Press, 2015 (pp. 24–25).
71 'Nine Ways to Stop Terrorism,' *Global Research*, November 18, 2015.
72 'CIA Red Cell special memorandum on "What If Foreigners See the United States as an 'Exporter of Terrorism'",' *Wikileaks*, February 2, 2010 (https://file.wikileaks.org/file/us-cia-redcell-exporter-of-terrorism-2010.pdf).
73 Richter, Monika L., 'The Kremlin's Platform for "Useful Idiots" in the West: An Overview of RT's Editorial Strategy and Evidence of Impact,' *European Values: Protecting Freedom,* September 18, 2019.
'America's exposure to Russian information warfare,' *Financial Times,* December 19, 2018.
*Putin's Asymmetric Assault on Democracy in Russia and Europe: Implications for U.S. National Security*, A Minority Staff Report Prepared for the Use of the Committee on Foreign Relations, United States Senate, One Hundred and Fifteenth Congress, Second Session, January 10, 2018.
74 Abrams, A. B., *Immovable Object: North Korea's 70 Years At War with American Power*, Atlanta, Clarity Press, 2020 (Chapter 19: Information War: The Final Frontier).
75 Assange, Julian, 'Google Is Not What It Seems,' *Wikileaks,* 2016.

76 Nixon, Ron, 'U.S. Groups Helped Nurture Arab Uprisings,' *New York Times,* April 14, 2011.
   Cartalucci, Tony, 'Twitter Targets Hong Kong in US-backed Regime Change Operation,' *Ron Paul Institute for Peace and Prosperity,* October 15, 2019.
   Blum, William, *Rogue State: A Guide to the World's Only Superpower,* London, Zed Books, 2006 (Chapter 19: Trojan Horse: The National Endowment for Democracy).

77 Geers, Kenneth, *Cyber War in Perspective: Russian Aggression against Ukraine,* Tallinn, NATO CCD COE Publications, 2015 (Chapter 10: Russian Information Warfare: Lessons from Ukraine).

78 Soloviev, Andrei, 'NED, просто NED. США вложили в "печеньки" на Майдане почти $14 млн,' [NED, just NED. The United States invested almost $14 million in "cookies" on the Maidan], *Sputnik,* July 15, 2015.
   Moniz Bandeira, Luiz Alberto, *The World Disorder: US Hegemony, Proxy Wars, Terrorism and Humanitarian Catastrophes,* Cham, Springer, 2019 (pp. 191–192).

79 Wei, Xinyan and Zhong, Weiping, 'Who is behind Hong Kong protests?,' *China Daily,* August 17, 2019.
   Cartalucci, Tony, 'Twitter Targets Hong Kong in US-backed Regime Change Operation,' *Ron Paul Institute for Peace and Prosperity,* October 15, 2019.

80 *Libya: Examination of intervention and collapse and the UK's future policy options,* House of Commons Foreign Affairs Committee, Third Report of Session 2016–17, September 14, 2016.

81 Nixon, Ron, 'U.S. Groups Helped Nurture Arab Uprisings,' *New York Times,* April 14, 2011.

82 Clemons, Steve, 'The Arab Spring: "A Virus That Will Attack Moscow and Beijing",' *The Atlantic,* November 19, 2011.

83 Shorrock, Tim, 'Did the CIA Orchestrate an Attack on the North Korean Embassy in Spain?,' *Foreign Policy,* May 2, 2019.
   Cho, Yi Jun, 'Who Is Anti-N.Korean Guerrilla Leader?,' *Chosun Ilbo,* April 4, 2019.

84 Taylor, Adam and Kim, Min Joo, 'The covert group that carried out a brazen raid on a North Korean embassy now fears exposure,' *Washington Post,* March 28, 2019.

85 Abrams, A. B., *Immovable Object: North Korea's 70 Years At War with American Power,* Atlanta, Clarity Press, 2020 (Chapter 19: Information War: The Final Frontier).
   Epstein, Susan B., 'CRS: Radio Free Asia: Background, Funding, and Policy Issues, July 21, 1999,' *Wikileaks,* February 2, 2009.
   Graham Ruddick, 'BBC braces for backlash over North Korea service,' *The Guardian,* August 20, 2017.
   '30–40% of NK thought to be tuning into pirate radio: how do we reach more?,' *Daily NK,* September 14, 2015.

86 Foster-Carter, Aidan, 'Obama Comes Out as a North Korea Collapsist,' *The Diplomat,* January 20, 2015.

87   The National Military Strategy of the United States of America 2015, The United States Military's Contribution to National Security, June 2015.

88   MacAskill, Ewen, 'US confirms it asked Twitter to stay open to help Iran protesters,' *The Guardian*, June 17, 2019.

89   Assange, Julian, 'Google Is Not What It Seems,' *Wikileaks*, 2016.

90   Schmidt, Eric and Cohen, Jared, 'The Digital Disruption, Connectivity and the Diffusion of Power,' *Foreign Affairs*, November/December 2010.

91   Assange, Julian, *When Google Met Wikileaks*, New York, OR Books, 2014 (pp. 22, 46).

92   Assange, Julian, *When Google Met Wikileaks*, New York, OR Books, 2014 (pp. 22, 45, 46).
     Miller, Greg, 'Revolving door from CIA to Blackwater,' *Los Angeles Times*, August 21, 2009.
     Vincent, James, 'The revolving door between Google and the White House continues to spin,' *The Verge*, January 14, 2016.
     'Google's Revolving Door (US),' *Tech Transparency Project*, April 26, 2016.

93   Assange, Julian, *When Google Met Wikileaks*, New York, OR Books, 2014 (p. 55).

94   'Behaviour Reform: Next Steps for a Human Rights Strategy,' *Wikileaks*, April 28, 2009 (https://wikileaks.org/plusd/cables/09DAMASCUS306_a. html).

95   Becker, Jo and Shane, Scott, 'Secret "Kill List" Proves a Test of Obama's Principles and Will,' *New York Times*, May 29, 2012.

96   *Al Thawra*, September 22, 2008.

97   Ahmed, Nafeez, 'Syria intervention plan fuelled by oil interests, not chemical weapons concern,' *The Guardian*, August 30, 2013.

98   Matthews, Dale, 'Study: austerity helped the Nazis come to power,' *Vox*, December 12, 2017.

99   Pernin, Christopher G. and Nichiporuk, Brian and Stahl, Dale and Beck, Justin and Radaelli-Sanchez, Ricky, 'Unfolding the Future of the Long War: Motivations, Prospects, and Implications for the U.S. Army,' *RAND Corporation*, 2008.

100  Nixon, Ron, 'U.S. Groups Helped Nurture Arab Uprisings,' *New York Times*, April 14, 2011.

101  Alliance of Youth Movements Summit, Attendee Biographies, 3–5 December 2008, New York City (http://allyoumov.3cdn.net/f734ac45131b2bbcdb_ w6m6idptn.pdf).

102  'Clinton Emails Show State Department's Close Relationship With Google,' *CBS News*, March 21, 2016.

103  Bolton, Doug, 'Google Planned to Help Syrian Rebels Bring Down Assad Regime, Leaked Hillary Clinton Emails Claim,' *The Independent*, March 22, 2016.

104  Assange, Julian, 'Google Is Not What It Seems,' *Wikileaks*, 2016.

105  'Syria: is it possible to rename streets on Google Maps?,' *The Guardian*, February 15, 2012.

106  Gunnar, Ulson, 'The Lingering Danger of Google & Facebook,' *New Eastern Outlook*, April 30, 2016.

107 Assange, Julian, 'Google Is Not What It Seems,' *Wikileaks, 2016.*

108 Keller, Jared, 'How The CIA Uses Social Media to Track How People Feel,' *The Atlantic,* November 4, 2011.

109 Gibbs, Samuel, 'Facebook apologises for psychological experiments on users,' *The Guardian,* July 2, 2014.

110 'Facebook boosted US election turnout via psychology experiment, company reveal,' *RT,* November 4, 2014.

111 Kramer, Adam D. I. and Guillory, Jamie E. and Hancock, Jeffrey T., 'Experimental evidence of massive-scale emotional contagion through social networks,' *PNAS,* June 2, 2014.

112 O'Carroll, Chad, 'YouTube deletes North Korean state media channel featuring vlogger Un A,' *NK News,* December 11, 2020.

113 'Facebook Bans All Myanmar Military-Linked Accounts and Ads,' *The Diplomat,* February 25, 2020.

114 'British scholar tells the truth about deleted social media accounts related to Hong Kong issues,' *CGTN,* September 18, 2019.

115 'Twitter blocks accounts of Raúl Castro and Cuban state-run media outlets,' *The Guardian,* September 12, 2019.
Sweeney, Steve, 'Cuban journalists condemn Twitter's mass blocking of their accounts,' *Morning Star,* September 12, 2019.
'YouTube shuts down pro-Syrian government channels,' *Al Jazeera,* September 10, 2018.
'YouTube Censors Iranian Press, HispanTV, Press TV Targeted,' *Telesur,* April 19, 2019.
'Google "disables" Press TV's YouTube account,' *Islamic Republic News Agency,* April 19, 2019.
'Twitter suspends Iran Leader's accounts,' *Press TV,* March 31, 2020.
Solon, Olivia, 'YouTube shuts down North Korean propaganda channels,' *The Guardian,* September 9, 2017.
Zimmerman, Max, 'Facebook to Remove Pro-Soleimani Posts on Instagram, CNN Reports,' *Bloomberg,* January 11, 2020.

116 Fielding, Nick and Cobain, Ian, 'Revealed: US spy operation that manipulates social media,' *The Guardian,* March 17, 2011.

117 Ibid.

118 'Department of Defense Authorization for Appropriations for Fiscal Year 2012 and the Future Years Defense Program,' Committee on Armed Services, March 1, 2011 (p. 199).

119 Iannelli, Jerry, 'U.S. Government Has Plans to Spread Hidden Facebook Propaganda in Cuba,' *Miami New Times,* August 21, 2018.
'"Imperial arrogance": Fake FB accounts spewing US propaganda at Cubans fit the pattern,' *RT,* August 29, 2018.
Norton, Ben, 'US Government Admits It's Making Fake Social Media Accounts to Spread Propaganda in Cuba,' *The Real News,* August 27, 2018.

120 Sengupta, Kim, 'New British Army unit "Brigade 77" to use Facebook and Twitter in psychological warfare,' *The Independent,* January 31, 2015.
'Leaked papers allege massive UK govt effort to co-opt Russian-language anti-Kremlin media & influencers to "weaken Russian state",' *RT,* February 18, 2021.

121  Cole, Juan, 'How the United States helped create the Islamic State,' *Washington Post*, November 23, 2015.
Sly, Liz, 'The hidden hand behind the Islamic State Militants? Saddam Hussein's,' *Washington Post*, April 4, 2015.
Abdulrazaq, Tallha, 'Invasion of Iraq: The original sin of the 21st Century,' *Al Jazeera*, March 20, 2018.
122  'We finally know what Hillary Clinton knew all along – U.S. allies Saudi Arabia and Qatar are funding Isis,' *The Independent*, October 14, 2016.
123  'Department of Defense Information Report, Not Finally Evaluated Intelligence – Iraq,' May 3, 2012 (http://www.judicalwatch.org/wp-content/uploads/2015/05/Pg.-2991-Pgs.-291.-287-2993-JW-v-DOD-and-State-14-812-DOD-Release-2015-04-10-final-version11.pdf).
124  Perry, Tom, 'Defying U.S., Hezbollah stronger than ever,' *Reuters*, July 14, 2008.
125  Final (Third) Presidential Debate of 2012 U.S. Presidential Election, October 22, 2012.
126  'Syrian protesters turn on Iran and Hezbollah,' *France24*, March 6, 2011.
127  Ahmed, Nafeez, 'Peak oil, climate change and pipeline geopolitics driving Syria conflict,' *The Guardian*, May 13, 2013.
128  Ibid.
129  Orenstein, Mitchell A. and Romer, George, 'Putin's Gas Attack,' *Foreign Affairs*, October 14, 2015.
Chang, Chris, 'Is the fight over a gas pipeline fuelling the world's bloodiest conflict?,' *news.com.au*, December 5, 2015.
'Syria's Pipelineistan war,' *Al Jazeera*, August 6, 2012.
Dr. Jill Stein on Twitter, 'This explains so much: there are 2 proposed pipelines through Syria – 1 supported by US, 1 supported by Russia,' October 22, 2016.
130  Kennedy, Robert F., Jr., 'Why the Arabs Don't Want Us in Syria,' *Politico*, February 22, 2016.
131  'Venezuela: Former American soldiers jailed over failed coup,' *BBC News*, August 9, 2020.
Vulliamy, Ed, 'Venezuela coup linked to Bush team,' *The Guardian*, April 21, 2002.
132  Prashad, Vijay, 'China's links with Morales figure in Bolivia coup,' *Asia Times*, November 13, 2019.
'Morales claims US orchestrated "coup" to tap Bolivia's lithium,' *Al Jazeera*, December 25, 2019.
'"We will coup whoever we want": Elon Musk sparks online riot with quip about overthrow of Bolivia's Evo Morales,' *RT*, July 25, 2020.
Dogantekin, Vakkas, 'Former US senator hints at CIA role in Bolivia,' *Andalou News Agency*, November 11, 2019.
133  'Deepening Crisis: Sudan Marks One Year Since Coup Ejected Popular Strongman From Power,' *Military Watch Magazine*, April 11, 2020.
134  '"ISIS in Afghanistan is U.S. tool to cause trouble in the whole region" – ex-Afghan President Karzai to RT,' *RT*, October 19, 2017.
135  'U.S. Aircraft Evacuates Over 20 Daesh Commanders From Deir ez-Zor – Source,' *Sputnik*, September 7, 2017.

136  '"ISIS in Afghanistan is U.S. tool to cause trouble in the whole region" – ex-Afghan President Karzai to RT,' *RT*, October 19, 2017.

137  Barrett, Richard, 'Beyond the Caliphate: Foreign Fighters and the Threat of Returnees,' *The Soufan Center*, October 2017.

Sanderson, Thomas, 'Russian-Speaking Foreign Fighters in Iraq and Syria: Assessing the Threat from (and to) Russia and Central Asia,' *Center for Strategic and International Studies*, December 2017.

Jones, Seth G. and Harrington, Nicholas and Bermudez Jr., Joseph S., 'Dangerous Liaisons: Russian Cooperation with Iran in Syria,' *Center for Strategic and International Studies*, July 16, 2019.

Trenin, Dimitri, 'Putin's Syria gambit aims at something bigger than Syria,' *The Tablet*, October 13, 2015.

Lister, Charles, *The Syria Jihad*, London, Hurst, 2015 (pp. 3, 75).

138  Barrett, Richard, 'Beyond the Caliphate: Foreign Fighters and the Threat of Returnees,' *The Soufan Center*, October 2017.

139  Blanchard, Ben, 'Syria says up to 5,000 Chinese Uighurs fighting in militant groups,' *Reuters*, May 11, 2017.

Al-Ghadhawi, Abddullah, 'Uighur Jihadists in Syria,' *Center For Global Policy*, March 18, 2020.

Lin, Meilian, 'Xinjiang terrorists finding training, support in Syria, Turkey,' *Global Times*, July 1, 2013.

Clarke, Michael, 'Uyghur Militants in Syria: The Turkish Connection,' *Jamestown Foundation*, February 4, 2016.

# Chapter 3

# War in Syria:
# The Initial Stages

## Preparing for War

Available evidence indicates that Western plans to topple the Syrian government through support for an insurgency date back to at least 2009 – the first year in office of the Barack Obama administration. During that time the State Department adopted a very different strategy towards engaging target states in the Middle East – one which would not require a costly 'boots on the ground' approach as the Bush administration's strategy had. Alongside the aforementioned information warfare efforts (see Chapter 2), the first signs of which appeared in 2009, French Foreign Minister Ronald Dumas noted that Britain had been preparing for very offensive forms of covert action against Syria from that year. The minister stated to this effect: "I was in England two years before the violence in Syria on other business... I met with top British officials, who confessed to me that they were preparing something in Syria. This was in Britain, not in America. Britain was preparing gunmen to invade."[1] Cables and reports from American, Saudi and Israeli intelligence agencies indicate that it was not only Britain, but the U.S. and its two closest Middle Eastern strategic partners, which by the end of 2009 had begun preparations for operations to forcefully topple the Syrian government through destabilisation.[2]

Leaked 2011 emails from leading private intelligence firm Stratfor, which included notes from a meeting with Pentagon officials, fully confirmed that the war in Syria was from the outset being waged as part of a subversive operation by NATO members Britain, France, the U.S. and Turkey – alongside Jordan which played a key role in the war's initial stages. All of these parties had deployed special forces to Syrian territory to support anti-government forces from the war's outset, with the explicit purpose of forcing a "collapse" of the state "from within."[3] The documents further showed that Western air operations against Syria to tip the balance in the favour of anti-government militant groups were under serious consideration from the war's earliest days, although a number of factors including the advanced capabilities of the country's dense air defence network and its strategic missile and chemical deterrents made this difficult.[4] Syria's North Korean supplied ballistic missiles, armed with either chemical or conventional warheads, could reach NATO territory. This included Turkey and Cyprus, which would be key staging grounds for NATO attacks, as well as American airbases in Jordan and Iraq and population centres in Israel, which seriously complicated planning for a Western offensive.[i] The Stratfor emails also stressed that the Pentagon believed further demonisation of the Syrian state, namely through "media attention on a massacre" by government forces, would be vital to facilitating an air attack.[5] When evidence of atrocities were not forthcoming, they would later be fabricated to provide the Western powers with the pretext needed intervene in force in support of the insurgency, which would play a significant role in the war's later stages (see Chapter Seven and Conclusion).

Operations to topple the government in Damascus under the Obama administration followed on from the Bush administration's authorisation of CIA operations targeting Hezbollah, Syria and Iran from 2007 – an escalation of hostilities carried out largely in response to Hezbollah's troubling military success in 2006.[6] Referred to as "a major shift in American policy," or "a new strategic alignment in the Middle East," policy in Bush's final two

---

i   This contrasted strongly with Libya, which in the 2000s had renounced its ballistic missile program and all weapons of mass destruction, had allowed highly intrusive Western inspections of its military facilities, and had begun to neglect military modernisation, meaning there was little to deter NATO from launching an offensive air campaign from March 2011. (Kopp, Carlo, 'Operation Odyssey Dawn – the collapse of Libya's relic air defense system,' *Defence Today*, vol. 9, no. 1, 2011.)

years had involved clandestine operations in close cooperation with Saudi Arabia in particular to counter the 'Axis of Resistance.' This centred around the belief that Sunni radical groups such as Al Qaeda were now the 'lesser evil,' and that Iran and its allies should be the primary focus of American and allied attentions. Deputy Director for Research at the Washington Institute for Near East Policy, Patrick Clawson, was thus one of many experts to highlight the possibility of closer ties between the U.S. and Sunni jihadist groups, as had been the case in Afghanistan, Yugoslavia and elsewhere, to counter common enemies.[7] This major strategic shift was key to paving the way for the American war effort in Syria, which centred around an Afghan-style program to strongly support Sunni jihadists to topple a target government.

Many in the U.S. at the time had serious reservations regarding the new strategy which was materialising in early 2007, from Nebraska Senator Chuck Hagel to veteran journalist Seymour Hersh.[8] Hersh projected that it could lead to the U.S. deploying forces to either Syrian or Iranian territory from Iraq, which bordered both, under various pretexts.[9] Fast escalating rhetoric from the administration targeting Damascus and Tehran gave some cause to suspect this possibility, which would ultimately materialise in operations against Syria four years later. These operations involved not only American and allied special forces on the ground, but also a partnership with the 'lesser evil,' in the form of radical jihadist elements, against the Syrian state.

Vali Nasr, senior fellow at the Council on Foreign Relations, Dean of the Johns Hopkins School of Advanced International Studies and expert on conflict in the Middle East, observed in 2007 regarding the new strategy adopted by the Bush administration that Saudi Arabia and other Gulf States would play a major role in mobilising and supporting jihadist elements to back the U.S. and combat the 'Axis of Resistance.' He stated: "The Saudis have considerable financial means, and have deep relations with the Muslim Brotherhood and the Salafis," and were "able to mobilize the worst kinds of Islamic radicals." Regarding the Saudi position, he observed: "Their message to us was 'We've created this movement, and we can control it.' It's not that we don't want the Salafis to throw bombs; it's who they throw them at – Hezbollah, Moqtada Al Sadr, Iran, and at the Syrians, if they continue to work with Hezbollah and Iran."[10] This closely resembled the aforementioned description of CIA National Council on Intelligence's Deputy Director Graham E. Fuller, who advocated "The policy of guiding the evolution of Islam and of helping them against our adversaries" – manipulating jihadist elements to wage war in line with Western interests.[11]

As part of this new partnership, according to Seymour Hersh, "the Saudi government, with Washington's approval, would provide funds and logistical aid to weaken the government of President Bashir [Bashar] Assad." A former senior intelligence official and U.S. government consultant cited by Hersh testified at the time that the U.S. was "in a program to enhance the Sunni capability to resist Shiite influence, and we're spreading the money around as much as we can," with much of this ending up in the hands of radical jihadist groups with links to Al Qaeda, such as Fatah Al Islam and Asbat Al Ansar.[12] While Hezbollah and Iran were both Shiite, Syrian President Bashar Al Assad, although he came from the Alawite sect which was a non-mainstream offshoot of Shiism, ran a government in which Sunnis occupied most major positions.[ii] The Syrian Ba'ath Party had since its foundation rejected sectarianism and chosen its members based on ideology rather than faith or ethnicity, which had been reflected in the composition of Hafez Al Assad's inner circle since long before he ascended to the presidency.[13] Despite Syria's secular government and Sunni majority both among the population and in government, the sectarian paradigm promoted in the West for viewing regional conflict framed it as a collaborator with the Shiite world due to its position in the Axis of Resistance and its joint stance with Iran and Hezbollah against Western regional hegemony.

---

ii  Prominent positions held by Sunnis included, among others, Prime Minister, Religious Minister, Foreign Minister, Interior Minister and presidential National Security Advisor. Sunnis were better represented in government than any other religious group, reflecting their majority status as well as the lack of sectarian division or institutional religious discrimination in Syria.

The policy of supporting radical jihadist groups was strongly advocated by Walid Jumblatt, a prominent figure in Lebanese politics, the leader of its sizeable Druze minority and a close confidant of the Bush administration. Highlighting Syria as a promising target, Jumblatt and his colleagues advised during meetings with U.S. Vice President Richard Cheney that the Syrian Muslim Brotherhood would be "the ones to talk to" if seeking to take action against the country. "We told Cheney that the basic link between Iran and Lebanon is Syria – and to weaken Iran you need to open the door to effective Syrian opposition," Jumblatt said. While acknowledging that some U.S. allies such as Egypt would oppose the idea of supporting the Muslim Brotherhood, Jumblatt stressed that it was necessary to seriously consider this option because "if you don't take on Syria we will be face to face in Lebanon with Hezbollah in a long fight, and one we [the West and Western-aligned parties] might not win."[14]

Regarding the possibility of U.S. and Saudi cooperation with the Syrian Muslim Brotherhood, Seymour Hersh noted in February 2007 after extensively investigating the nature of the Bush administration's new strategic shift:

> There is evidence that the Administration's redirection strategy has already benefitted the Brotherhood. The Syrian National Salvation Front is a coalition of opposition groups whose principal members are a faction led by Abdul Halim Khaddam, a former Syrian Vice President who defected in 2005, and the Brotherhood. A former high-ranking C.I.A. officer told me, "The Americans have provided both political and financial support. The Saudis are taking the lead with financial support, but there is American involvement." He said that Khaddam, who now lives in Paris, was getting money from Saudi Arabia, with the knowledge of the White House. (In 2005, a delegation of the Front's members met with officials from the National Security Council, according to press reports.) A former White House official told me that the Saudis had provided members of the Front with travel documents.[15]

The outbreak of a jihadist insurgency in Syria in 2011, spear-headed by groups linked to the Muslim Brotherhood and various Al Qaeda branches, was thus long in the making, and directly resulted from the Bush administration's strategic shift to make preparations for confrontation with the 'Axis of Resistance.' This offensive was supported by a number of allies – most notably Britain, France, Turkey, Jordan, Qatar and Saudi Arabia. While media across the Western world was quick to portray the outbreak of anti-government protests in the small Syrian border city of Daraa, just a few kilometres from the Jordanian border, as a spontaneous revolution demanding Western style political reforms, the background to Western and allied operations to lay the ground for an Afghan-style jihadist takeover of Syria painted a very different picture.

## The Beginnings of a Jihadist Insurgency

The beginnings of unrest in Syria saw the government forced to handle both attacks on its police and security forces from mid-March 2011,[16] which were particularly focused in the Turkish and Jordanian border areas where highly trained gunmen appeared to be crossing over, as well as street protests in several areas. The Qatari monarchy and its highly influential *Al Jazeera* satellite television channel, which had gained considerable credibility in the Arab world for its favourable coverage of Islamist resistance to Israeli operations in the Gaza Strip in previous years, played a leading role in backing calls for protest against the Syrian government and shortly afterwards in backing the emerging Islamist insurgency. This affected public opinion both within Syria and more broadly in the Arab world, with leaked documents later showing that the U.S. State Department had been able to directly exert an influence over *Al Jazeera's* news coverage.[17] A prominent paper from the Brookings Institute notably referred to *Al Jazeera's* coverage as part of the Qatari state's 'Islamist Soft Power,' with its support for jihadist uprisings against secular governments reflecting the state's own more radical tendencies.[18] These tendencies were also strongly reflected by Qatar's support for Al Qaeda in

Syria.[19] Among *Al Jazeera's* controversies, leaked emails from the news organisation were highlighted by a number of journalists as evidence of its practice of coaching eyewitnesses to give false testimony and fabricate information. Other major controversies included favourable coverage of terror attacks in Algeria, some of which were linked to Al Qaeda, and a strong general bias in favour of Islamist militant groups.[20]

A later paper from the Carnegie Endowment for International Peace highlighted the role of Qatari soft power in having "shaped the emerging narratives of protest through the Doha-based *Al Jazeera* media network." It "mobilized Arab support" for both the NATO war against Libya, after which a Western-aligned Islamist-leaning government was installed, and for the insurgency in Syria.[21] The paper further highlighted close ties between Qatar and both the Syrian and Egyptian branches of the Muslim Brotherhood, which both received state support to attempt to overthrow their countries' secular governments. Qatar's head of state, Sheikh Hamad bin Khalifa, would become the first in the Arab world to call for a foreign military intervention against Syria, and strongly implied the possibility of a Libyan-style Western attack.[22] This came after revelations Qatari special forces units had played a key role in the Western-led war effort against Libya, with hundreds of personnel deployed to launch attacks on Libyan government positions in coordination with Western forces.[23] A similar Qatari contribution to any potential Western military intervention against Syria remained likely. The secular Syrian state, like Libya before it, was thus a common target for both Islamists seeking to impose their theocratic rule, which included the Qatari royal family who set the agenda for *Al Jazeera,* and for the Western Bloc which sought the elimination of a decades-old adversary – the Syrian Ba'ath Party. Media channels in other Western-aligned Arab states, from Saudi Arabia to Jordan, quickly followed *Al Jazeera's* example with highly positive portrayals of the insurgency and multiple hit pieces targeting the Syrian state, the presidency, the military and the Ba'ath Party.

Western expectations for mass protests in major Syrian cities such as Damascus and Aleppo were dashed early on, despite extensive attempts to use American social media sites Facebook and Twitter to stoke them,[24] with unrest initially relegated to the border regions. U.S. ambassador in Damascus, Robert Ford, quickly began to play a very active role in nurturing the few seeds of rebellion that did exist and was one of many Westerners present in Syria at the time who did so.[iii] As *Washington Post* reporter Joby Warrick observed: "Since the early weeks of the uprising, Robert Ford's senior staff had held low-key meetings with opposition leaders and posted carefully worded encouragement on the U.S. Embassy's Facebook page." Ford would appear in the country's fourth-largest city, Homs, at a time when it was playing a central role in the ongoing unrest as the largest city to see any significant protests. According to Warrick the ambassador was "traveling uninvited to the uprising's bloody epicentre," where he "held a series of discreet meetings with opposition leaders, away from the glare of TV cameras." The Syrian Foreign Ministry slammed these activities, stating: "The presence of the U.S. ambassador in Hama without previous permission is obvious proof of the implication of the United States in the ongoing events, and of their attempts to increase tensions."[25]

Concerns about both rising income inequality and corruption were serious issues which fuelled the anti-government protests that emerged in some areas. These were problems which had grown under Bashar Al Assad's presidency with increasingly conspicuous shows of wealth by his inner circle, including by his billionaire cousin Rami Makhlouf who had reportedly made a fortune using government connections to receive kickbacks from a several lucrative business deals.[26] By the standards of the Arab world, however, corruption was not particularly severe in Syria and had been an issue raised since at least the 1990s, although the

---

iii It subsequently became an increasingly common practice for Western diplomats in countries outside the Western sphere of influence to openly encourage protests and unrest against their governments, at times marching in the street and organising the provision of food and other material support to encourage the youth in particular to remain on the streets. Another notable example in the Arab world was the British ambassador in Sudan, Irfan Siddiq, who played an instrumental role in the unrest of 2019, which paved the way for a coup that year that brought down the Sudanese government.

neoliberal reform process under the new presidency was widely credited with making the issue not only more serious but also much more visible to the public.[27] This was particularly clear in fields such as housing, where a growing segment of the population was forced to live in informal accommodations, while a new elite largely connected to the government resided in increasingly conspicuous luxury properties which exacerbated popular discontent.[28] Nevertheless, by comparison to Arab states which could not rely on fossil fuel exports to boost their economies such as Lebanon, Morocco or Jordan, or to neighbouring Iran or Turkey, housing issues in Syria were far less serious.[29]

While the rise in both corruption and conspicuous income inequality were important factors, much more serious was the aforementioned growing divide between the urban and rural populations, particularly in terms of adherence to traditional Islamic values, and economic woes caused by years of drought and poor harvest. These factors in particular exacerbated discontent, which was effectively exploited by a number of anti-government actors to encourage the population to demand the government's fall. This was closely reflected in the distribution of protests, which were overwhelmingly concentrated in rural areas or in areas with high populations of rural migrants. A number of critical factors, including major media efforts by Western powers and Western-aligned Arab states, effective training provided to pro-Western activists for organising rallies and manipulating social media, and the sense of momentum for change after the overthrows of Arab governments in Tunisia and Egypt, further fuelled protests in many parts of Syria. In Damascus by contrast, to the dismay of Western observers, only mass pro-government rallies could be seen.[iv]

Much more seriously than the ongoing and initially mostly peaceful protests, in terms of a direct threat to national security,

iv  Although Damascus would see significant protests in the coming years, these hardly supported anti-government groups but rather criticised the government for not dealing with the jihadist insurgency more effectively, failing to keep large parts of the country out of the hands of foreign backed terror groups, or failing to secure the release of civilian hostages held by jihadists. (Barnard, Anne, 'Blamed for Rise of ISIS, Syrian Leader Is Pushed to Escalate Fight,' *New York Times,* August 22, 2014.)

were the mass attacks simultaneously being carried out against government buildings, police and military positions by militants pouring into the country. Although this aspect of the conflict's early stages is left out in the overwhelming majority of Western accounts, militants had been armed and prepared for operations in Syria long before the first signs of any unrest had appeared.[30] Former CIA Case Officer and Army Intelligence Officer Philip Giraldi, an expert on Middle Eastern security who served as a security consultant and as Executive Director of the Council for the National Interest, was one of the few in the West to attest to this, stating: "Syrian government claims that it is being assaulted by rebels who are armed, trained, and financed by foreign governments are more true than false."[31]

One of the earliest indicators that there had been a significant armed insurgency from the outset, contradicting Western and allied claims of a purely peaceful revolution, was a report from Syrian state media on March 23 that large quantities of illegal arms had been seized in the city of Daraa adjacent to Jordanian border. These were reportedly being stored in the Al Omari mosque, and were thought to have been delivered through Jordan, with similar reports regarding the flow of arms and militants across the Jordanian and Turkish borders emerging with growing frequency in the following weeks and months. While such claims were either ignored or dismissed in Western and Gulf media, the existence of the arms stash at Al Omari was later confirmed by the head of the Middle Eastern Centre for Strategic Studies, retired Saudi General Anwar Al Eshki. Al Eshki was a major supporter of the insurgency with close ties to Saudi and Western intelligence and to insurgent leaders, and indicated in an interview with the BBC that it was policy from the outset to provide militants with arms to "exhaust the army... drive government forces out of the cities and villages."[32]

Britain, France, the U.S., Turkey and Jordan had all deployed special forces to Syrian territory to support the covert military campaign, which was largely shielded from view by the chaos of mass protests.[33] There was little illusion among Syria's foreign adversaries that mass protests could topple the Ba'ath Party by themselves, with the protesting minority, no matter how well trained and vocal their organisers were, still relegated to outlying areas and holding few prospects of gaining support in the capital. What the protests did achieve, however, was to create enough confusion and disruption to allow Western-trained militants flowing across the borders to make serious gains. Al Qaeda commander Abu Mohammad Al Julani, who would later lead the most powerful anti-government militant group with strong foreign support, stated to this effect regarding the protests paving the way for a Syrian jihad: "Syria would not have been ready for us if not for the Syrian revolution... The revolution removed many of the obstacles and paved the way for us to enter this blessed land."[34] The Syrian government itself appeared to have been caught totally off guard by the need to respond to both civilian protests and major armed attacks simultaneously. It would take time to identify the primary threat as coming from an Islamist insurgency largely engineered and heavily sponsored by the West and its regional partners.

In the West the escalating clashes with Syrian government forces were widely portrayed as being carried out by a moderate opposition. Western media outlets and official government statements gave a strong impression that the nature of the war in Syria was one between an oppressed people aspiring for Western style political and economic reforms, and a tyrannical government which stood against the 'tide of history,' as it was often referred to, by opposing this drive towards inevitable change along Western lines. While this served a valuable propaganda role, for all intents and purposes the overwhelming majority of fighting on the ground was being done by jihadist militants, with non-Islamist elements of the insurgency comprising a negligible element. Even the most ardent Western supporters of 'moderate opposition' would come to admit this, and while secular elements did exist there was little illusion either among the Western Bloc's regional allies or in Europe or the U.S. themselves that any meaningful military gains against the government would be made by non-jihadist elements.[35] A U.S. Defence Intelligence Agency document from 2012 notably attested to this, stating that "Salafist, Muslim Brotherhood and

AQI [Al Qaeda]" were "the major forces driving the insurgency in Syria."[36]

The dominance of jihadist elements in the insurgency from its earliest days closely reflected the trend in Afghanistan, where there had been a small secular Maoist insurgency against the government which had clashed with the Soviet military. These non-Islamist militants could not be credited with even a single percentage of Afghan government or Soviet battlefield losses.[37] Had common western perceptions of jihadist militants been as negative in the 1980s as they were after the War on Terror in the 2010s, the Carter and Reagan administrations and their allies may well have sought to portray the war as one between 'moderate Maoist rebels' and a 'brutal Afghan regime' while putting little to no emphasis on the overwhelming and predominant jihadist element. This was precisely what was done throughout the Syrian conflict. A secular armed opposition fighting for Western style political change did exist in Syria, at least initially,[v] but even then, to an even greater degree than the Maoists in Afghanistan, it was minuscule and the role it played was totally negligible outside the propaganda purpose it served in Western coverage of the war effort.

## Who Were the Free Syrian Army?

In order to publicly justify intervention in Syria in support of the insurgency, either with economic and political measures to target the government or with military action, it was essential for the West to be able to portray some form of 'good side' in the war as a Westphilian alternative to the Ba'ath Party. With Al Qaeda and other jihadist groups having been effectively demonised in the preceding decade due to the War on Terror, jihadism could not be lionised as it had been in Afghanistan in the 1980s, which forced

---

v    The existence of even a small secular armed opposition in Syria was itself questioned by experts, with director of the Middle East Peace Institute and chairman of the Mortons Group political consulting firm Geoffrey Aronson, among others, indicating that it may never have existed at all. (O'Connor, Tom, 'China May Be the Biggest Winner of All If Assad Takes Over Syria,' *Newsweek*, January 19, 2018).

the West to rely heavily on portrayals of the Free Syrian Army (FSA) as the 'right side' in the war.

Formed in July 2011, the FSA was a loose coalition of many of the anti-government militias in Syria, rather than a centralised paramilitary organisation with a military chain of command, and included multiple terrorist groups in its ranks. Indeed, in the early stages of the war the Al Nusra Front jihadist group was a part of the Free Syrian Army – at a time when Al Nusra was an official branch organisation of Islamic State and an affiliate of Al Qaeda.[38] The *Washington Post* would refer to Al Nusra in late 2012 as the most aggressive and successful arm of the Free Syrian Army,[39] and according to the Russian Foreign Ministry they continued for years to be labelled as 'moderate opposition' by the United States.[40]

One of the significant benefits that Western patronage brought the FSA was highly favourable media coverage. It was far from uncommon from the war's earliest stages for crimes such as massacres to be blamed unanimously by Western media on the Syrian government or its partners, only for it to later emerge, often through investigations by Western reporters on the ground, that FSA insurgents were responsible.[41] When August 2012, for example, the massacre of 245 people in the Daraya suburb was reported Western media almost unanimously blamed "Assad's army," although, as was often the case, there was no substantial evidence for this claim.[42] British journalist Robert Fisk, who investigated the incident on the ground, found that the Free Syrian Army had been responsible and had massacred civilians and off-duty soldiers it had been holding prisoner.[43] In December that year, a massacre of 120 to 150 villagers in the town of Aqrab was also blamed on the Syrian Government, with the *New York Times* suggesting that "members of Assad's sect" were responsible.[44] After launching a thorough investigation including multiple inter-views with survivors, British journalist Alex Thompson reported that the FSA had been responsible, holding 500 villagers from the Alawite religious minority hostage for nine days before carrying out mass executions.[45] These cases exemplified a far wider trend which predominated throughout the war.[46] Britain notably played a leading role in the media campaign, and using former British diplomats, intelligence officers and army officers as intermediaries, it covertly established a network of journalists across Syria "in an attempt to shape perceptions of the conflict." These efforts were managed by the Ministry of Defence, and their aim was to bring about "attitudinal and behavioural change" with the goal of "reinforcement of popular rejection of the Assad regime." Media content produced by the network of journalists in the pay of the British government was supported to reach outlets such as *BBC Arabic* and *Al Jazeera*.[47]

The FSA was consistently portrayed in the West as being built from a core of large numbers of defecting soldiers opposing the Syrian government, although with defections largely exaggerated former soldiers were found to comprise only around 4% of the insurgent coalition's numbers even in the conflict's initial months. This figure would decline sharply over the course of the war.[48] In December 2012 the FSA announced the formation of the Supreme Military Council (SMC) to try to coordinate the many separate insurgent groups operating against the government. The project was a failure from the outset and was unable to bring a significant portion of the insurgents together under one banner. As Australian Middle East expert and *Foreign Policy* contributor Reese Erlich noted: "The SMC, which was supposed to be a general command, failed to incorporate the other major armed groups. The SMC became just one more fighting group. 'Every time they set up a council to oversee the war effort, it turns into a militia,' wrote one rebel in Deir ez-Zor."[49] Thus insofar as it did not represent a viable political opposition, the SMC's primary purpose was to serve as a propaganda tool for Damascus' adversaries which gave the impression that there was some kind of moderate governing body ready to take power once the Syrian government was overthrown.

An FSA co-ordinator going by the name of Abu Haidar notably stated regarding the role of Al Nusra in the revolution the Free Syrian Army was professing to lead that the Al Qaeda affiliate "have experienced fighters who are like the revolution's elite commando troops,"[50] with the radical jihadist group receiving widespread praise from among the leadership of the FSA.[51]

"We are all Al Nusra Front," FSA forces in the Damascus suburbs would chant in December 2012 in protest against claims the Al Qaeda affiliate was a terrorist organisation – a particularly telling revelation regarding the nature of the supposedly moderate coalition.[52] Twenty-nine of the militant groups which comprised the FSA, including fighting brigades and civilian committees, signed a petition calling for mass demonstrations in support of Al Nusra, which was highly regarded throughout the coalition for its effectiveness.[53] The fact that Al Nusra was accepted into FSA ranks, not only as a partner but as an integral member of the coalition, reflected the organisation's strongly Islamist orientation which was well concealed by the media coverage of its foreign sponsors.

Although Al Nusra would eventually break with the FSA, relations overall remained positive with the two conducting multiple joint operations. Much of the material support including heavy equipment which other FSA factions received as aid from foreign sponsors was notably sold on to Al Nusra.[54] Some of the other jihadist groups that fought under or alongside the Free Syrian Army included the Suqour Al Sham Brigades, the Army of Mujahideen, and Jaysh Al Islam, although Al Nusra was the largest and most powerful. Some Western analysts contended that U.S. and European portrayals of the FSA as moderate opposition were the result of their having been deceived by the Syrian insurgents themselves – rather than a conscious effort by Western powers to disguise the nature of the radicals they were backing. The West had supposedly been "blindsided by the conniving tactics of the so-called 'opposition' who were only fundamentalist Islamists masquerading as secular fighters of the non-existent FSA," according to one prominent Australian assessment, which echoed widespread Western claims to similar effect.[55] This line of argument was highly questionable however, considering among other factors the large numbers of NATO forces operating covertly in Syria including those embedded in FSA units, the alliance's vast intelligence gathering capabilities, and the West's aforementioned long history of backing jihadist groups to undermine secular states which were outside the Western sphere of influence.

Alongside Al Qaeda, the Islamic State would emerge as the leading insurgent group in Syria from 2014 and notably also benefitted from ties to the Free Syrian Army, which included frequent large-scale defections of personnel who took significant military supplies with them to join IS ranks.[56] A large portion of the FSA's fighting strength was absorbed by IS in this way, and under a better organised and significantly more capable militant group these FSA defectors contributed to more serious gains against the Syrian government than they would have under their original organisation.[57] High level Islamic State commander Abu Yusaf said in August 2014 that Free Syrian Army militants who had been trained by the U.S., Turkey and various Arab states were joining IS in large numbers. As a result, he stated: "In the East of Syria, there is no Free Syrian Army any longer. All Free Syrian Army people have joined the Islamic State." This was partly attested to by the fast growing number of trained IS personnel from early that year.[58] IS' reliance on arms from Western backed insurgents was highlighted to by Professor Max Abrahms, fellow at the Combating Terrorism Center at West Point Military Academy and John Glaser, director of foreign policy studies at the Cato Institute, who observed in December 2017 that the Islamic State "imploded right after external support for the 'moderate' rebels dried up."[59] Multiple assessments, such as the study conducted by the London based investigative organization Conflict Armament Research at the behest of the European Union and the German Federal Foreign Office, consistently found that external support for groups such as the Free Syrian Army "significantly augmented the quantity and quality of weapons available to [IS] forces." This was a result of the nature of the relationship between IS and the supposedly moderate insurgents.[60]

Retired Jordanian general Fayez Al Dweiri, an expert on the Syrian conflict, was one of many to observe that by November 2014, except for small pockets southern Syria and around Aleppo, "the FSA has been effectively decimated and no longer effectively exists."[61] The group's power would only further diminish afterwards,[62] but this would not end persistent references across the Western media to an FSA 'moderate opposition' as if it remained, or had ever been, a major player in the conflict. The remnants of the Free Syrian Army would increasingly openly display their radical jihadist tendencies, leading *Foreign Policy* to issue an unprecedentedly down to earth assessment[63] of the group previously referred to as the "West's last hope" for a positive outcome in the Syrian War.[64] The Free Syrian Army, according to the prominent American magazine, were "Turkish-backed proxy forces with ties to extremist groups," "a decentralized band of Syrian rebels that has been linked to extremist groups," and were responsible for "killing scores of unarmed civilians" – highlighting their years long ties to various Al Qaeda affiliates. Although none of these aspects of the Free Syrian Army were at all new, the beginnings of a realistic Western portrayal of the group in 2019 came as the Western powers were increasingly cutting their losses with the FSA and relying more heavily on working with other insurgent groups.

Alongside the Free Syrian Army, a separate coalition known as Jaysh Al Islam was established in the war's early months and received funding from many of the same sources.[65] The coalition was generally much better organised and centrally controlled than the FSA, and had explicitly genocidal goals in regards to Syria's minorities. The group's founder and leader, Zahran Alloush, was an extremist Islamist scholar heavily influenced by Saudi Arabia's Wahhabist Islam, and in one instance in pledged of his fighters: "The jihadists will wash the filth of the *rafida* [a slur for Shiites] from Greater Syria, they will wash it forever, if Allah wills it."[66] Similar sentiments were widely expressed by Jaysh Al Islam and Free Syrian Army personnel throughout the war, with Syrian minorities such as the Druze, Alawites and Christians suffering harsh persecution as a result. Jaysh Al Islam would notably also copy the style of the Islamic State in many of its later propaganda videos, including publishing footage of mass executions of prisoners.[67] Despite its jihadist credentials, Western media would generally underemphasize the extremist nature of Islamist insurgent groups and often attempted to place positive spins on their victories.[68]

## The Jihad Gains Ground

As fighting intensified the Syrian government sought to rally
its support bases in major cities, with the *New York Times* reporting on October 19, 2011, that "large crowds of Syrians rallied
in the northern city of Aleppo in support of the government of
President Bashar Al Assad" – a sign that the government "can still
command support." Syrian estimates placed the size of the rallies
at over a million people, and while this was not verified, even the
more conservative estimates placed the figures in the hundreds
of thousands.[69] While jihadists could find some support in rural
areas, the fundamentalist Islamist nature of the insurgency only
further bolstered support for the government in major cities, and
particularly among religious minorities such as Christians and
non-Sunni Muslim sects who were all at risk of effective genocide
if forced to live under the militants' rule. Targeting of minorities
by militants, which were increasingly empowered by Western,
Gulf and Turkish support, included the destruction of places of
worship and holy sites, massacres, torture and sale of women
into slavery.[70] Several conservative leaders in the United States
opposed the war effort precisely on the grounds that the very
jihadist forces the Western world had unleashed were eradicating
Syria's ancient Christian communities, and had much praise for
the Syrian government for its defence of minorities. These voices
remained a minority in America, however, and an even smaller
minority in the wider Western world.[71]

TV stations owned by Western-aligned Arab monarchies,
which had used their immense oil wealth to buy ownership of
almost all of the Arab world's leading media outlets, aired allegations almost daily that the Syrian government was massacring
civilians. This played a key role in inspiring support for anti-government jihadist groups and recruiting legions of willing fighters
from across the Arab world to join the war. The Syrian War was
thus effectively demonstrating the true power of controlling news
and popular media. As Pulitzer Prize winning *Washington Post*
reporter Joby Warrick noted regarding the response:

sympathetic Arabs began donating cash, gold jewellery, and supplies to the Syrian Islamists' cause. Arab governments secretly sent aid as well, usually the lethal kind. In Kuwait, one of the biggest providers of private funding, a preacher named Hajjaj Al Ajmi, launched a Twitter campaign to persuade his 250,000 followers to donate money to special bank accounts set up to help the rebels. "Give your money to the ones who will spend it on jihad, not aid," Al Ajmi exhorted donors in a video pitch posted to YouTube in 2012. Other supporters held Twitter 'auctions' to sell off cars, boats, vacation properties – anything that could be exchanged for cash to help the Syrian rebels. A few wealthy donors – sometimes called 'angel investors' by those who benefitted – arranged visits to the battlefield to hand-deliver suitcases full of cash, and were sometimes rewarded by having a rebel brigade rename itself in the patron's honour.... young Muslim men from around the world were beginning to stream across the Syria-Turkey border to join the fight, evoking the great migrations of volunteer fighters into Afghanistan and Iraq in decades past. To encourage them, Al Nusra's leaders set up Twitter and Facebook accounts offering everything from theological pep talks to practical advice on what to wear and bring. From Western Europe came hundreds, then thousands of young men.[72]

Jordan's King Abdullah II would refer to the militants receiving massive infusions of Arab funds, war materials and recruits, with the sanction of government officials in several Western-aligned kingdoms, as "jihadists whose central aim is to create a seventh-century theocracy in the heart of the Middle East."[73] This assessment was supported by a range of prominent sources, with Senior Fellow at the Cato Institute and former Special Assistant to President Ronald Reagan, Doug Bandow, referring in *Forbes* to U.S. and allied policy as "turning Syria over to a mix of radicals, jihadists, and terrorists."[74]

Qatar in many ways took the lead among Western client states in the offensive against Syria, much as it had done to great effect in Libya, using both media and special forces among other means,[75] although other Gulf States would begin to catch up from 2012. The country would become one of the first to recognise Islamist forces waging war on the Syrian government as the official representatives of the Syrian nation, granting the SMC their first embassy in Doha[76] and spearheading efforts to grant them the Syrian seat at the Arab League.[77] Qatar also provided considerable material support to a growing body of Islamist insurgents which were massing in Turkey, a country which was also under a strongly Islamist oriented government. A Qatari Air Force C-130 heavy transport aircraft landed in Esenboga Airport near Ankara on January 3, 2012, one of the first of many large arms shipments from the Western client states in the gulf to supply the insurgency that became publicly known. CIA officers notably assisted Qatar in procuring weapons, while others posted in Turkey worked with Turkish intelligence to channel the weapons to various insurgent groups. Saudi Arabia is thought to have begun to supply jihadist groups soon afterwards, and by March 2013 over 160 military cargo flights from Saudi Arabia and Qatar had landed in Turkey and Jordan. Hugh Griffiths, of the Stockholm International Peace Research Institute, referred to this massive supply effort as "a well-planned and coordinated clandestine military logistics operation," placing its payload at 3,500 tons of military equipment at a conservative estimate.[78]

Saudi Arabia stepped up support for all manner of jihadist militants in Syria from 2012,[79] going so far as to allow death row inmates to go free if they joined the 'Syrian jihad' to further swell the numbers of the militant forces with hardened criminals.[80] Saudi intelligence maintained close contacts with many of these groups, with a top-secret U.S. National Security Agency document leaked by whistleblower Edward Snowden showing that several attacks carried out by jihadist militants on Syrian soil were directly ordered from Saudi Arabia. The coordinated rocket attacks on Damascus International Airport, the Presidential Palace and a government security compound to mark the two-year anniversary of the war on March 18, 2013, were notable examples. These had been personally ordered by Prince Salman bin Sultan, the son of the Saudi defence minister. Salman had procured 120 tons of explosives and other weaponry for militias in his pay, who were instructed to "light up Damascus" and "flatten" the airport.[81] This was hardly the only time jihadist forces operating with foreign support succeeded in striking the heart of the Syrian state, with a suicide car attack directed at the National Security headquarters in Damascus exactly eight months prior killing the Syria's Defence Minister Daoud Rajha and several heads of the country's intelligence agencies – a major blow.[82]

Plentiful supplies of funds, manpower and munitions, which even the jihadist forces in Iraq, Afghanistan and Yugoslavia could only have dreamt of, allowed militants to intensify their offensives. They relied heavily on roadside bombs, ambushes and mass assaults on isolated outposts to place large parts of rural Syria under their full control. Insurgents benefitted not only from material support, but also from the ability to shelter, rearm and regroup safely across the Turkish and Jordanian borders, which was a major asset in the war's initial stages when fighting was concentrated to the border areas. This closely resembled the use of access to Pakistani territory by Afghan jihadists in the 1980s to evade attacks by the Afghan military and the Soviet armed forces, with the role played by Pakistan in the former and Turkey in the latter conflicts in many ways highly comparable. An early example of this was on June 6, 2011, when Islamist militiamen ambushed Syrian forces near the city of Jisr Al Shugur around 10km from the Turkish border before evading a large counterattack by the Syrian Arab Army by crossing over into Turkey. These kinds of hit-and-run attacks by radicalised and very heavily armed militants were very common and took a heavy toll on Syrian forces in the border regions, with Turkey providing more active support for jihadist forces from October by openly allowing insurgents to operate command and control headquarters from inside Turkish territory. This allowed the militants coordinate attacks against Syrian forces while safe from retaliation.[83]

After leading calls for a NATO invasion of Syria in 2011,[84] and briefly attempting to organise a government in exile,[85] Turkey continued to play a leading role in supporting jihadist forces. The Turkish National Intelligence Organization (TINO) was given full responsibility for coordinating operations with militant groups and overseeing the transit of their manpower and supplies across Turkish territory and into Syria. This policy was in line with the agenda of its ruling Islamist Justice and Development Party (AKP), with Turkish police and prosecutors facing intimidation, dismissal and at times incarceration if they investigated or interfered with these operations.[86] The UN's Analytical Support and Sanctions Monitoring Team reported that Turkey intentionally turned a blind eye to the shipment of arms to Al Qaeda affiliated militant groups in Syria,[87] and according to Turkish military sources, TINO further took an active role in shipping weapons to Al Qaeda.[88] Further evidence of this was presented to Turkish courts in the form of testimonies from drivers responsible for transporting arms to jihadists in Syria.[89] As jihadist groups such as the Islamic State[vi] later moved to capture Syrian oil fields, Turkey would become the leading client for black market oil which would directly finance terrorist activities on Syrian soil,[90] while reportedly also providing vital spare parts to keep IS-held oil fields operational.[91] Support for the insurgency in Turkey was so significant that Al Nusra Front slogans notably began to appear at major intersections of Istanbul from 2014,[92] with jihadists receiving free treatment in Turkish hospitals before being allowed to return to Syria.[93]

The jihadist insurgency made very considerable gains in its second year, with the Al Nusra Front[vii] recognised as the most formidable insurgent group on the battlefield from the outset.[94] Its greater ideological fanaticism, which made its fighters particularly

---

vi Considerable further evidence of close Turkish ties to Islamic State in particular was reportedly obtained by the U.S. from IS flash drives and documents captured in a special forces raid on the jihadist group in 2015. (Chulov, Martin, 'Turkey sends in jets as Syria's agony spills over every border,' *The Guardian*, July 26, 2015.)

vii Al Nusra would change its name to Jabhat Fateh Al Sham in 2016. For simplicity, Al Nusra Front is used throughout this work when referring to the organization.

ruthless and effective, and its greater access to experienced personnel and material support, contributed to its effectiveness and reputation. Much like in Afghanistan four decades prior, the channelling of foreign material support to the more radical insurgent groups shaped the nature of the insurgency towards greater radicalism and ultimately forced the targeted government to deal with a more violent and extremist opposition.

Al Nusra was first established as a separate branch of the Al Qaeda in Iraq terror group in January 2012 and unified a number of jihadist militias into a single organisation with a strong initial focus on the Turkish and Jordanian border regions. Otherwise known as the Islamic State (IS), this Al Qaeda group had already built up a major power base in Iraq after exploiting the power vacuum left by the overthrow of the country's Ba'athist government in 2003. IS in Iraq was able to transfer of arms and ammunition to its new Syrian branch from across the Iraqi border to supplement material support being sent through Turkey and Jordan abroad.[95] Regarding the nature of Al Nusra as a branch of IS created to expand operations into Syria, Islamic State leader Abu Bakr Al Baghdadi professed: "Al-Nusra Front was only an expansion of the Islamic State of Iraq, and part of it," which would remain the case until late 2013.[96]

According to the U.S. State Department Al Nusra was responsible for a disproportionately high number of frontline engagements, taking territory at a much faster rate than other jihadist factions.[97] Like most Islamist militant groups operating in Syria, Al Nusra's call to jihad was transnational,[viii] and the bulk of its elite fighters came from outside the country including Chechens,[98] Dagestanis, Central Asians,[99] Africans, Europeans, Arabs,[100] and even Uighurs from China's Xinjiang province.[101] Its tactics ranged from car and suicide bombings[102] to direct attacks on Syrian military bases.[103] The jihadist group gained considerable material support from U.S. allies such as Turkey,[104] Saudi Arabia[105] and

---

viii  According to Syria's UN ambassador by September 2016 jihadists operating in Syria had come from 101 of the UN's 193 member states – reflecting the truly international nature of the Islamist insurgency. ('Syria's Ambassador Bashar Jaafari Talks to Caleb Maupin,' September 24, 2016.)

Qatar,[106] as well as from the American CIA itself.[107] The idea of an Islamist state governed under 'God's law' as opposed to secular law, of ensuring orthodox Sunni rule at the expense of Alawites, Christians and other religious minorities, and of achieving this by holy war much as had been done in Afghanistan, had a strong appeal to many Islamists across the world. The material benefits of arms, salaries and training provided by the insurgency's foreign sponsors, and the opportunity Syria presented to build up a power base to export jihad elsewhere in the world, was also a significant factor. By the end of 2013 Al Nusra had established a presence in 11 of Syria's 14 governates,[108] and would only be challenged in its position as the most ruthless and most powerful jihadist group in Syria when the Iraqi branch of the Islamic State sent its own forces into the country in force in 2014.

The conflict would continue to escalate throughout 2012, with the ranks of insurgents swelling and the Syrian Arab Army increasingly forced to rely on heavier equipment such as battle tanks, artillery, attack helicopters and combat aircraft to engage well-armed and trained militants. To counter Syrian Mi-24 attack helicopters and MiG-21 and MiG-23 fighter jets – many of the same aircraft used by Afghan and Soviet forces against Western-backed jihadists 30 years prior – Islamist insurgent groups were supplied with a range of Soviet designed air defence systems. Most notable were the ZU-23 autocannon and the 9K32 Strela-2 (NATO reporting SA-7) and 9K38 Igla (NATO reporting both SA-16 and SA-24) handheld surface to air missile systems.[109] These weapons limited the Syrian Arab Army's ability to apply air power effectively, and complicated efforts to press a counteroffensive against militant strongholds. They were also used by jihadists against international non-military aircraft, which forced civilian airliners to cease operations over Syrian airspace.[110] The preponderance of Soviet-designed equipment in the insurgents' arsenals was not limited to air defences, and reflected the fact that the bulk of supplies were being drawn from the substantial reserves of Eastern European NATO member states which had formerly been in the Soviet-led Warsaw Pact alliance.[111] Much of these were purchased and transferred by the Pentagon itself,[112] and were not only obtained cheaply, but also facilitated a faster transition for newer NATO member states towards using standardised alliance hardware produced in the U.S. and Western Europe by selling off their pre-NATO inventories. Azerbaijan's Silk Way Airlines, which provided diplomatic flights free from inspection, was hired for several of these transfers, with arms handed to militants operating in Syria.[113]

According to Pentagon sources cited by journalist Seymour Hersh, Soviet-origin arms also reached Syrian insurgents in considerable quantities through Libya where, following the defeat of the government in 2011, much of the country's arsenal was put at the disposal of the Western-backed militias. A primary purpose of the American consulate, which was quickly set up in Benghazi after the victory of U.S.-backed forces, was to organise arms transfers to Syria, with Britain, Turkey, Qatar and Saudi also playing major roles in supporting the operation.[114] The primary operation to arm Syrian insurgents was Operation Timber Sycamore, carried out by the CIA with support from the U.S., British, Qatari, Saudi and Jordanian intelligence services and the U.S. Defence Department. The program saw relatively little regulation of who the arms went to, and lacked accountability, as weaponry very consistently ended up in the hands of UN recognised terrorist organisations such as Al Qaeda and IS.

Despite multiple ceasefire attempts by the United Nations, the radical and fundamentalist nature of the clash between jihadist forces and the Syrian state meant that these would all be short lived with both sides blaming the other for violations. Considering the discrepancy in material support which the two sides were receiving, and the continuous and massive flow of arms and personnel to insurgent forces primarily through Turkey and Jordan, ceasefires strongly benefitted jihadist groups and allowed them to cement their control over newly occupied territories and strengthen their power bases within Syria's borders. The conflict escalated from October 2012, following the failure of the last of the ceasefire agreements, with insurgent groups making major gains on all fronts, which led to particularly fierce fighting in the Turkish border regions. Turkish and Syrian forces exchanged artillery fire for six days starting on October 2, which was one of several forms of overt Turkish support the insurgents received. The Turkish Air Force notably forced a Syrian civilian airliner to land on Turkish soil on October 10, where Russian communications equipment onboard was illegally appropriated by Turkish forces.[115] Extensive Turkish support, reportedly including limited deployments of Turkish personnel to Syrian territory to oversee offensive operations,[116] would lead to all border regions falling under insurgent control.

Fighting from the final quarter of 2012 also saw insurgents push hard to take Syria's two largest cities, Damascus and Aleppo, with protracted months long battles in the suburbs of the former and at the very heart of the latter. On December 12 one of the most prolific early videos of jihadist atrocities was released on the internet, showing an unarmed and immobilised prisoner beheaded by a child using a machete. Insurgents surrounding him gathered to shout 'Allahu Akbar' – Allah is Greatest – and displayed two bodies with severed heads. The militants were thought to be members of the Khalid ibn Al Waleed brigade – part of the Free Syrian Army and the so-called 'moderate opposition' – and claimed to have beheaded 80 other prisoners.[117] Such massacres were common from the war's outset, much as the Arab Mujahideen in Afghanistan had been well known for such killings in the 1980s, but this incident was notable in that it was filmed for dramatic effect. The very next day President Barack Obama announced that the Free Syrian Army would be recognised as the legitimate representative of Syria by the United States,[118] closely following France[119] and Britain[120] which had both done so the previous month. Recognition would facilitate the provision of material assistance to jihadist forces through official channels, supplementing the massive supplies already being provided unofficially primarily by the CIA. The U.S. and Britain announced plans to provide non-lethal aid such as food and armoured vehicles early in 2013[121] with the U.S. Senate subsequently deciding to provide lethal aid in May.[122] Israel also announced in April that official aid to anti-government forces was under consideration,[123] with its Prime Minister, Benjamin Netanyahu, also personally conducting "intense lobbying" for the U.S. to provide greater material support to the insurgency.[124]

With jihadist militias continuing to make gains, and demonstrating the capability to strike deep into Damascus from bases in the suburbs,[125] Russia's deputy foreign minister Mikhail Bogdanov gave an objective assessment on December 13 that the Syrian government was losing the war.[126] The government would continue to lose ground after the new year and into 2013, with insurgents focusing on the Aleppo and Damascus governates, prioritising the targeting of airbases and air defence sites, and carrying out major bombings of civilian targets. A bomb attack on Aleppo University on January 15 caused over 200 civilian casualties including 87 dead, one of the larger of multiple similar terror attacks occurring almost daily across the country.[127] Militants would continue to take ground in Damascus, but particularly quickly in Aleppo, including key checkpoints, military facilities and roads.[128] Aleppo was much closer to the Turkish border, from where jihadist groups were receiving the bulk of their external material and manpower support, placing it at the focus of offensive operations. The momentum of the jihadist offensive would only dissipate in May 2013 after an unexpected defeat at the battle of Qusayr, with considerable ground gained until then.

## International Dimensions to Syria's Conflict: The Looming Shadow of Direct Foreign Intervention

The shadow of a possible Western military intervention had hung over the Syrian conflict throughout much of 2012, following the successful application of NATO air power in cohesion with Islamist elements on the ground to topple a longstanding opponent of Western hegemony on the African continent – the Libyan Arab Jamahiriya. The three Western permanent members of the United Nations Security Council, Britain, France and the United States, had all pressed for a resolution to protect Libyan civilians, and when the council's only two non-Western permanent members failed to veto this, the resolution was subsequently abused. NATO launched large scale air and missile strikes against the country for several months, assassinated its longstanding leader Muammar Gaddafi and much of the national leadership,[129] and imposed a short lived pro-Western government after forcefully toppling its independent predecessor. The meaning of 'protecting civilians' was spun to mean a full-scale Western assault on their country which would destabilise it for over a decade.

Evidence that Libyan civilians were ever in danger from their government was highly questionable, with *Foreign Policy* among others noting that the Western claim of an imminent massacre by government forces unless NATO launched an offensive "does not stand up to even casual scrutiny."[130] With the NATO campaign initiated under a false humanitarian pretext, the subsequent Western victory over the Libyan government caused great suffering for the population of the formerly affluent African country. Consequences included a sharp decline in stability and living standards – leaving it "a completely failed state" in the words of the former U.S. ambassador.[131] Racially motivated massacres, torture and mass rapes of black Africans by the anti-government militias the West had supported, often killing tens of thousands at a time, effectively ethnically cleansed the country's black communities.[132] The emergence of widespread human trafficking, open slave markets,[133] and greater freedom of action for Western soldiers to deploy to Libyan soil at will,[134] were among the further direct consequences of the West's success. The response from Moscow in particular was outrage,[135] and ultimately the Libyan example led Russia, alongside China, to draw a zero-tolerance line against Western drafted resolutions against Syria at the United Nations. By the end of 2020 15 separate Western sponsored resolutions had been vetoed with none passing.

While a veto at the United Nations closed off the only legal avenue for a Western attack on Syrian government forces this far from guaranteed the country's safety, with the Western powers having previously violated international law multiple times to attack several UN member states without UN authorisation or any other legal basis. Notable examples included the U.S. invasions of Panama[136] and Grenada,[137] large scale NATO attacks on former Yugoslavia in the 1990s,[138] and the U.S. and British led invasion of Iraq in 2003.[139] These military interventions, and others like them, violated the UN charter, lacked justification under international law, and constituted crimes of aggression – the supreme international crime.[140]

Western sources widely speculated that Syria could use its chemical weapons arsenal against insurgents and claimed this would provide the Western powers with a moral pretext, although not a legal one, to launch an attack. Syrian Foreign Ministry spokesman Jihad Makdissi stated at a televised news conference on July 23, 2012, that "Any stock of WMD [weapons of mass destruction] or unconventional weapons that the Syrian Army possesses will never, never be used against the Syrian people or civilians during this crisis, under any circumstances. These weapons are made to be used strictly and only in the event of external aggression against the Syrian Arab Republic." Earlier that month, in a private meeting with the UN's special envoy for Syria, Kofi Annan, President Assad had similarly told him that any chemical weapons were stored safely, had not been mixed for use, and would not be deployed except in the case of foreign invasion.[141] These statements served both to preclude a possible Western pretext for attack, and to warn the Western powers that they could become targets for chemical strikes if they were to launch an illegal attack against Syria.[ix]

U.S. President Barack Obama vowed in August 2012 to take direct action if Syria used its suspected chemical weapons arsenal against insurgents,[142] a red line strongly supported by his European allies which would have significant consequences the following year. This was followed by unverified claims over several months by anti-government groups that chemical weapons were being actively used against them, although the veracity of these claims remained in serious doubt given the clear incentive militants had to make such allegations and thereby effectively call in Western airstrikes against the Syrian Arab Army.[143] Nevertheless, the

---

ix  Described in some circles as the 'poor man's nuclear weapons,' Syria's chemical arsenal was developed largely to complement its strategic ballistic missile deterrent in order to counter Israel's own very large nuclear weapons arsenal by deterring its use.

possibility of minor chemical attack on insurgent positions could not be ruled out entirely at the time. The Syrian government had warned in early December 2012 that insurgents could use chemical weapons after capturing an associated factory near Aleppo, although it was open to speculation whether this warning was genuine or was intended to be used as a cover for chemical attacks by government forces in future.[144]

On March 19, 2013, it was widely reported that sarin nerve gas, a medium grade chemical weapon, was employed in the Syrian town of Khan Al Assal, with the Damascus-based Syrian Arab News Agency (SANA) reporting 25 deaths.[145] Although anti-government forces blamed the Syrian government for the attack, the fact that it targeted a village held by the Syrian Army seriously undermined this claim and supported the government's assertions that the strike had been carried out by insurgents. Senior U.S. intelligence officials indicated that there was a "high probability" that Syria had used chemical weapons, largely on the basis that insurgents were not known to have such a capability, but final verification was still needed.[146] The incident was subsequently used as a pretext to escalate support to insurgent groups by the U.S. including arming them through official channels.[147] U.S. Secretary of Defence Chuck Hagel claimed in April that American intelligence had concluded "with some degree of varying confidence" that the Syrian Government used sarin gas during the war, echoing previous statements made by Britain, France, and Israel.[148] Western allegations that the Syrian government was using chemical weapons would come to play an increasingly significant role in the conflict as prospects for a swift victory by insurgent groups began to recede.

## Israel Joins the War

The year 2013 would see a major escalation in direct external involvement in the Syrian conflict, with what had initially primarily been a proxy war by the Western Bloc, the Gulf States and Turkey against the Syrian government through support for Islamist militants now more prominently adopting a new aspect – a clash between Israel and the 'Axis of Resistance.' This would involve not only Israeli support for the insurgency, both militarily and materially, but also the two other Axis members, Hezbollah and Iran, in support of the Syrian government and in opposition to Western, Turkish, Saudi, Qatari and Israeli interests.

Although far less threatening than the prospects for a full-scale Libya- or Iraq-style Western military intervention, Syria in 2013 faced an immediate threat of direct attacks by neighbouring Israel. If mishandled, these risked expanding the scope of the conflict to a full-scale war with the nuclear armed and strongly Western backed country. Tel Aviv indicated on January 27, 2013, that it was considering the possibility of pre-emptive strikes against Syrian targets to prevent the country's chemical weapon stockpiles falling into the hands of Hezbollah.[149] Although there was no indication that Hezbollah had any intention to acquire chemical weapons or the ability to store them, and the militia had much more efficient means to obtain them than to drive them across the Lebanese border through the Syrian warzone, this narrative was nevertheless used as a pretext for Israel to strike Syrian territory. There was even a possibility that the Israeli Air Force could brave Syria's air defences to weaken the country's ballistic missile and chemical deterrents, which would help to pave the way for subsequent U.S. and European strikes against a wider range of targets once Syria was unable to strike back. The fact that air defence sites were being made a priority target by insurgents on the ground would make such attacks considerably easier than they would have been before the war.

The Israeli Air Force struck Syrian territory on January 30, attacking what it alleged was a convoy transporting conventional arms to Hezbollah.[150] Some Israeli sources claimed that the actual target was a Syrian Scientific Studies and Research Centre which, according to Western sources, was responsible for developing chemical weapons.[151] This was the first of multiple Israeli strikes carried out throughout the conflict, usually under the pretext of combatting Hezbollah, which in many cases was highly questionable. Further airstrikes were carried out later in the year including twice in May[152] and once each in July[153] and October,[154] with the latter two respectively targeting weapons deliveries to the Syrian Arab Army from Russia and an SAA military base. The Syrian government claimed that the strikes in May targeted the Jamraya Military Facility near Damascus, a nearby weapons depot and an anti-aircraft unit – all targets totally unrelated to Hezbollah – and accused Tel Aviv of coordinating its attacks with jihadist groups on the ground.

By eroding the Syrian Arab Army's fighting capacity from the air, the Israeli Air Force was providing direct air support to insurgent fighters. It usually did so flying F-16 fighters, notably the same aircraft Pakistan had flown against Afghanistan in the 1980s for much the same purpose, drawing another parallel between the two conflicts and the roles played by American client states bordering the target states. These operations were calibrated to avoid the risk of a full-scale war and managed to neutralise multiple targets without serious escalation. Israel placed further pressure on the Syrian government by providing material support, including arms, to Islamist insurgent groups in the country. For seven years, starting in 2012, Tel Aviv claimed that it was a neutral party in the Syrian conflict and that it was providing no armaments and was supplying only medical aid to Syrians. Many of the recipients were notably from the Al Qaeda affiliated Islamist militias such as the Al Nusra Front.[155] It had been widely speculated by a range of sources since 2012, however, that the country was arming anti-government militants to bolster the insurgency against the Syrian state, with UN observers highlighting evidence for such claims on a number of occasions.[156] Multiple analysts, most notably Senior Fellow at the Foreign Policy Research Institute Elizabeth Tsurkov, made strong cases that there were such Israeli operations underway and provided considerable supporting evidence.[157] In a highly unusual move, the Palestinian Authority Foreign Ministry had also claimed in 2017 that Israel was arming Al Qaeda – a reference to the terror group's regional affiliate the Al Nusra Front.[158]

In February 2019 Israel Defence Forces Chief of Staff Lieutenant General Gadi Eisenkot broke from the policy of the past seven years by admitting that Israeli policy had been to arm and support anti-government insurgents in Syria.[159] Writing for the prominent Israeli newspaper *Haaretz*, British expert on the Syrian conflict Daniel J. Levy noted regarding the significance of this revelation: "in short, none other than Israel's most senior serving soldier has admitted that up until his statement, his country's officially stated position on the Syrian civil war was built on the lie of non-intervention.... For years, Israel has religiously adhered to the official party line that the country's policy was non-intervention, and this has now been exposed as a lie." Levy was among several analysts to highlight evidence pointing to the presence of Israeli officers embedded among anti-government militias in Syria, much as officers from other U.S. allies, in particular Turkey, had been.[160]

Israel's support for the Islamist insurgency in Syria notably included not only provision of armaments, which were often found on the battlefield by the Syrian Arab Army, but also the embedding of officers in militant units, paying of monthly salaries to militants, and providing further financing for purchases of black market arms.[161] This close relationship fostered with Islamist groups created an expectation among many that they would receive direct protection from the Israeli Defence Forces, much as Turkey and the U.S. began to provide to militants which they were sponsoring in the latter stages of the war, although such direct assistance was often not forthcoming. At the height of its assistance program, however, Israel was sponsoring multiple militant groups comprised of thousands of combatants, and Israeli financing allowed many militant groups to add significant numbers of new jihadists to their ranks. *Foreign Policy* would note regarding the relationship between Israeli forces and the commanders of militias on the ground: "commanders would communicate with Israeli officials by phone and occasionally meet them face to face in the Israeli-occupied Golan. When commanders switched groups and locations, Israeli assistance followed them."[162] These activities, paired with an intensifying frequency of airstrikes on Syrian and allied targets from 2013, made Israel a very active participant in the Syrian War.

# The Battle of Al Qusayr:
# Hezbollah and Iran's Entry into the War

Seven years after fighting the Israeli Defence Forces to a halt in southern Lebanon, Hezbollah would also begin a direct military intervention in the Syrian conflict in 2013. The Lebanese militia was reported in August 2012 by official U.S. sources to have begun assisting the Syrian war effort, not with a direct personnel contribution but rather with provision of "training, advice and extensive logistical support."[163] With the Syrian Arab Army heavily oriented towards fighting a major conventional war with a hostile state's armed forces, such as those of Turkey, Israel or the United States, it was ill prepared to handle a jihadist insurgency. Assistance from Hezbollah's battle-hardened militia units, which were particularly accustomed to unconventional warfare and city fighting, was thus of great benefit. The cost to Hezbollah of entering such a chaotic theatre of operations outside its own territory, even when operating in a limited capacity, was high, and by the end of 2012 two of its commanders had been killed in Syria.[164]

Hezbollah only began to play a direct role in the conflict in Syria in the spring of 2013,[x] when it operated alongside the Syrian Arab Army and (North) Korean People's Army advisors to capture the strategically located city of Al Qusayr from the Al Nusra front and affiliated militias. After a two-week battle, the capture of the city in the first week of June was widely seen as a key turning point in the war, allowing Syrian forces to link the major cities of Homs and Damascus, to reinforce the former of these, and to connect SAA units to their key supply hub at the port of Tartus. Control of Al Qusayr had previously allowed insurgents

---

x   Following its intervention in Syria Hezbollah's military wing was almost immediately designated a terrorist organisation by the European Union, meaning it was considered a terror group by all Western countries except Switzerland, Norway and Iceland, as well as by Israel, Japan and a number of Arab states. Hezbollah is not classified as a terrorist organisation by the United Nations or the vast majority of UN member states, however, and has considerable public support and several parliamentary seats in Lebanon. It has formed close ties with a number of countries including Russia, China and North Korea among others.

to isolate Damascus, to cut supply routes between Hezbollah and Syrian government positions, and to reinforce militants' positions in Homs. Its loss to the SAA ultimately facilitated swift military action by government forces to recapture the Homs governate, while also weakening the insurgents' hold on Aleppo.[165]

Associate fellow at Chatham House's Middle East and North Africa Programme, Christopher Phillips observed regarding the importance of Hezbollah's contribution at Al Qusayr: "Given Hezbollah's reputation as the most impressive military force in the Arab world, this sapped rebel morale and boosted the regime. By offering expertise that Assad lacked, such as light infantry and urban warfare expertise, training, or directing military tactics, from 2013 the Party of God [Hezbollah] became a vital component of Assad's forces and greatly shaped the conflict."[166] Hezbollah units played a key role in spearheading the offensive, supported by Syrian air and artillery strikes, and managed to gain ground quickly despite jihadist positions being heavily fortified with underground bunkers, an extensive tunnel network, booby traps and multiple high up sniper positions.[167] This served as a demonstration of its expertise in city fighting. Hezbollah subsequently negotiated a withdrawal plan with insurgent groups, allowing survivors to leave without being attacked, which significantly reduced civilian casualties and prevented further damage to the city. Insurgents fighting in Al Qusayr stressed the significant discrepancy in capabilities between Hezbollah and Syrian Arab Army units, stating that they particularly feared combat with the former. One member of an Islamist insurgent brigade stated to this effect regarding Hezbollah's performance in the field: "None of them were under 35 years old. They were very professional and tough fighters. You can tell they are superior fighters from the way they move in battle and how they fight."[168]

A paper from the Combating Terrorism Center at West Point referred to the Battle of Al Qusayr as having "marked the beginning of a broader campaign by the Syrian Arab Army to restore control over key strategic areas that had fallen to rebel hands," and as "a significant blow to the armed opposition, perhaps more in terms of morale and perception than strategic value." The latter point was reinforced by subsequent Syrian gains across the country.[169] The key battle was referred to by British analysts in 2016 as the Syrian War's "defining battle," [170] with Professor Alexandre Mansurov at the Johns Hopkins University's School of Advanced International Studies calling it a "significant military and symbolic victory" which "potentially changes the Syrian civil war dynamics."[171] The battle turned the tide after a months' long retreat by the Syrian Arab Army.

Al Qusayr also represented a turning point for Hezbollah in terms of its involvement in Syria. Within a week of the battle's outbreak in late May, Hezbollah General Secretary Hassan Nasrallah had pledged that the militia would stand by the Syrian government. He warned that the fall of Damascus would usher in a "dark period" in the Middle East and highlighted the threat posed by jihadist insurgents to Lebanon's security. "Syria is the back of the resistance, and the resistance cannot stand, arms folded while its back is broken... If Syria falls into the hands of America, Israel and takfiris [jihadists], the resistance will be besieged and Israel will enter Lebanon and impose its will," he warned.[172] This marked the beginning of official provision of direct support by Hezbollah for Syria's war effort through deployment of infantry and special forces for combat operations. Despite playing a significant and growing role in the Syrian War, Hezbollah could not afford to fully commit to the war effort due to its conflict with Israel on Lebanon's southern border. The conflict's ongoing nature was illustrated by an ambush conducted against an elite Israeli unit which had penetrated 400 meters across the Lebanese border two months after the battle of Al Qusayr ended, causing four casualties.[173] This was hardly the only low-level clash between the two longstanding antagonists in Lebanon during the course of the Syrian War.[174] Hezbollah's direct involvement to the Syrian War notably gave Israel an even greater incentive than before to support Islamist insurgent groups, forcing the Lebanese militia to fight on a second front for as long as possible and at greater cost to itself.

Alongside Hezbollah, which after victory at Al Qusayr would place a heavy emphasis on operations to remove the presence of

Al Qaeda linked groups from Aleppo, Iran would also begin to play an increasingly prominent role in the Syrian conflict. The Iranian Revolutionary Guards Corps' (IRGC) Al Quds Force, the branch responsible specifically for overseas operations, played a major role from 2012 in retraining and reorganising militias from Syria's pro-government Popular Committees. This effort was directly overseen by Quds Force Commander Qasem Soleimani. By mid-2013, the Popular Committees had been formed into a well-structured 60,000-strong National Defence Force serving as an effective and much valued auxiliary to the regular army. Their strength would later rise to 100,000, and these militias were assigned roles such as manning checkpoints, conducting patrols and performing a supporting role in counter-insurgency operations. Some of the more promising militiamen were arranged into special units and trained in urban guerrilla warfare by both the Quds Force and by Hezbollah.[175]

Syrian militia units would come to play a growing role in the country's defence as the war progressed, with some benefitting from embedded Quds Force officers and most working with Damascus under a unified command structure. These came from to a range of sects and ideologies, from the Jaysh Al Muwahhideen formed by the Druze minority to the Sootoro, made up of Assyrian Christians, the Shabiha comprised primarily of Alawites, and the Arab nationalist Ba'ath Brigades. The shared fear of total eradication should the country fall under the control of the Islamist insurgents was a strong motivator for unity and cooperation. The need to rely on these irregular units, however, and on Iranian officers to train them, reflected poorly on the capabilities of the Syrian Arab Army itself and highlighted its lack of preparation for counterinsurgency operations.

Iranian officials would stress the importance of the country's commitment to Syria's defence, particularly after jihadist forces began to take significant ground in 2012 and pose a real threat to Damascus. Senior Advisor for Foreign Affairs to Iran's Supreme Leader, Ali Akbar Velayati, stated on January 6, 2012: "The chain of resistance against Israel by Iran, Syria, Hezbollah, the new Iraqi government and Hamas passes through the Syrian highway," referring to Syria as "the golden ring of the chain of resistance."[176]

The head of Iran's Supreme National Security Council, Saeed Jalili, stated to the same effect eight months later: "What is happening in Syria is not an internal issue, but a conflict between the Axis of Resistance and its enemies in the region and the world. Iran will not tolerate, in any form, the breaking of the Axis of Resistance, of which Syria is an intrinsic part."[177] Nevertheless, much as with Hezbollah, there were no signs of direct Iranian support for the Syrian war effort until 2013, with IRGC commander Ali Jafari stating in September 2012 that the Guard Corps "is offering assistance in planning, as well as financial help, but does not have a military presence."[178] Commander of the IRGC's Quds Force, Qasem Soleimani, reportedly played a major role in reorganising the Syrian military in 2013, heading a command centre in Damascus which oversaw operations by the Syrian Arab Army, Hezbollah, and several Quds Force trained militias.[179]

Iranian involvement in Syria facilitated support from a number of Iranian affiliated groups from both Afghanistan and Iraq. The Fatemiyoun Brigade, comprised primarily of Shiites from Afghanistan's Hazara minority, was formed in 2014 with support from Iran's Quds Force to bolster the SAA in counterinsurgency operations. The Hazara faced severe religious and ethnic discrimination in Afghanistan after Western and Gulf Arab backed jihadist groups toppled the Afghan People's Republic in 1992, and the minority were frequently targeted for brutal mass killings in subsequent years with tens of thousands massacred.[180] Over three million Hazara were subsequently forced to flee to Iran. Recruits were largely drawn from this refugee community, with some also being recruited in Afghanistan itself, and they had a longstanding grudge against Wahhabist jihadist groups which could be settled on the battlefield in Syria.[xi]

---

xi Deployment of Hazara militias to Syria represented one of many ways in which the Syrian War could be considered a direct successor to the Afghan War of the 1980s. The Hazaras had been granted fully equality and occupied high ranks in both the military and the government including the Prime Ministership under Afghanistan's Soviet-aligned People's Republic. Both in the military and as part of independent militias, Hazaras had clashed frequently with foreign backed jihadist groups and were singled out for targeting by groups such as the Arab Mujahideen and later the Taliban due to their Asiatic appearances and Shiite faith.

The Fatemiyoun had an estimated size of 10–20,000 personnel,[181] and was founded with the official purpose of defending the holy shrine of Sayyida Zainab Bint Ali, granddaughter of the Prophet Muhammed, from Al Qaeda linked militants. Such shrines were particularly valued in the Shiite faith, and were frequently targeted by anti-government jihadist groups who considered maintaining Islamic historical sites for pilgrimage to be a form of idolatry. The Iraqi government of Premier Nouri Al Maliki notably permitted Iraqi Shiite volunteers, also trained by the Quds Force, to deploy to Syria under the pretext of protecting the shrine of Sayyida Zainab.[182] Iraqis deployed in considerable numbers under units organised by the Quds Force, such as Liwa Dhulfiqar and Liwa Al Imam Al Hussein, and provided a much needed manpower contribution to the war effort.[183] Baghdad further authorized oil shipments to Syria at 50% below market price,[184] which was particularly valued given that a great many Syrian oil producing facilities had fallen into the hands of Islamist insurgent groups. The Iraqi government also resisted very considerable Western pressure to close its airspace to Iranian and later to Russian aircraft flying supply missions to Syria. Despite extensive Western influence in the country and a major Western military presence on its soil, the common animosity between Baghdad and Damascus to Al Qaeda and its affiliates led Iraq to show strong solidarity with Syrian counterterrorism efforts.[185]

## North Korea in the Syrian War

North Korea's defence partnership with Syria dates back over half a century, with its armed forces, the Korean People's Army (KPA), fighting alongside the Syrian Arab Army in all its major wars since the Six Day War in 1967 including the Yom Kippur and Lebanon wars. Bolstering Syria represented part of a broader Korean effort to push back against Western interests in the third world and was one of multiple KPA overseas operations conducted since the country had first gone to war with the United States in 1950. These had seen its personnel deployed to battlefields far and wide from Angola and Egypt to Vietnam and

Lebanon.[186] Pyongyang was among the first to offer Damascus its support once the Islamist insurgency had escalated, and was one of just twelve states to vote against UN General Assembly Resolution 66/253 condemning the Syrian state in February 2012. There the Korean representative warned of "attempts by imperial powers and their allies" to force the Syrian government's overthrow "even at the cost of further bloodshed." Russian attempts to revise and moderate the text of the resolution were also condemned and rejected flatly by the Koreans as unwarranted intervention in internal Syrian affairs, making Pyongyang appear as Damascus' most resolute supporter at the Assembly.[187]

The KPA set up a command and control logistical assistance centre to support the Syrian war effort,[xii] with Korean officers deployed to multiple fronts including the frontlines in major battles such as Aleppo and Homs.[188] Western sources claimed, regarding the Korean role at Qusayr, that "Arab-speaking North Korean military advisors were integral to the operational planning of the surprise attack and artillery campaign execution during the battle for Qusayr."[189] Representatives of the insurgency claimed in 2013 that Korean pilots were flying Syrian Air Force aircraft in combat, which had some plausibility considering the significant shortages of trained pilots Syria had faced since the mid-1990s. Other reports by anti-government figures indicate that two KPA special forces units had deployed to Syria to engage jihadist forces, named Chalma-1 and Chalma-7, and that these units proved "fatally dangerous" on the battlefield. [190]

Deployment of Korean special forces overseas provided the KPA with valuable experience in modern warfare including in mountainous terrain and urban areas. Former Chief of Staff for the U.S. Special Operations Command Korea David Maxwell, among

---

xii It is important to note that these reports have emerged from Western backed anti-government sources which have openly sought a Western-sponsored overthrow of the government Syria and have not been independently verified. There is an incentive for Damascus and Pyongyang to underplay the extent of their defence cooperation, much as the Western Bloc and their allies have a strong incentive to exaggerate it. More verifiable details of the extent of Korean involvement in the current conflict are likely to remain elusive for many years to come.

others, expressed great concern at the benefits such overseas experience would bring North Korea.[191] These elite forces have been described in British reports as "highly motivated, politically well indoctrinated and well trained…. units are expected to seek the initiative continuously, to turn all unforeseen events to their advantage, and advance all to achieve their objectives regardless of cost."[192] Their notoriously rigorous training programs reportedly included "skills, such as abseiling, mountain climbing, swimming, martial arts, airborne, demolition, and rigorous physical fitness, and training designed to produce individual initiative, creativity, flexibility and aggressiveness."[193] North Korea fielded by far the largest special forces in the world with an estimated 180,000–200,000 personnel,[194] which had proven highly capable in clashes with South Korean forces during a 1996 infiltration incident[195] and were expected to be a highly formidable asset to Syrian counterinsurgency operations.

North Korea had provided considerable support for Syria's armed forces throughout the 1990s and 2000s, with frequently reported shipments of missile components and other military equipment vital to modernising the SAA's inventories.[196] This partnership strengthened following the outbreak of the Syrian War, with North Korea being a leading supplier of arms to the SAA as well as to Iran and Hezbollah themselves[197] and to several Iranian backed militia groups using the Quds Force as an intermediary.[198] Korean experts played a central role in Syrian efforts to maintain its defence industries and upgrade its deterrent capabilities during the war, with some details of this support emerging after an Israeli airstrike on the Syrian Scientific Studies and Research Centre. Korean engineers were reportedly killed in the attack, and had been tasked with producing solid fuel composites for ballistic missiles.[199] In what was speculated to be retaliation for Korean assistance to the Syrian state, hackers linked to the Islamic State jihadist insurgent group would compromise a webpage of the national airline, Air Koryo. The page was covered with jihadist propaganda, which described Korean leader Kim Jong Un as a "crying pig," and threatened that the "thug nation" of North Korea would "pay a price for their collaboration with the enemies of the muwahideen [jihadists]."[200]

Giving considerable insight into the nature of Korean support for Damascus' position, Syrian ambassador to Pyongyang Tammam Sulaiman stated in 2017: "In every meeting, every function, every symposium, every international meeting, the DPRK [Democratic People's Republic of Korea – North Korea's official name] expresses support to us, they express solidarity – not only the media, even from the people. It is not only a policy issue, it is a massive popular thing for the Korean people to stand in support of Syria, with the Syrian people."[201] The two states held "a bi-annual joint high-level ministerial commission that meets once in Pyongyang and once in Damascus. And then there are agreements in the economic field, in the cultural, educational, tourism, sports, and many other things," according to the ambassador.[202] Sulaiman highlighted that the both faced a common struggle against Western economic and military pressure, which he referred to as "the same colonial problem."[203] Korean officials in the same vein referred to the two states as "facing a common enemy which is seeking to undermine the independence of their two countries."[204] The two moved to considerably expand parliamentary cooperation from mid-2018,[205] and according to multiple statements from Syrian officials, bilateral ties in the economic and cultural fields expanded quickly throughout the war period.[206]

North Korean Defence Minister Kim Kyok Sik, an artillery officer and fluent Arabic speaker, visited Syria in 2013 and was one of the highest-ranking officials from any country do so at the time. Multiple agreements for closer defence cooperation and arms deals are thought to have been signed at this time to facilitate greater Korean support for the Syrian war effort. Korean Foreign Minister Ri Su Yong visited Damascus the following year and met with President Assad, and several high-level delegations were subsequently exchanged between the two states. At a time when Syria faced growing isolation, North Korea stood as its strongest state supporter alongside Iran. Korean embassy staff paid several visits to wounded Syrian soldiers, as the country provided considerable humanitarian assistance including the construction and full staffing of three hospitals by mid-2016.[207] Syria in turn opened a Kim Il Sung Park in honour of the country's founding father in 2015, adjacent to Kim Il Sung Street in Damascus, which was seen as a wartime tribute in thanks for Pyongyang's extensive assistance during the crisis. At the park's opening ceremony, which marked the 70th anniversary of the ruling Korean Workers' Party, Syria's deputy Foreign Minister Faisal Mikdad praised the Korean leader Kim Jong Un and the ruling Korean Workers' Party for "standing with Syria against terrorism."[208]

There is a strong argument to be made that North Korea has been Syria's closest strategic partner in the 21st century.[xiii] Unlike Iran and Hezbollah, with which Syria faces an ideological rift between its secular party state and their religion-based ideology, and in contrast to post-Soviet Russia which adopted political and economic models that could be called 'Western liberalism with Russian characteristics,' the two party states of North Korea and Syria have much less separating them. While there are concerns that Tehran or Moscow could seek to use their greater influence in post-war Syria to respectively 'Islamicise' or 'liberalise' the state, much as the former did in Iraq and the latter sought to do in Belarus,[209] there is little possibility that Pyongyang will attempt to move Syria away from a party state system and remake it in a different image. Tammam Sulaiman stated to this effect in 2017: "Of course, we belong to different cultures in the Arab and Asian regions, but we have a lot in common to address the issues that really are at stake in the current times. The relations are strong, basically, because we share the same values: the same suffering, the same mentality, the same orientation."[210] Syrian officials have repeatedly expressed considerable admiration for North Korea and particularly the resilience of its political and economic systems. This may influence the nature of governance of post-war Syria, which has proven less capable that its East Asian partner of dealing with many similar challenges in fields ranging from

---

xiii  Syria is one of just two North Korean partners not to recognise or have any diplomatic ties with South Korea, the other being Cuba, while Pyongyang had reciprocated by refusing to recognise the State of Israel.

industry and military performance to infrastructure and economic and information warfare.

# Notes

1 Ahmed, Nafeez, 'Syria intervention plan fuelled by oil interests, not chemical weapons concern,' *The Guardian*, August 30, 2013.
2 Kennedy, Robert F., Jr., 'Why the Arabs Don't Want Us in Syria,' *Politico*, February 22, 2016.
3 'INSIGHT – military intervention in Syria, post withdrawal status of forces,' *Wikileaks*, March 6, 2012 (https://wikileaks.org/gifiles/docs/16/1671459_insight-military-intervention-in-syria-post-withdrawal.html).
Thomson, Alex, 'Spooks' view on Syria: what wikileaks revealed,' *Channel 4*, August 28, 2013.
Giraldi, Philip, 'NATO Vs. Syria,' *The American Conservative*, December 19, 2011.
4 'INSIGHT – military intervention in Syria, post withdrawal status of forces,' *Wikileaks*, March 6, 2012 (https://wikileaks.org/gifiles/docs/16/1671459_insight-military-intervention-in-syria-post-withdrawal.html).
5 Ibid.
6 Ahmed, Nafeez, 'Syria intervention plan fuelled by oil interests, not chemical weapons concern,' *The Guardian*, August 30, 2013.
7 Hersh, Seymour M., 'The Redirection,' *The New Yorker*, February 26, 2007.
8 Ibid.
9 Ibid.
10 Ibid.
11 Congressional Record, Volume 151, Part 17, 109th Congress, 1st Session, October 7 to 26, 2005, U.S. Congress.
12 Hersh, Seymour M., 'The Redirection,' *The New Yorker*, February 26, 2007.
13 Seale, Patrick, *The Struggle for Syria: A Study of Post-War Arab Politics, 1945–1958*, London, Oxford University Press, 1965 (pp. 36–37, 39).
14 Hersh, Seymour M., 'The Redirection,' *The New Yorker*, February 26, 2007.
15 Ibid.
16 'State-run Syrian TV says 19 police officers and security forces have been killed in southern city of Daraa,' *AP Archive*, April 27, 2011 (http://www.aparchive.com/metadata/youtube/af7b6fd4a026b87e9a164d24f88c2cf4).
Holliday, Joseph, *The Struggle for Syria in 2011: An Operational and Regional Analysis*, Middle East Security Report 2, Institute for the Study of War, December 2011 (pp. 15–16, 21).
17 Chatriwala, Omar, 'What Wikileaks Tells Us About *Al Jazeera*,' *Foreign Policy*, September 19, 2011.
'After Disclosures by WikiLeaks, *Al Jazeera* Replaces Its Top News Director,' *New York Times*, September 20, 2011.
'Wikileaks: *Al Jazeera* Chief Linked to US Defense Department,' *Press TV*, September 12, 2011.

18  Roberts, David B., 'Reflecting on Qatar's "Islamist" Soft Power,' *Brookings Institute,* April 2019.
19  'Fighting, While Funding, Extremists,' *New York Times,* June 19, 2017.
    Osnos, Evan, 'The Biden Agenda,' *The New Yorker,* July 28, 2014.
    Kirkpatrick, David D., 'Qatar's Support of Islamists Alienates Allies Near and Far,' *New York Times,* September 7, 2014.
    Blair, David and Spencer, Richard, 'How Qatar is funding the rise of Islamist extremists,' *The Telegraph,* September 20, 2014.
    Mohammed, Riyadh, 'How Qatar Is Funding al-Qaeda – and Why That Could Help the US,' *The Fiscal Times,* December 29, 2015.
    'Funding Al Nusra Through Ransom: Qatar and the Myth of "Humanitarian Principle",' *CATF,* December 10, 2015.
20  'Al-Jazeera Gets Rap as Qatar Mouthpiece,' *Bloomberg,* April 9, 2012.
    Chatriwala, Omar, 'What Wikileaks Tells Us About *Al Jazeera*,' *Foreign Policy,* September 19, 2011.
    'الجزير «ليست بخير: استقالات.. والأجندة»' [*Al-Jazeera:* "It's not okay: resignations … and the agenda"], *Al Sagheet,* April 3, 2012.
    'Ex-employee: *Al Jazeera* provided Syrian rebels with satphones,' *RT,* April 4, 2012.
    'An exclusive interview with a news editor of Al-Jazeera Channel,' *Axis of Logic,* January 6, 2013.
21  Ulrichsen, Kristian Coates, 'Qatar and the Arab Spring: Policy Drivers and Regional Implications,' *Carnegie Endowment for International Peace,* September 2014.
22  'Qatar's Emir Suggests Sending Troops to Syria,' *Al Jazeera,* January 14, 2012.
23  Black, Ian, 'Qatar admits sending hundreds of troops to support Libya rebels,' *The Guardian,* October 26, 2011.
24  '"Day of Rage" for Syrians Fails to Draw Protesters,' *New York Times,* February 4, 2011.
25  Warrick, Joby, *Black Flags: The Rise of ISIS,* New York, Doubleday, 2015 (Chapter 6).
26  'Crony Capitalism, Syria Style,' *NPR,* May 22, 2012.
27  'Corruption in Syria on the Rise,' *Institute for War and Peace Reporting,* October 18, 2008.
28  Goulden, Robert, 'Housing, Inequality, and Economic Change in Syria,' *British Journal of Middle Eastern Studies*, vol. 38, no. 2, August 2011 (pp. 187–202).
29  'Slums of the World: The face of urban poverty in the new millennium,' Nairobi, *UN Habitat,* 2003.
    Goulden, Robert, 'Housing, Inequality, and Economic Change in Syria,' *British Journal of Middle Eastern Studies*, vol. 38, no. 2, August 2011 (pp. 187–202).
30  Ahmed, Nafeez, 'Syria intervention plan fuelled by oil interests, not chemical weapons concern,' *The Guardian,* August 30, 2013.
    Kennedy, Robert F., Jr., 'Why the Arabs Don't Want Us in Syria,' *Politico,* February 22, 2016.

31  Giraldi, Philip, 'NATO Vs. Syria,' *The American Conservative*, December 19, 2011.

32  'Interview with Anwar Al Eshki,' *BBC Arabic,* April 10, 2012 (https://www.youtube.com/watch?v=FoGmrWWJ77w).

33  'INSIGHT – military intervention in Syria, post withdrawal status of forces,' *Wikileaks,* March 6, 2012 (https://wikileaks.org/gifiles/docs/16/1671459_ insight-military-intervention-in-syria-post-withdrawal.html).
Thomson, Alex, 'Spooks' view on Syria: what wikileaks revealed,' *Channel 4,* August 28, 2013.
Giraldi, Philip, 'NATO Vs. Syria,' *The American Conservative*, December 19, 2011.

34  Warrick, Joby, *Black Flags: The Rise of ISIS,* New York, Doubleday, 2015 (Chapter 19).

35  Walter, Barbara F., 'The Extremist's Advantage in Civil Wars,' *International Security,* vol. 42, no. 2, Fall 2017 (pp. 7–39).
Walter, Barbara F., 'The New New Civil Wars,' *Annual Review of Political Science*, vol. 20, 2017 (pp. 469–486).
Lucente, Adam and Al Shimale, Zouhir, 'Free Syrian Army decimated by desertions,' *Al Jazeera,* November 11, 2015.
Hersh, Seymour M., 'The Redirection,' *The New Yorker,* February 26, 2007.
'Syria Conflict: Rebels, Army Battle Over Taftanaz Airbase,' *The Huffington Post*, November 3, 2012.
'Jabhat al-Nusra's rising stock in Syria,' *Al Jazeera,* May 19, 2013.
Holmes, Oliver and Dziadosz, Alexander, 'Special Report: Syria's Islamists seize control as moderates dither,' *Reuters,* June 19, 2013.

36  'Department of Defense Information Report, Not Finally Evaluated Intelligence – Iraq,' May 3, 2012 (http://www.judicalwatch.org/wp-content/ uploads/2015/05/Pg.-2991-Pgs.-291.-287-2993-JW-v-DOD-and-State-14- 812-DOD-Release-2015-04-10-final-version11.pdf).

37  Ibrahimi, Niamatullah, 'Ideology without Leadership: The Rise and Decline of Maoism in Afghanistan,' *Afghanistan Analysts Network,* August 2012.

38  Ignatius, David, 'Al-Qaeda affiliate playing larger role in Syria rebellion,' *Washington Post*, November 30, 2012.

39  Ibid.

40  Isachenkov, Vladimir, 'US asks Russia to not hit Nusra Front in Syria, Moscow says,' *AP News*, June 3, 2016.

41  May 2012 Houla Massacre:
Blame on Government: Chulov, Martin, 'The Houla massacre: reconstructing the events of 25 May,' *The Guardian*, June 1, 2012.
Evidence of Insurgent Perpetration: Hermann, Rainer, 'Syrien. Eine Auslöschung' [Syria. An extinction], *Frankfurter Allgemeine Zeitung*, June 13, 2012.
August 2012 Daraya Massacre:
Blame on Government: Mahmood, Mona, 'Syria's worst massacre: Daraya death toll reaches 400,' *The Guardian*, August 28, 2012.
Evidence of Insurgent Perpetration: Fisk, Robert, 'Inside Daraya – how a failed prisoner swap turned into a massacre,' *The Independent,* August 29, 2012.

December 2012 Aqrab Massacre:
Blame on Government: Stack, Liam and Mourtada, Hania, 'Members of Assad's Sect Blamed in Syria Killings,' *New York Times*, December 12, 2012.
Evidence of Insurgent Perpetration: Thompson, Alex, 'Was there a massacre in the Syrian town of Aqrab?' *Channel Four*, December 14, 2012.

42   Oweis, Khaled Yacoub, 'Syria activists report "massacre" by army near Damascus,' *Reuters*, August 25, 2012.

43   Fisk, Robert, 'Inside Daraya – how a failed prisoner swap turned into a massacre,' *The Independent*, August 29, 2012.

44   Stack, Liam and Mourtada, Hania, 'Members of Assad's Sect Blamed in Syria Killings,' *New York Times*, December 12, 2012.

45   Thompson, Alex, 'Was there a massacre in the Syrian town of Aqrab?' *Channel Four*, December 14, 2012.

46   The abduction of an *NBC News* team in Syria in December 2013 was initially blamed on a pro-government militia until a *New York Times* investigation revealed that the culprits were "a Sunni criminal element affiliated with the Free Syrian Army." (Somaiya, Ravi and Chivers, C. J. and Shoumali, Karam, 'NBC News Alters Account of Correspondent's Kidnapping in Syria,' *New York Times*, April 15, 2015.)

47   Cobain, Ian and Ross, Alice, 'The British government's covert propaganda campaign in Syria,' *Middle East Eye*, February 19, 2020.

48   Kainikara, Sanu, *In the Bear's Shadow: Russian Intervention in Syria*, Canberra, Air Power Development Center, 2018 (p. 43).

49   Erlich, Reese, *Inside Syra: The Backstory of Their Civil War and What the World Can Expect*, Amherst, Prometheus Books, 2014 (Chapter 5: The Uprising Begins).

50   Mojon, Jean-Marc, 'Syria revolt attracts motley foreign jihadi corps,' *Daily Star*, August 18, 2012.

51   LaFranch, Howard, 'For newly recognized Syrian rebel coalition, a first dispute with US,' *Christian Science Monitor*, December 12, 2012.

52   'Syrian protesters slam U.S. blacklisting of jihadist group,' *The Daily Star*, December 14, 2012.

53   Sherlock, Ruth, 'Syrian rebels defy US and pledge allegiance to jihadi group,' *The Telegraph*, December 10, 2019.

54   Cafarella, Jennifer, 'Jabat al-Nusra in Syria,' *Institute for the Study of War*, December 2014.
Mazzetti, Mark and Goldman, Adam and Schmidt, Michael S., 'Behind the Sudden Death of a $1 Billion Secret C.I.A. War in Syria,' *The New York Times*, August 2, 2017.

55   Kainikara, Sanu, *In the Bear's Shadow: Russian Intervention in Syria*, Canberra, Air Power Development Center, 2018 (p. 44).
Ripley, Tim, *Operation Aleppo: Russia's War in Syria*, Lancaster, Telic-Herrick Publications, 2018 (p. 10).

56   Mekhennet, Souad, 'The terrorist fighting us now? We just finished training them,' *Washington Post*, August 18, 2014.
Statement by Mr. Vladimir V. Putin, President of the Russian Federation, at the 70th session of the UN General Assembly, September 28, 2015.

57 'The terrorists fighting us now? We just finished training them,' *Washington Post*, August 18, 2014.
58 Ibid.
59 Abrahms, Max and Glaser, John, 'The pundits were wrong about Assad and the Islamic State. As usual, they're not willing to admit it,' *Los Angeles Times,* December 10, 2017.
60 *Weapons of the Islamic State – A three-year investigation in Iraq and Syria,* London, Conflict Armament Research, 2017.
   Sands, Phil and Maayeh, Suha, 'Death of a Syrian arms salesman,' *The National,* August 7, 2016.
61 Perry, Tom, 'Syria rebels in south emerge as West's last hope as moderates crushed elsewhere,' *Reuters,* November 13, 2014.
62 Lucente, Adam and Al Shimale, Zouhir, 'Free Syrian Army decimated by desertions,' *Al Jazeera,* November 11, 2015.
63 Seligman, Lara, 'Turkish-Backed Forces Are Freeing Islamic State Prisoners,' *Foreign Policy,* October 14, 2019.
64 Perry, Tom, 'Syria rebels in south emerge as West's last hope as moderates crushed elsewhere,' *Reuters,* November 13, 2014.
65 Hassan, Hassan, 'The Army of Islam Is Winning in Syria and That's Not Necessarily a Bad Thing,' *Foreign Policy*, October 1, 2013.
66 Hudson, John, 'US Weighing Closer Ties with Hardline Islamists in Syria,' *Foreign Policy*, December 17, 2013.
67 'Syrian rebels filmed shooting Islamic State militants,' *BBC News*, July 1, 2015.
   Zielinski, Caroline, 'Syrian rival jihadi group, Jaysh al-Islam, execute ISIS fighters in brutal role reversal video,' *News.com.au,* July 5, 2015.
68 Hassan, Hassan, 'The Army of Islam Is Winning in Syria: And that's not necessarily a bad thing,' *Foreign Policy,* October 1, 2013.
69 'Pro-Assad Rally Shows Syrian Government Can Still Command Support,' *New York Times*, October 20, 2011.
70 Sherlock, Ruth, 'Dispatch: Syria rebels "burned down churches and destroyed Christian graves",' *The Telegraph*, January 3, 2015.
   'Report: Over 120 Syrian churches damaged by war since 2011,' *Associated Press,* September 10, 2019.
   'Syria's beleaguered Christians,' *BBC News,* February 25, 2015.
   'Remarks by the Vice President at In Defense of Christians Solidarity Dinner,' *The White House,* October 25, 2017.
   'We finally know what Hillary Clinton knew all along – U.S. allies Saudi Arabia and Qatar are funding Isis,' *The Independent*, October 14, 2016.
71 'Va. senator travels to Syria, shakes hands with Bashar al-Assad,' *Washington Post,* April 28, 2016.
   Congressman Dana Rohrabacher at the House Foreign Affairs Committee, May 3, 2017.
   Wilkie, Christina, 'Rand Paul: Assad "Protected Christians" in Syria, Rebels "Attacking Christians",' *Huffpost,* September 1, 2013.
   Paul, Ronald, 'Ron Paul: Donald Trump's Disastrous Syria Attacks,' *Fitsnews,* April 16, 2018.

'Rep. Tulsi Gabbard Votes Against Efforts to Overthrow Syrian Government – H.Con.Res.75,' *Website of Congresswoman Tulsi Gabbard*, March 14, 2016.

72  Warrick, Joby, *Black Flags: The Rise of ISIS*, New York, Doubleday, 2015 (Chapter 20).

73  Ibid (Chapter 20).

74  Bandow, Doug, 'U.S. Should Stay Out Of Syria: "Safe Zones" Aren't Safe For Americans,' *Forbes*, February 1, 2017.

75  Roberts, David, 'Behind Qatar's Intervention In Libya,' *Foreign Affairs*, September 28, 2011.
Black, Ian, 'Qatar admits sending hundreds of troops to support Libya rebels,' *The Guardian*, October 26, 2011.
Starr, Barbara, 'Foreign forces in Libya helping rebel forces advance,' *CNN*, August 24, 2011.

76  'Syrian opposition opens embassy in Qatar,' *CNN*, March 27, 2013.

77  'Opposition takes Syria seat at Arab League summit,' *BBC News*, March 26, 2013.

78  Chivers, C. J. and Schmitt, Eric, 'Arms Airlift to Syria Rebels Expands, With Aid From CIA,' *New York Times*, March 25, 2013.

79  Barnard, Anne, 'Syrian Rebels Say Saudi Arabia Is Stepping Up Weapons Deliveries,' *New York Times*, September 12, 2013.

80  'Report: Saudis sent death-row inmates to fight Syria,' *USA Today*, January 21, 2013.

81  Hussain, Murtaza, 'NSA Document says Saudi Prince directly ordered coordinated attack by Syrian Rebels on Damascus,' *The Intercept*, October 24, 2017.

82  Reals, Tucker, 'Syria Defense Minister Gen. Dawoud Rajha, two other top ministers killed in explosion in Damascus,' *CBS News*, July 18, 2012.

83  İpek, Yezdani, 'Syrian rebels: Too fragmented, unruly,' *Hürriyet Daily News*, September 1, 2012.

84  Giraldi, Philip, 'NATO Vs. Syria,' *The American Conservative*, December 19, 2011.

85  Mahfudh, `Aqeel, 'Syria and Turkey: A turning point or a historical bet?,' *Arab Center for Research & Policy Studies*, February 2012 (pp. 68–69).

86  Uslu, Emrullah, 'Jihadist Highway to Jihadist Haven: Turkey's Jihadi Policies and Western Security,' *Studies in Conflict and Terrorism*, vol. 39, no. 9, 2016 (p. 787).
'Erdoğan'ın emri ile ISID'e silah gonderildi' [Weapon sent to ISIS on the orders of Erdoğan], *Cumhuriyet*, July 23, 2014.
'Iste silah tasıyan MIT tırlarıyla ilgili yayın yasagı getirilen belgeler' [Documents against publication ban on MIT trucks carrying guns], *BirGun*, January 14, 2015.

87  'Ankara Refutes UN Report Claiming Turkey Route for Arms to al-Qaeda,' *Hurriyet Daily News*, December 30, 2014.
Uslu, Emrullah, 'Jihadist Highway to Jihadist Haven: Turkey's Jihadi Policies and Western Security,' *Studies in Conflict and Terrorism*, vol. 39, no. 9, 2016 (pp. 781–802).

88  Taştekin, Fehim, 'Turkish Military Says MIT Shipped Weapons to al-Qaeda,' *Al-Monitor*, January 15, 2015.

89  Uslu, Emre, 'Has Turkey helped ISIS?,' *Today's Zaman*, August 31, 2014.

90  Sanger, David E. and Hirschfeld Davis, Julie, 'Struggling to Starve ISIS of Oil Revenue, U.S. Seeks Assistance From Turkey,' *New York Times*, September 13, 2014.
Yayla, Ahmet S. and Clarke, Colin P., 'Turkey's Double ISIS Standard,' *Foreign Policy*, April 12, 2018.
Uslu, Emrullah, 'Jihadist Highway to Jihadist Haven: Turkey's Jihadi Policies and Western Security,' *Studies in Conflict and Terrorism,* vol. 39, no. 9, 2016 (pp. 781–802).
'One of 2 Russian pilots shot down by Turkey rescued, back to airbase in Syria,' *RT,* November 25, 2015.

91  Phillips, Christopher, *The Battle For Syria: International Rivalry in the New Middle East,* New Haven, Yale University Press, 2016 (p. 199).

92  Uslu, Emre, 'ElKaide, IHH, TIR vs...,' *Taraf,* January 2014.

93  Yayla, Ahmet S. and Clarke, Colin P., 'Turkey's Double ISIS Standard,' *Foreign Policy*, April 12, 2018.
'Turkey opposition accuses govt of protecting ISIS militants,' *France 24,* June 17, 2014.
Gokce, Dincer, 'ISID uyesi Sanlıurfa'da tedaviedi liyor iddiası,' [The allegation that ISID members did not receive treatment in Sanlıurfa], *Hurriyet,* September 22, 2014.

94  Ignatius, David, 'Al-Qaeda affiliate playing larger role in Syria rebellion,' *The Washington Post*, November 30, 2012.
Abouzeid, Rania, 'The Jihad Next Door,' *Politico*, June 23, 2014.
'Syria Conflict: Rebels, Army Battle Over Taftanaz Airbase,' *The Huffington Post*, November 3, 2012.

95  'Who is supplying weapons to the warring sides in Syria?,' *BBC News*, June 14, 2013.

96  'Mosul Study Group: What the Battle for Mosul Teaches the Force,' *U.S. Army*, 2017 (p. 4).

97  Ignatius, David, 'Al-Qaeda affiliate playing larger role in Syria rebellion,' *The Washington Post*, November 30, 2012.

98  Hauer, Neil, 'Chechen and north Caucasian militants in Syria,' *Atlantic Council,* January 18, 2018.

99  'Russia air strikes targeting Chechen jihadists in Syria,' *Middle East Online,* July 10, 2015.

100 Alami, Mona, 'The New Generation of Jordanian Jihadi Fighters,' *Carnegie Endowment For International Peace*, February 18, 2014.

101 Shih, Gerry, 'AP Exclusive: Uighurs fighting in Syria take aim at China,' *Associated Press*, December 23, 2017.
Volodzko, David, 'China's New Headache: Uyghur Militants in Syria,' *The Diplomat*, March 8, 2016.

102 'Jihadist group claim responsibility for Damascus blasts,' *ITV News*, May 12, 2012.
'Syria unrest: Aleppo bomb attacks "kill 28",' *BBC News*, February 10, 2012.

'At least 50 pro-Assad forces killed in Syria suicide bombing, activists say,' *Haaretz*, November 5, 2012.

Fahim, Kareem and Saad, Hwaida, 'Suicide bombers kill 14 in Damascus,' June 11, 2013.

103 'Syria Conflict: Rebels, Army Battle Over Taftanaz Airbase,' *The Huffington Post*, November 3, 2012.

'Militant group says was behind Aleppo air defense base assault,' *Reuters*, October 20, 2012.

104 Sengupta, Kim, 'Turkey and Saudi Arabia alarm the West by backing Islamist extremists the Americans had bombed in Syria,' *The Independent*, May 12, 2015.

Bozkurt, Abdullah, 'US Defense Intelligence Agency says Turkey, Qatar supported al-Nusra Front,' *Nordic Monitor,* December 10, 2019.

Hersh, Seymour, 'Military to Military,' *London Review of Books,* vol. 38, no. 1, January 2016 (pp. 11–14).

Uslu, Emrullah, 'Jihadist Highway to Jihadist Haven: Turkey's Jihadi Policies and Western Security,' *Studies in Conflict & Terrorism*, vol. 39, no. 9, 2016 (pp. 781–802).

Tanis, Tolga, 'Al-Assad in his last six months, US estimates,' *Hürriyet Daily News*, January 17, 2013.

105 Sengupta, Kim, 'Turkey and Saudi Arabia alarm the West by backing Islamist extremists the Americans had bombed in Syria,' *The Independent*, May 12, 2015.

106 'Fighting, While Funding, Extremists,' *New York Times,* June 19, 2017.

Kirkpatrick, David D., 'Qatar's Support of Islamists Alienates Allies Near and Far,' *New York Times,* September 7, 2014.

Blair, David and Spencer, Richard, 'How Qatar is funding the rise of Islamist extremists,' *The Telegraph,* September 20, 2014.

Mohammed, Riyadh, 'How Qatar Is Funding al-Qaeda – and Why That Could Help the US,' *The Fiscal Times,* December 29, 2015.

'Funding Al Nusra Through Ransom: Qatar and the Myth of "Humanitarian Principle",' *CATF,* December 10, 2015.

107 'Stop Arming Terrorists,' *Website of Congresswoman Tulsi Gabbard* (https://gabbard.house.gov/news/StopArmingTerrorists).

108 Glenn, Cameron, 'The Nusra Front: Al Qaeda's Affiliate in Syria,' *Wilson Center,* June 17, 2016.

109 Chivers, C. J., 'Videos From Syria Appear to Show First Confirmed Hit of Aircraft by Surface-to-Air Missile,' *New York Times,* November 27, 2012.

'Syrian rebels muster new air power,' *The Australian,* November 30, 2012.

Borger, Julian, 'Arms and the Manpads: Syrian rebels get anti-aircraft missiles,' *The Guardian,* November 28, 2012.

Boxx, Eddie and White, Jeff, 'Responding to Assad's Use of Airpower in Syria,' *Washington Institute for Near East Policy*, November 20, 2012.

Boxx, S. Edward, 'Observations on the Air War in Syria,' *Air & Space Power Journal*, March–April 2013 (p. 153).

110 'Missiles Fired At Passenger Jet Over Syria,' *Sky News,* April 29, 2013.

'Russia bans flights over Syria after airliner targeted by missiles,' *Traveller*, May 1, 2013.

Sterman, Adiv, 'Syrian rebels claim Iranian plane shot down,' *Times of Israel,* March 28, 2013.

111  Angelovski, Ivan and Marzouk, Lawrence, 'Revealed: the £1bn of weapons flowing from Europe to Middle East,' *The Guardian,* July 27, 2016.
'US, Allies Supply Arms to Nusra, Daesh Through Third Countries – Damascus,' *Sputnik,* September 4, 2018.

112  Angelovski, Ivan and Marzouk, Lawrence, 'Revealed: The Pentagon Is Spending Up To \$2.2 Billion on Soviet-Style Arms for Syrian Rebels,' *OCCRP,* September 12, 2017.
Angelovski, Ivan and Marzouk, Lawrence, 'The Pentagon's \$2.2 Billion Soviet Arms Pipeline Flooding Syria,' *Balkan Insight,* September 12, 2017.

113  Dilyana, Gaytandzhieva, '350 diplomatic flights carry weapons for terrorists,' *TRUD,* August 2, 2017.
'Report: Saudi, UAE weapons end up with armed groups,' *Al Jazeera,* August 27, 2017.

114  Hersh, Seymour M., 'The Red Line and the Rat Line,' *London Review of Books,* vol. 36, no. 8, April 2014.

115  Barnard, Anne and Arsu, Sebnem, 'Turkey, Seeking Weapons, Forces Syrian Jet to Land,' *New York Times,* October 10, 2012.

116  'Turkey and Syria trade fire as border skirmishes continue,' *France24,* October 7, 2012.
'Syrian Troops Arrest 4 Turkish Pilots in Aleppo: Report,' *Al Manar,* December 31, 2012.

117  'Syrian rebels use a child to behead a prisoner,' *Human Rights Investigations,* December 10, 2012 (http://humanrightsinvestigations.org/2012/12/10/syrian-rebels-use-a-child-to-behead-a-prisoner/).

118  Landler, Mark and Gordon, Michael R., 'Obama Says U.S. Will Recognize Syrian Rebels,' *New York Times,* December 11, 2012.

119  Erlanger, Steven and Gladstone, Rick, 'France Grants Its Recognition to Syria Rebels,' *New York Times,* November 13, 2012.

120  Spencer, Richard, 'Britain officially recognises new Syrian rebel coalition as country's "legitimate" government,' *The Telegraph,* November 20, 2012.

121  'Syria rebels to get direct non-lethal support from U.S. for 1st time, Secretary Kerry announces,' *CBS News,* February 28, 2013.
'William Hague offers Syrian rebels armoured vehicles and body armour,' *The Telegraph,* March 6, 2013.

122  Zengerle, Patricia, 'Senate panel backs arming Syria rebels,' *Reuters,* May 22, 2013.

123  Federman, Joseph, 'Israeli PM doesn't rule out helping Syrian rebels,' *News Daily,* April 18, 2013.

124  Mazzetti, Mark and Goldman, Adam and Schmidt, Michael S., 'Behind the Sudden Death of a \$1 Billion Secret C.I.A. War in Syria,' *New York Times,* August 2, 2017.

125  Ben Zion, Ilan, 'Five dead, dozens injured in Damascus triple bombing,' *Times of Israel,* December 12, 2012.
'Car bomb hits Damascus petrol station, 11 killed,' *Reuters,* January 4, 2013.

'At least 24 killed in car bombs in Syria's Idlib: monitoring agency,' *Reuters,* January 16, 2013.

126  Harding, Luke and Elder, Miriam and Beaumont, Peter, 'Assad losing Syria war, Russia admits for first time,' *The Guardian,* December 13, 2012.

127  Ben Zion, Ilan, 'Five dead, dozens injured in Damascus triple bombing,' *Times of Israel,* December 12, 2012.
'Car bomb hits Damascus petrol station, 11 killed,' *Reuters,* January 4, 2013.
Holmes, Oliver, 'Coordinated car bombs kill 24 in north-west Syria,' *Reuters,* January 16, 2013.
'Syria bomb kills 42, including top cleric,' *Australia World News,* March 22, 2013.

128  'Syrian activists say rebels are advancing near Aleppo airport,' *CTV News,* February 2, 2013.
'Syrian troops battle rebels around Damascus,' *Al Jazeera,* February 8, 2013.
'Syrian rebels "capture" air base in Aleppo,' *Al Jazeera,* February 12, 2013.
'Syrian rebels cut major desert road,' *Al Arabiya,* May 11, 2013.
'Syrian rebels enter northern air base,' *Yahoo News*, May 5, 2013.

129  'Air strike hit 11 vehicles in Gaddafi convoy – NATO,' *Reuters,* October 21, 2011.
Harding, Thomas, 'Col Gaddafi killed: convoy bombed by drone flown by pilot in Las Vegas,' *The Telegraph,* October 20, 2011.

130  Bosco, David, 'Was there going to be a Benghazi massacre?,' *Foreign Policy,* April 7, 2011.
Kuperman, Alan, 'Lessons from Libya: How Not to Intervene,' *Harvard Kennedy School Belfer Center,* September 2013.
Bosco, David, 'A Model Humanitarian Intervention? Reassessing NATO's Libya Campaign,' *Harvard Kennedy School Belfer Center,* Summer 2013.
Pedde, Nicola, 'The Libyan conflict and its controversial roots,' *European View,* vol. 16, 2017 (pp. 93–102).
'5 things the U.S. should consider in Libya,' *USA Today,* March 22, 2011.

131  '"Libya becoming completely failed state" – former U.S. Ambassador,' *RT,* May 30, 2017.

132  Hoff, Brad, 'Hillary Emails Reveal True Motive for Libya Intervention,' *Foreign Policy Journal,* January 6, 2016.
'Libyan rebel ethnic cleansing and lynching of black people,' *Human Rights Watch,* July 7, 2011.
'Black Africans "forced to eat Gaddafi's flag" in Libya,' *The Telegraph,* March 6, 2012.
'African viewpoint: Colonel's continent?,' *BBC News,* February 25, 2011.
Forte, Maximilian C., *Interventionism, Information Warfare, and the Military-Academic Complex,* Montreal, Alert Press, 2011 (pp. 153–155).

133  'African migrants raped & murdered after being sold in Libyan "slave markets" – UN,' *RT,* April 11, 2017.
Osborne, Samuel, 'Libya: African refugees being sold at "regular public slave auctions",' *The Independent,* April 11, 2017.

134 'U.S. ground troops are in Libya, Pentagon admits,' *RT*, August 12, 2016.
Donaghi, Rory, 'Britain is at war in Libya and nobody thought to tell us,' *The Independent*, May 28, 2016.

135 Bryanski, Gleb, 'Putin: Libya coalition has no right to kill Gaddafi,' *Reuters*, April 26, 2011.
Osborn, Andrew, 'Vladimir Putin lashes out at America for killing Gaddafi and backing protests,' *The Telegraph*, December 15, 2011.

136 Rothschild, Matthew, 'In Panama, An Illegal and Unwarranted Invasion,' *Chicago Tribune*, December 21, 1989.
Maechling Jr., Charles, 'Washington's Illegal Invasion,' *Foreign Policy*, no. 79, Summer, 1990 (pp. 113–131).
Henkin, Louis, 'The Invasion of Panama Under International Law: A Gross Violation,' *Columbia Journal of Transnational Law*, vol. 29, issue 2, 1991 (pp. 293–318).

137 Waters, Maurice, 'The Invasion of Grenada, 1983 and the Collapse of Legal Norms,' *Journal of Peace Research*, vol. 23, no. 3, September 1986 (pp. 229–246).
Berlin, Michael J., 'U.S. Allies Join in Lopsided U.N. Vote Condemning Invasion Of Grenada,' *Washington Post*, November 3, 1983.

138 Wintour, Patrick, 'MPs say Kosovo bombing was illegal but necessary,' *The Guardian*, June 7, 2000.
Erlanger, Steven, 'Rights Group Says NATO Bombing in Yugoslavia Violated Law,' *New York Times*, June 8, 2000.

139 Hughes, David, 'Chilcot report: John Prescott says Iraq War was illegal,' *The Independent*, July 9, 2016.
Kramer, Ronald and Michalowski, Raymond and Rothe, Dawn, '"The Supreme International Crime": How the U.S. War in Iraq Threatens the Rule of Law,' *Social Justice*, vol. 32, no. 2, 2005 (pp. 52–81).
Jones, Owen, 'The war in Iraq was not a blunder or a mistake. It was a crime,' *The Guardian*, July 7, 2016.

140 Broomhall, Bruce, *International justice and the International Criminal Court*, Oxford, Oxford University Press, 2003 (p. 46).
*Judgment of the International Military Tribunal for the Trial of German Major War Criminals: The Nazi Regime in Germany*, The International Military Tribunal for Germany, September 30, 1946, The Avalon Project, Yale University (https://avalon.law.yale.edu/imt/judnazi.asp#common).

141 MacFarquhar, Neil and Schmitt, Eric, 'Syria Threatens Chemical Attack on Foreign Force,' *New York Times*, July 23, 2012.

142 'Obama warns Syria not to cross "red line",' *CNN*, August 21, 2012.

143 Barnard, Anne, 'Syria and Activists Trade Accusations on Chemical Weapons,' *New York Times*, March 19, 2013.

144 'Rebels could resort to chemical weapons, Syria warns,' *France24*, December 8, 2012.

145 'Dueling Claims In Syria After Unconfirmed Reports About Chemical Weapons,' *NPR*, March 19, 2013.

146 '"High probability" Syria used chemical weapon,' *CNN*, March 20, 2013.
Barnard, Anne, 'Syria and Activists Trade Charges on Chemical Weapons,' *New York Times*, March 19, 2013.

147 Wintour, Patrick, 'Putin dashes G8 hopes for Syria breakthrough,' *The Guardian,* June 18, 2013.
148 Gearan, Anne and Whitlock, Craig, 'U.S. intelligence believes Syria's Assad used chemical weapons "on a small scale",' *Washington Post*, April 25, 2013.
149 Rudoren, Jodi and Barnard, Anne, 'Israel Girds for Attacks as Syria Falls Apart,' *New York Times,* January 27, 2013.
150 'Israel strikes Syrian weapons en route to Hezbollah,' *The Jerusalem Post,* January 30, 2013.
151 Lappin, Yaakov, 'Analysis: Syria center long been on Israel's radar,' *The Jerusalem Post,* January 31, 2013.
152 Barnard, Anne and Gordon, Michael R. and Rudoren, Jodi, 'Israel Targeted Iranian Missiles in Syria Attack,' *New York Times*, May 4, 2013.
Cohen, Gili, 'Israel overnight strike targeted Iranian missile shipment meant for Hezbollah,' *Haaretz*, May 5, 2013.
153 'Report: Israel behind recent strike on Syria missile depot, U.S. officials say,' *Haaretz*, July 12, 2013.
154 'Israeli warplanes attack military base in Syria,' *The Independent,* November 1, 2013.
155 'Israel Treats Wounded Syrians Along Frontier,' *ABC News*, February 16, 2013.
Sengupta, Kim, 'Priti Patel visited a hospital that treats jihadis – this is in Israel's interests, but not the UK's,' *The Independent*, November 9, 2017.
Cohen, Gili, 'Israel Halts Medical Treatment for Members of Syria's Nusra Front,' *Haaretz*, July 20, 2015.
156 Ravid, Barak, 'UN Reveals Israeli Links With Syrian Rebels,' *Haaretz,* April 10, 2018.
157 Tsurkov, Elizabeth, 'Israel's Deepening Involvement with Syria's Rebels,' *War on the Rocks*, February 14, 2018.
Tsurkov, Elizabeth, 'Inside Israel's Secret Program to Back Syrian Rebels,' *Foreign Policy,* September 6, 2018.
158 Lieber, Don, 'Palestinian Authority claims Israel backs al-Qaeda in Syria,' *Times of Israel,* November 5, 2017.
159 Gross, Judah Ari, 'IDF chief finally acknowledges that Israel supplied weapons to Syrian rebels,' *Times of Israel,* January 14, 2019.
Levi, Daneil J., 'Israel Just Admitted Arming anti-Assad Syrian Rebels. Big Mistake,' *Haaretz,* February 3, 2019.
160 Levi, Daneil J., 'Israel Just Admitted Arming anti-Assad Syrian Rebels. Big Mistake,' *Haaretz,* February 3, 2019.
161 'Report: Israel armed rebels in south Syria for years, in effort to block Iran,' *Times of Israel*, September 6, 2018.
Jones, Rory, 'Israel Gives Secret Aid to Syrian Rebels,' *Wall Street Journal*, June 18, 2017.
162 Tsurkov, Elizabeth, 'Inside Israel's Secret Program to Back Syrian Rebels,' *Foreign Policy,* September 6, 2018.
163 'Treasury Designates Hizballah Leadership,' *US Department of the Treasury,* press release, September 13, 2012.

164 Dehganpisheh, Babak, 'Hezbollah Increases Support for Syrian Regime, U.S. and Lebanese Officials Say,' *Washington Post*, September 26, 2012.
Kennedy, Elizabeth A., 'Official: Hezbollah Fighters Killed in Syria,' *Daily Star* (Beirut), October 2, 2012.

165 Kasapoğlu, Can, 'The Syrian Civil War: Understanding Qusayr and Defending Aleppo,' *Centre for Economics and Foreign Policy Studies*, June 28, 2013.
Blanford, Nicholas, 'The Battle for Qusayr: How the Syrian Regime and Hizb Allah Tipped the Balance,' *Combatting Terrorism Center at West Point*, vol. 6, issue 8, 2013.

166 Phillips, Christopher, *The Battle For Syria: International Rivalry in the New Middle East*, New Haven, Yale University Press, 2016 (p. 158).

167 Barnard, Anne, 'In Syrian Victory, Hezbollah Risks Broader Fight,' *New York Times*, June 5, 2013.

168 Blanford, Nicholas, 'The Battle for Qusayr: How the Syrian Regime and Hizb Allah Tipped the Balance,' *Combatting Terrorism Center at West Point*, vol. 6, issue 8, 2013.

169 Ibid.

170 Cavanaugh, Darien, 'Russia is teaching Hezbollah some terrifying new tricks,' *The Week*, January 27, 2016.

171 Mansourov, Anexandre, 'North Korea: Entering Syria's Civil War,' *38 North*, November 25, 2013.

172 Bassej, Mroue, 'Hezbollah chief says group is fighting in Syria,' *Associated Press*, May 25, 2013.
'Hezbollah vows to stand by Syrian regime,' *CBC News*, May 25, 2013.

173 Miller, Elhanan, 'Explosion that hurt troops was a Hezbollah ambush,' *Times of Israel*, August 8, 2013.
al-Amine, Ibrahim, 'The Lowdown on Hezbollah's Ambush in South Lebanon,' *al-Akhbar*, August 8, 2013.
Blanford, Nicholas, 'The Battle for Qusayr: How the Syrian Regime and Hizb Allah Tipped the Balance,' *Combatting Terrorism Center at West Point*, vol. 6, issue 8, 2013.

174 Eglash, Ruth, 'Hezbollah retaliates against Israel with a missile; Israel fires back at Lebanon,' *Washington Post*, September 1, 2019.

175 Hiro, Dilip, *Cold War in the Islamic World: Saudi Arabia, Iran and the Struggle for Supremacy*, Oxford, Oxford University Press, 2018 (p. 258).

176 Goodarzi, Jubin, 'Iran and Syria at the Crossroads: The Fall of the Tehran-Damascus Axis?,' *Wilson Center*, August 2013 (p. 1).

177 Ibid (p. 1).

178 Phillips, Christopher, *The Battle For Syria: International Rivalry in the New Middle East*, New Haven, Yale University Press, 2016 (p. 161).

179 Ibid (p. 161).

180 Ibrahimi, Niamatullah, *The Hazaras and the Afghan State: Rebellion, Exclusion and the Search for Recognition*, London, Hurst & Co., 2017.
Rashid, Ahmed, *Taliban: Islam, Oil and the New Great Game in Central Asia*, London, I.B. Tauris, 2002 (pp. 55–75).
Ibrahimi, Niamatullah and Maley, William, 'Afghanistan: the Hazaras are not safe,' *The Lowy Institute*, November 26, 2018.

Caroll, Rory, 'Pits reveal evidence of massacre by Taliban,' *The Guardian*, April 7, 2002.

181 Jamal, Ahmad Shuja, 'Mission Accomplished? What's Next for Iran's Afghan Fighters in Syria,' *War on the Rocks*, February 13, 2018.

182 Hiro, Dilip, 'Fall of Eastern Aleppo Marks Turning Point for Syrian Civil War,' *YaleGlobal Online*, December 13, 2016.

183 Smyth, Philip, 'Iraqi Shiite Foreign Fighters on the Rise Again in Syria,' *The Washington Institute*, May 29, 2015.

184 'Syria: the view from Iraq,' *European Council on Foreign Relations*, June 24, 2013.

185 Gordon, Michael R., 'Iran Supplying Syrian Military via Iraqi Airspace,' *New York Times*, September 4, 2012.
Grabell, Michael and Linzer, Dafna and Larson, Jeff, 'To Retrieve Attack Helicopters from Russia, Syria Asks Iraq for Help, Documents Show,' *Pro Republica*, November 29, 2012.

186 Abrams, A. B., *Immovable Object: North Korea's 70 Years At War with American Power*, Atlanta, Clarity Press, 2020 (Chapter 10: Proxy Wars: How North Korea and America Wage War Through Third Parties).

187 'General Assembly Adopts Resolution Strongly Condemning "Widespread and Systematic" Human Rights Violations by Syrian Authorities,' *United Nations*, February 16, 2012.

188 'Bechtol, Bruce E., *Military Proliferation to the Middle East in the Kim Jong-un Era: A National Security and Terrorist Threat*, Presentation at Shurat HaDin Law Center, March 5, 2016.

189 Gady, Franz-Stefan, 'Is North Korea Fighting for Assad in Syria?' *The Diplomat*, March 24, 2016.
Mansourov, Alexandre Y., 'North Korea Coming to Assad's Rescue,' *The Korea Times*, June 13, 2013.

190 Gady, Franz-Stefan, 'Is North Korea Fighting for Assad in Syria?' *The Diplomat*, March 24, 2016.

191 Bechtol, Bruce and Maxwell, David, 'North Korean Military Proliferation in the Middle East and Africa: A Book Launch,' Presentation at the Korea Economic Institute of America, September 25, 2018.

192 Bermudez, Joseph S., *North Korean Special Forces*, Coulsdon, Jane's Publishing, 1988 (p. 2).

193 Ibid (p. 2).

194 Fitzpatrick, Mark, *North Korean Security Challenges: A Net Assessment*, London, International Institute for Strategic Studies, 2011 (p. 50).

195 'North Korean Special Forces Simulate Rapid Assault Exercises; Why Pyongyang's Adversaries Fear the KPA's Elite,' *Military Watch Magazine*, August 26, 2017.

196 Berger, Andrea, *Target Markets, North Korea's Military Customers in the Sanctions Era*, Abingdon, Routledge, 2017 (pp. 67–69).

197 Abrams, A. B., *Immovable Object: North Korea's 70 Years At War with American Power*, Atlanta, Clarity Press, 2020 (Chapter 10: Proxy Wars: How North Korea and America Wage War Through Third Parties).

198 Trevithick, Joseph, 'Why These Really Strange North Korean Guns Are Turning Up Almost Everywhere,' *National Interest*, November 7, 2018.

Mitzer, Stijn, 'N. Korean Arms Found in Vessel Intercepted Off Coast of Oman,' *NK News*, March 16, 2016.

'Iranian delivered North Korean Type-73 machine guns sighted in Syria,' *Oryx*, March 9, 2016.

199 Roblin, Sebastien, 'Why Has Russia Not Been Stopping Israel's Attacks On Syria?,' *National Interest*, May 29, 2020.

'Belarusian, North Korean missile engineers killed or injured in Israel's air raid of Masyaf,' *Debka*, April 14, 2019.

200 'Pro-Isis hackers attack North Korean airline Facebook page,' *The Guardian*, January 14, 2015.

201 'Pyongyang: People of Syria and North Korea Face a Common Enemy,' *Syrian Arab News Agency*, April 21, 2015.

202 O'Carroll, Chad, 'A long way from Damascus: Life as Syria's ambassador to North Korea,' *NK News*, January 31, 2017.

203 Ibid.

204 'Pyongyang: People of Syria and North Korea Face a Common Enemy,' *Syrian Arab News Agency* April 21, 2015.

205 'Pyongyang: Syria, DPRK parliamentary relations based on firm principles,' *Syrian Arab News Agency*, 8 October, 2018.

'Sabbagh stresses need for consolidating parliamentary cooperation between Syria and DPRK,' *Syrian Arab News Agency*, March 12, 2019.

206 'Mikdad: Syria and DPRK relations steadily growing,' *Syrian Arab News Agency*, September 10, 2018.

207 'DPRK Ambassador affirms his country's readiness to support health sector in Syria,' *Syrian Arab News Agency*, July 25, 2016.

208 'Syria names park in capital after N Korea Founder,' *Al Jazeera*, August 31, 2015.

209 'Russia pressures Lukashenko to change constitution,' *Deutsche Welle*, November 26, 2020.

210 O'Carroll, Chad, 'A long way from Damascus: Life as Syria's ambassador to North Korea,' *NK News*, January 31, 2017.

# Chapter 4

# Internationalising the War Effort: Escalation of Direct Foreign Intervention in the Syrian War

## Holding the West at Bay:
## Russia Responds to Third Party Threats Against Syria

The battle of Qusayr which ended in early June 2013 was a major turning point in the Syrian War, after which the SAA and its partners including Hezbollah, Quds Force trained militias, and both Korean and Iranian advisors would begin to turn the tide against the insurgents and push back against their positions across the country. Where early 2013 had seen the beginnings of much more direct involvement in the war by Iran and Hezbollah, the second half of the year would see the conflict's further internationalisation as the Western powers, observing unfavourable power trajectories on the ground,[1] looked to launch a direct offensive against the Syrian state. Russia, too, would begin to play a larger role in the conflict from this time and would start to commit itself more strongly to supporting its oldest regional strategic partner.

Following the first confirmed Israeli airstrikes against Syrian government positions in January and May, and amid escalating talk in the West of potential direct attacks on Syria under the pretext of responding to the alleged use of chemical weapons, Russia would itself escalate its involvement and begin to emerge as a major supporter of Damascus. Three major factors appear to have influenced this shift. The first was the fact that Israeli involvement, and more significantly the possibility of direct Western involvement, internationalised the conflict and ended prior perceptions in many circles that the war was an internal affair. Although the

Western powers and their partners in the gulf and Turkey had been heavily involved in creating, supporting and shaping the course of the Islamist insurgency from the outset, the nature of the threat to the Syrian state as external, rather than originating within its borders, was becoming increasingly clear.

The second factor was the very serious threat that a Western, Turkish and Gulf backed jihadist takeover of Syria would allow for the projection of destabilising Islamist forces not only against Hezbollah and Iran, but also into the Russian sphere of influence in Central Asia and into the Muslim regions of Russia itself. In one of his many warnings regarding this threat, President Putin highlighted that militants operating from Syria posed a "very real" threat and that they "did not come out of nowhere, and they will not vanish into thin air" should the Syrian War conclude. Muslim-majority areas in Russia reportedly contributed "whole brigades" worth of personnel to the jihadist insurgency, with the Islamic State group which would rise to prominence in 2014 recruiting particularly large numbers.[2] Russia had a bitter experience of Islamist insurgency, not only in Chechnya but also in neighbouring Afghanistan and Tajikistan, and supporting the Syrian government's war effort appeared to be the most effective means of averting this possibility.

A third factor influencing Russia to provide greater support to the Syrian war effort was the inauguration of Vladimir Putin as president in May 2012. This followed a four-year term where Putin had served as prime minister, during which the administration of President Dimitry Medvedev had taken a much softer line against Western interventionism in the Middle East and North Africa. Medvedev's administration, often lauded in the West, had allowed a Western-drafted resolution facilitating NATO attacks on the Libyan government to pass through the UNSC, while the president had personally frozen a major contract to supply Iran with S-300PMU-2 (NATO reporting SA-20) air defence systems in his first year in office. The latter move came at a time when Western or Israeli airstrikes against the country were being openly discussed.[3] Medvedev expressed confidence shortly after leaving office that the Syrian leadership would not survive the war,[4] a belief he appeared to have held while serving as president which was reflected in the very limited nature of Russian support for its longstanding strategic partner in the conflict's critical early stages. President Putin, by the standards of post-Soviet Russian leaders, was considered a hardliner who lacked the strongly Westphilian tendencies of the other two office holders. Due to the hyper-presidential nature of the Russian political system, with foreign policy shaped much more by the individual office holder than by a ruling party, in contrast to party states such as China, North Korea or Syria itself, a change in president could have a very drastic impact on the state's policies within a short period.

In mid-May 2013 it was announced that the Russian Navy had expanded use of its sole remaining overseas naval facility located at the Syrian port of Tartus. Although Russian ships had previously only periodically visited the port, in the last three months an average of 10–15 ships were reported to have been positioned near it at all times.[5] Armed with anti-ship cruise missiles and a range of advanced air defence systems, and likely supported by submarines, which were the most modern component of the Russian combat fleet and maintained a significant overseas presence, the continuous deployment of a naval contingent appeared to have been initiated at a time when the Western powers were considering direct military action. This allowed Moscow to take a hard line against this at any moment as needed. The chief of staff of the Free Syrian Army had in February 2013 announced that Russian ships, much like Iranian airliners, would be made targets by the insurgents as fighting drew closer to Tartus. The Russian General Staff had previously threatened "an appropriate response" to any attack, which may have also influenced the decision to escalate the country's military presence in the area.[6]

On May 30 the *Washington Post* reported that Syria had two months earlier requested a price quote "in the shortest time possible" for a wide range of equipment from Russia's state arms exporter Rosoboronexport. This included 20,000 AK-47 assault rifles, 20 million rounds of ammunition, grenades, grenade launchers, sniper rifles and other very standard infantry equipment.[7] All of these equipment types were readily available from

North Korea and Iran, and the Syrian decision to request such arms from Russia instead at this sensitive time, amid signs that Moscow was preparing to more strongly support the Syrian state, could well have been intended to increase Russian interest in the conflict and reinforce historical defence ties.

Russia also separately agreed in the final week of May to supply Syria with the S-300PMU-2 surface-to-air missile system, which would revolutionise its ability to intercept Western and Israeli air and missile strikes. Russian Deputy Foreign Minister Sergei Ryabkov highlighted that delivery of weapons systems such as the S-300 could "help restrain some 'hotheads' considering a scenario to give an international dimension to this conflict" – a thinly veiled reference to the Western powers discussing attacks on Syria at that very time.[8] The S-300 would allow Syrian forces to shoot down aircraft across Israel's entire territory with highly precise missiles travelling at over 14 times the speed of sound and capable of engaging targets up to 250km away.[9] This led Israel to place significant pressure on Russia to either cancel or postpone the deal, which Russia agreed to do before the end of the year despite Syrian air defence crews already having been trained.[10]

Although the S-300 deal was terminated, Russia also announced in May that Syria had been supplied with new variants of the Bastion anti-ship cruise missile system.[11] This weapons system was capable of hitting targets several hundred kilometres away with high precision and at over three times the speed of sound and benefitted from 'fire and forget' capabilities allowing launchers to remain constantly on the move. The missiles themselves had a terminal low-profile sea skimming trajectory to avoid interception, and leading-edge electronic warfare countermeasures. The Bastion could provide an asymmetric shore defence against much larger naval fleets, with the *Jane's International Defense Review* describing it as "a real ship killer" which could "deter foreign forces looking to supply the opposition from the sea, or from undertaking a more active role if a no-fly zone or shipping embargo were to be declared at some point."[12] With Syria having fielded a negligible naval capability, deployment of the Bastion allowed it to pose a very real threat to Western surface warships. The delivery at a time when the U.S. and its allies were contemplating attacks on Syria sent a powerful signal regarding Moscow's intentions.

In June at the G8 summit – convened by Japan, Russia and six Western powers including the U.S., France, Britain, Germany, Italy and Canada – Russia firmly opposed Western efforts to use the meeting to set out a plan for imposing a change of government on Syria. President Putin insisted he could not support peace talks convened on the assumption that President Bashar Al Assad would be removed from power. Foreign Minister Sergei Lavrov stated to similar effect regarding the nature of the intentions behind the Western peace plan: "We are categorically against ... assertions that the conference should be some kind of public act of capitulation by the government delegation followed by a handing over of power to the opposition."[13] The Western powers had long insisted that a removal of the Syrian government was a necessary precondition for any peace agreement, under the slogan 'Assad Must Go.' While this outcome was strongly in line with Western interests, the Western Bloc had no authority to impose such terms which was highlighted by Russia both at the G8 and at the United Nations.

Issuing a particularly harsh rebuke of British plans to significantly escalate material support to insurgent groups in Syria, President Putin stated on June 15 regarding the nature of the jihadist groups which were receiving Western support: "You will not deny that one does not really need to support the people who not only kill their enemies, but open up their bodies, eat their intestines in front of the public and cameras. Are these the people you want to support? Is it them who you want to supply with weapons? Then this probably has little relation to humanitarian values that have been preached in Europe for hundreds of years."[14] This referred to a recent video filmed by insurgents from the Free Syrian Army showing one of their personnel cutting open a fallen Syrian solder and eating his heart[i] – one of multiple brutalities committed by Western backed groups since the earliest days of the conflict.[15]

## No-Fly Zone or Full-Scale Airstrikes? Western Moves Towards a Direct Offensive Against Syria

June 2013 was highlighted by multiple analysts as a turning point in Western involvement in Syria towards a greater willingness to take direct military action, namely through imposition of a 'no-fly zone' in the country.[16] Under such a plan the Western powers would prevent Syrian partners from flying supplies into the country, would shoot down any Syrian aircraft preventing the air force from providing air support to ground troops or transporting men or supplies, and most likely would attack airfields across the country. All precedents suggested that this would be followed by both Western airstrikes on Syrian positions and provision of more active material and battlefield support to Islamist insurgent groups, which would continue indefinitely until an outcome to the war favourable to Western interests was achieved. Without authorisation from the UN Security Council, the Western powers had no legal mandate to interfere with Syria's use of its sovereign airspace or to violate it with Western warplanes – any more than Pakistan would have a mandate to shoot down air traffic over India, Angola over South Africa or Russia over Ukraine. This was due to the equality of all states under the UN Charter, with the use of force by member states against one other absolutely prohibited under Article 2(4) except as exercised in self-defence or when legitimized by a Security Council resolution. International law, however, had rarely been able to constrain Western ambitions to launch overseas attacks, and European and American perceptions

---

i    The insurgent committing the act stated "I swear to God we will eat your hearts out, you soldiers of Bashar. You dogs. God is greater!... we will take out their hearts to eat them." Although mutilation of corpses was contrary to orthodox interpretations of Islamic law, it was increasingly normalised among jihadist combatants when targeting other Muslims as also previously seen in Afghanistan when committed by Arab foreign fighters against government troops. (Akram, Assen, *Histoire de la Guerre d'Afghanistan*, Paris, Editions Balland, 1996 (pp. 227–277).)

of their own exceptionalism when it came to military interventionism made the West a very dangerous actor in the Syrian conflict.

The West's greater willingness to consider the 'no-fly zone'
option, and to discuss the possibility of conducting offensive
airstrikes outright to ensure a victory for the insurgency, notably
closely followed a key turning point in the Syrian War itself. This
was the pivotal defeat of Western-backed insurgents at Al Qusayr
and the further demonstration of Hezbollah's military prowess.
This crucial battle is thought to have heavily influenced the
Western powers towards favouring more direct action to prevent
the insurgency's defeat. In a 2013 report prepared for the U.S. Air
Force by the RAND Corporation think tank, it was emphasized
that the definition of a Western no-fly zone was often "stretched
to include" air attacks and operations to directly weaken enemy
forces on the ground, which it stated could well be the case in
Syria. The report noted that Syrian forces had made significant
gains in 2013, and that a no-fly zone could turn the tide of the war
in favour of anti-government forces and "potentially pave the way
for more extensive operations" against government forces.[17]

Retired U.S. Air Force Lieutenant General David A. Deptula,
who had overseen imposition of a no-fly zone over Iraq in the
1990s under Operation Northern Watch, indicated in May 2013
that operations in Syrian airspace after imposition of a no-fly zone
could be a means to cut the transfer of supplies between Syria,
Iran and Hezbollah in Lebanon. He further highlighted, citing
the Libyan precedent, that operations could also be conducted to
"target Syrian leadership and active military units" from the air,
which was another indication that the more benign 'no-fly zone'
had behind it Western intentions which were considerably more
aggressive still. He indicated, however, that Syria's air defence
network which was much more sophisticated than that of Iraq,
could make such operations difficult.[18] The *Washington Post* similarly highlighted that a no-fly zone would likely be just a first
step towards facilitating more active Western offensive operations
against the Syrian state. It stressed, as many publications across
the Western world did at the time, that conducting such offensive

operations against "the oppressor," as it referred to Damascus, was a moral obligation for Western countries.[19]

President Obama asked the Pentagon to draw up plans for imposition of a potential no-fly zone over Syria in the penultimate week of May.[20] The Pentagon had previously drawn up plans in April although the administration, despite significant pressure from within the Democratic Party and from lawmakers, had not asked to be shown them and took a much more conservative approach.[21] France and Britain, by contrast, had been strongly calling for a no-fly zone up to this point, and as had been the case in Libya and before in Yugoslavia, it appeared the European powers had the more interventionist and aggressive tendencies while the U.S. acted more cautiously and conservatively.[22] Turkey's then-Prime Minister Recep Tayyip Erdoğan was another leading advocate for Western military intervention, stating in an interview on May 9 when asked whether his country would actively support Western efforts to impose a no-fly-zone: "Right from the beginning ... we would say 'yes'."[23] Erdoğan had himself demanded the forceful removal of the Syrian government – in his words "the leaders who feed on blood"[24] – and his country was conducting the most active offensive operations on the ground of any state actor fighting against Syria. Western air support had the potential not only to seriously benefit Turkish-backed militants, but also to provide cover for the many Turkish officers embedded with militants in the field. Western defence partners in the Gulf Cooperation Council favoured imposition of a no-fly zone for similar reasons, with U.S. analysts highlighting that, much as was the case with Turkey, the Arab states hoped such operations would facilitate further more aggressive military operations and commit the U.S. more fully to forcefully overthrowing the Syrian government.[25]

Regarding his rationale for holding back, President Obama notably told aides that a no-fly zone "would require a much larger military operation than its proponents believe," with a number of significant factors often being overlooked, including the sizes of the Syrian air, air defence and ballistic missile forces and the involvement of third parties in support of the Syrian government.[26] He soon afterwards expressed scepticism that a no-fly zone alone would have any significant impact on the conflict.[27] The president's National Security Advisor Spokesman Benjamin Rhodes similarly appeared hesitant, stressing on multiple occasions that a no-fly zone was "not some type of silver bullet" that could resolve the conflict on its own, and that relative to Libya, "It's dramatically more difficult and dangerous and costly in Syria for a variety of reasons."[28] Chairman of the Joint Chiefs of Staff General Martin Dempsey stated to much the same effect that the danger of 'mission creep' meant a no-fly zone could lead the U.S. to commit to further offensive operations against the Syrian government. If Syria's aerial warfare capability was neutralized, he warned, "the question then becomes: If you eliminate one capability of a potential adversary, will you be inclined to find yourself in a position to be asked to do more against the rest?"[29]

Although the U.S. under Obama had shown few qualms about waging war on the Syrian state through large scale support for a major Islamist insurgency, the administration's greater caution regarding direct military action came largely as a result of its 'Pivot to Asia' foreign policy initiative and the need to divert attention away from the Middle East to other theatres which were much more consequential. North Korea, for one, had just tested a new miniaturised nuclear warhead of unprecedented power in March, and appeared poised to make a breakthrough in developing longer range missiles capable of delivering them to a wider range of American targets. This was a potential game changer in the country's then 63 year-long ongoing war with the United States.[30] China, for another, was poised to overtake the United States as the world's largest economy (measured by purchasing power adjusted GDP) which it would achieve in 2014.[31] The administration's strategy for tackling Beijing by isolating it from other East and Southeast Asian nations and drastically expanding the American military presence in the Asia-Pacific[32] was already being seriously undermined by the drag of Middle Eastern commitments.

The high opportunity cost of the U.S. wars of Afghanistan and Iraq in 2001 and 2003 had not only allowed China to continue its peaceful rise unimpeded, but was also credited with allowing North Korea to withdraw from the nuclear non-proliferation treaty and quickly develop a very formidable nuclear weapons capability without a significant American response.[33] As important as the Syrian conflict was, in the larger picture the primary challenges to America's position of post-Cold War global hegemony were not being issued by the Middle East, and likely never would. This was something the Obama administration appeared highly aware of, which made it essential to avoid overcommitting to the war effort against Damascus. As the president's advisor, Ben Rhodes, stressed, such operations in Syria "carry with it great and open-ended costs," something the relative decline in American power resulting from its overcommitting in Iraq and Afghanistan under the Bush administration had left the new administration highly cautious of.[34]

Joseph Holliday, a fellow at the Institute for the Study of War and expert on the Syrian conflict, stressed regarding a further difficulty of a direct U.S. military intervention that Syria retained "one of the densest air-defence systems in the world," while its air force had shown a growing degree of combat readiness in 2013 with intensified airstrikes. He further alluded to the threat posed by elite Syrian combat jets, namely the MiG-29A and the more dangerous MiG-25, which were not being used for airstrikes on insurgents and were instead being conserved for possible air defence operations in the event of a full-scale attack.[35] These were the two most formidable classes of Soviet jet ever exported during the Cold War in terms of air-to-air combat capabilities and had since been conservatively modernised. For air-to-ground operations, however, Syria favoured older and lighter MiG-23BN and MiG-21 jets throughout the war because they were cheaper to operate and had more suitable avionics. Syria also fielded a small fleet of Su-24M long range strike fighters which could deploy a range of advanced guided weapons. Two of these notably performed a show of force in early September by making a close approach at low altitude to Britain's RAF Akrotiri airbase in Cyprus, which demonstrated their ability to retaliate against key targets in the event of a Western attack.[36]

It is notable that none of the arguments against imposing a no-fly zone in Syria and attacking Syrian government forces without provocation raised by any major sources in the West, be they politicians, military officials or analysts, pertained to the total illegality of such action under international law. The idea of Western exceptionalism, and that international laws against crimes of aggression did not apply to Western countries launching military campaigns in the third world, was very widely accepted although rarely explicitly stated. It was raised by Russia several times, however, with Foreign Minister Sergei Lavrov stating on June 15, regarding reports that the U.S. had begun military deployments to Jordan to prepare for imposition of a no-fly zone over Syria: "you don't have to be a great expert to understand that this will violate international law."[37]

## Chemical Attack Near Damascus: The West's Questionable New Pretext to Attack Syria

The Obama administration remained undecided throughout much of the summer of 2013 regarding whether to pursue military action but faced strong pressure from its European and Middle Eastern partners to launch an attack as well as from much of the foreign policy establishment in the U.S. itself.[38] A major incident on August 21, however, would tip the balance in Washington and bring the U.S. to the brink of open war with the Syrian Arab Republic. After almost three months of major gains by Syrian and allied forces following the battle of Qusayr, a number of reports from Syrian anti-government sources emerged claiming that the Syrian Arab Army had attacked targets in the Eastern Ghouta, a suburban area in the Damascus governate, with chemical weapons. These sources claimed that up to 635 people were killed with sarin nerve gas,[39] which made this alleged attack several times larger than the one in June. The publication of footage, though unverified, of civilians affected by the attacks,[40] fuelled support in the West for offensive military action against the Syrian state.

Inspectors from the United Nations subsequently requested access to sites in Eastern Ghouta and a ceasefire surrounding the area, both of which were permitted by the Syrian government. Evidence led inspectors to confirm that sarin nerve gas had indeed been used, although investigators noted that insurgents controlling the sites before the UN arrived could have moved and manipulated evidence.[41] Although there was no evidence as to which party was responsible for the attack, Western governments would almost unanimously conclude that Damascus was the perpetrator. While Western and Western-aligned states would dismiss out of hand the possibility that any party other than the Syrian government was responsible for launching a chemical strike, however, there was significant evidence to support the claim that Islamist insurgents were the perpetrators. One of the most significant of these was circumstantial. The Syrian Arab Army had been gaining ground since early June and was now winning the war, and at a time when Western powers were hotly debating whether to use prior alleged chemical attacks as a pretext for an illegal attack on Syria, it would have made little sense for government forces to suddenly use chemical weapons on a much larger scale. Doing so would markedly increase the possibility that NATO forces would begin to provide air support to insurgent forces.

In contrast to the Syrian Arab Army, which had everything to lose by launching a chemical attack, jihadist groups seeking the state's overthrow had everything to gain. A mass violation of Syrian airspace by Western aircraft, followed by imposition of a no-fly zone and likely airstrikes as well, had the potential to turn the tide of the war in their favour. Beyond an incentive to use chemical weapons, there was significant evidence that militants had access to such weapons including sarin and that they had used them in the past. Former Chief Prosecutor of two United Nations international criminal law tribunals, and former Swiss attorney general and ambassador, Carla Del Ponte, served on the Independent International Commission of Inquiry on the Syrian Arab Republic in 2013 and reported in May that "opponents of the regime" in Syria were the ones conducting the sarin gas attacks.[42] Later that month, Turkish security forces arrested members of Syria's Al Qaeda affiliate, the Al Nusra Front, who were found to be in possession of 2 kilograms of sarin.[43] This arrest alone proved that Islamist insurgent elements in Syria had access to the very weapon the Syrian government would in August be accused of using in Eastern Ghouta. Considering the number of state actors supporting the insurgency with an interest in creating a pretext for Western intervention, from Qatar and Saudi Arabia to Turkey itself, it is very possible that militants had assistance in both acquiring and employing the deadly nerve agent.

The case for insurgents being responsible for the sarin attack was further strengthened by a study by Theodore A. Postol, a professor of science, technology and national security policy at the Massachusetts Institute of Technology, and Richard M. Lloyd, an analyst at the military contractor Tesla Laboratories, which was published by the *New York Times* in December. Based on an evaluation of the exteriors of the rockets which delivered the nerve agent, both analysts suggested that they were propelled by motors taken from BM-21 122mm artillery rockets which were used extensively by both the Syrian Arab Army and by insurgent forces. Calculating potential maximum ranges for the sarin-filled rockets, the experts concluded that the attack could not have been carried out from Syrian Arab Army positions as Western governments and media had previously asserted.[44]

Evidence for the insurgents' complicity continued to mount, with Associated Press correspondent Dale Gavlak and reporter Yahya Ababneh publishing the results of interviews with doctors, Ghouta residents and insurgent fighters who expressed widespread certainty that it was the Al Nusra front which had been responsible for the attack. The reports indicated that the chemical weapons used had been supplied by Saudi Arabian intelligence services, which had provided significant material support to the insurgency since early 2011. Although unverified, this report did closely corroborate with others regarding the Al Qaeda linked group's possession of chemical weapons and cannot be ruled out as a significant possibility.[45] The report would gain greater credibility in 2017, when leaked documents from the U.S. National Security Agency showed that Saudi sponsors were indeed able to order Syrian insurgents they had armed to carry out specific kinds of attacks and against very specific targets to achieve political ends.[46]

In December Pulitzer Prize-winning investigative journalist Seymour Hersh, who had risen to prominence for uncovering the My Lai Massacre in Vietnam and the secret U.S. bombing of Cambodia, reported, based on multiple interviews with U.S. intelligence officials and an extensive investigation, that the Obama administration had been dishonest in its portrayal of the Ghouta incident. He alleged that the administration had "cherry-picked intelligence" for its own ends, which were to implicate Damascus and provide a pretext for further hostile policies towards it. Hersh further highlighted that the administration buried intelligence on the Al Nusra Front, and never considered it a suspect despite its major presence in Eastern Ghouta, its strong incentive to carry out attacks, and knowledge that the terror group had access to sarin. He stated regarding his investigation:

> Barack Obama did not tell the whole story this autumn when he tried to make the case that Bashar Al Assad was responsible for the chemical weapons attack near Damascus on 21 August. In some instances, he omitted important intelligence, and in others he presented assumptions as facts. Most significant, he failed to acknowledge something known to the U.S. intelligence community: that the Syrian army is not the only party in the country's civil war with access to sarin, the nerve agent that a UN study concluded – without assessing responsibility – had been used in the rocket attack. In the months before the attack, the American intelligence agencies produced a series of highly classified reports, culminating in a formal Operations Order – a planning document that precedes a ground invasion – citing evidence that the Al Nusra Front, a jihadi group affiliated with Al Qaida, had mastered the mechanics of creating sarin and was capable of manufacturing it in quantity. When the attack occurred Al Nusra should have been a suspect, but the administration cherry-picked intelligence to justify a strike against Assad. … in recent interviews with intelligence and military officers and consultants past and present, I found intense concern, and on occasion anger, over what was repeatedly seen as the

deliberate manipulation of intelligence. One high-level intelligence officer, in an email to a colleague, called the administration's assurances of Assad's responsibility a "ruse." The attack "was not the result of the current regime," he wrote. A former senior intelligence official told me that the Obama administration had altered the available information – in terms of its timing and sequence – to enable the president and his advisers to make intelligence retrieved days after the attack look as if it had been picked up and analysed in real time, as the attack was happening. The distortion, he said, reminded him of the 1964 Gulf of Tonkin incident, when the Johnson administration reversed the sequence of National Security Agency intercepts to justify one of the early bombings of North Vietnam. The same official said there was immense frustration inside the military and intelligence bureaucracy: "The guys are throwing their hands in the air and saying, 'How can we help this guy' – Obama – 'when he and his cronies in the White House make up the intelligence as they go along?'"[47]

"The cherry-picking [of intelligence] was similar to the process used to justify the Iraq War... the White House's misrepresentation of what it knew about the attack, and when, was matched by its readiness to ignore intelligence that could undermine the narrative. That information concerned Al Nusra," Hersh concluded, citing considerable evidence that the Al Qaeda affiliate was responsible. He further cited a four-page top secret cable forwarded to David R. Shedd, deputy director of the Defence Intelligence Agency, on June 20, 2013, which confirmed previous reports that Al Nusra could acquire and use Sarin. This effectively collapsed the central Western argument for Syrian government culpability, which was that it was the only party with such a chemical weapons capability. "Already by late May, the senior intelligence consultant told me, the CIA had briefed the Obama administration on Al Nusra and its work with sarin," Hersh stated, highlighting a later intelligence document showing that the Al Qaeda affiliate had recruited expertise from the former Ba'athist Iraqi military, which had had a major chemical weapons program of its own. These assessments were complemented by an Operations Order by the Joint Chiefs of Staff for a potential deployment of U.S. forces to Syria, which warned that insurgent forces were capable of producing and employing sarin which could threaten U.S. troops on the ground.[48]

Hersh further highlighted, citing talks with U.S. National Security Agency and government officials, that America had an advanced early warning capability to alert itself to activities at Syrian chemical sites in preparation for a possible attack, including those as basic as low level exercises, as well as extensive surveillance of Syrian communications. None of these intelligence assets gave any indication that Syria was making preparations for a chemical attack in the lead-up to the Ghouta incident. With Al Nusra having operated in Eastern Ghouta at the time of the attack, there was a very strong case to be made that it was culpable.[49]

Further details regarding support from state actors to an insurgent chemical weapons program emerged in 2014. A former senior U.S. intelligence official with access to current intelligence told Seymour Hersh: "We knew there were some in the Turkish government who believed they could get Assad's nuts in a vice by dabbling with a sarin attack inside Syria – and forcing Obama to make good on his red line threat." Prime Minister Erdoğan was among those known to be strongly supporting Al Qaeda affiliates, and by the spring of 2013 Turkey was reportedly providing insurgents with training in chemical warfare. The official stressed that the attack was "a covert action planned by Erdoğan's people to push Obama over the red line... The deal was to do something spectacular. Our senior military officers have been told by the DIA and other intelligence assets that the sarin was supplied through Turkey – that it could only have gotten there with Turkish support. The Turks also provided the training in producing the sarin and handling it." This followed growing concerns in Ankara that the insurgency was fast losing the war, and stemmed from the belief that engineering a U.S. military intervention represented the most effective way to turn the tide.[50]

A classified brief issued by the U.S. Defense Intelligence Agency, also cited by Hersh, stated that Al Nusra maintained a sarin production cell. According to the paper, the jihadist chemical weapons programme was "the most advanced sarin plot since al-Qaida's pre-9/11 effort." "Turkey and Saudi-based chemical facilitators were attempting to obtain sarin precursors in bulk, tens of kilograms, likely for the anticipated large scale production effort in Syria," the brief further highlighted. Citing sources within the Pentagon, Hersh reported that British intelligence had obtained a sample of the sarin used in the Ghouta attack and confirmed that the gas used didn't match that known to exist in Syria's chemical weapons arsenal. He also highlighted, citing a source with knowledge of the UN's activities, that an investigation of the Khan Al Assal attack earlier that year in March by a UN mission had clearly shown insurgents to be responsible – although "It did not come out in public because no one wanted to know."[51]

Further evidence for insurgent culpability for the chemical weapons attack surfaced in December from the United Nations, which observed similarities between the Ghouta attack and an earlier use of sarin in Aleppo's Khan Al Assal district on a smaller scale, with both attacks bearing the "same unique hallmarks." It is notable that three of the five targets struck with sarin at Khan Al Assal were Syrian Arab Army soldiers, which indicated that the strike, and by extension the latter very similar attack in Ghouta, were carried out by Islamist insurgent groups and not by Syrian government forces. The UN report did not explicitly assign blame for chemical attacks to any party, but gave evidence strongly implicating anti-government militants.[52] This was supported by video evidence in 2014, which a number of analysts indicated showed chemical attacks by the Al Nusra front neutralising Syrian Arab Army soldiers.[53] UN Secretary General Ban Ki Moon would subsequently inform the Security Council in July that Syrian government forces had seized two cylinders of sarin nerve gas from insurgents – a further strong indication that anti-government forces had the capability to launch chemical attacks.[54] Kurdish militias operating in northern Syria would also show evidence the following year that jihadist insurgents they were in conflict with had a chemical weapons capability, seizing canisters as evidence.[55]

## Russia Averts a NATO-Syrian War

With France, the U.S. and Britain taking the lead among the Western powers in placing blame on the Syrian government for chemical attacks in Eastern Ghouta, calls were significantly strengthened not only for a no-fly zone but also for more direct and comprehensive attacks on Syria to forcefully topple its government. Warships from the British Royal Navy and the United States Navy were deployed close to Syrian territory within a week. By August 26 these included the British Invincible Class light aircraft carrier *HMS Illustrious*, the last of three ageing ships which had led the country's military campaign against Argentina in the 1980s now on its last mission, as well a small Albion Class assault ship, two Norfolk Class frigates, an attack submarine, and four American Arleigh Burke Class heavy destroyers.[56] British Foreign Secretary William Hague stated that day that diplomacy over Syria had failed, and that military action against the country would be considered even without authorisation from the United Nations.[57] A fifth American destroyer entered the theatre the following day,[58] followed by an amphibious landing dock a day later.[59] The joint campaign being planned was reportedly intended to "completely eradicate any military capabilities Assad had" – as opposed to neutralising a specific weapons facility or sending a message with a limited strike. Targets would include every known logistics and weapons depot, command and control facility, and military and intelligence building under Syrian government control, and would also extensively target key civilian infrastructure including electric power grids and oil and gas depots.[60]

Covering the British deployment, British media widely reported that the country was ready to launch the first attacks against Syria. The *Telegraph* cited government sources on August 25 stating that talks were ongoing with the U.S. and other Western partners but that strikes could begin within a week.[61] Officials from both the U.S. and European nations cited moral obligations as reasons to launch the attack, although some highlighted that it was still unclear whether a military intervention would be intended to weaken the Syrian Arab Army or to see through a decisive victory for anti-government forces.[62] Reflecting widespread perceptions in the West that Europe and the United States had the right to violate international law in pursuing their foreign policy objectives, if done in the name of Western values or a perceived moral cause, the *New York Times* published an opinion piece on August 27 stressing that "ethics, not only laws, should guide policy decisions." It was fittingly titled 'Bomb Syria, Even If It Is Illegal.'[63] It was hard to find a similar sense of self-righteousness and open willingness to commit acts of illegal aggression anywhere else in the world. In the eyes of analysts across the Western world, as expressed in multiple papers and editorials, if Western foreign policy contravened international law, it was because the law was too constrained, not because the Europeans or Americans could ever be wrong to attack non-Western countries.[64] This extreme outlook, driven by the ideology of Western supremacism, would force Damascus and its partners to resort to more active means than reliance on the law to prevent Syria from enduring the same fate as Afghanistan had in 1992 – when its capital was overrun by Western-backed jihadists, and economic and social progress in the country was set back generations.

Despite strong rhetoric, the U.S. appeared hesitant regarding launching a military intervention for a number of aforementioned reasons, with advisor Benjamin Rhodes noting regarding the president's apprehensions: "He did not see where a more interventionist military option led us, other than being deeper and deeper in a conflict that is extraordinarily complex and shows no signs of having a military solution." Plans presented to Obama "didn't feel fully baked," according to Rhodes, with much uncertainty regarding the consequences an attack could have.[65] The Pentagon estimated that should the Syrian government be toppled, 70,000 U.S. personnel on the ground would be required to secure the country's sizeable chemical and ballistic missiles arsenals to prevent them from being acquired by Al Qaeda or other hostile elements. Assurances made by proponents of the attack that Damascus could be toppled without American boots on the ground were thus ultimately hollow.[66] This likely played a significant role in preventing a U.S. attack, as the need to commit tens of thousands of troops to Syria would have been disastrous for the American position in East Asia, much as the Iraq War had been, and could well unravel the Pivot to Asia initiative entirely. Syria's strategic deterrent was thus indirectly proving effective by providing a major disincentive for attacking the country.

President Obama refused to issue an executive order for an attack and instead announced that he would seek authorisation from the U.S. Congress. Several members of the Senate Foreign Relations Committee appeared to share the president's concern that Syria could turn into 'another Iraq,' which was unaffordable given America's already overstrained commitments to counter challenges to its dominance in East Asia in particular. These concerns were reflected in the draft resolution for the war which limited operations to just 60 days and made clear that the U.S. would not deploy ground forces. Divisions over the course of action still remained, however, with Secretary of State John Kerry opposing the ruling out of deploying American ground troops while others such as Senator Tom Udall pressed for a greater "guarantee that our military actions will be limited." Udall stressed that Americans were "understandably weary after the fiasco in Iraq and over a decade of war," and highlighted the likelihood that undermining the Syrian government would "allow rebels allied with Al Qaeda to gain a stronger foothold in Syria."[67] These multiple concerns, and the lack of a united vision for action, would pervade Washington throughout the Syrian conflict.

With uncertainty regarding whether a U.S.-led attack would be launched, Russia stepped up its support for the Syrian state and drew a hard line against a possible Western strike. As early as June 17 when Western imposition of a no-fly zone was first being considered,[68] over two months before the East Ghouta attacks, the Russian Foreign Ministry issued a statement that it "fundamentally will not allow" such actions. The ministry highlighted prior Western use of a no-fly zone as a precursor to more active measures to overthrow the government of Libya two years prior, stressing that Western discourse regarding violation of Syrian territory came as "a direct consequence of a lack of respect for international law."[69]

Referring to the U.S.-led attack on Iraq ten years prior, launched illegally[70] without UN authorisation and under the false pretext of eliminating its weapons of mass destruction, the Russian Foreign Ministry now warned that "Attempts to bypass the [UN] Security Council, once again to create artificial groundless excuses for a military intervention in the region are fraught with new suffering in Syria and catastrophic consequences for other countries of the Middle East and North Africa." Foreign Minister Sergey Lavrov, referring to possible attack as "a crude violation of international law," highlighted that the U.S. had yet to even produce any evidence implicating the Syrian government in the Ghouta attack.[71] Other Russian officials would refer to the proposed Western attack as a repetition of the invasion of Iraq, with Deputy Prime Minister Dmitry Rogozin stating regarding the cavalier and seemingly lawless behaviour of the Western powers in the region: "The West behaves in the Islamic world like a monkey with a grenade."[72]

The U.S. and Britain both faced ongoing divisions and significant popular and legislative resistance regarding a prospective attack on Syria, in both cases largely influenced by the negative experience of Iraq and the need to balance support for the war effort against Syria with other foreign policy concerns. In an attempt to win support for military action, U.S. Secretary of State John Kerry would insist that there was no presence of Al Qaeda in the Syrian insurgency, leading to further criticism of his position both domestically and internationally with his unsubstantiated claim directly contradicting available intelligence.[73] A major turning point was a vote in the British parliament of 285 to 272 against endorsing military action targeting Syria, which was an unexpected setback for the proponents of military action that also significantly influenced the debate in the United States. The primary cause for this outcome appeared to be concern that attacking Syria would draw Britain into a conflict with the country's allies, with Hezbollah, Iran and Russia respectively mentioned 11, 43 and 68 times when the vote was being discussed in parliament.[ii] As parliamentarian Sarah Wollaston noted, the case against attacking was primarily motivated by "risks of such action exploding into a wider military conflict." [74]

On September 9, amid fast receding support for a possible attack in the U.S., Sergey Lavrov proposed that Syria place its chemical weapons arsenal under international control for destruction. Moscow thereby sought to prevent military action by finding a face-saving solution for the Obama administration to respond to the alleged chemical attacks without violating international law or bringing America directly to blows with Syria. President Obama referred to the proposal as "a potentially positive development," pledging to "engage with the Russians and the international community to see, can we arrive at something that is enforceable and serious."[75] The carrot of a way out of the crisis was paired with the stick of Russian threats to respond to a Western attack on its long-standing strategic partner. The chief of the Russian parliament's foreign affairs committee, Alexei Pushkov, warned on September 11 that while he hoped Washington would support plans to disarm Syria of chemical weapons peacefully, if America went through with plans to attack the country Russia would consider drastically increasing arms sales to Iran. These had been heavily restricted since 1992, and more so since 2007, under Western pressure. Pushkov further warned that Moscow would seriously consider revising the contract allowing the U.S. Military to supply its forces in Afghanistan by transiting through Russian territory in the event of American aggression against Syria.[76] Russian President Putin further indicated that an American attack would undermine future cooperation on the Iranian nuclear weapons program, with Moscow having many more drastic cards to play to bolster Tehran, the Western Bloc's primary regional adversary, should Syria come under attack.[77]

---

ii  The British Ministry of Defence later found what was widely seen as a 'work around' to the parliament's vote by embedding pilots in U.S. and Canadian units which operated in Syria ('Syria air strikes conducted by UK military pilots,' *BBC News*, July 17, 2015.)

On September 12, in an apparent attempt to further sway Western opinion which was then poised in a delicate balance regarding whether or not to initiate an attack against Syria, President Putin took the unusual step of personally publishing an opinion piece in the *New York Times*. Coming a year before the Ukrainian crisis, which saw Western portrayals of all aspects of Russian politics take a sharply negative turn in what many in America termed the beginning of a new Cold War,[78] Putin was at the time considered a respected voice on international politics particularly in conservative circles in the West. His personal appeal over Syria thus had the potential to significantly influence discourse surrounding a possible offensive.[79] The Russian President would "speak directly to the American people" through his opinion piece, arguing that a unilateral attack on Syria could leave the United Nations, as a body for multilateral action, increasingly obsolete, "throw the entire system of international law and order out of balance," and "unleash a new wave of terrorism" including waves of Al Qaeda linked militants returning to both Europe and Russia "with experience acquired in Syria."[80]

Regarding Russia's rationale for opposing a Western attack on Syria, Putin further stated:

> We need to use the United Nations Security Council and believe that preserving law and order in today's complex and turbulent world is one of the few ways to keep international relations from sliding into chaos. The law is still the law, and we must follow it whether we like it or not. Under current international law, force is permitted only in self-defense or by the decision of the Security Council. Anything else is unacceptable under the United Nations Charter and would constitute an act of aggression.... It is alarming that military intervention in internal conflicts in foreign countries has become commonplace for the United States.[81]

Regarding the chemical attacks in Eastern Ghouta, and their implications for international security, Putin stated: "No one doubts that poison gas was used in Syria. But there is every reason to believe it was used not by the Syrian Army, but by opposition forces, to provoke intervention by their powerful foreign patrons, who would be siding with the fundamentalists." He went on to highlight reports that jihadist militants would carry out further chemical attacks beyond Syria, thereby presenting an attack on the Syrian state as a wholly inappropriate option and warned that Western attacks on sovereign states led a growing number of actors to perceive international law as insufficient to protect them. This in turn fuelled the proliferation of nuclear weapons which would only accelerate if Damascus came under Western attack.[82]

The U.S. and its European partners would officially accept the proposal to disarm Syria of its chemical arsenal two days later, through a Framework Agreement signed on September 14 and agreed to by all members of the UN Security Council under Resolution 2118. A joint mission of the Organisation for the Prohibition of Chemical Weapons and the United Nations was subsequently established on October 16, and by June 23 Syria's entire chemical arsenal had been neutralised. While this was considered a major foreign policy success for Russia, preventing a Western attack and effectively upholding international law against crimes of aggression without needing to deploy any significant military forces or even threatening to do so, it cost Syria its only strategic deterrent other than its ballistic missile arsenal. This left it in a weaker position to face future threats of Western, Turkish or Israeli attacks.

## After Ghouta: The War Changes

While not intervening directly in the conflict, Russia had arguably achieved something far more important by preventing a direct U.S.-led military intervention and mass airstrikes on Syrian government positions. All precedents of Western intervention indicate that the U.S. and its European partners would otherwise have launched an intensive bombardment of the country targeting military facilities, Ba'ath Party affiliated buildings, key infrastructure and population centres. Attacks would have continued until the government was toppled, and likely would have seen highly toxic munitions such as depleted uranium used in civilian areas, as was the case in Yugoslavia[83] and Iraq.[84] By averting such an attack, Russia gave Syria a chance to avoid the dark fates of those countries the West had targeted before, allowing the Syrian Arab Army and its partners on the ground to continue their counteroffensive against insurgent forces and retake the ground lost over the past year.

Syria notably gained another political victory when a successful military coup was launched in early July, backed by mass popular protests, in neighbouring Egypt.[85] The most populous Arab state had been under Muslim Brotherhood rule since June the year before, with the Islamist group having cut all Cairo's diplomatic ties with Damascus within days of coming to power.[86] While in power the Muslim Brotherhood had been a leading advocate for the Syrian government's overthrow,[87] while also seeking to place pressure on Iran to cut ties to the country[88] and supporting a Western military intervention to realise Damascus' defeat.[89] The Brotherhood government had affiliated closely with radical preachers calling for violence against Shiite Muslims, leading to killings of Egyptian Shiites by Islamist mobs,[90] and had called for Egyptians to join the 'holy war' in Syria and support jihadist groups fighting against the Syrian Arab Army.[91] Egyptian President Mohamed Morsi, who had aligned his government closely with Turkey and Qatar and maintained strong relations with the Western powers,[92] had also attempted to order the Egyptian Armed Forces to launch an attack on the Syrian state. With the country's military leadership refusing to launch an unprovoked invasion of another Arab country, however, the Brotherhood's hopes for such an offensive were dashed.

The clash between Egypt's Muslim Brotherhood and its armed forces had strong implications for the outcome of the war in Syria, and the Brotherhood's defeat was of major benefit to Syrian interests.[93] While Egypt under Islamist rule had undermined Syrian security,[94] which had it not been for the strongly non-interventionist stance taken by the military against the presidency could have been considerably worse, the Egyptian military council which took power after the Muslim Brotherhood's removal began to establish close ties with Damascus[95] as well as with Russia.[96] The shift in Cairo led it to strongly oppose Western plans to attack Syria over the Ghouta incident,[97] with interim President Adly Mansour highlighting that such offensives would be conducted "without the approval of the UN Security Council and without commitment to international legitimacy."[98] Egypt subsequently voted with Russia at the United Nations on Syria-related resolutions,[99] and undermined[100] efforts by Western-aligned Arab states to isolate Syria in the Arab world.[iii]

One of the SAA's first operations after the threat of Western attack had receded was to recapture the demographically Christian historic town of Maaloula. The town had been taken over by insurgents who had reportedly threatened residents who did not convert to Islam with execution and destroyed several historical sites.[101] SAA armored units played a key role in recapturing Maaloula with few casualties, with the battle providing one of many examples where Syria's religious minorities were protected by the government from intense persecution. The primary thrusts of the broader Syrian counteroffensive were towards liberating the Damascus suburbs, where insurgents were heavily entrenched, and towards the country's largest city Aleppo, which largely by virtue of being only around 50km from the Turkish border had become a major stronghold of jihadist forces. Operation Northern Storm was launched in early October to reopen a key supply route linking central Syria to central Aleppo, and with support from Hezbollah officers, special forces and heavy air support the strategically critical village of Khanasir, a key checkpoint, was captured along with surrounding villages within eight days. After pushing closer to Aleppo, taking all required targets, and thwarting an attempted counteroffensive by insurgents, the operation

iii Ties between the parallel conflicts in Egypt and Syria were symbolised by the actions of the prominent U.S. Senator John McCain, who after entering Syria earlier in the year and meeting with jihadist militants to call for their victory over Damascus, would fly to Egypt after the coup to campaign for the release of Muslim Brotherhood prisoners and criticise the actions of the military government there. ('Egypt dismisses US senators' call for releases,' *Deutsche Welle*, August 8, 2013.)

concluded on December 1. It paved the way for a second offensive to cut supply lines to Aleppo city under Operation Canopus Star which was launched six days later. Major victories across multiple other more minor fronts were being gained simultaneously.

While the Syrian Arab Army continued to make gains, the various Islamist groups waging war against it would increasingly begin to fight among themselves, with each blaming others for the war effort's failure and seeking to impose its will on the wider jihad in the belief that this could turn the tide against Damascus. Shortly after prospects were dashed for an immediate and direct Western military intervention against the Syrian government, a new Islamist insurgent faction, Islamic State (IS), would begin to play a larger role which would heavily shape the conflict over the following two years. IS had formerly been part of the same terror group as the Al Nusra Front, although the two had split in April 2013. The leader of the Al Nusra front, Abu Mohammad Al Julani, was notably a former commander under IS who had headed operations in northern Iraq's Nineveh Governorate. The split between the two branches of the terror group occurred after Abu Bakr Al Baghdadi, commander of the Islamic State, had announced a full merger of IS with the Al Nusra Front for joint operations in both Iraq and Syria, with the two previously having divided operations between the two countries. The following day, Al Julani announced that he had not been informed of the merger, and that he would continue to lead Al Nusra as a separate branch organisation. He further demanded that the international leader of Al Qaeda and mentor of Osama Bin Laden, Ayman Al Zawahri, mediate the disagreement between Al Nusra and the Islamic State.[102]

Amid rising tensions between the two factions Al Zawahri, thought to be based between Afghanistan and Pakistan as Bin Laden had been, renounced the merger and allowed Al Julani to remain at the head of the Al Nusra Front in Syria.[103] Despite his senior position, Islamic State would question the authenticity of Al Zawahri's arbitration before rejecting it outright, with Al Baghdadi declaring that the creation of a unified Islamic State of Iraq and Syria was there to stay. IS' break with the international Al

Qaeda movement, and Al Nusra's refusal to be absorbed into IS, led each to see the other as illegitimate and would result in fierce clashes between them in the coming years.[104]

IS would make its first major entry into the Syrian conflict in mid-2013, and after cooperating with other Islamist groups operating under the Free Syrian Army to jointly occupy the town of Al Dana in the Idlib Governorate, it would turn on and eliminate these forces, behead their leader and occupy the town completely. The military commander of the rival Islamist faction there and his brother were both beheaded and their headless bodies dropped in the town's central square.[105] IS subsequently kept a low profile until mid-September, when it assaulted and captured the town of Azaz near the Iraqi border, a key transit point for war materials from Iraq, from rival militants.[106] IS' campaign to absorb the territory, manpower and arms of rival insurgent groups in northern Syria would intensify from January 2014, with the increasingly formidable insurgent group taking Syria's eastern provincial capital, Raqqa city, in early November[107] and clashing fiercely with rival jihadist militants occupying Aleppo.

The Islamic State's military leadership was comprised largely of veterans from Iraq's years of conflict, who had fought Iranian-backed militias, Kurdish separatists and the Iraqi government for a decade since the country had been destabilised by a U.S.-led invasion in 2003. The militant group could draw on a power base across the Iraqi border to project power into Syria. With the Syrian Arab Army having only a very limited presence in the country's northern regions near Turkey and Iraq, which had been under insurgent control for some time, IS at first appeared to only be fighting against Damascus' enemies. This fuelled a number of conspiracy theories among anti-government activists in the Arab world in particular – namely that the two were working together or else that the Syrian government had somehow created the terror group.[108] This impression was strengthened by Islamic State's relegation to Syria's desert peripheries near the Iraqi border, in contrast to groups such as Al Nusra and other Al Qaeda affiliates which controlled the much more critical heartlands such as Homs, Aleppo and the Damascus suburbs, meaning that IS had remained a low priority target for Syrian air attacks until it began to expand more aggressively in the latter half of 2014.

Although the rise of the Islamic State was initially seen to be benefitting the Syrian government by exacerbating conflict among the jihadist insurgent groups, it would prove to be the greatest danger on the ground to the Syrian state's continued survival. As the Islamic State emerged as without question the most powerful militant group in Syria, it would absorb jihadists from multiple other groups,[109] many of which took their substantial Western, Gulf and Turkish-provided training and supplies with them.[110] The result was that the insurgency across much of Syria came to be effectively unified under a single particularly ruthless ideology and a single command structure.

# Notes

1   'Casey Statement Regarding Administration Announcement on Syria,' *Website of Senator Bob Casey,* June 13, 2013.
    Hafezi, Parisa and Solomon, Erika, 'U.S. considers no-fly zone after Syria crosses nerve gas "red line",' *Reuters*, June 14, 2013.
    Blanford, Nicholas, 'The Battle for Qusayr: How the Syrian Regime and Hizb Allah Tipped the Balance,' *Combatting Terrorism Center at West Point*, vol. 6, issue 8, 2013.
2   de Carbonnel, Alissa, 'Insight: Russia fears return of fighters waging jihad in Syria,' *Reuters,* November 14, 2013.
    Allison, Roy, 'Russia and Syria: explaining alignment with a regime in crisis,' *International Affairs,* vol. 89, no. 4, 2013 (pp. 795–823).
3   'Report: Moscow freezes sale of S-300 to Iran,' *Jerusalem Post,* February 18, 2009.
4   'Medvedev: Assad's chances of retaining power in Syria are shrinking,' *The Guardian,* January 27, 2013.
5   'Russia raises stakes in Syria,' *Wall Street Journal,* May 17, 2013.
6   Allison, Roy, 'Russia and Syria: explaining alignment with a regime in crisis,' *International Affairs* vol. 89, no. 4, 2013 (p. 807).
7   DeYoung, Karen and Warrick, Joby, 'Russia sends arms to Syria as it tries to reassert its role in region,' *Washington Post,* May 30, 2013.
8   Williams, Carol J., 'Russians hedging their bets on prospects for Syrian peace accord,' *Los Angeles Times,* May 29, 2013.
    DeYoung, Karen and Warrick, Joby, 'Russia sends arms to Syria as it tries to reassert its role in region,' *Washington Post,* May 30, 2013.

9 'Deterring the West: Russia Bolsters Iranian Air Defences With New Missiles for S-300 Systems – Reports,' *Military Watch Magazine,* July 18, 2020.

10 'Syria Will Deploy the S-300 Within Two Weeks; Russian Defence Ministry Takes Response to Israeli Actions Into Its Own Hands,' *Military Watch Magazine,* September 24, 2018.

11 Gordon, Michael R. and Schmitt, Eric, 'Russia Sends More Advanced Missiles to Aid Assad in Syria,' *New York Times,* May 16, 2013.

12 'Russia Sends More Advanced Missiles to Aid Assad in Syria,' *Atlantic Council,* May 17, 2013.

13 Wintour, Patrick, 'Putin dashes G8 hopes for Syria breakthrough,' *The Guardian,* June 18, 2013.

14 Roberts, Dan and Wintour, Patrick, 'Obama and Putin at odds over Syria after cool exchange at G8 summit,' *The Guardian,* June 17, 2013.

15 Abdelaziz, Salma and Yan, Holly, 'Video: Syrian rebel cuts out soldier's heart, eats it,' *CNN,* May 15, 2013.

16 Allison, Roy, 'Russia and Syria: explaining alignment with a regime in crisis,' *International Affairs,* vol. 89, no. 4, 2013 (p. 796).

17 Mueller, Karl P., 'Denying Flight: Strategic Options for Employing No-Fly Zones,' *RAND Corporation,* 2013 (p. 13).

18 'Prospects for Syrian No-fly Zone Assessed at USIP,' *United States Institute of Peace,* May 30, 2013.

19 Cooper, Scott, 'A Syrian no-fly zone is the moral and strategic thing to do,' *Washington Post,* April 5, 2013.

20 Simpson, Connor, 'Obama Wants His No-Fly Zone War Plan for Syria,' *The Atlantic,* May 28, 2013.

21 Stolberg, Sheryl Gay, 'Lawmakers Call for Stronger US Action in Syria,' *New York Times,* April 28, 2013.
Entous, Adam, 'Inside Obama's Syria Debate,' *Wall Street Journal,* March 29, 2013.

22 Simpson, Connor, 'Obama Wants His No-Fly Zone War Plan for Syria,' *The Atlantic,* May 28, 2013.

23 'Turkey PM "will support" Syria no-fly zone,' *Al Jazeera,* May 10, 2013.

24 'Syria crisis: Erdoğan steps up Turkey pressure on Assad,' *BBC News,* November 15, 2011.

25 'Prospects for Syrian No-fly Zone Assessed at USIP,' *United States Institute of Peace,* May 30, 2013.

26 Simpson, Connor, 'Obama Wants His No-Fly Zone War Plan for Syria,' *The Atlantic,* May 28, 2013.

27 De Luce, Dan, 'Obama's Criticism of No-Fly Zone and Humanitarian Corridors Options for Syria,' *Atlantic Council,* June 18, 2013.

28 Hughes, Dana, 'Will a No-Fly Zone Really Work in Syria?,' *ABC News,* June 15, 2013.

29 Ibid.

30 Abrams, A. B., *Immovable Object: North Korea's 70 Years At War with American Power,* Atlanta, Clarity Press, 2020 (Chapter 13: The 21st Century and Renewed "Maximum Pressure").

Bell, Larry, 'Indefensible Policies: Our Commander-in-Chief Retreats As Putin's Missile Programs Advance,' *Forbes,* June 14, 2013

Bell, Larry, 'Obama's North Korean And Iranian Missile Defense Trajectories: Course Corrections; Russian Re-Set Dud,' *Forbes,* May 24, 2013.

31  Fray, Keith, 'China's leap forward: overtaking the US as world's biggest economy,' *Financial Times,* October 8, 2014.

Allison, Graham, 'China Is Now the World's Largest Economy. We Shouldn't Be Shocked.,' *National Interest,* October 15, 2020.

32  Abrams, A. B., *Power and Primacy: The History of Western Intervention in the Asia-Pacific,* Oxford, Peter Lang, 2019 (Chapter 15 and Chapter 17).

33  Abrams, A. B., *Immovable Object: North Korea's 70 Years At War with American Power,* Atlanta, Clarity Press, 2020 (pp. 406–407).

Cristopher, Warren, 'Iraq Belongs on the Back Burner,' *New York Times,* December 31, 2002.

Rachman, Gideon, *Easternisation, War and Peace in the Asian Century,* New York, Vintage, 2017 (pp. 77–78).

34  Hafezi, Parisa and Solomon, Erika, 'U.S. considers no-fly zone after Syria crosses nerve gas "red line",' *Reuters,* June 14, 2013.

35  'Prospects for Syrian No-fly Zone Assessed at USIP,' *United States Institute of Peace,* May 30, 2013.

'Soviet MiG-25 Foxbat vs. American F-15 Eagle: Which Was Better in Air to Air Combat?,' *Military Watch Magazine,* October 15, 2020.

36  Nelson, Nigel, 'Syrian warplanes flee after testing defences at British air base in Cyprus,' *The Mirror,* September 8, 2013.

37  'Syria no-fly zone would violate international law, says Russia,' *The Guardian,* June 15, 2013.

38  Everett, Burgess, 'McCain, Graham call for no-fly zone,' *Politico,* June 13, 2013.

39  Sheva, Arutz, 'Syria: Up to 635 Reported Dead in Chemical Attack,' *Israel National News,* August 21, 2013.

40  Ibid.

41  'UN: "Convincing evidence" of Syria chemical attack,' *New York Post,* September 16, 2013.

42  Mcelroy, Damien, 'UN accuses Syrian rebels of chemical weapons use,' *The Telegraph,* May 6, 2013.

43  'Turkey arrests 12 in raids on "terrorist" organization,' *Reuters,* May 30, 2013.

44  Chivers, C. J., 'New Study Refines View of Sarin Attack in Syria,' *New York Times,* December 28, 2013.

45  Gavlak, Dale and Ababneh, Yahya, 'Syrians In Ghouta Claim Saudi-Supplied Rebels Behind Chemical Attack,' *Mint Press News,* August 29, 2013.

46  Hussain, Murtaza, 'NSA Document Says Saudi Prince Directly Ordered Coordinatted Attack By Syrian Rebels on Damascus,' *The Intercept,* October 24, 2017.

47  Lee, Adrian, 'Seymour Hersh Alleges Obama Administration Lied on Syria Gas Attack,' *The Atlantic,* December 8, 2013.

48  Ibid.

49  Ibid.

50  Hersh, Seymour M., 'The Red Line and the Rat Line,' *London Review of Books,* vol. 36, no. 8, April 2014.

51  Ibid.

52  'Report on Chemical Weapons Attacks in Syria,' UN Human Rights Council, February 2014.

53  Turbeville, Brandon, 'New Video Evidence Points To al-Nusra Chemical Attack Against Syrian Soldiers,' *Brandon Turbeville*, May 5, 2014.

54  '"Abandoned" barrels containing deadly sarin seized in rebel-held Syria,' *RT,* July 8, 2014.

55  Akbar, Jay, 'More evidence emerges of ISIS using chemical weapons as Kurdish fighters seize chlorine canisters after suicide bomb attack that left them "dizzy, nauseous and weak",' *Daily Mail,* March 14, 2015.

56  LaGrone, Sam, 'U.S. and U.K. Move Ships Closer to Syria,' *USNI News,* August 26, 2013.

57  'Syria crisis: Diplomacy has not worked, says William Hague,' *BBC News,* August 26, 2013.

58  'Official: 5th destroyer headed to the Med,' *Navy Times*, August 29, 2013.

59  Shalal-Esa, Andrea, 'Sixth U.S. ship now in eastern Mediterranean "as precaution",' *Yahoo News*, August 30, 2013.

60  Hersh, Seymour M., 'The Red Line and the Rat Line,' *London Review of Books,* vol. 36, no. 8, April 2014.

61  Ross, Tim and Farmer, Ben, 'Navy ready to launch first strike on Syria,' *The Telegraph,* August 25, 2013.

62  'John Kerry: Syria's Chemical Attacks "A Moral Obscenity",' *The Atlantic,* August 26, 2013.
    'Syria crisis: UK draws up contingency military plans,' *BBC News,* August 27, 2013.

63  Hurd, Ian, 'Bomb Syria, Even if It Is Illegal,' *New York Times,* August 27, 2013.

64  'Syria, chemical weapons and the limits of international law,' *The Conversation*, April 16, 2018.
    Sterio, Milena, 'Syria and the Limits of International Law,' *ILG2,* April 12, 2018.
    Partlett, William, 'Does it matter that strikes against Syria violate international law?,' *Pursuit: University of Melbourne,* April 16, 2018.

65  Warrick, Joby, *Black Flags: The Rise of ISIS,* New York, Doubleday, 2015 (Chapter 20).

66  Sanger, David E. and Schmitt, Eric, 'Pentagon Says 75,000 Troops Might Be Needed to Seize Syria Chemical Arms,' *New York Times,* November 15, 2012.
    'Securing Syrian Chemical Sites May Require 75,000 Troops: U.S. Military,' *NTI,* November 16, 2012.
    Martosko, David, 'Revealed: Pentagon knew in 2012 that it would take 75,000 GROUND TROOPS to secure Syria's chemical weapons facilities,' *Daily Mail,* September 5, 2013.

Foust, Joshua, 'Obama's Wrong, Syria's Chemical Weapons Require Boots on the Ground,' *Defense One,* September 11, 2013.

Lee, Adrian, 'Seymour Hersh Alleges Obama Administration Lied on Syria Gas Attack,' *The Atlantic,* December 8, 2013.

67   Smith, Matt and Levs, Josh and Smith-Spark, Laura, 'Draft resolution on Syria would limit strike to 60 days,' *CNN,* September 4, 2013.

68   Hafezi, Parisa and Solomon, Erika, 'U.S. considers no-fly zone after Syria crosses nerve gas "red line",' *Reuters,* June 14, 2013.

69   'Russia says it will not allow Syria no-fly zones,' *Reuters,* June 17, 2013.

70   MacAskill, Ewen and Borger, Julian, 'Iraq war was illegal and breached UN charter, says Annan,' *The Guardian,* September 16, 2004.

'Iraq War Was Illegal, Ex-deputy PM Prescott Says,' *Newsweek,* October 7, 2016.

71   'Syria crisis: Russia and China step up warning over strike,' *BBC News,* August 27, 2013.

72   Radia, Kirit, 'Russia Warns of "Catastrophic Consequences" If US Meddles in Syria,' *ABC News,* August 27, 2013.

73   Hosenball, Mark and Stewart, Phil, 'Kerry portrait of Syria rebels at odds with intelligence reports,' *Reuters,* September 5, 2013.

'Vladimir Putin calls John Kerry a liar over al-Qaeda in Syria claims,' *The Telegraph,* September 4, 2013.

74   Glazebrook, Dan, 'The British parliament only likes to attack the weak,' *Asia Times,* September 6, 2013.

75   Gordon, Michael R. and Myers, Steven Lee, 'Obama Calls Russia Offer on Syria Possible "Breakthrough",' *New York Times,* September 10, 2013.

76   'Russia threatens to arm Iran if US strikes Syria,' *Los Angeles Daily News,* September 11, 2013.

Anishchuk, Alexei, 'Russia could boost Iran arms sales if U.S. strikes Syria: Putin ally,' *Reuters,* September 11, 2013.

77   Putin, Vladimir V., 'A Plea for Caution From Russia,' *New York Times,* September 12, 2013.

78    Black, J. and Johns, Michael, *The Return of the Cold War: Ukraine, the West and Russia.* London, Routledge, 2016.

Mamlyuk, Boris N., 'The Ukraine Crisis, Cold War II, and International Law,' *The German Law Journal,* vol. 16, no. 3, 2015 (pp. 479–522).

79   Nussbaum, Matthew and Oreskes, Benjamin, 'More Republicans viewing Putin favorably,' *Politico,* Decemmber 16, 2016.

Tharoor, Ishaan, 'Why U.S. conservatives love Russia's Vladimir Putin,' *Washington Post,* August 25, 2014.

Horsey, David, 'Conservatives harbor an odd admiration for Vladimir Putin,' *Los Angeles Times,* March 7, 2014.

Chhor, Khatya, 'Trump, Farage, Le Pen: Why Western conservatives love Vladimir Putin,' *France 24,* November 15, 2016.

Michel, Casey, 'Beyond Trump and Putin: The American Alt-Right's Love of the Kremlin's Policies,' *The Diplomat,* October 13, 2016.

Zimmerman, Jonathan, 'It's not just Trump who's fond of Putin: Why social conservatives have a thing for the Russian strongman,' *New York Daily News,* March 6, 2017.

80   Putin, Vladimir V., 'A Plea for Caution From Russia,' *New York Times*, September 12, 2013.

81   Ibid.

82   Ibid.

83   '"Up to 15 tons of depleted uranium used in 1999 Serbia bombing" – lead lawyer in suit against NATO,' *RT*, June 13, 2017.

84   Edwards, Rob, 'U.S. fired depleted uranium at civilian areas in 2003 Iraq war, report finds,' *The Guardian*, June 19, 2014.

85   Kingsley, Patrick, 'Protesters across Egypt call for Mohamed Morsi to go,' *The Guardian*, June 30, 2013.
     'Egypt crisis: Mass protests over Morsi grip cities,' *BBC News*, July 1, 2013.

86   'Egypt cut ties to Assad regime and calls for support of rebels,' *Financial Times*, June 16, 2013.

87   'Morsy backs Syrian calls for al-Assad to face war crimes trial,' *CNN*, January 7, 2013.
     'Morsi criticises Syria at Tehran meeting,' *Al Jazeera*, August 30, 2012.
     'Egypt's Morsi calls on Assad to step down,' *France24*, September 5, 2012.

88   Spencer, Richard, 'Morsi tells Iran that Syria's Assad must go,' *The Telegraph*, August 30, 2012.
     Peralta, Eyder, 'At Nonaligned Conference, Egypt's Morsi Slams Iran Over Syria Position,' *NPR*, August 30, 2012.

89   'Morsi Cuts Egypt's Syria Ties, Backs No-fly Zone,' *Voice of Asia*, June 15, 2013.

90   Marshall, Tim, 'Egypt: Attack On Shia Comes At Dangerous Time,' *Sky News*, June 25, 2013.

91   Hendawi, Hamza, 'Morsi seen to endorse holy war on Syria,' *Times of Israel*, June 17, 2013.
     'Morsi role at Syria rally seen as tipping point for Egypt army,' *Irish Times*, July 2, 2013.

92   Pierce, Anne R., 'US "Partnership" with the Egyptian Muslim Brotherhood and its Effect on Civil Society and Human Rights,' *Society*, vol. 51, no. 1, 2014 (pp. 68–86).
     Ibrahim, Raymond, 'Egyptians Enraged by U.S. Outreach to Muslim Brotherhood,' *Middle East Forum*, August 9, 2013.

93   Evans, Dominic, 'Syria's Assad says political Islam being defeated in Egypt,' *Reuters*, July 3, 2013.

94   'Syria hails ouster of Egypt's Morsi as "great achievement",' *The National*, July 4, 2013.

95   Kessler, Oren, 'Egypt Picks Sides in the Syrian War,' *Foreign Affairs*, February 12, 2017.
     Ghosh, Rudroneel, 'Collective Responsibility: Egyptian President Sisi's support for Assad is rooted in UN principles,' *Times of India*, November 24, 2016.
     'Egypt's Sisi expresses support for Syria's military,' *Al Jazeera*, November 23, 2016.

96   Saleh, Heba and Farchy, Jack, 'Egypt and Russia to boost trade ties as US influence wanes,' *Financial Times*, March 26, 2014.

97   'Egypt rejects military intervention in Syria,' *Ahram Online,* August 27, 2013.
98   'Demo in Cairo against military intervention in Syria,' *Ahram Online,* September 6, 2013.
99   'Saudi anger as Egypt votes with Russia in UN vote,' *Middle East Eye,* October 13, 2016.
100  Ramesh, Randeep, 'Iran "wanted Egypt at Syria talks" as Middle Eastern alliances shift,' *The Guardian,* October 20, 2016.
101  'Syrian village is "liberated" by rebels... who then forced Christians to convert to Islam,' *Daily Mail,* September 8, 2013.
     'Activists: Syrian rebels take Christian village,' *Daily Star*, September 8, 2013.
     'Battle for Syria Christian town of Maaloula continues,' *BBC News,* September 11, 2013.
102  al-Mustapha, Hamza, 'The al-Nusra Front: From Formation to Dissension,' *Arab Center for Research & Policy Studies,* 2014 (pp. 16–18).
103  'الظواهري يلغي دمج «جهاديي» سوريا والعراق' [Al-Zawahiri abolishes the merger of the "Jihadists" of Syria and Iraq], *Al Jazeera,* June 9, 2013.
104  al-Mustapha, Hamza, 'The al-Nusra Front: From Formation to Dissension,' *Arab Center for Research & Policy Studies,* 2014 (pp. 16–18).
105  Roenblatt, Nathaniel, 'ISIS' Plan To Govern Syria – And What The US Should Do About it,' *War on the Rocks,* October 31, 2013.
106  Karam, Zeina and Mroue, Bassem, 'Al-Qaida militants capture town in northern Syria,' *Associated Press*, September 19, 2013.
     Wood, Paul, 'Isis seizure of Syria's Azaz exposes rebel rifts,' *BBC News,* September 19, 2013.
107  Walsh, Nick Paton and Razek, Raja and Tuysuz, Gul, 'Inside Syrian town living under al Qaeda reign of fear,' *CNN,* November 5, 2013.
108  Abrahms, Max and Glaser, John, 'The pundits were wrong about Assad and the Islamic State. As usual, they're not willing to admit it,' *Los Angeles Times,* December 10, 2017.
     Walsh, Nick Paton and Razek, Raja and Tuysuz, Gul, 'Inside Syrian town living under al Qaeda reign of fear,' *CNN,* November 5, 2013.
     Cockburn, Patrick, *The Rise of Islamic State: ISIS and the New Sunni Revolution,* London, Verso Books, 2015 (Kindle: L431).
     Roenblatt, Nathaniel, 'ISIS' Plan To Govern Syria – And What The US Should Do About it,' *War on the Rocks,* October 31, 2013.
     Barnard, Anne, 'Blamed for Rise of ISIS, Syrian Leader Is Pushed to Escalate Fight,' *New York Times,* August 22, 2014.
109  Williams, Lauren, 'Syrians adjust to life under ISIS rule,' *The Daily Star*, August 30, 2014.
     Ripley, Tim, *Operation Aleppo: Russia's War in Syria,* Lancaster, Telic-Herrick Publications, 2018 (p. 138).
110  Statement by Mr. Vladimir V. Putin, President of the Russian Federation, at the 70th session of the UN General Assembly, September 28, 2015.

# Chapter 5

# Turning Points

## The Islamic State Turning Point

The Syrian Arab Army and its partners would continue to make major battlefield gains into 2014, although tensions between Damascus and the external supporters of the Islamist insurgency would also continue to escalate. On March 18 the United States officially closed the Syrian embassy in Washington, suspending operations of all consulates and expelling all diplomats.[1] This apparently unprovoked action appeared to be a result of the Obama administration's shrinking list of options to place further pressure on its Middle Eastern target in the face of mounting domestic pressure to 'get tough on Assad.' The following day, in retaliation for an alleged Syrian attack which caused four military casualties, the Israeli Air Force launched multiple airstrikes on Syrian Arab Army positions.[2] This was followed four days later by a Turkish attack on a Syrian MiG-23 fighter operating on a strike mission against Turkish backed militants near the border.[3] Despite these clashes, Syrian forces overall were holding their own and making gains throughout the first half of 2014.

Looking to Syria's international situation, the Western-backed overthrow of the government of Ukraine[4] and subsequent Russian annexation of the Crimean Peninsula in March not only pushed the Syrian conflict further down the Obama administration's already long list of urgent foreign policy priorities, but also soured relations between Moscow and the Western Bloc. The crisis escalated what many analysts referred to as a new Cold War between Russia and the West,[5] increasing tensions and leading to mutual imposition of economic sanctions.[6] This not only reduced Western leverage over Russia, but also meant that the former superpower would be better inclined to support its oldest strategic partner in the Middle East against future Western offensive actions. On the Syrian domestic front, the first week of May saw government forces capture the city of Homs, the third largest in the country, which had been referred to in the West as the 'cradle of the Syrian uprising.'[7] This marked the most significant victory since the pivotal battle at Qusayr eleven months prior. Syria's position in the first half of 2014 thus appeared to be steadily improving, although this would be short lived with the security situation taking a drastic turn for the worse from July.

The Islamic State insurgent group had notably made major gains of its own in early 2014, taking the major Iraqi city of Fallujah in the first week of January[8] which provided it with the expanded power base needed to make a major push into Syria. Despite some initial cooperation with Islamist groups fighting under the Free Syrian Army, IS would carve a swathe through their territory and win large numbers of new recruits to its cause through its demonstrated battlefield prowess. January would see IS make a major push into the territory of rival groups, reportedly redeploying over 1000 veterans from Iraq including elite special forces units to bolster its Syrian front.[9] Making extensive use of suicide car explosions, Islamic State forces were able to capture a number of key targets including the Al Jarah military airport, the cities of Manbij and Jarabulus[10] in the Aleppo governate and most of the governate of Raqqa, including its capital Raqqa city.[11] It also began to press into the Homs governate in central Syria. In February the militant group consolidated its hold over Aleppo, attacking the headquarters of the Al Qaeda affiliated[12] Al Tawhid Brigade, which further increased tensions between IS and the global Al Qaeda network.

Al Qaeda elder statesman Abu Khalid Al Suri, a personal emissary of the group's leader, Ayman Al Zawahri, who had been sent to Syria to mediate disputes between various Al Qaeda branches and end conflict between Al Nusra and IS, was assassinated on February 21. Al Suri had notably received extensive funding from the founder of the Swiss-based human rights NGO Alkarama, the Qatari human rights advocate Abd Al Rahman Al Naimi, representing one of multiple cases in the Syrian conflict where human rights groups were found to be affiliated with jihadist activities.[13] The death of the veteran jihadist, who had obituaries written for him by Islamist groups across much of the world, was widely attributed to the Islamic State. Although this was not definitively proven it permanently soured relations between IS and Al Qaeda leading to further fierce clashes on Syrian territory. Al Nusra, moving to declare war on IS within a week of the assassination,[14] led the fight against its new adversary in the Deir ez-Zor governate, which placed the area largely under the Al Qaeda affiliate's control by the end of the month.

Pressing an offensive into Iraq from early June, Islamic State forces were quickly able to overrun and establish a stronghold in the country's third largest city Mosul,[15] vanquish four Iraqi Army divisions, and take over multiple major military installations including the largest in western Iraq. This gave the insurgent group control of nearly a third of Iraq's territory. By late June IS held territory over triple the size of the state of Qatar, including valuable assets such as oil wells and refineries, military bases, arms depots, factories and banks needed to establish the beginnings of a jihadist state. By July the former Al Qaeda affiliate controlled one third of Syrian territory and almost all the country's oil and gas production facilities.[16]

IS' military prowess stemmed not only from its ideological conviction, but also from its effective organisational skills and its access to highly experienced personnel. These included both veteran jihadist militants from across the world and former Iraqi military officers from before the country's armed forces had been disbanded in May 2003. True to its name, IS was organised as an actual state with institutions, a defence industry and a military divided into separate types of battalions for specific roles. These included elite 'Special Tasks Platoons' and heavy armour and artillery units which were assigned complementary roles in the jihadist group's campaigns. Its defence industry's tasks ranged from modifying hundreds of armoured vehicles, many for suicide attacks, to equipping civilian drones with bomb racks for combat missions.

The primary targets of the Islamic State's initial advances were rival Islamist insurgents, as these groups operated in proximity to the Iraqi border regions which lay between Syria's Turkish and Jordanian borders. Attacking other Islamist groups provided IS with the opportunity to swell its ranks, with rival jihadists increasingly seeing defections to join IS. From July 2014, however, IS forces would begin to lay siege to a Syrian Arab Army garrison in Deir ez-Zor after eliminating rival insurgent groups in the area.[17] From August IS began to more broadly engage Syrian government forces, resulting in intensified airstrikes by the Syrian Air Force against the jihadist group's positions in Raqqa and Deir ez-Zor. That month also saw the beginning of engagements around Syria's largest city, Aleppo, which was in the hands of Al Qaeda affiliated groups and which both the government and Islamic State were seeking to capture.

On July 15, the day of President Bashar Al Assad's inauguration into a third term as president, Islamic State launched a major assault in the Homs governate and captured the Shaer Gas Field, with the SAA and supporting militias taking heavy losses.[18] Although the Syrian president had faced no viable opposition, and the Western powers and their regional allies had gone to considerable lengths to ban Syrians residing overseas from voting in order to deny the election legitimacy,[19] Islamic State's attack soured what had still been seen as a moment of triumph for Syria's ruling Ba'ath Party. Shaer was quickly recaptured after ten days by the SAA, with special forces leading a renewed assault, but IS would quickly follow this with further offensives. By the end of the month Islamic State had captured the SAA's Division 17 headquarters in Raqqa after causing heavy losses with multiple suicide bombings, with several soldiers captured in the aftermath subsequently beheaded.[20] The jihadist group had also laid siege to and captured part of the Kwayres Airbase, which was a strategically vital SAA position located just 30km from Aleppo city.[21]

Clashes between Syrian and Islamic State forces from June to August saw the former take heavier manpower losses than at any other time in the war so far. This bore testament to the effectiveness of the new jihadist group, which proved even more capable and ruthless on the battlefield than the Al Nusra Front.[22] By mid-August Islamic State controlled the lion's share of Syria's oil and gas fields,[23] and had also taken effective control of the Raqqa governate. IS fighters succeeded in capturing Raqqa's most vital military installation, Tabqa Airbase,[24] a target no other insurgent group had ever managed to seriously threaten, and two other major military installations. Syrian forces had relied heavily on air attacks to counter Islamic State attacks in Raqqa, and although they reportedly managed to evacuate all aircraft from Tabqa the loss of the facility still represented a serious blow.[25] The MiG-21 jets deployed there had increasingly become the workhorses of the Syrian air campaign, and although they could fly high and fast they were extremely cheap to operate, required little fuel or spare parts and could often fly more than three sorties per day – something newer, more complex and heavier jets such as the MiG-23BN could not do.[26] On August 28 the Syrian Air Force struck back with an attack on an IS headquarters building in Muhasen, acting on intelligence that there was a major meeting between its military leaders and sharia judges, and succeeded in causing critical losses. A second airstrike on that day on an IS camp in Raqqa caused dozens of casualties, which was followed by further intensive strikes on targets in Raqqa and Deir ez-Zor the following week again causing heavy losses.[27]

The connection between the parallel but separate campaigns being waged in Syria and Iraq against Islamic State led a number of analysts to refer to them as a single 'Syraq War.'[28] This was symbolised by IS' abolition of the border between the two countries on the basis that it was an artificial colonial imposition, with the jihadist group's gains in each country strengthening its hand in the other.[29] An Iraqi helicopter assault targeted IS positions in Syria in late April,[30] which was hardly the last Iraqi strike on the terror group on Syrian soil,[31] while Syrian fighter jets bombed IS positions in Iraq in late June.[32] Both countries were reliant on significant Iranian Quds Force support, which played a major role in the campaign to contain IS and reverse its gains on both fronts.

The 'Syraq' phenomenon[i] was also reflected in the growing debate in the United States regarding whether or not to strike the Islamic State on Syrian soil, with proponents highlighting the ineffectiveness of targeting one half of its territory and leaving the other off limits.[33] The case for going through with such a bombing campaign was strengthened considerably by the beheadings of U.S. journalist James Foley on August 20 and journalist Steven Sotloff on September 2, and the perception that IS posed a global threat beyond the 'Syraq' theatre particularly given its not inconsiderable support base among Muslim minorities in the Western world.[34]

The U.S. decision to begin bombing Islamic State forces in Syria, alongside a sizeable coalition of Western partners, placed Damascus in a dangerous position. Although Syria was willing to work with potential partners against the jihadist group, the Western powers refused to recognise the Syrian government despite its broad international recognition across the non-Western world and its representation as a member state at the United Nations. This meant that when the first Western warplanes entered Syrian airspace, although they were not attacking government positions, they were operating in violation of Syria's territorial sovereignty. While Syria had the legal right to shoot down the Western aircraft violating its airspace, doing so would open it up to the prospects of escalated clashes when it was already hard pressed to defend itself and faced no immediate threat from the Western jets. Furthermore, it would likely lead to accusations that Damascus was providing a shield for Islamic State which in turn could build further support in Europe and the U.S. to target it directly. The weakness of the Syrian government's position ultimately forced it to at least temporarily tolerate an extensive Western presence in its skies.

Paving the way for an air campaign which at least at first would exclusively target IS, the U.S. Air Force began conducting

---

i   In February 2021 the U.S. would strike Iranian-backed militias in Syria to respond to attacks on American forces by affiliated militias in Iraq – an action which demonstrated the extent to which the U.S. had accepted the 'Syraq' phenomenon and considered the two countries as a single conflict zone. (Horton, Alex, 'Biden administration conducts strike on Iranian-linked fighters in Syria,' *Washington Post,* February 25, 2021.)

surveillance flights over Syrian airspace from the final week of August while making a point of not requesting Damascus' permission.[35] The Western attacks commenced on September 23, and while they were overwhelmingly led by the U.S., they would also come to include Australia,[36] Belgium,[37] Britain,[38] Canada,[39] Denmark,[40] France[41] and the Netherlands.[42] America's regional allies Bahrain, Jordan, Saudi Arabia and the United Arab Emirates reportedly also participated in a minor supporting role – a type of contribution American leaders had historically referred to as the non-Western "token force" which was vital "to lend real moral standing to a venture that otherwise could be made to appear as a brutal example of imperialism."[43] The token participation of Western-aligned Arab monarchies made the large scale and daily violation of Syrian airspace appear less like illegal Western violation of a third world state's sovereignty and more like action on the basis of international consensus.

With the Western Bloc countries taking advantage of the pretext of countering Islamic State to operate military aircraft freely and in large numbers over Syrian skies, they were now in a much stronger position to pursue offensive actions against the Syrian government. Now that the Western powers effectively had a foot in the door, the options they could exercise ranged from airdrops to insurgents, to imposition of an illegal no-fly zone, or even airstrikes on government positions. Worse still for Syria was the apparent ineffectiveness of Western bombardment of the Islamic State, whether by design or otherwise, meaning the threat of having aircraft from hostile countries in its airspace was not compensated for by any significant slowing of the jihadist group's offensive into government held territory.[44] Indeed, when comparing the intensity of Western bombings to other campaigns such as Yugoslavia or Desert Storm, the firepower being brought to bear against IS positions was negligible. This strengthened the argument that Western bombing of IS' Syrian positions was much more a pretext to gain access to the country's airspace than an end in and of itself.

Beyond the initiation of an air campaign, a $500 million program was also approved in Washington to train and arm 'moderate'

Syrian insurgents under the pretext of responding to IS' gains. Such 'moderates' had been few and far between even in 2011, and by mid-2014 were almost impossible to find.[45] Despite planning to train 5,400 personnel within a year only 60, or 1.1% of the target number, were ready, with the program subsequently declared a failure. Genuine moderates were harder to find than expected and, unlike the CIA which oversaw other insurgent training programs, the Pentagon, which oversaw this particular program, appeared genuinely unwilling to openly train jihadists.[46]

## Slow Retreat

After losing Raqqa to Islamic State forces the Syrian Arab Army would continue to lose ground, not only to the powerful new insurgent group, which in less than a year had expanded from a minor presence among anti-government forces to the undisputed leader, but also to Al Nusra and other Al Qaeda affiliates. As IS pushed forward from the east, other Islamist insurgent groups attacking from the south captured significant ground from the Syrian Arab Army in the Jordanian border region from September 9. This stripped the SAA of a key transport route between the Quneitra and Daraa governates, giving insurgents control over most of Quneitra. On September 23, the day after U.S.-led coalition forces began operations in Syrian airspace, the Syrian Air Force lost one of its precious few Su-24M heavy strike fighters to Israeli military action, with the Israeli Defence Force claiming the jet had violated its airspace.[47] Only around twenty of these aircraft, with long ranges and relatively modern precision strike capabilities, were in service.[48]

On October 1 jihadist forces conducted one of the most successful suicide bombing attacks of the war, targeting an elementary school in Homs and causing over 100 casualties including 41 child deaths. It was unclear which of the many insurgent groups was responsible.[49] Low level fighting against Islamic State forces was ongoing, particularly around Deir ez-Zor where a small Syrian garrison would remain besieged for two more years, as well as in the Damascus suburbs where the SAA gained some ground from

Al Qaeda linked groups. Against the tide of losses one significant gain, which again saw the SAA operate with support from
Hezbollah advisors, was the capture of the key town of Murak
in the Hama governate. The battle to control the town had lasted
almost nine months and seen Al Nusra and its affiliates such as
the Sham Legion[50] and the Islamic Front put up a resolute defence
before suffering a decisive defeat on October 23.

The Syrian Arab Army went on to win a number of isolated
victories, most notably the garrison at Deir ez-Zor's repelling of
multiple IS assaults, encircling a large army of the Jaysh Al Islam
insurgent group in Jobar city and capturing its east district, and
sustaining a slow but steady push to take Aleppo. Syria would
also gain a significant public relations victory following its longstanding claims of collusion between Israel and Al Qaeda linked
jihadist groups, when UN peacekeepers deployed to the Israeli-
Syrian border regions officially testified to having witnessed
multiple interactions between the Israeli military and Al Nusra
Front militants. This included observing Israeli provision of arms
to Al Nusra. Referring to Al Nusra as terrorists, UN Secretary-
General Ban Ki Moon reported this interaction to the United
Nations Security Council on October 27.[51] On December 7, Israel
proceeded to carry out a new round of airstrikes against Syrian targets, attacking two military facilities near Damascus, seemingly
without provocation.[52]

These gains notwithstanding, the second half of 2014 had
overall seen major setbacks for the Syrian government's war effort
particularly in its final two months. These included the loss of
Nawa city to the Al Nusra Front in early November,[53] considerable SAA losses to and the capture of 120 soldiers by the Islamic
Front militant group in mid-December,[54] and the capture of the
key Wadi Deif and Hamidiyeh military bases in an Al Nusra
Front led attack. The last of these losses ceded key positions on a
highway linking the cities of Aleppo, Idlib and Damascus to the
insurgents.[55] Perhaps more concerning still was the formation of a
new united front of jihadist militias on December 25, with groups
including the Islamic Front, the Asala Wa Al Tanmiya Front,
the Mujahideen Army and Fastaqim Kama Umirt among others

coming together to confront the Syrian Arab Army and making important advances on the Aleppo front.[56] With the SAA already under tremendous pressure from both Islamic State and the other Islamist forces, an official union of many of the latter boded ill for its ability to hold ground.

## Heavy Losses and the Threat of a Western-Imposed Partitioning of Syria

The year 2015 would see Islamic State continue to make territorial gains, and under pressure from it and other jihadist groups the Syrian Arab Army would be pressed harder than ever before. Key to facilitating IS' successes were its absorption of other groups' fighters and war materials and the prestige of its victories which gained it considerable support both financially from donors in the Gulf States and in terms of manpower from inspired Islamists across the world. Furthermore, simultaneous IS advances into Iraq had left Iran's Quds Force and its affiliated militias more thinly stretched, with these units now forced to contain the jihadist threat on two separate fronts. The Gulf States and Turkey had also escalated support for insurgent groups in Syria, with Ankara working particularly closely with Qatar and Saudi Arabia to empower various proxy forces against Damascus.[57] Furthermore, following major losses to the Syrian government in the first half of 2014 and then to Islamic State in the latter half, other insurgent groups began to reduce infighting among themselves and cooperate more closely, which allowed them to carry out more effective offensives into government-controlled territory. These factors, combined with the threat of ever-present Western aircraft overhead from September 2014, made Syria's security situation in 2015 particularly dire.

On January 25 the SAA lost the Brigade 82 military base in the Daraa governate near the Jordanian border, which had formed a key part of the southern line of defence protecting Damascus and was one of its last strongholds in the area. The loss caused significant subsequent logistical issues and left the nearby town of Sheikh Maskeen isolated, which allowed insurgent forces to seize it after multiple failed prior attempts. In mid-February an attempt to cut the flow of jihadists and materials from Turkey saw Syrian government forces capture strategically located towns and villages such as Ratyan and Bashkoy in northern Aleppo near the border. Insurgents succeeded in retaking the former within 48 hours and would quickly launch counteroffensives which undercut the gains made by government forces. Fighting in Aleppo also grew particularly fierce at this time, with an attempted SAA offensive in northern Aleppo stalling on February 17 [58] and Al Nusra fighters launching a large-scale counterattack two days later, which gained them considerable ground. Losses on both sides were heavy. [59]

In the first week of March Al Nusra and affiliated jihadist groups set off explosives under the Syrian Air Force Intelligence headquarters in Aleppo's Jamiat Al Zahra district, before launching a large scale attack in which the SAA and Hezbollah took significant losses. [60] Although the attack was ultimately a failure, Syria's growing reliance on air operations as pressure on its ground forces grew, and the Air Force Intelligence's position as the elite of its intelligence apparatus, meant the loss of several highly trained personnel at the headquarters was a major blow. Al Nusra would launch a second assault on the intelligence headquarters on April 13, again using tunnel bombs and causing significant government losses but failing to gain ground. [61] Jihadist militants claimed to have caused heavy losses among government forces in Aleppo in late April, and in June and July they went on to make significant gains in the fiercely contested area as hopes for a swift recapture by the SAA dimmed.

With government forces hard pressed and increasingly on the defensive against Al Nusra and its affiliates in Aleppo to the north, Islamic State launched a major assault in the Homs governate to the south. This took place in May, and gained the jihadist group control of the ancient city of Palmyra on the 21st. IS proceeded to demolish the World Heritage site located there and conducted mass executions of captured soldiers and over 400 civilian supporters. [62] The insurgent group also gained control of several nearby oil fields and two nearby towns, with the Syrian government responding with multiple air strikes. [63] With continuing momentum from its prior offensive, Islamic State forces captured the strategically located town of Hassia in early June which lay on the main road between Damascus, Homs and Latakia.[64] In the final week of that month IS forces launched two parallel offensives, the first against Kobani city (see Chapter 6) and the second against government-held parts of Al Hasakah city, going on to capture the latter's vital Regiment 121 military base. The militant group's push into government-controlled territory would continue into August, with the SAA's heavy losses and IS' publication of videos of gruesome mass executions of captured soldiers shaking Syrian morale.

On July 26 President Assad publicly conceded that the SAA was facing a manpower shortage and had been forced to withdraw from some regions under jihadist assault in order to prioritise the defence of others.[65] In parallel to Syrian government losses to Islamic State, Hezbollah was also increasingly hard pressed to hold ground in 2015, with the militia having suffered a serious blow in January to a targeted Israeli air strike. The attack took the lives of field commander Mohamad Issa, Iranian Quds Force Brigadier General Mohammad Ali Allahdadi, and five regular Hezbollah fighters.[66] A renewal of direct hostilities from the Israeli front led Hezbollah to retaliate, firing an anti-tank missile at an Israeli convoy which caused nine casualties including two deaths. This in turn led Israel to retaliate with artillery fire which killed a single UN peacekeeper in Lebanon.[67] These low-level hostilities highlighted that, while Hezbollah was fighting jihadist militant groups being armed and funded by Israel and its regional and Western partners, the threat posed by the Israeli Defence Force itself was ever present.

Also in early January the buffer zone held by Hezbollah near the Lebanese border came under concerted attack by both the Al Nusra front and affiliated insurgent groups operating under the Free Syrian Army. Although Hezbollah's positions in the Qalamoun Mountains were well fortified, insurgent groups boasting significant numerical advantages and access to heavy firepower managed to make significant gains with heavy casualties reported on both sides. Jihadist control of Qalamoun would allow them to cut Syrian government supply routes between Damascus and Homs city, possibly in preparation for an assault to again place the latter under insurgent control, as well as cutting Hezbollah supply routes into Syria. It would have also allowed jihadists to project power into southern Lebanon and expand the Syrian War into Lebanese territory with direct attacks on Hezbollah's heartlands. General Secretary Hassan Nasrallah emphasized the seriousness of the threat, and referred to the attacks on the area by Al Qaeda affiliates as "a real aggression that exists every hour, every day, every night."[68] The potential for a takeover of the area by Islamist militant groups reportedly bolstered local Lebanese support for Hezbollah due to its role as the primary force preventing this.[69]

The Al Qaeda assault on Qalamoun notably followed the Islamic State takeover of the Lebanese border town of Arsal but represented a much more sensitive target which Hezbollah would devote much greater efforts to countering. The Lebanese militia would begin to sharply reverse all losses by May with SAA support, but the cost of intensified fighting against jihadists who enjoyed a seemingly endless supply of manpower and heavy weapons flowing across the Turkish and Jordanian borders still exacted a heavy toll.[70]

By August Iran's Quds Force, Hezbollah,[71] the North Koreans and the various Quds Force trained militias in Syria were thinly stretched to bolster the faltering Syrian Arab Army, with major further gains for the Islamic State, Al Nusra and other jihadist groups expected at the expense of the Syrian government. A jihadist push towards Latakia and Hama appeared set to cut Damascus off from the coast entirely, which would make a potential siege of the capital a great deal easier. Meanwhile all of Deir ez-Zor except for small SAA holdouts had been lost, the large majority to Islamic State which was continuing to rapidly push westwards. On a third major front to the south insurgents benefitting from a flow of manpower and supplies from the Jordanian border were gaining ground in a push northwards into government held territory.

By the beginning of August jihadist groups had made unprecedented gains, and begun a push into the Syrian government's key heartlands in the Sahl Al Ghab plains.[72] This was followed

by a separate but similarly troubling development for Syria as
Islamic State forces began an assault on the southern outskirts
of Damascus, clashing with rival Islamist fighters which already
occupied the area.[73] While significant information was available
on the Syrian Arab Army and Hezbollah, with the two being
relatively transparent about the general nature of their operations
and positions, details on the operations of other parties supporting
Damascus, be they the Afghan Fatemiyoun Brigade or the Korean
People's Army, are scarce given the much greater secrecy under
which they operated. It can be assumed based on the battlefield
circumstances, however, that much like the SAA and Hezbollah
these parties too were increasingly hard pressed as jihadist offensives grew larger and more persistent.

Worsening an already dire situation for Damascus, growing
calls began to emerge among Syria's state adversaries to take
direct military action against the Syrian government. On August
15 Turkish Prime Minister Ahmet Davutoglu, who had assumed
office after Recep Tayyip Erdoğan ascended to the presidency,
called for imposition of a no-fly zone over Syria. Davutoglu further
raised the possibility of deploying Turkish troops to Syrian territory to create a 'safe zone' – an area under the control of foreign
powers to house refugees and provide a safe haven for the training
of insurgents.[74] This followed a statement in the final week of July
by Foreign Minister Mevlut Cavusoglu that Turkey planned to use
military force to form safe zones in northern Syria.[75]

Turkey was hardly alone in working towards the imposition
of safe zones on Syrian territory, with the U.S. agreeing to support the creation of such zones in the country's northeast where
insurgents would be protected. From there they would be allowed
to exercise separate governance and continue to wage war on the
Syrian state. Official American statements portrayed theses safe
zones as intended to counter the Islamic State, making little men-
tion of the Syrian government despite it being the primary party
adversely affected. As the *New York Times* among others noted,
the safe zone would likely also be covered by a NATO no-fly
zone, meaning Syrian aircraft would be targeted if they attempted
to access certain parts of their own airspace deemed 'off limits'

by the Western powers.[76] Jordan, which provided the second major crossing point into Syria for Western-backed insurgents after Turkey, had announced as early as June 29 that it intended to create a similar zone on Syrian soil under its own control, which would be manned by Western-backed anti-government militants many of whom were trained in Jordan itself.[77]

Creation of safe zones was seen by several analysts as the first step towards partitioning Syria. Once NATO forces, either Western or Turkish, had established their occupation in a part of the country and allowed insurgents to set up their own armed forces, institutions and political systems there, the chances were very slim that these would ever be returned to the control of the internationally recognised Syrian government. This partly supported assertions made by Hezbollah leader Hassan Nasrallah, among others, that Syria's adversaries had long held designs for imposing a partitioning of the country, for which creation of safe zones would be the clearest path. In 2007, four years before the outbreak of the war, Nasrallah predicted, regarding Western designs to partition the most powerful and ethnically and religiously diverse states in the Arab Middle East, that the intention was:

The drawing of a new map for the region. They want the partition of Iraq. Iraq is not on the edge of a civil war – there is a civil war. There is ethnic and sectarian cleansing. The daily killing and displacement which is taking place in Iraq aims at achieving three Iraqi parts, which will be sectarian and ethnically pure as a prelude to the partition of Iraq.... I can say that President [George W.] Bush is lying when he says he does not want Iraq to be partitioned. All the facts occurring now on the ground make you swear he is dragging Iraq to partition. And a day will come when he will say, 'I cannot do anything, since the Iraqis want the partition of their country and I honour the wishes of the people of Iraq.'

In Syria, according to Nasrallah, the West sought to push the country "into chaos and internal battles like in Iraq." In Lebanon, "There will be a Sunni state, an Alawi state, a Christian state, and a Druze state... I do not know if there will be a Shiite state."[78]

Nasrallah had not been the only one to highlight the possibility before the outbreak of the Syrian War that Damascus' adversaries could seek to partition the country along sectarian lines. Most notably, senior Israeli Foreign Ministry official and advisor to then Defence Minister Ariel Sharon, Oded Yinon, had highlighted as early as 1982 that the dissolution of Syria and other potentially hostile Arab states could be pursued to enhance Israeli security. Referring to pursuit of this objective as a "strategy for Israel," his paper was published in the prominent *Kivunim* journal and was also published by the World Zionist Organization's department of information in Jerusalem. Yinon stated that if this strategy was pursued:

> Syria will fall apart, in accordance with its ethnic and religious structure, into several states such as in present day Lebanon, so that there will be a Shi'ite Alawi state along its coast, a Sunni state in the Aleppo area, another Sunni state in Damascus hostile to its northern neighbour, and the Druzes who will set up a state, maybe even in our Golan, and certainly in the Hauran and in northern Jordan... This state of affairs will be the guarantee for peace and security in the area in the long run, and that aim is already within our reach today.[79]

While Israel was set to benefit considerably from a partitioning scenario, and its actions did support such an outcome, it was far from solely responsible. The vast majority of the war effort against the Syrian government, from information operations to funding, training, arming and motivating insurgent groups, and finally creating the 'safe zones,' had been carried out by the Western Bloc countries and their regional client states in the Gulf and Turkey. Israel's smaller responsibility reflected its more limited involvement.

In early 2016 Israeli Defence Minister Moshe Ya'alon notably again highlighted the likelihood of a partitioning scenario, stating that Syria would not return to its pre-war position as a unified state and would be divided into small warring enclaves.[80] "We should realise that we are going to see enclaves – 'Alawistan,' 'Syrian Kurdistan,' 'Syrian Druzistan.' They might cooperate or fight each other," he predicted.[81] General Director of Israeli Intelligence, Ram Ben-Barak, referred to a partitioning scenario not only as a likely outcome, but as "the only possible solution" to the conflict. "I believe that in the end, Syria must be divided into regions controlled by whoever is there; Alawites rule their regions, and Sunnis rule theirs," he stated.[82] The Washington-based Middle East Institute would similarly call explicitly for the partitioning of Syria into spheres of influence – this time granting Russia responsibility for government-controlled areas on the condition that President Assad was removed from power, and splitting the other two thirds of the country between the U.S. and Turkey.[83] Former U.S. general and CIA director David Petraeus stated to much the same effect that it was "increasingly appearing likely that Syria may not be able to be put back together again," highlighting that a de-facto partition along sectarian lines was likely.[84] The benefits for the West, Turkey and Israel were clear given their decades long histories of conflict with a unified nationalist Syria which had stood in the path of all three parties' designs for the region. Western and allied support for the insurgency, and subsequent creation of 'safe zones,' would be key to realising the outcome of an eventual partitioning.

## Russia's Swift and Decisive Expedition Changes the Syrian War

How Damascus' adversaries planned for the war effort against Syria to proceed in the final quarter of 2015 and into the Obama administration's final year will likely never be known. A no-fly zone over various safe zones could be gradually expanded to cover more and more of the country, and eventually to facilitate limited airstrikes against Syrian combat jets on the ground while the massive flow of funds, recruits and arms to Al Nusra and other insurgent groups continued. Syria, Iran, North Korea and their non-state supporters were by this point too thinly stretched to mount much of a response, and likely would have been unable to oppose the creation of the first safe zones on Syrian soil. As it was, however, Syria's oldest defence partner Russia, which since the collapse of the Soviet Union had had a largely ambiguous stance towards Damascus' security, committed to its first military intervention outside the territory of the former USSR since the 1980s. In doing so, it turned the tide of the war decisively in favour of the Syrian government.

In late August 2015 Russia began low key deployments of warplanes, T-90 battle tanks, artillery and several hundred personnel to Khmeimim Airport in Syria's Latakia governate.[85] From that time cargo planes carrying military equipment and building supplies began arriving frequently, with housing for approximately 1500 personnel constructed, defences improved, the runway re-laid and a new aircraft control tower built. It was later reported that a treaty had been signed between Russia and Syria on August 26 stipulating conditions for use of Khmeimim Airport, which would soon be known as Khmeimim Airbase and serve as the heart of Russian military operations in the theatre.[86] Russian Air Force spokesman Colonel Igor Klimov would later elaborate regarding this process: "A system of engineering, technical, and other support has been created at the Khmeimim Airbase. Dozens of facilities for the field infrastructure were set up quickly, including refuelling points, warehouses, field kitchens, and a bakery."[87] Work to transform the modest airport into a major military facility continued into September, and Russia would set up a joint information centre alongside Syria, Iran and Iraq to coordinate operations – with Hezbollah unofficially also joining either at this stage or soon afterwards.[88] Facilities were protected by modern T-90 tanks, BTR-82 armoured vehicles and Russian marines from the Black Sea Fleet. The marines were veterans of the Crimean campaign a year before and soon saw action ambushing and neutralising jihadist militants threatening Khmeimim before the end of the month.[89]

Unlike the Western and Turkish military presences on Syrian soil, which lacked either UN authorisation or the permission of the Syrian government meaning they were illegal, Russia had received Syrian permission to deploy its forces. According to some sources, this had been specifically requested by Damascus in July. Other reports indicate that Iranian Quds Force Major General Qasem Soleimani had personally visited Moscow that month and laid out plans for a coordinated counteroffensive between the SAA and its partners and the Russian Military to reverse the tide of the war against the insurgency, which were agreed to by both Damascus and Moscow.[90] Soleimani was considered the second most powerful man in Iran only to Supreme Leader Ali Khamenei, and is widely credited by Israeli, Iranian and Western analysts with having conveyed to Russian policymakers[ii] the seriousness of the situation in Syria and helped persuade them to take military action to decisively turn the tide.[91] While the exact nature of Russia's decision making process regarding its intervention in Syria are uncertain, the urgency conveyed by both Syrian and Iranian requests for assistance and by advocates of intervention within Russia itself reflected both the looming threat of direct intervention by hostile states to establish safe zones and no-fly zones in Syria, and months of mounting and very serious battlefield losses.

On September 30 a Russian three-star general arrived at the U.S. Embassy in Baghdad and informed the Americans that Russian airstrikes on specific insurgent targets in Syria were set to begin imminently, and that any U.S. forces present in the targeted areas must leave immediately.[92] Although there was a risk that U.S. special forces embedded with militant groups could be present in some of the targeted areas the warning, which caught Washington on the back foot, also served as a formal announcement that Russia would begin an air campaign later that day. Russian air

---

ii  According to Hassan Nasrallah, Soleimani had received a two-hour audience with Russian President Vladimir Putin where he explained the military situation on the ground in Syria in detail and showed how limited Russian support could turn the tide of the war, after which Putin, who had previously been undecided, agreed to commit to a Russian intervention. ('Interview with Hassan Nasrallah,' *Al Mayadeen Programs*, December 27, 2020.)

strikes against insurgent positions were particularly vigorous in their initial stages, and benefitted from fresh pilots, sophisticated aircraft and access to considerable quantities of precision guided air-to-ground weapons of which the Syrian Air Force had barely had any. With an abundance of fuel, spare parts and other supplies, and without the shortage of trained pilots which had become a serious issue for Syria after the Cold War, the small contingent of around three dozen Russian combat jets could conduct airstrikes at a far greater rate and do much more damage than the entire Syrian Air Force had been able to. Insurgent positions across the country were targeted, with strikes in the first 48 hours engaging militants in Homs and Hama, Raqqa and Deir ez-Zor with groups such as IS, Al Nusra, the jihadist Army of Conquest and others taking substantial losses.[93]

When the Russian Air Force first joined the war it was notably made as public and dramatic as possible by the country's media outlets, as well as those owned by Iran, Hezbollah and Syria itself, with definitive signs that the former superpower was fully committing to supporting Damascus seen as a remedy to the fast faltering morale of the Syrian Arab Army. Although they often had significant battlefield impacts, the subsequent deployments of Russian warships, heavy bombers and even an aircraft carrier over the following months were also intended largely for dramatic effect in order to boost Syrian morale, intimidate the insurgents and their backers, and ultimately reverse the highly unfavourable psychological dynamic of the war. Russian combat aircraft involved in the first round of attacks included 12 Su-24M and 4 Su-34 strike fighters, 12 Su-25 attack jets, 4 Su-30SM multirole fighters and 12 Mi-24P attack helicopters. The presence of just four of the powerful new Su-30 jets, the very first to arrive in Syria, was described by British analysts as having "immediately changed the balance of power over Syria and the Eastern Mediterranean," with the fighters notably armed with air-to-air missiles which sent a strong signal to Damascus' state adversaries.[94] The arrival of Russian aircraft had been met with an escort of Syrian MiG-29A jets, the country's newest fighters, which had been supplied by the USSR shortly before its collapse, and their welcoming gesture would be followed by multiple joint operations by the two air forces.[95] A surge in supplies of Russian parts and munitions to the Syrian Air Force notably accompanied the Russian intervention, possibly supplied free of charge as a cost effective means of complementing its own air campaign, which allowed the Syrian Air Force to increase its rate of air strikes by 40% in October.[96]

The Russian Air Force carried out 20 combat missions in its first day of operations in Syria on September 30, flying aircraft almost continuously, and would maintain this very high tempo over the coming weeks.[97] Russia's new Su-34 strike fighters, which had only entered service in March the previous year, had arrived in Syria just one day before military operations began.[98] Arguably the most important of the deployed aircraft, the jets were widely considered the world's most capable strike fighters, and having been designed to strike heavily defended targets across the European continent from bases in Russia their high endurances allowed them to carry very heavy weapons payloads when operating in the much smaller Syrian theatre.[99] Two of the Su-34's first targets were an Islamic State headquarters building in the Idlib governate[100] and a fortified bunker in the Hama governate,[101] with the jets using specialised penetrative bombs to neutralise hardened targets.[102] Russian state media subsequently referred to the new aircraft as the "ultimate ISIL-crushing machine,"[103] and eight more would be deployed to Khmeimim Airbase three weeks later on November 20 to further escalate the air campaign. These were accompanied by a full squadron of Su-27SM3 air superiority fighters.[104]

Western media reports highlighted the fact that many of the insurgent groups being targeted were receiving CIA backing,[105] leading to widespread allusions to a proxy war as Russia again found itself bombing CIA-backed Islamists to protect a strategic partner as it had in Afghanistan in the 1980s. Indeed, the chairman of the Senate Armed Forces Committee, John McCain, who had met with insurgent leaders in Syria two years prior near the Turkish border,[106] would not only call the conflict a proxy war but also advocate drastic escalation. This included increased arms supplies to the insurgents and creation of a no-fly zone to impede

Syrian and Russian air operations.[107] The *New York Times* reported that shortly after the beginning of Russian operations, insurgent forces quickly began to receive large quantities of American anti-tank weapons. "We get what we ask for in a very short time," one commander of an insurgent group interviewed by the *Times* stated regarding U.S. arms provided, with another stating that Russian intervention had led to a very significant increase in arms supplies from Western states. "We can get as much as we need and whenever we need them. Just fill in the numbers," he said. "U.S. weaponry is turning Syria into proxy war with Russia," the *Times* summarised, highlighting that insurgents had also increasingly requested supplies of surface-to-air missiles which was something Turkey appeared particularly eager to provide.[108] Alongside Western parties, Western-aligned Gulf Arab states would also step up arms supplies to insurgent groups to counter the Russian intervention.[109]

When the U.S. announced a month after the Russian intervention that it would deploy additional special forces personnel to "train, advise and assist" insurgent groups in the field, the Russian Foreign Ministry warned that this posed a risk of escalation to an effective proxy war.[110] While the presence of American troops on Syrian soil was illegal, the U.S. move to disperse American personnel among insurgents so shortly after the Russian bombing campaign began appeared to be intended to provide cover for these groups, since the Russian Air Force was expected to avoid targeting areas where Americans were present in order to avoid risking an incident if they were killed.

Although the air campaign was portrayed by Russian officials[111] and state media as the country "going to war with ISIS,"[112] the most immediate goal of Russia's military intervention was widely seen in the West to be pre-empting Western designs to undermine the Syrian state through imposition of illegal no-fly zones and safe zones. Indeed, according to a senior European diplomat interviewed by the *Financial Times* in the first week of August, the Russian military intervention was seen as a direct response to Western plans for "enforcing no-fly zones, safe zones," which were imminently to be put into effect when the Russian Air

Force began its campaign.[113] Research analyst at the Royal United Services Institute, Justin Bronk, assessed regarding the impact the Russian intervention would have on the future of Western operations in Syria:

> The Russian forces now in place make it very, very obvious that any kind of no-fly zone on the Libyan model imposed by the U.S. and allies is now impossible, unless the coalition is actually willing to shoot down Russian aircraft... The Russians are not playing ball at deconfliction – they are just saying, 'keep out of our way.' The coalition's operations in Syria will be vastly more complex from a risk assessment point of view and from a mission-planning point of view.[114]

NATO's supreme military commander in Europe, U.S. General Phillip Breedlove, warned in the final week of September that the Western powers were "worried about another A2/AD [anti-access area denial] bubble being created in the eastern Mediterranean." Through the deployment of a range of advanced aerial warfare and anti-shipping systems, Russia could effectively deny Western military aircraft and warships access to strategically important territories much as had been done in Crimea in 2014.[115] The 'A2/AD bubble' would largely materialise with the deployment of Su-30SM and Su-27SM3 modern heavyweight fighters, two of the most capable in the Russian inventory for air-to-air combat, and with the deployment of the navy cruiser *Moskva* which was armed with an S-300F long range ship-to-air missiles with 64 vertical launchers and a powerful sensor suite. These assets represented only the beginnings of a Russian A2AD presence in Syria, the capabilities of which would be multiplied manifold from December.

Despite Russian intervention, there were still significant calls in the U.S., including from several presidential candidates such as Hillary Clinton, to impose a no-fly zone over at least some parts of Syrian territory.[116] Senator Lindsey Graham, a longstanding advocate of a no-fly zone, stressed that Russia was "walking over

Obama like a small child" and that more assertive policies in Syria were needed.[117] Governor Jeb Bush, a frontrunner in the election's early days and brother of the 43rd president, stressed that Syria was "a place where American leadership is desperately needed," pledging: "My first phone call would be to Vladimir [Putin], and I'd say to him, 'Listen, we're enforcing this no-fly zone... And I mean we're enforcing it against anyone, including you. So don't try me. Don't try me. 'Cause I'll do it.'"[118] New Jersey Governor Chris Christie highlighted that a no-fly zone was vital precisely because Russian forces had entered Syria "because we must make it crystal clear to Russia, they do not get to move into the Middle East" – supposedly an exclusive right of the Western powers.[119] Others in the American leadership issued multiple statements to much the same effect. President Obama himself however, focused keenly on East Asia where he would come close to initiating a much larger and more serious war against North Korea the following year,[120] opposed the idea of using U.S. forces to directly escalate hostilities in Syria.[121]

It was highly questionable how genuine calls for further illegal military action against Syria were now that Russian fighters were flying overhead, with Moscow having effectively pre-empted and blocked possible Western efforts to initiate further hostilities against the Syrian government. Research fellow at the Heritage Foundation Luke Coffey stated to this effect regarding proposals for imposing a no-fly zone in Syrian airspace: "It makes for a nice tweet, it sounds good, it sounds like a policy idea. But when you get down into the details, you see why it's not really going to work." Senior fellow at the Council on Foreign Relations Micah Zenko similarly commented: "If you want to be a politician and give the appearance of doing something... nothing looks more impressive and is more responsive than U.S. military power." He noted that advocating such a policy was a political play which "allows you to appear tough, and to appear different" from President Obama, but that implementation of such policy was "unserious on so many levels." The nature of the American political system meant that, to gain support from a public largely ignorant of the intricacies of foreign policy but looking for signs of strength and resolve, there was a strong incentive for politicians to make such statements.[122]

The majority of experts appeared to come to the same conclusion, with senior political scientist at the RAND Corporation, Karl P. Mueller, stressing that the Russian Air Force's involvement "changes things significantly," and that "initiating armed combat with the Russian Air Force is a very big thing" – something imposing a no-fly zone would inevitably require. "In the past, when there's been talk about no-fly zones, usually what people have meant is we're going to force the Syrian Air Force to stay on the ground. With the Russians in the country, that gets significantly more complicated, because now you're talking about grounding or shooting down Russian aircraft, or intimidating them into not flying, or not attacking certain targets in certain areas," he stated.[123] U.S. Director of National Intelligence James Clapper similarly warned that a consequence could be the Russian Air Force simply shooting down American aircraft over Syria.[124]

The Chairman of the Joint Chiefs of Staff, Marine General Joseph Dunford, would spell out the implications of what politicians from across the political spectrum, including the sitting State Secretary John Kerry and his predecessor Hillary Clinton, had been virulently advocating. While referring to Russia as "the most significant threat to our national interests," Dunford highlighted regarding calls for a no-fly zone that: "For now, for us to control all the airspace in Syria would require us to go to war with Syria and Russia. That's a pretty fundamental decision that certainly I'm not going to make."[125] What was seemingly obvious – that attempting to illegally enter UN member state's airspace, deny it the ability to use its own airspace, and shoot down any aircraft which refused these demands, was in fact both illegal and an act of war – apparently needed to be spelled out. The presence of the Russian Air Force thus played a critical strategic role, beyond the considerable tactical implications its bombing campaign would have.

## Hezbollah and Iran Join the Russian Counteroffensive

The tactical significance of the Russian air offensive came not only from the sheer firepower it brought to bear, but also because operations were conducted in close coordination with parties on the ground, including the Syrian Arab Army, the Quds Force and Hezbollah. While Iran's Quds Force had played a major role in planning the offensive in Moscow,[126] this included from the outset the intention for SAA and allied units to make advances on the ground with Iranian support and in coordination with Russian air support.

The Russian deployment at Khmeimim airbase in preparation for an air campaign was paired with a strengthening of the Iranian military presence in Syria in preparation for an advance on land in parallel to the air campaign. According to a Reuters report from the first week of October:

> In the biggest deployment of Iranian forces yet, sources told Reuters last week that hundreds of troops have arrived since late September to take part in a major ground offensive planned in the west and north-west. Around 3,000 fighters from the Iranian-backed Lebanese group Hezbollah have also mobilized for the battle, along with Syrian army troops, said one of the senior regional sources. The military intervention in Syria is set out in an agreement between Moscow and Tehran that says Russian air strikes will support ground operations by Iranian, Syrian and Lebanese Hezbollah forces, said one of the senior regional sources.[127]

According to an unnamed U.S. official quoted by Fox News regarding the counteroffensive launched in October 2015: "It has always been understood... that the Russians would provide the air force, and the Iranians would provide the ground force in Syria."[128] Alongside ground units, Iran had deployed C-130 aircraft purchased from the United States in the 1970s to drop supplies to besieged allied holdouts in northwest Syria. The aircraft were temporarily based at Damascus International Airport, which was the first time the Islamic Republic had ever deployed its air force from a facility outside its own territory. Iran would also deploy reconnaissance and attack drones to support its partners in Syria, but beyond this its contribution to the air campaign was restricted to refuelling Russian Su-25 attack jets in transit at airfields in Iran, and flying F-14 jets as escorts for Russian bombers crossing its territory as a purely symbolic show of solidarity.[129] Iran's lack of modern fighter aircraft which could have had a significant impact on operations, and the need to avoid escalation and the possibility of a serious air war with neighbouring Israel, are thought to have influenced its decision to focus on the ground campaign.

While Iran's Quds force had been involved in an advisory role since at least 2012, with Iranian officers reportedly even having been provided full command over SAA units in some cases,[130] its lack of a frontline combat role had been reflected in its low casualties, which were estimated by Western sources at under 100 by January 2015.[131] This would reportedly change from October that year with the Quds Fore involving itself more directly, albeit on a relatively conservative scale. Reuters reported on October 1, citing sources on the ground, that hundreds of Iranian troops had arrived in Syria in preparation to support a major ground offensive, alongside the SAA and Hezbollah.[132] Casualty numbers indicated that fighting in early October was particularly intense and that Iranian participation was considerable. Looking to senior officers alone: Qasem Soleimani's deputy, brigadier general Hossein Hamadani, was killed on October 7 by Islamic State forces in Aleppo,[133] with the deaths of two more senior Quds Force commanders, Hamid Mokhtarband and Farshad Hassounizadeh, reported four days later by Iranian media.[134]

As the most capable conventional force on the ground, Hezbollah cooperated closely with Russia with the two reportedly establishing joint operations rooms in Latakia and Damascus.[135] While well accustomed to defensive semi-guerrilla tactics and city fighting, which it had trained in extensively and had applied very effectively against Israel in 2006, fighting in Syria forced Hezbollah to prepare for and operate in a number of new roles.

This provided it with experience in offensive manoeuvre warfare, mountain assault, and fighting under friendly rather than enemy air superiority. Hezbollah would gain greater operational flexibility in Syria and critical combat experience, which was repeatedly highlighted by both Western and Israeli analysts as a major long-term threat to Israeli and allied interests.[136]

A Hezbollah officer speaking anonymously to U.S. media under the pseudonym 'Commander Bakr' elaborated in 2017 regarding the nature of the Hezbollah-Russian partnership, particularly after September 2015: "We are strategic allies in the Middle East right now – the Russians are our allies and give us weapons... Without their air force we can't advance and they couldn't give us air support without our information from the ground." Highlighting close cooperation between the two, he said that Russia relied on Hezbollah for intelligence and target selection and had worked more closely with the Lebanese militia since 2012, which was the year a new administration had taken power in Moscow and began to more actively support the Syrian government.[137] Russian Deputy Foreign Minister Mikhail Bogdanov had notably met with Hezbollah General Secretary Hassan Nasrallah in December 2014 for discussions regarding the situation in Syria.[138] Close cooperation with Russia in the Syrian theatre from September 2015 would provide Hezbollah with valuable new experience in how a very high end conventional military waged war, including in fields such as surveillance, reconnaissance, special operations tactics, operational planning and joint operations between air and ground units.

Russia, too, had taken a keen interest in how Hezbollah fought, and in its merger of guerrilla and conventional tactics and city fighting techniques. Speaking anonymously, a Hezbollah commander stationed in Aleppo confirmed close cooperation with Russia in the theatre and that Russian officers at times accompanied Hezbollah units to observe them in combat. "Our relationship with the Russians is better than excellent... In some parts of Aleppo, Russian officers are present. They go to strategic areas overlooking the battlefield and watch Hezbollah engage with rebel forces and carry out reconnaissance missions. Sometimes they film these operations." He continued "The Russians are impressed with the way we fight; how we handle our weapons; our tactics and our esprit de corps... When the Russians see Hezbollah on the battlefield, they stop, talk to us, and show respect for our work. They do not have the same opinion of the Syrian army units." [139]

Hezbollah's origins as a revolutionary resistance group against foreign occupation, rather than a national military, had a profound ideological influence which largely facilitated its high morale, spirit of self-sacrifice, and emphasis on high combat readiness. While this gave it much in common with the Korean People's Army, it set it apart from the armed forces of Syria, Russia and Iran. Not only were there significant ideological and foundational similarities between Hezbollah and North Korea, but also a direct and profound Korean influence on the organisation since its formation in the 1980s. Much of Hezbollah's central leadership, including Secretary General Nasrallah, Security and Intelligence chief Ibrahim Akil and head of counter-espionage operations Mustapha Badreddine, were trained in Korea, and the militia's intelligence sharing, command structures and security apparatus continued to closely reflect this influence. Two generations of Hezbollah's special forces and officer corps were also Korean trained.[140] Israeli experts thus described Hezbollah as "a defensive guerrilla force organized along North Korean lines," [141] with its 2006 war effort having relied heavily on both a Korean-constructed underground bunker and tunnel network, mirroring that on the North Korean border with South Korea,[142] and on assistance from Korean advisers.[143] The effectiveness of Hezbollah's tight security network, its emphasis on use of complex and often extremely deep underground tunnel and bunker networks, and its subsequent deployment of vast arsenals of rocket artillery and ballistic missiles, many North Korean sourced,[144] all closely reflected both influences and active assistance from the East Asian state.

## Retaking Syria Under Russian Protection

The Syrian Arab Army and its partners on the ground would launch a major counteroffensive to reverse territorial losses of previous years on October 7 – a week after the Russian air campaign had begun. The offensive sought to push back simultaneously against Islamic State forces in the east and against other militant groups to the West, and would begin to gain ground in the Aleppo, Latakia, Idlib and Hama regions simultaneously. The Russian Navy fired the opening shots of the offensive on the first morning, launching 26 3M-14T Kalibr cruise missiles against insurgent targets from a light frigate and corvettes in the Caspian Sea. This was the first time Russia had demonstrated this very long range precision strike capability, and was the first combat use of any variant of the Kalibr missile which travelled over 1,500km crossing both Iranian and Iraqi airspace to reach its targets.[145] Referred to by Western analysts as "an amazingly capable new weapon,"[146] the Kalibr strikes were seen as a troubling game changer in Western military circles and a sign of the rapid progress Russia had made in modernising its conventional forces and recovering from over 15 years of post-Cold War military decline.[147] Only the United States and Britain had ever conducted such missile strikes in the past, but none had ever shown a capability to do so from tiny corvette-sized ships. This was a capability no Western navy had, which made the Russian strikes particularly outstanding.[148]

The Russian Air Force conducted at least 40 air strikes on the first day of the assault alone, which rose to over 60 daily in the next two days,[149] and in the coming weeks would at times reach almost 90 strikes a day.[150] Their precision and efficiency was highlighted as a major source of concern in the West, and contrasted sharply with Russia's military performances in prior wars with Western backed forces in Chechnya and Georgia.[151] Indeed, a report for the European Council on Foreign Relations highlighted that the Russian Military's performance in Syria showed that its military transformation in the period after the Georgian War was the most rapid since the 1930s, when the country had first industrialised.[152] Russian night fighting, damage assessment, logistical capabilities and its ability to launch expeditionary forces were also major surprises to Western analysts, which were perceived with much concern.[153]

With this considerable firepower now targeting their adversaries from the air and sea, the SAA and its allies focused their ground assault on an area straddling the northern Hama governate and the southern Idlib governate, where insurgents held high ground that threatened positions in the vital coastal areas. Al Nusra bore the brunt of the attacks, leading to widespread criticisms in the West that Russia was only claiming to target Islamic State, but the campaign it was supporting was primarily targeting the Turkish,[154] Gulf,[155] Israeli,[156] and CIA-backed[157] Al Qaeda-linked group. The Russian campaign was in fact targeting a wide range of insurgent groups, some overtly Western backed and others covertly supported by the Americans and Europeans or their regional allies. Considering that supporting armed militants to overthrow a foreign government, especially militants with connections to UN-recognised terrorist organisations, was effectively an act of war, Russia was within its rights to attack any militants it saw fit so long as it had Damascus' permission.

By October 8 the SAA had succeeded in pushing 40km into the Hama governate, while making significant but slower gains on other fronts. Russia claimed the following day to have struck 60 Islamic State targets, killing approximately 300 militants, while also destroying the headquarters of the Liwa Al Haqq jihadist group in Raqqa which, given the tempo of operations, were believable claims.[158] On October 14 an unnamed U.S. intelligence official lamented that up to 150 CIA-backed insurgents had been killed in deliberate Russian airstrikes, stating in what was widely interpreted as a warning regarding the possible provision of anti-aircraft weapons to jihadist elements: "Putin might not look so tough if a Russian helicopter were downed or some Russian soldiers captured... In the modern age of social media, one captured Russian soldier paraded by extremists could shock the Russian population."[159] This came amid ongoing appeals from insurgents for provision of handheld surface-to-air missiles.[160] With arms transfers between even the most 'moderate' insurgent groups and radical insurgents such as Al Nusra[161] and Islamic State[162] well known at the time through both sales and defections, however, doing so carried with it the considerable risk that such missiles could threaten civilian airliners across the world.[163] Despite this risk, an improved insurgent air defence capability would gradually begin to be observed as U.S. officials indicated over the following months a growing willingness to supply such weapons.[164]

One leading insurgent group operating in the Damascus sub-urbs, Jaysh Al Islam, resorted to a different means of guarding itself from air strikes, and on November 2 displayed civilians in cages who were being explicitly used as human shields.[165] Four days later a separate insurgent group, Ajnad Al Sham, would attempt to undermine the morale of the SAA by sharing pictures of a beheaded officer on Twitter and Facebook using derogatory labels.[166] The Syrian and allied offensive would gather further momentum and accelerate in November, with the most notable gain being the ending of a two year siege by Islamic State forces on Kuweires Airbase near Aleppo city.[167] Within four days the SAA had captured 408 square kilometres of territory in Southern Aleppo,[168] which was the largest gain it had made in the area in two years. By the end of the month government forces had come close to eliminating the insurgent presence in the Latakia governate on the west coast, where Khmeimim Airbase was located, and had neared the Aleppo-Latakia highway. The final insurgent bastion in the Latakia governorate, the town of Salma, was captured on January 12, ending concerns which had emerged the previous year that Russian military facilities and key ports and airfields located in the coastal province could come under threat.[169]

Russia sought to escalate the campaign against jihadist groups and demonstrate a number of new capabilities in mid-November, with a terror attack on October 31 connected to its presence in Syria providing an effective pretext. The attack saw a Russian A321 civilian airliner brought down over Egypt's Sinai Peninsula and 219 Russian tourists killed. After a popular coup had removed the Muslim Brotherhood from power in 2013, Egypt's new mili-tary-led government had expressed support for the Russian mili-tary intervention in Syria within its first week, which represented a tectonic shift from Cairo's staunchly pro-Western position of the previous 40 years.[170] With Egypt moving to begin free trade agreements with the Russian-led Eurasian Economic Union[171] and purchasing large quantities of high-end Russian arms,[172] and with both countries taking a strong stance against Western-backed Islamist groups, the attack was seen to be targeting both countries in response.

After accusing Islamic State of perpetrating the Sinai attack,[173] the ensuing round of Russian strikes against it beginning on November 17 appeared to be as much intended as a show of force aimed at NATO as it was as an attempt to retaliate against the insurgent group. The Air Force first dispatched a dozen Tu-22M bombers from airfields in Russia to drop gravity bombs on Raqqa and Deir ez-Zor, followed by heavier Tu-95 and Tu-160 strategic bombers equipped with long range cruise missiles.[174] These were two of the largest combat aircraft in the world, and the latter deployed Kh-101 radar evading cruise missiles which had extremely long ranges, very high precision, and could be armed with nuclear warheads.[175] The strike was the first time the Kh-101, the Tu-95 or the Tu-160 had ever been used in combat, and was followed three days later by the launch of 18 Kalibr cruise missiles against targets in Raqqa, Idlib and Aleppo from submarines and light corvettes in the Caspian Sea.[176] These were followed by multiple further bomber strikes over the following days, concluding in a raid on November 20 by two Tu-160 bombers which flew 1300km from an Arctic airbase, around Ireland and through the Straits of Gibraltar before firing cruise missiles over the Mediterranean and returning to Russia over Iraqi and Iranian airspace. The final strike caught NATO totally off guard and was initially widely dismissed by Western officials as phantastic before being confirmed several hours later.[177]

One of the most significant incidents during the Russian military intervention in Syria, and the first time in decades a Russian combat aircraft was shot down by an enemy fighter jet, was a Turkish Air Force attack on a Su-24M strike fighter operating near the Syrian-Turkish border. Turkey, which alongside Qatar appeared to be the most fervent regional supporter of the insurgency, had been particularly alarmed by the major shift the Russian military intervention was producing on the battlefield and on November 24 took direct action to show its displeasure. The means by which Turkey had been supporting the insurgency in Syria in many ways closely resembled Pakistani support for the insurgency Afghanistan thirty years prior, with both influenced by a similar combination of strategic and ideological motives. Thus, much as Pakistan had sent F-16 fighters into Afghanistan to engage Afghan and Soviet aircraft, so too did a Turkish F-16, the standard low cost lightweight fighter sold to America's export clients, take to the offensive to provide air support to Turkic jihadist militias operating in the border regions.

Turkey claimed the Su-24M it attacked had violated its airspace for 17 seconds, although this was hotly disputed with Russia publishing satellite data showing the jet was operating 1000 meters inside Syrian airspace.[178] Many observers, from the writers at *Forbes* to Iraqi Vice President Nouri Al Maliki, highlighted that the pretext for the Turkish attack on the basis of a minor airspace violation was highly unusual – particularly when considering that Turkish military aircraft almost daily conducted much more serious violations of Syrian, Iraqi and Greek airspace.[179] The Su-24M was purely a strike fighter, and was not only taken by surprise but also had no significant anti-aircraft weapons even for basic defence. The aircraft's two crew managed to eject, but the pilot was subsequently killed by Turkish-backed jihadists on the ground. Possibly acting on intelligence provided by Turkey, militants subsequently shot down a search and rescue helicopter and killed one of the marines sent by Russia to find the aircraft's weapons systems officer – the second crew member. The officer would eventually be rescued by Syrian and Hezbollah commandos, who carried out a joint operation through a nearby wooded area while the Russian Air Force agreed to provide a distraction with large scale bombardments of militant positions.[180]

Russian President Vladimir Putin issued a statement soon after the shootdown referring to it as a "stab in the back by terrorist accomplices."[181] Putin warned of serious consequences,[182] and Moscow quickly introduced a broad range of economic sanctions against Turkey which were particularly damaging for its agriculture and tourism sectors.[183] Russian Lieutenant General Sergey Rudskoi warned regarding the country's assets in Syria that "every target posing a potential threat will be destroyed,"[184] and almost immediately, on November 25, the Russian cruiser *Moskva* was deployed near the Syrian-Turkish maritime border.[185] The large warship was armed with the S-300F surface-to-air missile system and over five dozen associated launch cells, which provided missile coverage deep into Turkish territory and radar coverage considerably further still. The cruiser was replaced by its sister ship, the *Varyag,* in January 2016, ensuring that the Russian Navy's check on Turkish air power remained in place. With the Turkish Air Force fielding no post-1990s air to air missiles, and no modern fighters other than the F-16 which was the lightest and cheapest American fighter on offer, and these too being older variants no longer in production, the country was poorly placed to counter Russia on a peer level.[186]

The Su-24M shootdown incident was capitalised on by Russia as a further opportunity to massively escalate its military presence, specifically its aerial warfare assets, in the Syrian theatre. This was to the detriment not only of Turkish interests, but also those of other Syrian adversaries which operated illegally on the country's territory including the Western powers and Israel. By November 26 the deployment of a full unit of S-400 (NATO reporting SA-21) surface to air missile systems to Syria's Latakia governate was under way,[187] closely followed by a second.[188] These systems had powerful sensor suites and electronic warfare countermeasures designed to counter the Western Bloc's most advanced stealth aircraft such as the F-22 Raptor, and were capable of intercepting manoeuvrable hypersonic missiles at long ranges.[189] The deployment left the air fleets of regional powers such as Turkey and Israel, which relied on much less capable fighter aircraft than those the S-400 was designed to counter, in a poor position to engage them. Each S-400 could engage up to 80 targets simultaneously with up to 160 missiles.[190] The S-400s were complemented by the S-300V4 (NATO reporting SA-23), a newer air defence system with many of the same features but a higher mobility and superior capabilities against cruise missiles.[191] Both had an engagement range of 400km,[192] giving them coverage from Latakia over most of Syria and much of Turkey, and a detection range against large aircraft of around 600km.[193] Under the cover of these air defences, the Russian Air Force would deliver further punishment to Turkey by heavily bombarding militant positions in the immediate border areas and escalating attacks on their supply routes, many of which led to Turkey.

It is no exaggeration to say that the deployment of Russia's most advanced air defence systems, which even compared to the latest Chinese and American systems had several very significant performance advantages, would cast a long shadow over the remainder of the conflict. It multiplied manifold the anti-aircraft firepower Russia deployed to watch over the theatre and provided an extremely high degree of situational awareness across most of Syria. These would be complemented by a range of other assets including Pantsir-S1/S2 and BuK-M2 (NATO reporting SA-17) short and medium range air defence systems, 3K55 Bastion anti-ship cruise missile systems and, later on, even Iskander ballistic missiles. While many had hoped that Russia's deployment of these assets would end illegal air attacks against Syrian government forces, Russia made clear that they were deployed exclusively for the protection of its own assets in the region. Nevertheless, having such a formidable capability deterred any party from again threatening Russian forces from the air, which in turn allowed Russia to intervene a number of times to block third party attacks on Syrian government forces. Overall, however, Russia's military intervention remained focused on counterinsurgency and self-defence, and while it heavily bombarded their proxies it would not immediately attempt to directly confront other state actors operating in Syria.

On November 30 Russia announced that its Su-34 strike fighters in Syria had begun flying combat missions while armed with air-to-air missiles, with images released shortly afterwards confirming that this had been implemented.[194] Within a month the Russian Air Force had deployed A-50 airborne early warning and control aircraft, informally known as 'flying radars,' to monitor NATO and Israeli aircraft across the Syrian theatre and beyond. If necessary these could be used to guide friendly anti-aircraft missiles to their targets with greater precision.[195]

This was followed in January by the first deployments of Su-35 jets, Russia's prime fighter for air-to-air combat which had entered service alongside the Su-34 in 2014.[196] The Su-35 was, according to some U.S. reports, more capable than any American fighter other than the F-22 – a design fielded exclusively by the U.S. Air Force – and would have several run-ins with the elite American aircraft during its time in Syria.[197] As noted by Tim Ripley, correspondent for *Jane's Defence Weekly*, other than the F-22, the Su-35 and Su-30SM were "more than a match for anything else flying around the Middle East" – which at the time included many of the most advanced Western fighters such as the F-16E, F-15SA, Eurofighter and F-18E jets.[198] The deployment also marked the debut of the R-77 active radar guided air-to-air missile in Russian service, with the missiles used to equip the Su-35s.[199] The R-77 had far superior capabilities to the much older missiles relied on by the Turkish Air Force, and comparable ones to the AIM-120C missiles used by U.S. and Israeli fighter units. The Su-35 built on the already formidable air and air defence contingent in place and allowed Russia to test its new high end aircraft in combat conditions, provide pilots with combat experience, and give feedback to its defence sector to further refine the fighter's design.[200]

Deployment of modern aircraft and air defences had multiple significant advantages for Russia beyond its immediate interests in the Syrian conflict. As the only country able to permanently station powerful state of the art ground-based radar systems in Syria, Russia was able to closely observe the operations of other states' air units in the country. This had particularly significant implications when American fifth generation fighters, its newest jets with advanced stealth capabilities, began to deploy to the theatre. These included U.S. Air Force F-22 Raptors deploying from Al Dhafra Air Base in Abu Dhabi, and Israeli Air Force F-35A jets – a lighter and cheaper counterpart to the Raptor marketed for export. U.S. Air Force Lieutenant General VeraLinn Jamieson, the Deputy Chief of Staff for Intelligence, Surveillance and Reconnaissance, noted to this effect that F-22 operations over Syria "have really just been a treasure trove for them to see how we operate. Our adversaries are watching us, they're learning from us... Russia has gained invaluable insights and information with operating in a contested airspace alongside of us in Syria."[201] Israel notably attached special Luneberg Reflectors to its F-35s to mask their stealth profiles, preventing Russia from studying them, but this also meant they could not utilise their stealth capabilities in combat.[202]

Russia would gain further information on American air operations, apparently with a keen interest in its F-22 fighter, from run-ins between them and its own aircraft including multiple mock air battles. Elaborating on this, Russian Aerospace Forces Major Maksim Makolin noted: "When meeting our partners from the Western coalition in the air, we always found ourselves 'on their tails' as the pilots say, which means victory in a dogfight."[203] This claim was substantiated by images of thermal scans of an F-22 taken from the rear, reportedly by a Russian Su-35.[204] The ability to prove their high performances in an active war zone had the added effect of increasing foreign interest in purchasing high-end Russian weapons systems.[205]

Russia used its military deployment in Syria to test all of its major combat aircraft classes, and alongside the aircraft previously mentioned it would carry out strike missions with aircraft carrier based Su-33 and MiG-29K fighters in 2016. From September 2017 it deployed MiG-29SMT medium fighters for their first ever combat missions,[206] and from February 2018 advanced prototypes of its Su-57 next generation fighter carried out multiple brief combat tests in the theatre. Up to four of the jets were stationed at Khmeimim Airbase at any one time – around half of all combat capable prototypes Russia had.[207] Various helicopters, including the Mi-24P,[208] Mi-35[209] and new Ka-52[210] dedicated attack platforms and the Mi-8MTPR-1 electronic warfare platform,[211] similarly saw combat tests in the theatre, as did a number of new air launched missiles such as Kh-59KM2,[212] Kh-55[213] and the aforementioned Kh-101. Attempts to test new combat robots in the field notably proved far less successful.

Russia also used the Syrian campaign as an opportunity to provide its airmen and other officers with valuable first-hand combat experience.[214] As the *National Interest* noted three years later in November 2018: "Approximately two-thirds of Russian tactical air assets have rotated through Syria. General officers, staff officers, and rank-and-file soldiers have gained valuable lessons on modern warfare and developed new ideas to implement in future conflicts." The conflict allowed the Russian Military to compare its armaments to those of its NATO adversaries in the theatre, and to resolve multiple organizational and technical issues which only surface in real wartime situations. With Russian forces deployed on a much more conservative scale, the ability of NATO forces to make similar evaluations was more limited.

The benefit of experience in coalition management was also a significant boon for Russia, particularly given efforts to integrate its military more closely with strategic partners in Asia and North Africa.[215] With Islamist militants on the ground deploying significant numbers of surface-to-air missiles, the war provided an important 'trial by fire' for the various defence systems on Russian aircraft,[216] with none of its high-end heavyweight jets lost to surface fire by the time of writing.

Elaborating on the rotations of personnel from across the Russian armed forces for combat tours in Syria, Russian Defence Minister Sergei Shoigu stated in March 2017: "86% of the flight personnel received combat experience, including 75% of the long-range crews, 79% of the operational-tactical, 88% of the military transport and 89% of the army aviation." He further highlighted the key role played by Russian special forces in "eliminating the leaders of terrorists and destroying critical enemy targets," with these also having gained valuable experience from the war.[217] Regarding the intensity of Russian air strikes relative to those being carried out by Western forces against Islamic State targets, the Defence Minister highlighted that the although the Russian Air Force had, relative to NATO, deployed: "several times fewer planes, [it] performed three times as many sorties and inflicted four times as many missile and bomb strikes."[218] Regarding the benefits to Russia of establishing a military presence in Syria, Shoigu stated that not only were terrorist organizations dealt a serious blow and the collapse of the Syrian state averted, but also "a grouping of the Russian Armed Forces has been created on the southern flank of NATO, which has radically changed the strategic alignment of forces in the region."[219]

The Russian military intervention in Syria was historically significant not only for shaping the future of its Middle Eastern ally and preventing Damascus from suffering the same fate as Kabul had in 1992, but it was also as a turning point for how Russia fought wars and would assert its power overseas. Russia was a centuries old land power and traditionally, from the Great Northern War to the Second World War and wars in Afghanistan and Chechnya, the country had relied heavily on vast armies on the ground to achieve its foreign policy objectives. Russia had to an extent begun to emerge as a major sea power from the mid-1960s, under a naval modernisation program overseen by the famous Admiral Sergey Gorshkov, which allowed the Soviet Navy to influence conflicts from Libya[220] and Egypt[221] in the late 1960s to the Indian Ocean the following decade.[222] Construction of large and even medium sized surface ships had effectively ground to a halt after the Soviet Union's collapse, however, which partly explained why small frigates and corvettes as well as submarines were responsible for the Russian Navy's missile strikes in Syria.

The Syrian campaign's central focus on air power was thus unprecedented in Russian military history, and reflected a broader overall shift as conscript numbers continued to be cut and the emphasis on the army was reduced.[223] Indeed, there were more Soviet infantry deployed in East Germany alone in the final years of the Cold War than there were Russian infantry in the entire world in 2015 – a testament to the magnitude of the shift away from a large land force.[224] Russia would continue to rely heavily on aerial warfare assets as foreign policy tools, notably beginning to substitute port visits to friendly nations by large cruisers or destroyers with visits by Tu-160 intercontinental range bombers – which were similarly if not more iconic symbols of national power.[225] Russia would similarly rely heavily on deployment of aircraft and long range air defences to draw a hard line against Western attacks against neighbouring North Korea in 2017, rather than using warships which was more common.[226]

# Notes

1   Gordon, Michael R., 'U.S. Orders Syrian Embassy and Consulates to Suspend Operations,' *New York Times*, March 18, 2014.

2   Smith-Spark, Laura and Schwartz, Michael, 'Israel retaliates in Syria after roadside bomb attack against Israeli troops,' *CNN*, March 19, 2014.

3   Spencer, Richard, 'Syrian jet shot down by Turkey,' *The Telegraph*, March 23, 2014.

4   'Ukraine crisis: Transcript of leaked Nuland-Pyatt call,' *BBC News*, February 7, 2014.
    Milne, Seamus, 'It's not Russia that's pushed Ukraine to the brink of war,' *The Guardian*, April 30, 2014.

5    Black, J. and Johns, Michael, *The Return of the Cold War: Ukraine, the West and Russia*, London, Routledge, 2016.
    Mamlyuk, Boris N., 'The Ukraine Crisis, Cold War II, and International Law,' *The German Law Journal*, vol. 16, no. 3, 2015 (pp. 479–522).

6   'Указ Президента РФ от 6 августа 2014 г. N 560 "О применении отдельных специальных экономических мер в целях обеспечения безопасности Российской Федерации"' [Presidential Decree of 6 August 2014 N 560 "On the application of certain special economic measures to ensure the security of the Russian Federation"], *Kremlin.ru*, August 6, 2014.
    Herszenhorn, David S., 'Putin extends counter-sanctions against EU,' *Politico*, June 30, 2017.

7   Evans, Dominic, 'Rebels evacuated from Homs, cradle of Syrian uprising,' *Reuters*, May 7, 2014.

8   'Iraq government loses control of Fallujah,' *Al Jazeera*, January 4, 2014.

9   'Lex Runderkamp: 1300 Isis-soldaten onderweg naar Aleppo' [Lex Runderkamp: 1300 Isis soldiers on their way to Aleppo], *NOS News*, January 5, 2014.

10  Dziadosz, Alexander, 'Syrian rebels push Qaeda affiliate from northwest stronghold,' *Reuters*, January 17, 2014.

11  'ISIL recaptures Raqqa from Syria's rebels,' *Al Jazeera*, January 14, 2014.

12  Roggio, Bill, 'Free Syrian Army units ally with al Qaeda, reject Syrian National Coalition, and call for sharia,' *The Long War Journal*, September 26, 2013.

13  'Treasury Designates Al-Qa'ida Supporters in Qatar and Yemen,' *Treasury. gov*, December 18, 2013.

14  Mortada, Radwan, 'Syria: al-Nusra Front declares war on ISIS,' *Al Akhbar*, February 26, 2014.

15  Al-Salhy, Suadad and Arango, Tim, 'Sunni Militants Drive Iraqi Army Out of Mosul,' *New York Times*, June 10, 2014.

16  Cockburn, Patrick, 'ISIS Consolidates,' *London Review of Books*, vol. 36, no. 16, August 2014 (pp. 3–5).

17  'Islamic State expels rivals from Syria's Deir al-Zor: activists,' *Reuters*, July 14, 2014.

18  '"Hundreds killed" in Syrian gas field capture,' *Al Jazeera*, July 19, 2014.

19  'Syria election: Refugees vote in Lebanon and Jordan,' *BBC News*, May 28, 2014.

20  'ISIS take over Syria army base, behead soldiers: Activists,' *The Daily Star,* July 26, 2014.

21  Hubbard, Ben, 'ISIS Tightens Its Grip With Seizure of Air Base in Syria,' *New York Times,* August 24, 2014.

22  Phillips, Christopher, *The Battle For Syria: International Rivalry in the New Middle East,* New Haven, Yale University Press, 2016 (p. 199).

23  Mekhennet, Souad, 'The terrorists fighting us now? We just finished training them,' *Washington Post,* August 18, 2014.

24  'Islamic State Captures Major Air Base in Syria From Government,' *Wall Street Journal,* August 24, 2014.

25  'سقوط مطار الطبقة: كل الرقة خارج السيادة السورية!' [The fall of al-Tabqa airport: all of Raqqa is outside Syrian sovereignty!], الأخبار, August 25, 2014.

26  '"Strong & safe": Syrian Air Force pilots say veteran Soviet fighter jets are effective against jihad,' *RT,* November 7, 2015.

27  'Syrian army kills 18 foreign Islamic State fighters, including one American jihadist,' *Jerusalem Post,* September 5, 2014.

28  Cohen, Roger, 'The Diplomacy of Force,' *New York Times,* June 19, 2014.
    Niglia, Aalessandro and Sabaileh, Amer Al, *Countering Terrorism, Preventing Radicalization and Protecting Cultural Heritage,* Amsterdam, IOS Press, 2017 (p. 48).
    Al-Marashi, Ibrahim, 'Iraq in turmoil: The rise of "Syraq",' *Al Jazeera,* June 17, 2014.
    Escobar, Pepe, 'The partition of "Syraq",' *RT,* June 19, 2015.
    Bhadrakumar, M.K., 'U.S. Takes Israel's Advice for Unified "Syraq" Strategy,' *Asia Times,* January 13, 2019.

29  Doyle, Neil, 'ISIS militants "destroy Iraq/Syria border crossing",' *ITV News,* June 12, 2014.

30  'Iraq hits "jihadist convoy" in Syria,' *BBC News,* April 27, 2014.

31  'Iraq bombs ISIS "operations room" in Syria,' *Reuters,* August 16, 2018.

32  Tawfeeq, Mohammed and Yan, Holly and Carter, Chelsea J., 'Syrian warplanes reportedly strike in Iraq, killing 57 civilians,' *CNN,* June 26, 2014.

33  Gordon, Michael R. and Cooper, Helene, 'U.S. General Says Raiding Syria Is Key to Halting ISIS,' *New York Times,* August 21, 2014.

34  Landler, Mark, 'Despite ISIS Horror, Congress Is Wary of U.S. Military Expansion,' *New York Times,* August 21, 2014.

35  Entous, Adam and Barnes, Julian E. and Nissenbaum, Dion, 'U.S. Lays Groundwork for Syria Strike,' *Wall Street Journal,* August 25, 2014.

36  'Australia launches first air strikes inside Syria,' *BBC News,* September 10, 2015.

37  Rubin, Alissa J., 'Belgium's Anti-ISIS Airstrikes Expand From Iraq Into Syria,' *New York Times,* May 13, 2016.

38  'RAF killed "4,000 fighters in Iraq and Syria",' *BBC News,* March 7, 2019.

39  Stout, David, 'Canadian Jets Have Begun Bombing ISIS Targets in Syria,' *Time,* April 9, 2015.

40  'Danish Warplanes Drop First Bombs Against ISIS In Syria,' *NDTV,* August 5, 2016.

41 Black, Ian, 'France more active than rest of the west in tackling Syria,' *The Guardian*, November 14, 2015.

42 Rubin, Alissa J., 'Belgium's Anti-ISIS Airstrikes Expand From Iraq Into Syria,' *New York Times*, May 13, 2016.

43 Eisenhower, Dwight, *The White House Years: Mandate for Change, 1953–1956*, New York, Doubleday, 1963 (p. 340).

44 Dilnian, Ken, 'Despite bombing, Islamic State is no weaker than a year ago,' *Associated Press*, July 31, 2015.
Beauchamp, Scott, 'America's Misplaced Faith in Bombing Campaigns,' *The Atlantic*, January 30, 2016.
Welna, David, 'After A Year Of Bombing ISIS, U.S. Campaign Shows Just Limited Gains,' *NPR*, August 7, 2015.
Byman, Daniel L., 'Limited Airstrikes Against ISIS a Bad Idea,' *Brookings Institute*, June 19, 2014.

45 'Congress approves mission to train, arm Syrian rebels,' *Fox News*, September 18, 2014.

46 Wright, Austin and Ewing, Philip, 'Carter's unwelcome news: Only 60 Syrian rebels fit for training,' *Politico*, July 7, 2015.
'US to abandon training new Syria rebel groups,' *BBC News*, October 9, 2015.

47 Smith-Spark, Laura, 'Israel says it shot down Syrian warplane over Golan Heights,' *CNN*, September 23, 2014.

48 International Institute for Strategic Studies, *The Military Balance*, Volume 114, 2014 (p. 345).

49 'Double bombing kills at least 41 children at school in Syria,' *ABC News*, October 2, 2014.

50 Lefevre, Raphael and El Yassir, Ali, 'The Sham Legion: Syria's Moderate Islamists,' *Carnegie Middle East Center*, April 15, 2014.

51 'UN Peacekeepers Observe IDF Interacting with Al Nusra in Golan,' *UN Tribune*, December 4, 2014.

52 'Israeli jets "strike near Damascus" – Syrian army,' *BBC News*, December 7, 2014.

53 'Syria rebels, Nusra capture key southern town: monitor,' *Daily Star*, November 9, 2014.

54 Holmes, Oliver, 'Around 180 Syrian soldiers, jihadists reported killed in battle for base,' *Reuters*, December 16, 2014.

55 Ghannam, Mohammad, '2 Military Bases in Syria Fall to Rebels,' *New York Times*, December 15, 2014.

56 Banco, Erin, 'Syrian Rebels Merge Into "Levant Front," Gain Ground In North,' *International Business Times*, December 26, 2014.

57 Tol, Gönül, 'Frustrated Turkey Turns to Onetime Ally Saudi Arabia,' *Middle East Institute*, March 17, 2015.

58 'Rebel counter-attack, storms halt Aleppo offensive,' *The Daily Star*, February 19, 2015.
'Syria regime forces launch new Aleppo offensive,' *Yahoo News*, February 17, 2015.

59 Barnard, Anne, 'Syrian Rebels Regain Territory Near Aleppo,' *New York Times*, February 18, 2015.

60  'Syria conflict: Blast hits Aleppo intelligence HQ,' *BBC News,* March 4, 2015.

61  Gebelly, Maya, 'Blast, fierce clashes rock Syrian regime Aleppo base,' *Yahoo News,* April 13, 2015.

62  Bolton, Doug, 'Just days after seizing Palmyra, Isis massacres 400 people in the ancient city,' *The Independent,* May 25, 2015.

63  'Syria conflict: Regime jets carry out air raids around IS-controlled city of Palmyra, monitor says,' *ABC News,* May 25, 2015.

64  Spencer, Richard, 'Assad's forces defeated on roads north and south,' *The Telegraph,* June 9, 2015.

65  Samaan, Maher and Barnard, Anne, 'Assad, in rare admission, says Syria's army lacks manpower,' *New York Times,* July 26, 2015.

66  Casey, Nicholas, 'Two Israeli Soldiers Killed in Attack Claimed by Lebanon's Hezbollah,' *Wall Street Journal,* January 29, 2015.

67  'Israel admits its fire killed Spanish UN peacekeeper,' *BBC News,* April 7, 2015.

68  Samaha, Nour, 'Why Qalamoun matters for Hezbollah,' *Al Jazeera,* May 11, 2015.

69  Ibid.

70  'Hezbollah and Syrian army make gains in Qalamoun,' *Al Jazeera,* May 13, 2015.
    Schenker, David and Alrifai, Oula A., 'Hezbollah's Victory in Qalamoun: Winning the Battle, Losing the War,' *Washington Institute,* May 20, 2015.
    Samaha, Nour, 'Why Qalamoun matters for Hezbollah,' *Al Jazeera,* May 11, 2015.

71  Schenker, David and Alrifai, Oula A., 'Hezbollah's Victory in Qalamoun: Winning the Battle, Losing the War,' *Washington Institute,* May 20, 2015.

72  'Syria conflict: Rebels advance on Assad heartland,' *BBC News,* August 11, 2015.

73  'Islamic State battles Syrian rebel forces in Damascus,' *BBC News,* September 1, 2015.

74  'Turkey PM: Syria no-fly zone needed,' *BBC News,* August 11, 2015.

75  'Turkey says parts of Syria to become "safe zones",' *Al Jazeera,* July 25, 2015.

76  Barnard, Anne and Gordon, Michael R. and Schmitt, Eric, 'Turkey and U.S. Plan to Create Syria "Safe Zone" Free of ISIS,' *New York Times,* July 27, 2015.
    De Young, Karen and Sly, Liz, 'U.S.-Turkey deal aims to create de facto "safe zone" in northwest Syria,' *Washington Post,* July 26, 2015.

77  Jones, Sam and Khalaf, Roula and Solomon, Erika, 'Jordan to set up buffer zone in southern Syria,' *Financial Times,* June 29, 2015.

78  Hersh, Seymour M., 'The Redirection,' *The New Yorker,* February 26, 2007.

79  Yinon, Oded and Beck, Yoram,  'אסטראטגיה לישראל בשנות השמונים'
    [A Strategy for Israel in the 1980s], Kivunim, vol. 14 (pp. 49–59).

80  'Syria Will Not Return to What It Was Before the Civil War, Ya'alon Says,' *Haaretz,* February 13, 2016.

81  Williams, Dan, 'Israel pessimistic on Syria ceasefire, talks up sectarian partition,' *Reuters,* February 14, 2016.

82 'Senior Israeli officials urge sectarian partition of Syria,' *Press TV,* February 15, 2016.

83 Koleilat Khatib, Dania, 'Syria should be divided into three zones of foreign influence,' *Middle East Institute,* June 4, 2020.

84 Smith, Alexander and Neubert, Michele, 'Syria Civil War: Petraeus Says Country May Never Reunify,' *NBC News,* October 6, 2016.

85 Luhn, Alec, 'Russia sends artillery and tanks to Syria as part of continued military buildup,' *The Guardian,* September 14, 2015.

86 Договор о размещении авиагруппы РФ в САР заключен на бессрочный период [Agreement on the Deployment of RF Air Force Group is Concluded For a Limitless Period], *RIA Novosti,* January 14, 2016.

87 'Russian Su-34s Can Precisely Strike Any ISIL Ground Target in Syria,' *Sputnik,* October 2, 2010.

88 Lister, Tim, 'Why Russia is pressing the "accelerate" pedal in Syria,' *CNN,* October 15, 2015.

89 Eckel, Mike, 'Evidence Suggests Key Russian Brigade In Crimea Seizure Deploying To Syria,' *Radio Free Europe,* September 11, 2015.
'СМИ: Боевики ИГИЛ атаковали морскую пехоту РФ в Сирии' [Media: ISIS fighters attacked the Russian marines in Syria], *Свежий Ветер,* September 20, 2015.

90 Bassam, Laila and Perry, Tom, 'How Iranian general plotted out Syrian assault in Moscow,' *Reuters,* October 6, 2015.
Solomon, Jay and Dagher, Sam, 'Russia, Iran Seen Coordinating on Defense of Assad Regime in Syria,' *The Wall Street Journal,* September 21, 2015.
'Interview with Hassan Nasrallah,' *Al Mayadeen Programs*, December 27, 2020.

91 Ripley, Tim, *Operation Aleppo: Russia's War in Syria*, Lancaster, Telic-Herrick Publications, 2018 (pp. 24–25).
Bassam, Laila and Perry, Tom, 'How Iranian general plotted out Syrian assault in Moscow,' *Reuters,* October 6, 2015.

92 Buncombe, Andrew, 'Syria bombing: Russian three star general warned US officials "we request your people leave",' *The Independent,* September 30, 2015.

93 'Russia jets strike Islamic State in northern Syria: al-Mayadeen TV,' *Reuters,* October 1, 2015.

94 Ripley, Tim, *Operation Aleppo: Russia's War in Syria*, Lancaster, Telic-Herrick Publications, 2018 (p. 29).

95 Cenciotti, David, 'According to our sources, some (if not all) the Russian Air Force formations that arrived in Syria were "greeted" by Assad's Mig-29 Fulcrums,' *The Aviationist,* September 25, 2015.

96 Ripley, Tim, *Operation Aleppo: Russia's War in Syria*, Lancaster, Telic-Herrick Publications, 2018 (p. 27).

97 'Russian Airstrikes Destroy ISIL HQ in Syria,' *Sputnik,* October 1, 2015.
'Russian Air Force Carries Out 394 Sorties, Hits 731 Targets in Three Days,' *Sputnik*, November 20, 2015.

98 Cenciotti, David, 'Six Russian Su-34 Fullback bomber have just arrived in Syria. And this is the route they have likely flown to get there,' *The Aviationist,* September 29, 2015.

99 Larson, Caleb, 'How Is Russia's Su-34 Fighter-Bomber So Good?,' *National Interest,* July 18, 2020.

100 'Russian Su-34 Strike Fighters Combat ISIL in Syria,' *Sputnik,* October 1, 2015.

101 'Russian Jets Destroy ISIL Command Post, Bunker in Syria,' *Sputnik,* October 2, 2015.

102 'Russia Air Force Destroys ISIL Command Center, Underground Depot Near Raqqa,' *Sputnik,* October 3, 2015.

103 'Su-34: Russia's Ultimate ISIL-Crushing Machine,' *Sputnik,* September 30, 2015.

104 'Russian Air Force Carries Out 394 Sorties, Hits 731 Targets in Three Days,' *Sputnik,* November 20, 2015.

105 'Russian air strikes hit CIA-trained rebels, commander says,' *Reuters,* October 1, 2015.
Pengelly, Michael, 'John McCain says US is engaged in proxy war with Russia in Syria,' *The Guardian,* October 4, 2015.

106 Shalal-Esa, Andrea, 'Senator McCain met with rebels in Syria: spokesman,' *Reuters,* May 27, 2013.

107 Pengelly, Michael, 'John McCain says US is engaged in proxy war with Russia in Syria,' *The Guardian,* October 4, 2015.

108 'U.S. Weaponry Is Turning Syria Into Proxy War With Russia,' *New York Times,* October 12, 2015.

109 Gardner, Frank, 'Gulf Arabs "stepping up" arms supplies to Syrian rebels,' *BBC News,* October 8, 2015.

110 'Syria conflict: Russia warns US of "proxy war risk",' *BBC News,* October 31, 2015.

111 'Russian Parliament Grants Putin Right To Use Military In Syria,' *Radio Free Europe,* September 30, 2015.

112 'Russia goes to war with ISIS: Why and how?,' *RT,* September 30, 2015.

113 'Moscow scuppers US coalition plans for no-fly zone in Syria,' *Financial Times,* October 4, 2015.

114 Ibid.

115 Gibbons-Neff, Thomas, 'Top NATO general: Russians starting to build air defense bubble over Syria,' *Washington Post,* September 29, 2015.
Goşu, Armand, 'The Seizure of Crimea – A Game Changer for the Black Sea Region,' *Journal of Baltic Security,* vol. 1, issue 1, 2015 (pp. 37–46).

116 O'Toole, Molly, 'From Reset to Realpolitik, Clinton's New Hard Line on Moscow,' *Foreign Policy,* September 22, 2016.
Gearan, Anne, 'Clinton joins some Republicans in breaking with Obama on Syria no-fly zone,' *Washington Post,* October 2, 2015.

117 Catsimaditis, John, 'Lindsey Graham Speaks at the CATS Roundtable Radio Show,' *Catsimaditis,* October 19, 2015.

118 Flores, Reena, 'Jeb Bush weighs in on Afghan strategy, Donald Trump,' *CBS News,* October 16, 2015.

119 Kaplan, Rebecca, 'Obama up against growing support for a no-fly zone in Syria,' *CBS News,* October 5, 2015.

120 Abrams, A. B., *Immovable Object: North Korea's 70 Years At War with American Power,* Atlanta, Clarity Press, 2020 (pp. 408–409).

Johnson, Jesse, 'Obama weighed pre-emptive strike against North Korea after fifth nuclear blast and missile tests near Japan in 2016, Woodward book claims,' *Japan Times,* September 12, 2018.

'Obama mulled preemptive attack on N. Korea: book,' *Yonhap,* September 12, 2018.

Sanger, David E. and Broad, William J., 'Trump Inherits a Secret Cyberwar Against North Korean Missiles,' *New York Times,* March 4, 2017.

121 Kaplan, Thomas, 'G.O.P. Candidates Leading Charge in Call for Syrian No-Fly Zone,' *New York Times,* October 19, 2015.

122 Ibid.

123 Ibid.

124 Ackerman, Spencer, 'Why Clinton's plans for no-fly zones in Syria could provoke US-Russia conflict,' *The Guardian,* October 25, 2016.

125 O'Toole, Molly, 'From Reset to Realpolitik, Clinton's New Hard Line on Moscow,' *Foreign Policy,* September 22, 2016.

126 Bassam, Laila and Perry, Tom, 'How Iranian general plotted out Syrian assault in Moscow,' *Reuters,* October 6, 2015.

Solomon, Jay and Dagher, Sam, 'Russia, Iran Seen Coordinating on Defense of Assad Regime in Syria,' *The Wall Street Journal,* September 21, 2015.

127 Bassam, Laila and Perry, Tom, 'How Iranian general plotted out Syrian assault in Moscow,' *Reuters,* October 6, 2015.

128 'Iranian troops prepare to aid Russia with Syrian ground assault, officials say,' *Fox News,* October 1, 2015.

129 Cenciotti, David, 'Watch this video of Iranian F-14 Tomcats escorting a Russian Tu-95 bomber during air strike in Syria,' *The Aviationist,* November 20, 2015.

Rogoway, Tyler, 'New Video Of F-14 Tomcat Escorts And Cruise Missiles As Russia Steps Up Syria Offensive,' *Foxtrotalpha,* November 20, 2015.

130 'Iran is taking over Assad's fight in crucial parts of Syria,' *Business Insider,* June 8, 2015.

131 'Iran's evolving policy in Iraq and Syria,' *The Economist Intelligence Unit,* January 8, 2015.

132 Bassam, Laila, 'Assad allies, including Iranians, prepare ground attack in Syria: sources,' *Reuters,* October 1, 2015.

133 Dearden, Lizzie, 'Iranian commander Brigadier General Hossein Hamedani killed by Isis while advising Syrian regime,' *The Independent,* October 9, 2015.

134 'Two more Iranian commanders killed in Syria,' *Al Jazeera,* September 13, 2015.

135 Corbeil, Alexander, 'Hezbollah is Learning Russian,' *Carnegie Endowment for International Peace,* February 26, 2016.

Katz, Muni and Pollak, Nadav, 'Hezbollah's Russian Military Education in Syria,' *Washington Institute,* December 24, 2015.

136 Katz, Muni and Pollak, Nadav, 'Hezbollah's Russian Military Education in Syria,' *Washington Institute,* December 24, 2015.

137 Rosenfeld, Jesse, 'Russia Is Arming Hezbollah, Say Two of the Group's Field Commanders,' *The Daily Beast,* April 13, 2017.

138 'Russian deputy FM visits Hezbollah chief before departing Lebanon,' *The Daily Star*, December 7, 2014.

139 Corbeil, Alexander, 'Russia is Learning About Hezbollah,' *Carnegie Endowment for International Peace*, January 11, 2017.

140 Dilegge, Dave and Bunker, Robert J. and Keshavarz, Alma, *Iranian and Hezbollah Hybrid Warfare Activities: A Small Wars Journal Anthology*, Amazon Media, 2016 (p. 258).

141 'Hezbollah a North Korea-Type Guerilla Force,' *Intelligence Online*, no. 529, August 25–September 7, 2006.
'Hezbollah As A Strategic Arm of Iran,' *Intelligence and Terrorism Information Centre at the Centre for Special Studies*, September 8, 2006.

142 'Hezbollah a North Korea-Type Guerilla Force,' *Intelligence Online*, no. 529, August 25–September 7, 2006.
'Hezbollah As A Strategic Arm of Iran,' *Intelligence and Terrorism Information Centre at the Centre for Special Studies*, September 8, 2006.
Spyer, Jonathan, 'Behind the Axis: The North Korean Connection,' *Jerusalem Post*, May 22, 2010.

143 'North Koreans Assisted Hezbollah with Tunnel Construction,' *Terrorism Focus*, *The Jamestown Foundation*, vol. III, issue 30, August 1, 2006.

144 Binnie, Jeremy, 'IDF corroborates Hizbullah "Scud-D" claims,' *IHS Jane's 360*, March 2, 2015.
Harel, Amos and Issacharoff, Avi, 'Syria Is Shipping Scud Missiles to Hezbollah,' *Haaretz*, April 12, 2010.
Badran, Tom, *Hezbollah's Growing Threat Against U.S. National Security Interests in the Middle East*, Hearing before House Foreign Affairs Committee Subcommittee on Middle East and North Africa, Washington D. C., March 22, 2016.

145 '4 Russian warships launch 26 missiles against ISIS from Caspian Sea,' *RT*, October 7, 2015.

146 Lee Myers, Steven and Schmitt, Eric, 'Russian Military Uses Syria as Proving Ground, and West Takes Notice,' *New York Times*, October 14, 2015.

147 'War game changer: Russia's launch of dozens of precision cruise missiles at Syria from 1500km away surprises military analysts,' *South China Morning Post*, October 8, 2015.
Campbell, Garrett I., 'Russia's military is proving Western punditry wrong,' *Brookings Institute*, October 23, 2015.
Bodner, Matthew, 'Russia Shows Early Success, New Capabilities in Syria,' *Defense News*, October 18, 2015.

148 Harshaw, Tobin, 'Putin's Navy Sends a Shot Across Obama's Bow,' *Bloomberg*, October 16, 2015.
Campbell, Garrett I., 'Russia's military is proving Western punditry wrong,' *Brookings Institute*, October 23, 2015.
Cavas, Christopher P., 'Is Caspian Sea Fleet a Game-Changer?,' *Defense News*, October 11, 2015.

149 'Сирийская армия не оправдывает надежд российских военных,' [The Syrian army does not live up to the hopes of the Russian military], *Vedamosti*, October 12, 2015.

150 Lee Myers, Steven and Schmitt, Eric, 'Russian Military Uses Syria as Proving Ground, and West Takes Notice,' *New York Times,* October 14, 2015.

151 Antidze, Margarita and Stubbs, Jack, 'Before Syria, Russia struggled to land air strikes on target,' *Reuters,* October 26, 2015.
Peck, Michael, 'Welcome to Syria, the Russian Air Force's Battle Lab,' *National Interest,* September 7, 2019.
Weir, Fred, 'In Georgia, Russia saw its army's shortcomings,' *Christian Science Monitor,* October 10, 2008.

152 Gressel, Gustav, 'Russia's quiet military revolution and what it means for Europe,' *European Council on Foreign Relations,* October 13, 2015.

153 Lee Myers, Steven and Schmitt, Eric, 'Russian Military Uses Syria as Proving Ground, and West Takes Notice,' *New York Times,* October 14, 2015.

154 Sengupta, Kim, 'Turkey and Saudi Arabia alarm the West by backing Islamist extremists the Americans had bombed in Syria,' *The Independent,* May 12, 2015.
Bozkurt, Abdullah, 'US Defense Intelligence Agency says Turkey, Qatar supported al-Nusra Front,' *Nordic Monitor,* December 10, 2019.
Hersh, Seymour, 'Military to Military,' *London Review of Books,* vol. 38, no. 1, January 2016 (pp. 11–14).
Uslu, Emrullah, 'Jihadist Highway to Jihadist Haven: Turkey's Jihadi Policies and Western Security,' *Studies in Conflict & Terrorism,* vol. 39, no. 9, 2016 (pp. 781–802).
Tanis, Tolga, 'Al-Assad in his last six months, US estimates,' *Hürriyet Daily News,* January 17, 2013.

155 Sengupta, Kim, 'Turkey and Saudi Arabia alarm the West by backing Islamist extremists the Americans had bombed in Syria,' *The Independent,* May 12, 2015.
'Fighting, While Funding, Extremists,' *New York Times,* June 19, 2017.
Kirkpatrick, David D., 'Qatar's Support of Islamists Alienates Allies Near and Far,' *New York Times,* September 7, 2014.
Blair, David and Spencer, Richard, 'How Qatar is funding the rise of Islamist extremists,' *The Telegraph,* September 20, 2014.

156 'Israel Treats Wounded Syrians Along Frontier,' *ABC News,* February 16, 2013.
Sengupta, Kim, 'Priti Patel visited a hospital that treats jihadis – this is in Israel's interests, but not the UK's,' *The Independent,* November 9, 2017.
Cohen, Gili, 'Israel Halts Medical Treatment for Members of Syria's Nusra Front,' *Haaretz,* July 20, 2015.
Ravid, Barak, 'UN Reveals Israeli Links With Syrian Rebels,' *Haaretz,* April 10, 2018.
Tsurkov, Elizabeth, 'Israel's Deepening Involvement with Syria's Rebels,' *War on the Rocks,* February 14, 2018.
Tsurkov, Elizabeth, 'Inside Israel's Secret Program to Back Syrian Rebels,' *Foreign Policy,* September 6, 2018.

157 'Stop Arming Terrorists,' *Website of Congresswoman Tulsi Gabbard* (https://gabbard.house.gov/news/StopArmingTerrorists).

158 'Russian air force hits 60 Islamic State targets in Syria, kills 300 jihadists,' *Times of India,* October 9, 2015.
159 'Official: Russia "deliberately targeting" US-backed forces in Syria,' *Fox News,* October 14, 2015.
160 'U.S.-backed Syrian rebels appeal for antiaircraft missiles,' *Washington Post,* October 2, 2015.
161 Cafarella, Jennifer, 'Jabat al-Nusra in Syria,' *Institute for the Study of War,* December 2014.
162 Mekhennet, Souad, 'The terrorists fighting us now? We just finished training them,' *Washington Post,* August 18, 2014.
163 Coghlan, Tom, 'Terror fears as rebels in Syria brandish anti-aircraft missiles,' *The Times,* April 19, 2016.
Ashkenazi, Michael and Amuzu, Mawuena and Grebe, Jan and Kögler, Christof and Kösling, Marc, 'MANPADS: A Terrorist Threat to Civilian Aviation?,' *Bonn International Center for Conversion,* April 2020.
164 Groll, Elias, 'The U.S. Wants To Design Safer Anti-Aircraft Missiles for Syria's Rebels,' *Foreign Policy,* April 20, 2016.
Dillow, Clay, 'Wanted: A Safer Anti-Aircraft Missile for Syrian Rebels,' *Fortune,* April 22, 2016.
165 'Syrian rebels using caged civilian captives as "human shields",' *The Telegraph,* November 2, 2015.
166 Fadel, Leith, 'U.S. Backed Moderate Rebels Proudly Post Images of Beheaded Syrian Soldiers in Northern Hama,' *Al Masdar News,* November 6, 2015.
167 Fisk, Robert, 'Inside the air base that held out against Isis for three years – and the death and destruction that was left behind,' *The Independent,* July 4, 2016.
168 Fadel, Leith, 'Syrian Army and Hezbollah Capture 408 Square Kilometers of Territory in Southern Aleppo,' *Al-Masdar News,* November 17, 2015.
169 Corbeil, Alexander, 'Hezbollah is Learning Russian,' *Carnegie Endowment for International Peace,* February 26, 2016.
170 'Egypt supports Russia's military moves in Syria,' *Al Arabiya,* October 4, 2015.
171 Putz, Catherine, 'Will Egypt Join the Eurasian Economic Union?,' *The Diplomat,* June 3, 2015.
172 'Egypt's Most Capable Aerial Warfare Assets,' *Military Watch Magazine,* December 15, 2019.
'May's top stories: Egypt MiG-29 aircraft, A400M crash,' *Air Force Technology,* June 4, 2015.
173 'Russia plane crash: "Terror act" downed A321 over Egypt's Sinai,' *BBC News,* November 17, 2015.
174 'Russia's Bombers Tu-160, Tu-95MS Go Through Baptism of Fire in Syria,' *Sputnik,* November 18, 2015.
Cenciotti, David, 'Russia Has Deployed Its MiG-29SMT Multirole Combat Aircraft To Syria For The Very First Time,' *The Aviationist,* September 13, 2017.
175 Egozie, Arie, 'Russian bombers deploy Kh-101 cruise missiles over Syria,' *Flight Global,* November 19, 2015.

Larrinaga, Nicholas, 'Russia launches long-range air sorties into Syria,' *IHS Jane's Defence Weekly*, November 17, 2015.

176 'Russia's Newest Weapons Used in Syria for the First Time,' *Sputnik*, November 20, 2015.
'Russia Releases Video of Missile Strikes on ISIL Targets From Caspian,' *Sputnik*, November 20, 2015.

177 Ripley, Tim, *Operation Aleppo: Russia's War in Syria*, Lancaster, Telic-Herrick Publications, 2018 (pp. 50–51).

178 'Russian Defense Ministry Video Proves Su-24 Never Entered Turkish Airspace,' *Sputnik*, November 24, 2015.

179 'Turkey risks sparking world war, says Iraq's Maliki,' *Yahoo News*, November 26, 2015.
McCarthy, Niall, 'Turkish Jets Violated Greek Airspace Over 2,000 Times Last Year,' *Forbes*, November 26, 2015.
Ruano, Christopher, 'Turkey breaches airspace of Greece 40 times in a day, triggering mock dogfights between the NATO allies,' *Stars and Stripes*, December 18, 2019.

180 'One of 2 Russian pilots shot down by Turkey rescued, back to airbase in Syria,' *RT*, November 25, 2015.

181 'Turkey downing of Russia jet "stab in the back" – Putin,' *BBC News*, November 24, 2015.

182 'Turkey downs Russian warplane near Syria border, Putin warns of "serious consequences",' *Reuters*, November 23, 2015.

183 Girit, Selin, 'Turkey faces big losses as Russia sanctions bite,' *BBC News*, January 2, 2016.
'Russian sanctions hit Turkey's tourism industry,' *RT*, February 1, 2016.
'Russian sanctions hit Turkish farmers hard,' *Deutsche Welle*, January 19, 2016.

184 'One of 2 Russian pilots shot down by Turkey rescued, back to airbase in Syria,' *RT*, November 25, 2015.

185 'Putin's furious act of retaliation,' *News.com.au*, November 11, 2014.

186 International Institute for Strategic Studies, *The Military Balance*, Volume 115, 2015 (p. 146).

187 'Россия развернула в Сирии ЗРК С-400' [Russia deployed S-400 air defense system in Syria], *Kommersant*, November 26, 2016.

188 Binnie, Jeremy and O'Connor, Sean, 'Second Russian S-400 in Syria confirmed,' *IHS Jane's Defence Weekly*, September 29, 2017.

189 Gady, Franz-Stefan, 'China's S-400 Air Defense System Intercepts "Ballistic Target" 250 Kilometers Away,' *The Diplomat*, December 28, 2018.

190 'Turkey to get Russian S-400 missile system "in July" amid row over US jets,' *BBC News*, June 12, 2019.
Episkopos, Mark, 'Russia's S-400: The Air Defense System NATO Fears Most?,' *National Interest*, December 16, 2020.

191 'События в Сирии приняли противовоздушный оборот' [Events in Syria took an anti-aircraft turn], *Kommersant*, October 4, 2016.
'Russia's Latest Specialised Air Defences Deployed to Syria; The Effect

of the S-300V4 and S-400 Missile Systems on the Balance of Power in the Syrian Conflict,' *Military Watch Magazine,* June 20, 2017.

192 Gady, Franz-Stefan, 'Russia Sends New Missiles for S-400 Air Defense System to China,' *The Diplomat,* April 30, 2019.
Bryen, Stephen, 'Why Russia's S-400 Anti-Air System Is Deadlier Than You Think,' *National Interest,* November 9, 2019.
'Russia Demonstrates S-400's Hypersonic Ballistic Missile Interception Capability at Full 400km Range,' *Military Watch Magazine,* May 1, 2020.

193 Zohuri, Bahman, *Radar Energy Warfare and the Challenges of Stealth Technology,* Cham, Springer, 2020 (p. 195).

194 'Russian SU-34 jets fly with air-to-air missiles in Syria for self-defense for first time,' *Reuters,* November 30, 2015.

195 Ripley, Tim, 'Russia operates "Mainstay" AEW&Cs over Syria,' *Jane's Defence Weekly,* January 13, 2016.

196 'Russia redeployed advanced Su-35S fighter jets to Syria – defense ministry,' *TASS,* February 1, 2016.
de Larrinaga, Nicholas and O'Connor, Sean, 'Russia deploys Su-35S fighters to Syria,' *IHS Jane's Defence Weekly,* February 3, 2016.

197 Watts, Barry, 'The F-22 Program in Retrospect,' *Center for Strategic and Budgetary Assessments,* August 2009.

198 Ripley, Tim, *Operation Aleppo: Russia's War in Syria,* Lancaster, Telic-Herrick Publications, 2018 (p. 45).

199 Cenciotti, David, 'Russian Su-35S deployed to Syria carry the AA-12 Adder air-to-air missile: a significant threat to NATO planes,' *The Aviationist,* February 14, 2016.

200 'Russia to upgrade Su-35C fighter,' *TASS,* June 5, 2017.
Nikolsky, Alexey, 'В боевых действиях в Сирии участвовали практически все летчики российских ВКС' [Almost all the pilots of the Russian Aerospace Forces took part in the hostilities in Syria], *Vedomosti,* May 24, 2017.

201 'U.S. General Claims Russia has Obtained a "Treasure Trove" of Data on the F-22 Raptor; Have Operations in Syria Compromised America's Most Capable Fighter?,' *Military Watch Magazine,* January 6, 2018.
'Russia Now Has "Treasure Trove" of Info About Stealthy F-22s – US General,' *Sputnik,* January 5, 2018.

202 Cenciotti, David, 'Image Of Israeli F-35 Flying Off Beirut (With Radar Reflectors) As Well As More Details About The Adir's First Strikes Emerge,' *The Aviationist,* May 24, 2018.
McLaughlin, Andrew, 'F-35 makes combat debut,' *ADBR,* May 25, 2018.

203 'U.S. General Claims Russia has Obtained a "Treasure Trove" of Data on the F-22 Raptor; Have Operations in Syria Compromised America's Most Capable Fighter?,' *Military Watch Magazine,* January 6, 2018.
'Russia Now Has "Treasure Trove" of Info About Stealthy F-22s – US General,' *Sputnik,* January 5, 2018.

204 Mizokami, Kyle, 'Unexplained Images Shows F-22 Raptor in Russian Fighter's Sights,' *Popular Mechanics,* September 24, 2018.

205 'Syria campaign raises interest in Russian weapons and naval hardware,' *TASS,* October 19, 2016.

'Russia's Success in Syria Helping Sukhoi Warplanes Soar in Global Market,' *Sputnik,* April 12, 2017.

206 'Russia's upgraded MiG-29 fighter jets to test new aircraft armament in Syria,' *TASS,* December 7, 2017.
Cenciotti, David, 'Russia Has Deployed Its MiG-29SMT Multirole Combat Aircraft To Syria For The Very First Time,' *The Aviationist,* September 13, 2017.

207 'Su-57 Contingent in Syria Doubles in Size; How Deployments of Fifth Generation Fighters to Combat Zones Can Facilitate Major Export Successes for the Russian Platform,' *Military Watch Magazine,* February 25, 2018.

208 Johnson, Henry, 'This Helicopter Is Putin's Weapon of Choice in Syria,' *Foreign Policy,* October 14, 2015.

209 Cenciotti, David, 'Russian Mi-35M gunship helicopter appears in Syria for the first time,' *The Aviationist,* December 14, 2015.

210 Karnozov, Vladimir, 'Russian Kamov Ka-52 "Alligator" Sees Combat Debut in Syria,' *AIN Online,* April 5, 2016.
'Russian Ka-52 Choppers Make Combat Debut In Syria,' *Defense Bureau,* April 12, 2016.

211 'Russia Deploys Advanced Electronic Warfare Systems to Syria,' *Military Watch Magazine,* March 24, 2018.

212 'Russian Su-57 reportedly fired cutting-edge Kh-59Mk2 cruise missile during tests in Syria,' *Ru Aviation,* May 29, 2018.

213 Larrinaga, Nicholas, 'Russia launches long-range air sorties into Syria,' *IHS Jane's Defence Weekly,* November 17, 2015.

214 'Two thirds of Russian air force personnel received in-theater experience in Syria,' *TASS,* August 11, 2018.

215 'The War in Syria Has Been a Boon for the Russian Military,' *National Interest,* November 8, 2018.

216 Nikolsky, Alexey, 'В боевых действиях в Сирии участвовали практически все летчики российских ВКС' [Almost all the pilots of the Russian Aerospace Forces took part in the hostilities in Syria], *Vedomosti,* May 24, 2017.

217 Ibid.

218 Ibid.

219 Ibid.

220 Goldstein, Lyle J. and Zhukov, Yuri M., 'A Tale of Two Fleets – A Russian Perspective on the 1973 Naval Standoff in the Mediterranean,' *Naval War College Review,* vol. 57, no. 2, Spring 2004 (pp. 12–14).

221 Popov, V. I., 'Desantnye korabli osvaivayut Sredizemnoye more' [Landing ships are mastering the Mediterranean Sea], *Taifun,* February 2002 (p. 45).

222 'In 1971, the U.S. Navy Almost Fought the Soviets Over Bangladesh,' *War is Boring,* July 19, 2016.

223 'An introduction to Russia's military modernisation,' *International Institute for Strategic Studies,* September 30, 2020.
Goble, Paul, 'Despite Cut in Draft Numbers, Russia Unlikely to Have Fully Professional Army Soon,' *Jamestown Foundation,* October 5, 2017.

224 'The Russian Way of Warfare' [Presentation], *Center for Strategic and International Studies*, CSIS Headquarters, Washington D.C., April 9, 2018.

225 'A New Field of Power Projection; Venezuelan Air Force Jets Escort Russian Tu-160 Bombers in Caribbean Patrols,' *Military Watch Magazine*, December 13, 2018.

'Russian Nuclear Weapons in Venezuela; Outflanking U.S. Air Defences and the Full Implications of Tu-160 Bombers in Caracas,' *Military Watch Magazine*, December 12, 2018.

Trevithick, Joseph, 'Russian Tu-160 Bombers Touch Down In South Africa In Historic First-Ever African Visit,' *The Drive*, October 23, 2019.

226 Abrams, A. B., *Immovable Object: North Korea's 70 Years At War with American Power*, Atlanta, Clarity Press, 2020 (pp. 463–466).

'Vicious Circle: How to Prevent "Guam Missile Crisis" Between US, N Korea,' *Sputnik*, August 12, 2018.

'How to Interpret Russia's Growing Surface-to-Air Missile Deployments Near the North Korean Border,' *Military Watch Magazine*, August 11, 2017.

# Chapter 6

# Aleppo and a New Phase of the War

## Battlefield: Aleppo

The Syrian Arab Army and its partners made significant advances into insurgent-held territory throughout December 2015 and into the following year, with militant groups taking heavy losses. In the Hama and Latakia governates heavily armed insurgents inflicted significant losses on advancing SAA armour, but in both cases Russian airstrikes and particularly operations by low-flying Mi-24P attack helicopters proved decisive. The helicopter was a heavily enhanced variant of that which had been feared by Islamist insurgents in Afghanistan,[1] and demonstrated even higher survivability in Syria. They often flew at under 100 feet to bombard militant positions more precisely with rockets. The Mi-24P proved useful in mountains, fields and even in the streets of villages, providing a very considerable firepower boost to the SAA's offensive. Russian ground personnel notably set up arming and refuelling points next to runways to reduce the turn-around time for Mi-24s.[2]

In Homs the SAA faced an ongoing offensive by Islamic State forces which, having captured Palmyra in May, continued to gain ground until it captured the town of Mahin and pressed towards Sadad – a strategically located Christian settlement just ten kilometres from the Damascus-Homs highway. Russian assistance played a key role in turning back IS forces, flying supply missions from late October and shipping in modernized T-72 tanks with advanced explosive reactive amour and BMP-2 armoured personnel carriers (APCs) which were then turned over to the Syrian Army's 4th Mechanised Division. While Russian advisors were dispatched to the local SAA headquarters, Mi-24P attack helicopters were also deployed to the nearby Shayrat Airbase.[3] The morale boost from new Russian-suppled tanks and air support may well have done as much to bolster Syrian forces as the added firepower itself did, and low-level rocket attacks by helicopters paired with airstrikes from Su-24M jets took a heavy toll on Islamic State forces, allowing the SAA to take to the offensive. IS was conclusively driven out of Mahin on December 29, with the SAA soon afterwards approaching Palmyra. The final stages of the offensive saw Russian special forces dispatched to the frontlines to serve as forward air controllers, increasing the precision of airstrikes by providing valuable targeting data at a time when helicopters were flying 20–25 attack missions per day. Russian-operated TOS-1A rocket artillery systems and Mi-28 attack helicopters were also deployed to the front, with the former firing special thermobaric rounds which used vacuum explosives to release shock waves that could rupture the lungs of all fighters in a targeted area.[4] A decisive breakthrough was made on March 18, and Palmyra was captured by the end of the month.

In parallel to gains made in Hama, Homs and Latakia, progress would also be made in the southern governate of Daraa where insurgents were receiving considerable support from across the Jordanian border. On January 26, 2016, Hezbollah, Russian special forces and elite SAA units spearheaded an assault to recapture the town of Sheikh Maskeen, the most vital near-term objective in Daraa, which split insurgent positions in the governate into eastern and western pockets and cut them off from areas of the Damascus suburbs which were under insurgent control.

In the first week of February, in an apparent bid to encourage Washington to intervene more assertively against Damascus, Saudi Arabia and the United Arab Emirates both pledged to send ground troops into Syria if they had U.S. support.[5] Considering their initiation of a military campaign in Yemen in March the previous year with massive Western frontline support,[6] which was hardly considered a success,[7] and the underwhelming capabilities of both countries' ground forces,[8] it was hardly a credible threat. Syria's Foreign Ministry nevertheless threatened to send any soldiers from the Gulf States "home in wooden coffins" if they entered Syrian territory.[9] The Saudi-Emirati offensive never materialised, although massive financial and other material support from the Gulf would continue to play a major role in sustaining the insurgency in partnership with the Western powers, Turkey and Israel.

While the SAA was committed to multiple offensives simultaneously, by far the most significant in the twelve months following the Russian military intervention was the push to recapture Syria's largest city Aleppo. Commencing in mid-October 2015, a joint offensive by the Syrian Arab Army and all its major partners on the ground, including the Quds Force and its affiliated militias, Hezbollah, the Palestinian nationalist Liwa Al Quds militia,[i] and the Korean People's Army, would initiate the most significant campaign of the war. This was largely made possible by the massive provision of assistance by Iran and the full commitment of the Russian Military to a Syrian victory from September, with Russian air units, advisors and special forces all participating.[10] These forces established a joint central command at the massive Al Safirah military base south east of Aleppo city, which formerly housed some of Syria's most valuable strategic weapons, and they would coordinate closely and act in unison throughout the duration of the campaign. Iranian Quds Force Commander Qasem Soleimani personally worked from Al Safirah to oversee the campaign, which was spearheaded by elite special forces units of the SAA, Hezbollah and sometimes even Russia, and was the primary focus of Russian air operations. These were all indicators of the campaign's vital importance to irrevocably turning the tide of the war. While the number of Quds Force personnel involved

---

i   Palestinian secular nationalist groups were among Damascus' most ardent wartime supporters, with the Gailiee Forces, As-Saiqa and Liwa Al Quds being the foremost among Palestinian militias backing the SAA and the third of these playing a significant role in the Aleppo campaign. Palestinian Islamist group Hamas notably supported the insurgency due largely to its strong ideological affinity with militant groups such as Al Nusra. (Ripley, Tim, *Operation Aleppo: Russia's War in Syria*, Lancaster, Telic-Herrick Publications, 2018 (pp. 111–112).) ('Military wing of Hamas training Syrian rebels,' *Jerusalem Post*, April 5, 2013.)

in the offensive is unknown, up to 3,000 were helping to plan and execute campaigns across Syria,[11] which given the Aleppo campaign's significance and the presence of General Soleimani means a large Quds Force contingent was likely involved.

The initial phases of the offensive, which began as early as October 26, 2015, required the capture of the Aleppo countryside and surrounding villages before a push into the governate's capital could finally be pursued. SAA and allied forces made only slow gains in the first two weeks and faced multiple dug in and heavily armed insurgent groups. The American TOW anti-armour missile was deployed in particularly large numbers, having been provided by the CIA, Saudi Arabia and other hostile parties, and proved dangerous against older Syrian tanks. The wire guided missiles were delivered from a CIA-run depot in Turkey, and militants only received replacements if they were able to provide CIA operatives running the operation with video evidence that the weapons had been used in combat. This resulted in several video clips appearing online showing TOW missile strikes against Syrian targets.[12] According to insurgents contacted by *Reuters*, their forces had received new batches of TOW missiles specifically to counter the SAA offensive in late 2015, which resulted in significant losses during the army's advance. As Issa Al Turkmani, a commander of the Western backed Sultan Murad Islamist group, which was heavily involved in combatting the SAA in the early stages of the Aleppo offensive, stated: "We received more supplies of ammunition in greater quantities than before, including mortar bombs, rocket launchers and anti-tank [missiles]. We have received more new TOWs in the last few days ... We are well-stocked after these deliveries."[13]

A sizeable counterattack from October 26 by Islamic State, which was operating in eastern Aleppo, further slowed initial progress by Syrian government forces. Although the primary belligerents occupying the Aleppo governate were Al Qaeda linked groups, most notably the Al Nusra Front, the Syrian plan to encircle and besiege the Aleppo city required eliminating Islamic State forces in governate's eastern regions. From November 27 the Syrian Arab Army offensive focused on capturing villages from

Islamic State forces in eastern Aleppo that surrounded Kuweires Airbase, with operations culminating in the capture of the base itself on January 15.[14] The base would be used as a staging ground for the SAA to press further into Islamic State held territory in Eastern Aleppo, and over the next month Syrian forces would make considerable gains before capturing the Aleppo Thermal Power Plant on February 20.[15] The remaining Islamic State forces had either withdrawn from Aleppo or been neutralised by February 22, marking a successful end to the three month sub-campaign, which had been part of the broader campaign to retake Syria's largest city. The offensive had seen the Syrian Arab Army's Tiger Force spearhead the push into Islamic State territory, in close coordination with supporting Quds Force officers, Ba'athist militias and Russian aerial units which often exacted a heavy toll on IS positions with Su-25 'flying tank' close support jets.

While Islamic State was only a peripheral player in Aleppo, with its heartlands lying in Raqqa, Deir ez-Zor, and western Iraq, the SAA and its partners were simultaneously engaging the Al Nusra Front and its affiliates. These were the primary occupying force in the governate and were much better armed and entrenched in the area. The positions of Al Nusra and its many partner jihadist groups in Aleppo were notably relatively close to the Turkish border, which was their primary source of material support. A key early SAA target in western Aleppo was the M5 highway, which linked Aleppo city with the Jordanian border and the cites of Damascus, Homs and Hama, meaning it would be a major loss to the insurgents if it were to fall under government control.[16] Thus while the Tiger Forces were spearheading a push into Islamic State territory to the east, Quds Force backed militias were at the centre of an offensive in western Aleppo to seize the M5.[17] The offensive initially faltered with casualties running high, leading Iran to deploy Shahed 129 attack drones to provide air support which, although beneficial, were not decisive. The result was months of protracted engagements in the area.

Meanwhile in northern Aleppo, the third major battlefront in the campaign, a major but brief sub-campaign was initiated against insurgent forces on February 1 which sought to cut supply routes from Turkey to Aleppo city. This was one of the most important gains made in the campaign, and without fresh material support and combatants from Turkey the jihadist insurgents' ability to hold the city was seriously undermined. Where the SAA's Tiger Forces had spearheaded the assault on Islamic State to the east, Hezbollah special units, widely considered more capable still, spearheaded the northern offensive. Other militias, including the Iranian-trained Afghan Liwa Fatemiyoun, were also heavily involved.[18] Fighting was particularly intense in the offensive's first three days, with jihadists fighting under the Army of Conquest launching multiple counterattacks to slow the Hezbollah-led advance. This led to the loss of two brigadier generals, one from the SAA and one from the Quds Force, as well as 11 Quds force military advisors. On February 4 Hezbollah broke the three-year jihadist siege of the towns of Nubl and Zahraa, cutting the insurgents' primary supply route from the Turkish border and paving the way for a further push towards Aleppo city.[19]

Playing a pivotal role in the northern Aleppo offensive were armoured offensives by Syrian T-90 tanks and effective use of special forces by Hezbollah. The Syrian Arab Army reportedly began to field T-90 tanks for the first time in December 2015, after older models of this advanced platform were delivered from Russia in small numbers primarily for use in Aleppo. The new tanks' improved survivability over older Syrian armour was particularly valuable for breaking through enemy defences where large numbers of modern anti-tank weapons were deployed. The SAA had previously relied on the T-72 as its foremost tank, a design which had served since the Lebanon War of the 1980s, although the army had lacked access to modern variants such as the T-73B3 which meant assaults on militant positions with large numbers of modern anti-tank weapons had often been costly. Operational Syrian T-72s all dated back to the Soviet era, the most modern of which were the T-72M1 and T-72B which were models from 1982 and 1985 respectively. Syria otherwise relied heavily on the ageing T-55 tank to form the bulk of its armoured units, although these were prized for their low maintenance needs and operational costs and many had been extensively upgraded with features such as laser range finders and improved armour by North Korean technicians. The T-90A was a very welcome addition which would spearhead offensives against heavily fortified insurgent positions for the remainder of the war, with British reports indicating that T-72B3 tanks were also delivered from Russia which had many comparable features to the T-90.[20]

Russia notably provided extensive air support against militant targets during the northern Aleppo offensive,[21] carrying out 280 airstrikes on a very narrow front over three days from the start of the offensive on February 1.[22] This represented one of the first cases in which Hezbollah and the Russian Air Force worked closely together on the battlefield. Speaking anonymously, a Hezbollah commander stationed in Aleppo would later state, regarding the value of working alongside Russian forces: "The Russians bring precision to the battlefield. Syrian airstrikes have terrible aim and go off target; the Russians are reliable."[23] The pairing of Hezbollah's city fighting expertise with Russia's formidable precision strike capabilities was thus a lethal one. Some reports also indicated that Russian personnel operated the aforementioned TOS-1A thermobaric artillery system, an ideal asset for neutralising fortified or dug in militants, to provide fire support on the frontlines, although this remained unconfirmed.[24]

With all sub-campaigns in Aleppo succeeding despite significant insurgent resistance, due in no small part to extensive Russian air support which the jihadist forces could do little to counter, Al Nusra and its affiliates were encircled and effectively cut off from external support. The Syrian Arab Army built up its elite Tiger Force to a strength of around 4000 men in the area from mid-June and deployed at least two elite armoured brigades from 4th Mechanised Division, before completing the encirclement of Aleppo city on July 27 and announcing a three-month amnesty for insurgent fighters who laid down their arms. Two days later Russia announced the opening of corridors from insurgent-held areas of the city to allow civilians to escape before the SAA launched its final offensive. Insurgents would briefly break through the encirclement with a successful attack on the Ramousah district, although this was retaken by the SAA on September 8 which ensured jihadist positions remained isolated. Russian and Syrian air strikes escalated from September 22 preceding a Tiger Force-led push into Eastern Aleppo, which lasted until October 18. The insurgents were subsequently again given a chance to surrender with Russia announcing a unilateral three-day ceasefire from this time. Insurgents operating from near the Turkish border to the west of Aleppo city would attempt to break the siege of the governate's capital on October 28, dispatching over 1,200 combatants and over 120 vehicles including tanks and suicide bomber trucks,[ii] but with a Russian Spetsnaz special forces team holding the line and soon reinforced with massive air support and Syrian T-72 tanks the jihadist offensive quickly lost momentum.

The SAA and Hezbollah began to move into eastern Aleppo city (from here referred to simply as eastern Aleppo) in mid-November and continued to receive external support. This included North Korean artillery experts, who were deployed to oversee strikes on insurgent held areas, as well as advisers from the Quds Force and from Russia's own special forces who had limited combat roles of their own.[25] Elite Syrian Republican Guard units, which had been held back in Damascus until the penetration of eastern Aleppo began, were also dispatched to the frontlines alongside a full armoured brigade. The Quds Force trained militias, meanwhile, were primarily tasked with holding the outer siege line to prevent insurgents outside the city from breaking the encirclement. Russian air support for frontline operations went far beyond strikes by fighters, bombers and helicopters, with the provision of intelligence also proving critical. As Tim Ripley, correspondent for *Jane's Defence Weekly* and expert on Middle Eastern security, noted in reference to operations by Russian Forpost surveillance drones:

> The rapid advance by the Syrian army through Aleppo was possible because the rudimentary distribution of

---

ii Use of suicide bombers in explosive-laden trucks was a common and often effective tactic of jihadist insurgents throughout the war, with one of the trucks dispatched to Aleppo creating a mushroom cloud several hundred meters high which could be seen across the whole city.

UAV [unmanned aerial vehicle] video imagery was enough to give the Tiger Force a huge combat advantage. Its commanders had the confidence to advance small units of troops boldly into the opposition held enclave with minimal flank support. Thanks to their Russian eyes in the sky, the Syrian troops could be confident that there was little risk of being attacked unexpectedly.

He further highlighted that Russian forces provided a theatre-wide computer display showing the positions of aircraft across Syria, so SAA commanders would know when Russian aircraft would be providing support.[26] It is likely that Hezbollah units, which had joint command centres with the Russian military, received similar support.

The intelligence gathering capabilities of Forpost drones was complemented by the deployment of one of Russia's most capable surveillance aircraft, the Tupolev Tu-214R, which had been stationed at Khmeimim Airbase from February. The aircraft's radar could track all vehicle movement across a wide area of Syria in real time and produce three-dimensional radar pictures of tanks or other vehicles in areas of interest including those concealed in forested or urban environments. Its long-range thermal cameras provided further valuable intelligence on enemy positions, which was extremely useful for coordinating offensives and air strikes.[27]

Air strikes resumed on November 15, with the SAA capturing the northern part of the insurgent-held eastern Aleppo enclave and making rapid advances which shrunk insurgent-held territory by more than a third. A further swift day-long advance from the north from December 5 left insurgents trapped in a small southern portion of the enclave, placing 75% of eastern Aleppo including the historic Old City under SAA control. This was followed six days later by further Syrian advances, capturing Aleppo's Sheikh Saeed district and further tightening the noose around the remaining insurgents in the city's south east. With insurgents by this point having lost 90% of eastern Aleppo, they would agree on December 13 to abandon their remaining territory in exchange for guarantee of safe passage to the Idlib governate – the country's leading jihadist stronghold straddling the Turkish border.[28] Insurgents and those civilians who chose to go with them were evacuated by bus, giving up control of the remainder of the city peacefully with Russian soldiers and monitors from the Red Cross supervising the process. The evacuation was confirmed complete by the Red Cross on December 23.[29]

Although it was scarcely mentioned in Western media reports, jihadist forces occupying eastern Aleppo, the Al Nusra Front foremost among them, were widely accused of holding the population hostage and using them as human shields. This was an accusation levelled by the United Nations Syria Envoy, Staffan de Mistura, among others.[30] Mistura had also warned that other forms of insurgent misconduct towards civilians in Aleppo could amount to war crimes.[31] Syrian government reports that militants had ensured their 'human shields,' the civilian population of eastern Aleppo, did not leave through the humanitarian corridors by issuing threats of violence, were later confirmed both by a UN investigation and by interviews carried out with residents by foreign media.[32] Sharply contradicting the Western, Turkish and Gulf Arab narrative that the SAA was leading an offensive to subjugate Aleppo's population and end the rule of the purportedly virtuous and popular 'freedom fighters,' the response of the population to Aleppo's liberation showed their overwhelming support for the Syrian government.

British correspondent Tim Ripley described the ceasefire and evacuation deal as a "dual victory" for Damascus, stating: "Not only had the rebel fighters been driven from the city but the vast majority of the population of the enclave had opted to stay with the government troops." 110,000 elected to remain under Damascus' rule while 34,000 left with the insurgents, giving a clear sign of the state's popular legitimacy.[33] Social media was often "full of pictures and videos of thousands of civilians coming out of their homes to greet the advancing Syrian troops," he highlighted, and that "in the battle for hearts and minds of the Syrian population, the Damascus government had scored a major success. Although the western news media gave this aspect of the battle minimal coverage...the majority of the population of Aleppo 'voted with their feet' to back the Syrian government and not the rebels." Regarding Western coverage of the campaign and the conduct of the SAA towards civilians, Ripley noted that despite the fighting occurring in densely populated areas, the number of civilian casualties was "nowhere near some of the claims made during the height of the battle" and "significantly less than during the U.S.-led coalition forces operation to capture Mosul in Iraq, which was playing out at the same time as the Battle for Aleppo."[34] Western activists and human rights organisations, many with close ties to governments hostile to Damascus, tended to portray a brutal massacre where there was considerable evidence that none had taken place.

Ripley stated regarding the popularity of the returning SAA and the decision of the large majority to live in areas under government control:

> The framing of Syrian military operations in this way is difficult for many outside observers, particularly in the West, to appreciate. A near-continuous flow of international news reports, based largely on opposition or opposition-influenced sources, portrayed the population of eastern Aleppo as universally supporting the rebel fighters who controlled the enclave. The idea that a significant chunk of the enclave's population might welcome the Syrian army as 'liberators' just did not compute for many in the western media.

The Western powers would strongly protest operations to restore Syrian government control over the country's largest city, which ranged from repeated demands for Russia to cease its air campaign[35] and harsh criticisms at the United Nations to the raising of prospects for a no-fly zone by Western media outlets.[36] A European resolution at the United Nations Security Council in October notably demanded a no-fly zone over Aleppo to end both SAA and Russian air campaigns and provide a key respite to insurgent forces, although this was predictably vetoed by Moscow meaning any Western intervention would have to be unilateral and illegal. The tabling of the resolution appeared primarily intended to give Western powers a forum to criticise Russia and Syria and demonise their campaign against hardened jihadists on the ground.[37] Short of a direct military confrontation with Russia, however, there was little more the West could do beyond its provision of considerable material support, military advisors and favourable media coverage to the insurgency.

With Aleppo recaptured the economic and demographic core in western Syria was now decisively out of insurgent hands.[38] The offer to ferry militants and their families by bus to the Idlib governate had proven successful in the campaign's final stages, and a similar strategy was simultaneously attempted successfully in the Damascus suburbs. The imminent return of Aleppo to government control was seen as a major blow to the insurgency's already faltering morale, with Russian support in particular making a jihadist victory seem increasingly impossible. The Aleppo campaign thus had knock-on effects across the Syrian theatre, and increasingly led insurgents to withdraw or else seek to negotiate. The capture of Aleppo effectively ended hopes for an Afghanistan-style insurgent takeover of Syria, albeit one dominated far more by foreign fighters than the Afghan insurgency had been, and forced the Western powers and their regional partners to re-define their objectives.

## Russian Carrier Group and Ballistic Missiles Join the War

The period of the Aleppo offensive also saw an expansion of the Russian military presence in the Syrian theatre. This was widely interpreted by analysts as a Russian effort to gain combat experience with more of its new weapons systems, to further demoralise the insurgency with more conspicuous shows of force, and to accelerate counterinsurgency efforts to gain a stronger position before the new year. This final point was critical due to the expected inauguration of Hillary Clinton as U.S. president in January 2017, who was a hardliner promising a much more assertive stance against Damascus and Moscow. With the first six months of operations in Syria having cost only 66 billion roubles[39] ($464 million at the time) and taken the lives of only five servicemen, a rather incredible feat given the intensity of the fighting,

Russia had every incentive to continue to escalate. The country would deploy three new attack helicopter classes for combat operations, including the Ka-52, Mi-28 and Mi-35 which all played major roles in the Homs campaign against Islamic State forces in Palmyra. Also deployed was the Iskander hypersonic ballistic missile,[40] which had a sufficient range to strike targets across most of Syria and much of Turkey from launchers near Khmeimim Airbase.

In August the Russian Air Force made an unprecedented deployment of Tu-22M[41] bombers and Su-34[42] strike fighters respectively to the Hamedan and Nojeh air bases in western Iran, after having previously deployed aircraft exclusively from Russian territory and from Khmeimim Airbase in Syria. The short-lived deployment was seen in the West as an unprecedented sign of Russian-Iranian cooperation, and of an increasingly united front to protect their mutual ally Damascus.[43] Use of Iranian territory allowed Tu-22M bombers to strike targets in Syria with greater efficiency due to the shorter ranges required, and also allowed the Russian Air Force to bring more Su-34 jets to the theatre as the aircraft would have struggled to loiter in Syrian airspace if flying from bases in Russia itself.[iii] The deployment was the first of foreign aircraft to Iran since 1979, although sharp controversy in the Iranian parliament due to strict interpretations of the country's law against allowing foreign military bases on its territory (Article 146 of Iran's constitution) meant that bombers would be made to leave within two weeks.[44]

In November 2016 the only carrier strike group ever launched for combat by post-Soviet Russia began operations in Syria. The

---

iii Russia would later significantly expand Khmeimim Airbase itself to accommodate large bombers, and deployed its first Tu-22Ms there in May 2021. This provided a valuable staging ground for potential strikes on NATO territory from its southern underside, which was particularly valuable since the bulk of the Western alliance's defences in Europe were focused eastwards. The bombers drastically increased the amount of firepower the airbase could put out in the event of major war, with each Tu-22M able to employ over 23,500kg of munitions when on shorter ranged missions. (Newdick, Thomas, 'Russian Tu-22M3 Backfire Bombers Appear Over Syria And They Could Be There To Stay,' *The Drive,* May 24, 2021.)

Soviet Union had in the late 1980s begun construction of three Kuznetsov Class heavy aircraft carrying cruisers, closely followed by two Ulyanovsk Class supercarriers,[45] in an attempt to revolutionise its surface fleet's power projection capabilities. The state's untimely collapse, however, meant only one of these ships was ever completed domestically – a single Kuznetsov Class ship – which was subsequently converted into a carrier with cruise missiles removed to make space for more aircraft.[46] The Kuznetsov was unable to launch aircraft with high fuel and weapons loads as the Ulyanovsk would have[47] and as American supercarriers did,[48] and had a very limited endurance due to its lack of nuclear propulsion systems. With funds for modernisation remaining low, its air wing was unsophisticated compared to the latest Su-34 and Su-35 jets deployed to Khmeimim Airbase, and the poor state of the country's austere post-Soviet investment in carrier aviation would become evident in the eastern Mediterranean.

The imposing size of Russia's Kuznetsov Class carrier, which took several weeks to reach Syria, nonetheless served as something of a psychological weapon against militants held up in Aleppo in particular, whom it was hoped would be persuaded by the approaching carrier group to accept ceasefire terms and withdraw peacefully to Idlib. The carrier was accompanied by a Kirov Class battlecruiser, the largest class of surface combat ship in the world, as well as by two anti-submarine warfare ships and multiple small supporting vessels – an imposing albeit slightly old strike force from the late 1980s. The *Kuznetsov* and its escorts cause a storm in British media, as while NATO states were accustomed to sailing their own carriers and destroyers across the world the transit of a Russian carrier group through the English Channel was viewed with fear and indignation. The U.S. and Britain notably tried to impede the strike group's journey by preventing it from refuelling in Cueta in the western Mediterranean, although Algeria, a close defence partner of both Russia and Syria, would instead provide this service which totally undermined these Western efforts.[49]

Many of Russia's latest weapons systems had significant performance advantages over their Western counterparts, from the manoeuvrability and endurance of its fighter jets to the firepower of its attack helicopters, the speed of its anti-ship cruise missiles and the range and mobility of its air defence systems. In the field of carrier aviation, however, the Russian Navy was soundly out-matched. Shortly after beginning operations a MiG-29K fighter from the *Kuznetsov* fell off the deck due to problems with arresting gear on November 14,[50] followed on December 3 by the loss of a more costly Su-33 fighter in the same way,[51] which forced the Navy's air wing to deploy from an airstrip on land for some time. Fighters subsequently returned to deck and faced no further issues.

The carrier air wing took a heavy toll on jihadist positions and heavily targeted forces in the west of the Aleppo governate that were attempting to break the siege on Aleppo city from the outside. Four hundred and twenty sorties were carried out over two months, striking 1252 insurgent targets,[52] and to compensate for the carrier-based fighters' lack of modern targeting pods an effective kill chain was built using surveillance drones to allow the jets to effectively neutralise mobile targets. These operations were supported by a Tu-95 bomber strike from bases in the Arctic, with the aircraft flying around Scotland and Ireland and through the Straits of Gibraltar before launching Kh-101 cruise missiles – the first time these aircraft had used this weapon in combat.[53] This again caused a major stir in Britain, with the Defence Ministry denying the bombers had flown past the country, until this claim was thoroughly disproven by recordings. As British correspondent Tim Ripley noted regarding the coverup by British Defence Secretary Michael Fallon: "Apparently, Fallon had ordered the media blackout on the Russian bombers because he felt all the publicity that had been given the *Admiral Kuznetsov* had backfired and made the British government look weak."[54]

## After Aleppo

Aleppo's return to government control was a major turning point in the war, and seemed at the time to mark the beginning of the end of the conflict as the insurgency faltered across the country. Within six months the UN refugee agency reported that more than

440,000 internally displaced Syrians and around 31,000 of those who had fled abroad had now returned home, the majority to areas which the SAA had recently cleared of insurgents primarily in the Aleppo, Hama, Homs and Damascus governates. This indicated that the war was widely seen to be ending.[55]

Russia would play a significant role in stabilising Syria's largest city in the aftermath of the battle, and arguably more than any of its allies, it placed a heavy emphasis on winning the hearts and minds of the population as part of a long-term investment in stabilising the country. The 100,000 refugees who chose to escape to government-controlled territory from eastern Aleppo enclave, for example, saw a particularly stark contrast to their treatment under Syrian government and Russian protection than they had received when living under the insurgents. British journalist Vanessa Beeley, who visited the Jibreen refugee shelter where many of these were housed, reported the people there were receiving hot food 24/7 from a Russian field kitchen. After conducting several interviews, she stated regarding their perceptions: "They had been told by the people who held sway in the [eastern Aleppo] enclave that they would be killed by the 'Shia militia,' a lie that had made them afraid to leave... The people said Jibreen was heaven compared to life in East Aleppo. They could just not believe how well they were being treated – the Russians were hugely appreciated."[56] Russia was at the time shipping 2000 tons of humanitarian aid supplies to Syria per day.[57]

As part of its efforts to win popular support for the war effort, Russian senior officers were frequently seen across the country giving Syrian soldiers medals and visiting frontline units as a sign of support and to bolster morale. Russia would also make its first large scale ground force deployment to Syria after Aleppo's capture, stationing an estimated 400–600 military police, many of them of Muslim Chechen origin, to the city in a non-combat role to stabilise the city. These were accompanied by approximately 200 personnel deployed for de-mining operations and several dozen more medical personnel, none of whom were tasked with combat operations but all of whom played an important and highly sensitive role in restoring stability to Syria's largest city.

The senior commander of the Chechen military police, Numakhadjiev Ruslan Mukhashevich, notably stated when interviewed that a predominantly Muslim battalion had likely been chosen because they were "closer in faith and traditions" to the local population. He highlighted that the Syrian population's impression of Chechens had been extremely negative before the deployment due to the conduct of Chechen jihadists who fought among the insurgents. "To them a Chechen is a barbarian, a thief, a bandit. They speak very badly about the Chechens whom they saw before us," he stated, highlighting that good conduct towards locals by Chechen police officers was "a chance to rectify this error." "They are coming to greet us, hug us... they wouldn't know there are different Chechens if not for us," he concluded.[58] Again, winning over the public appeared to be a priority.

By the summer of 2017 four Russian military police battalions like the one in Aleppo had been stationed to monitor de-escalation zones across Syria in the wake of major advances by the SAA. Military policemen interviewed consistently appeared touched by the appreciation of the local population, with one stating: "The most memorable moment happened when we were handing out humanitarian aid. We could see it in their eyes, the people were very grateful, very happy. Some of them even learned a few words in Russian. And when the crowds were shouting, for real, 'love Russia, love Russi, thank you Russia.' That was really gratifying and something that every one of us will remember it for a long time."[59] Russian personnel deployed to Syria had many Arabic speakers among them and were under orders to connect with the population at cultural, linguistic and social levels and behave non-threateningly. They were seen attending music concerts, living in Syrian army camps and shopping in local bazaars, as part of an effective 'soft offensive' which was key to winning public opinion. The fact that all personnel deployed were professional contract soldiers, rather than reluctant conscripts, made this considerably easier.[60]

The Aleppo campaign was hardly the only major incident which took place in 2016 in the aftermath of the Russian military intervention, with the SAA's capture of Palmyra and much of Homs being other major gains. Efforts had also been made to reclaim the Damascus suburbs and much of the Hama governate and to use air power to erode the fighting capacities of insurgent groups across the country. While the SAA made significant gains on multiple fronts, the threat to Syrian sovereignty in the north-western border regions had seriously escalated as Turkey, which had long occupied the area through various proxy forces who were armed, trained and fed by Ankara, began a full-scale military operation on Syrian territory. Operation Euphrates Shield saw Turkish forces backed by insurgent auxiliaries push into the country for seven months from August 24, 2016, capturing 2,055 square kilometres of territory[61] and 230 villages,[62] while also significantly expanding the territory controlled by Turkish backed insurgents. Although this invasion weakened both the Islamic State and local Kurdish militias, it posed a much greater challenge to Damascus and its partners. While jihadists could be bombed and their towns and cities brought to siege, as had just been done in Aleppo and as the SAA was doing against Islamic State in Homs, an illegal military occupation by a NATO member state brought with it the risk of full-scale war if measures were taken to expel its presence.

September 2016 had also seen a major direct clash between Western and Syrian forces after the Syrian garrison at Deir ez-Zor, which had been besieged by Islamic State for two years and was increasingly losing ground, came under intensive bombardment from the air on September 17. U.S. Air Force A-10 Warthog attack jets, British MQ-9 Reaper attack drones, and F-16 and F-18 fighters from the Danish and Australian air forces respectively, all took part in the joint Western strike. The attack caused over 150 SAA casualties,[63] the majority of them deaths. While the perpetrators would claim it was accidental, Western analysts from the Atlantic Council, *Time* and other major papers highlighted that such air attacks near SAA positions, even if they were not targeting Syrian forces explicitly, were highly unusual if not unprecedented.[64] The foreign ministries of both Russia and Syria stated the attack was evidence that the U.S. was protecting and supporting the Islamic State,[65] while Syrian and Russian analysts speculated that it seemed to be well coordinated with an IS offensive to place further pressure on the Syrian garrison.⁶⁶ The fact that the U.S. officer at the hotline for emergency Russo-American communications in Syria was conveniently away from his desk for 27 minutes during the attack, after a Russian officer tried to contact him demanding the U.S. stop striking the SAA, hardly helped make the case that the attack was accidental.⁶⁷ The incident would be followed by three further direct attacks on Syrian forces by Western aircraft in the first half of 2017.⁶⁸

Closely coinciding with the end of the Aleppo campaign, Islamic State would also launch a major offensive in Homs in December and recaptured ground which it had lost in the first half of the year including Palmyra which was recaptured on December 11. A multi-pronged assault appeared to take the SAA and the Russians totally off guard, with over 4,000 militants backed by armoured units having been drawn from Raqqa and Deir ez-Zor,⁶⁹ which indicated that IS was prioritising reasserting control of Homs over its other objectives. The SAA and its partners were in a much stronger position to respond and push back against IS after Aleppo was secured, and prioritised this over combatting Al Nusra and its affiliates in Idlib near Turkey.

The threat to Syrian security was made all the more severe by the growing U.S. military presence in the north of the country, where American special forces backed by considerable air support had been deployed to back various militant groups under the banner of the Syrian Democratic Forces (SDF). This was a new coalition of Western-backed militia groups (see below) focused on taking territory from the Islamic State. For Damascus and its partners, this development made it imperative to take back central Syria from IS as quickly as possible. The more Islamic State territory taken by the U.S.-backed SDF, the more difficult it would be to reunify the country in the aftermath of the jihadist group's defeat, and the more likely it would be that the Western powers could seek to partition Syria by creating a Kosovo-type northern state under their protection. While the Islamic State's defeat in the long term was assured, a race had now begun between rival state actors to determine which could take and hold more of its territory the fastest.

In preparation for a counterassault to recapture Palmyra and subsequently push back further against IS forces in Homs, Syrian and Russian forces built up assets heavily around the large Tiyas Airbase a little over 100km from Palmyra. Islamic State forces had come close to capturing this key facility in December 2016, before being turned back with the assistance of Syrian Republican Guard reinforcements and Russian special forces. Units deployed included Russian operated TOS-1A thermobaric rocket artillery systems and 152mm heavy artillery guns, over 900 Syrian marines, two SAA armoured divisions, a mechanised infantry division, a desert commando regiment, and various local militia units. Elite Hezbollah and Tiger Forces units would also participate, with some Western sources alleging that Russian private military contractors fighting under the Wagner Group were also present and played a role in frontline fighting – although this was unconfirmed.[70]

With manpower remaining a major issue, Russian and Syrian forces had begun to work towards establishing a new all-volunteer formation known as the 5th Corps.[71] Unlike the four pre-war SAA corps, this would not be assigned a particular area of operations but was instead tasked with responding to threats across the country. A network of training bases began to be set up for the corps in late 2016, and it was provided with arms from the Russian Military's own surpluses including T-62M tanks and BMP-1 personnel carriers.[72] Although inferior to the higher end hardware such as T-90 tanks provided to the Tiger Force, these armaments were much easier to operate and maintain and still had an above average performance for the SAA's inventory. After its initial engagements the 5th Corps began receiving much more advanced T-72B3 tanks from Russia, as its capabilities continued to grow with experience which allowed it to absorb more advanced hardware. Extensive support for the 5th Corps specifically for offensive roles reflected Moscow's desire to accelerate the push against the jihadist group by helping the SAA to take ground faster. An estimated five 5th Corps brigades and several artillery units reinforced frontlines across Syria in the following months, with a mixed performance to be expected of a hastily assembled formation using relatively simple ageing hardware.

Further reinforced by over 1000 personnel from the 5th Corps, the SAA would launch an offensive on January 13, 2017, with the initial phases of the operation intended to drive IS forces back from around Tiyas Airbase. Russian Mi-28 and Ka-52 attack helicopters with advanced night fighting capabilities provided close air support while the air force contingent further away at Khmeimim launched multiple strikes. Fighting in desert areas where little cover was available left IS forces at a major disadvantage, with tanks and attack helicopters sweeping the area of any militant forces and facilitating a much faster advance. Syrian troops avoided close combat with IS militants, even at the expense of time, and relied heavily on rocket attacks to clear dug in forces. Jihadist forces were well motivated and proved surprisingly effective despite overwhelming material disadvantages, and five weeks into the campaign managed to kill four Russian advisors and wound two more in a single attack on February 16. This was the heaviest Russian loss of the war, and it was later confirmed that a Russian major general, Pyotr Milyukhin, was seriously wounded in the attack.[73]

After faltering in the initial week, the SAA made slow but steady progress over the next six. It concluded the campaign on March 2 after capturing 52 settlements and 1,702 square kilometres of territory, including Palmyra itself.[74] With some of the world's most capable offensive weapons systems deployed, namely Ka-52 and Mi-28 helicopters and TOS-1A artillery pieces, each one of which could be considered a game changer, and with IS having no air support and a massive inferiority in firepower on the ground, the jihadist group had not stood much of a chance. The second loss of Palmyra spelt the beginning of an accelerated decline of Islamic State, which was increasingly forced to retreat in future battles and to stage fewer counterattacks with supplies and morale declining fast. The Palmyra campaign's final stages had seen Russian special forces play a pivotal role in capturing the city. As well as operating in independent units, several special forces advisors were also embedded among SAA armoured and infantry units bolstering morale, providing key field guidance, and operating as forward air controllers to guide fighter and helicopter strikes. The campaign's success had depended particularly heavily on the Russian military.

Islamic State forces fleeing Palmyra were pursued eastwards, where they had entrenched themselves in nearby hills around the village of Arak. Russian special forces again played a significant role in neutralising jihadist defences, with some embedded among Republican Guard and 5th Corps forces, and others deploying as independent teams. The hills were cleared in early June, and the advance would continue into early August despite an attempted IS counterattack using armoured and artillery units.

Simultaneously to the battle at Palmyra, a second major struggle between the SAA and Islamic State was being waged at Deir ez-Zor where the jihadist group initiated a renewed assault closely coinciding with the beginning of the Palmyra offensive. With IS taking serious losses in both Iraq and Syria, taking the small but well-fortified SAA outpost at Deir ez-Zor had the potential to provide a much-needed boost to the jihadist group's war effort. Capturing this SAA holdout would provide IS with access to key road junctions, bridges and arms caches under SAA control, as well as improving jihadist morale. Deir ez-Zor by this stage had become one of the most prominent sieges in post-Second World War history, rivalled only by Dien Bien Phu in the French colonial war in Vietnam, with the SAA garrison having been encircled since 2013 and having taken heavy losses to the aforementioned Western air strike in September 2016. The garrison was receiving supplies only by air, and on maps appeared to be surrounded by vast seas of black representing IS-held territory which spanned far and wide across multiple governates.

A surprise IS offensive from January 14, 2017, cut the road between Deir ez-Zor's airbase and its main garrison and captured several points around the base, before attempting to capture strategic points including an overlooking mountain, the central Al Assad Hospital and a powerplant. With nowhere to run, and facing a brutal massacre if defeated, the SAA's garrison's 'victory or death' situation fuelled fierce resistance. The Russian Air Force launched Tu-22M bombers from its own territory to provide air support to the garrison at Deir ez-Zor from January 21, at least some of which were backed by Su-30 or Su-35 fighters,[75] while its surveillance drones overhead provided key intelligence to the Syrian Army. These were followed by supply drops using Mi-17 helicopters, and on February 17 Tu-95 bombers would place further pressure on IS forces by striking key targets in its self-proclaimed capital Raqqa.[76] U.S. media reported[iv] that Russia took the clashes at Deir ez-Zor as an opportunity to test its Iskander hypersonic ballistic missile system deployed at Khmeimim airbase, launching four missiles across the breadth of Syria from the west coast to strike Islamic State targets in the far eastern border region.[77] Missile strikes and air support allowed the SAA garrison to re-establish a defensive perimeter and take back many of the key sites lost to IS. Sustaining the holdout at Deir ez-Zor not only prevented a massacre, and sustained a major disruption for Islamic State, but it also preserved a potentially major asset for any future SAA push to retake eastern Syria from the insurgent group. Government forces' total recapture of Homs would pave the way for such an operation.

Also coinciding with the end of hostilities in Aleppo, the SAA and Hezbollah launched an offensive to capture the Wadi Barada valley near Damascus, which housed a valuable water spring, from jihadist groups including Al Nusra and Jaysh Al Islam. This target was prioritized due to the intentional pollution of the water supplies flowing from there to the capital by the insurgents.[78] With militants allegedly pouring diesel into the water from the Al Fija spring located in the valley, which was relied on heavily by Damascus' population, this made neutralizing their hold over Wadi Barada all the more urgent. The area was captured on January 29. The poisoning of water supplies was a sign of the insurgents' growing desperation, as was the assassination of the Syrian Army's chief negotiator after he held peace talks

---

iv Reports of Iskander use were later indirectly verified in a statement by Russian Deputy Prime Minister Yury Borisov, who said it had proven its effectiveness in combat in Syria. ('Russian Aviation in Syria Carried Out Up to 100 Sorties Per Day – Minister,' *Sputnik*, December 17, 2018.)

in the valley.[79]As had been the case in Aleppo, and increasingly elsewhere, the government used offers of safe passage to Idlib to minimise loss of life and clear the area of insurgents, which they were willing to accept when placed under enough military pressure. This was one of several major SAA gains made in the fight for the wider Damascus governate at the time.

## The Kurds' War and Western Boots on the Ground

The Russian military intervention in support of the Syrian government from September 2015, alongside a major escalation in Iranian military involvement in the conflict in coordination with Moscow, spelled the end of prospects for a jihadist takeover of the country. This had become clear to all serious observers after the swift and wholly unexpected capture of Aleppo and other major gains made against insurgents on all other fronts in 2016. Russia's military presence not only facilitated a fast pushback against Western, Turkish, Gulf Arab and Israeli backed militants, but also deterred the Western powers and their partners from providing insurgents with more direct protection by imposing no-fly zones or safe zones on Syrian soil. These factors combined strengthened an already prevailing trend, which was for the Western Bloc to seek to work more directly with parties other than jihadist groups to achieve its ends in the country. To this end closer ties were forged with ethno-nationalist paramilitary groups from Syria's Kurdish minority, which sought autonomy from Damascus and which had been active from the war's early stages defending Kurds from jihadist attacks.

The Kurdish ethnic minority was divided between four countries – Iran, Syria, Iraq and Turkey – with the populations in the latter two having historically been particularly politically active and frequently calling for autonomy or full separation. Support for Kurdish nationalist groups had long provided an effective means for parties hostile to a state with a Kurdish minority to undermine it, a notable example being Iranian, Israeli and U.S. efforts to do so in Iraq in the 1970s.[80] Iran did so again to undermine Baghdad during the Iran-Iraq war in the 1980s,[81] and Israel later cultivated relationships with such groups in Syria and Iran to collect intelligence on both countries.[82] Syria for its part had supported the Patriotic Union of Kurdistan (PUK), Iraq's Kurdish nationalist party, throughout the 1980s during a period of high tensions with Baghdad. Damascus had also supported Turkey's Kurdish nationalist party, the Kurdistan Workers' Party (PKK), and provided it with safe haven in its own Kurdish regions.[83] This support was withdrawn in 1998, at a time of improving relations with both Ankara and Baghdad, with disaffected Kurdish nationalists in Syria subsequently founding the Democratic Union Party (PYD) in 2003 in violation of Syrian law.

The PYD would notably take an independent stance after the outbreak of the Syrian conflict, criticising both the Syrian government and the opposition, and highlighting that the latter was acting as a proxy for Turkish interests in Syria and was opposed to Kurdish autonomy. Amid a growing threat posed by jihadist insurgents to Kurdish civilian areas in 2012, Kurdish nationalist groups formed a network of People's Protection Units (YPG) on the basis that a decline in the Syrian Arab Army's presence had left these areas vulnerable. The PYD quickly established itself as the leading Kurdish nationalist group in Syria, placing local militias under its control,[84] and showed increasingly separatist tendencies. This culminated in the announcement of an independent Kurdish government in northern Syria with a separate constitution – the Autonomous Administration of North and East Syria which was better known as the Rojova.

The Rojova's existence was not initially an existential threat to Damascus' position, with its resistance holding Gulf Arab and Turkish ambitions for a jihadist ruled Syria partly in check by denying the insurgency much of the territory of northern Syria which was protected by the YPG. The YPG would begin to see intensive combat in 2012 when the Al Nusra Front, which was receiving Turkish, Gulf, CIA and Israeli support, assaulted the Rojova. Al Nusra was later joined by another Al Qaeda affiliate, the Ghurbada Al Sham militia. The Battle of Ras Al Ayn was one of the larger engagements and saw the jihadists, including many Islamist militias fighting under the Free Syrian Army, decisively defeated after attempting to capture YPG held positions. The Syrian Air Force provided some limited support to Kurdish forces during the battle. Kurdish nationalist groups, committed to their own defence and increasingly seeing a common enemy with Damascus in the insurgency, were waging a parallel war for their own survival much as secularists, Ba'athists and members of all Syria's religious minorities were by supporting the Syrian Arab Army. The aggressive growth in the power of the Islamist insurgency threatened the eradication of all these groups – with Kurds being among the groups targeted for ethnic cleansing.[85]

Turkey in particular was opposed to the existence of the Rojova, and sought its subjugation as well as that of Damascus through massive support for radical jihadist groups. With Turkey's Kurdish minority denied autonomy domestically, many Kurdish nationalists moved from Turkey to the Rojova which led to close ties between it and the PKK.[86] The latter was listed as a far left terrorist organisation by Turkey, Israel, NATO and the EU. Rojova-PKK ties, and the threat of a Kurdish autonomous region on Turkey's border which could potentially inspire its own Kurdish minority to rebel, fuelled Ankara's hostility towards the Kurdish nationalist movement in Syria. Cross-border pan-Kurdish nationalism was seen by many Western and Turkish analysts to have contributed to mounting violence by the PKK in Turkey's southeast, particularly after talks between it and the Turkish government broke down in July 2015.[87] Turkey sought to counter this perceived threat by supporting jihadist groups which frequently launched attacks on both the Rojova and the Syrian government, with Islamist militants participating in the offensive at Ras Al Ayn notably admitting to receiving Turkish backing.[88] With Damascus unable to provide any significant support, the new self-declared Kurdish autonomous region was left isolated against a mounting jihadist threat, leading the Rojova to eventually turn to the United States for support.

U.S. policy regarding which groups it was willing to support in Syria was very far from consistent, and it was far from unheard of for separate jihadist militant groups supported by the Pentagon and CIA to go to war with one another.[89] The CIA's backing of Al

Qaeda linked groups,[90] and Washington's turning a blind eye to its allies' support for Islamic State,[91] were prominent examples. The only consistent factor between the various parties which received American backing was their lack of affiliation with the Syrian government or its partners. Washington was thus willing to work with the Rojova and its YPG militias to further its own objectives and gain a better foothold in Syria, particularly after Russian intervention in 2015 had made the defeat of Islamist militias appear inevitable. The U.S. would begin limited military cooperation with the YPG in 2014 with an initial focus on countering Islamic State. Kurdish militias, which included PKK units from Turkey, did the bulk of the fighting at the Battle of Kobani in response to Islamic State attempts to press into YPG-held territory. American backing came in the form of intensive airstrikes, with U.S. Air Force B-1B heavy bombers supported by F-15E strike fighters bringing considerable firepower which turned the tide of the battle.[92] While Western airstrikes against IS were generally seen to be ineffective and lacked the intensity needed to turn the tide against the jihadist group, particularly compared to those later carried out by Russia, in the case of Kobani and protecting the Kurdish autonomous region U.S. attacks were unusually intense. This indicated a strong American interest in preserving the Rojova.[93] The battle ended in mid-March 2016 with a YPG-led victory – the most intensive combat the Kurdish militias ever faced – and cemented ties between the Rojova and the U.S.[94] The common threat posed by Islamic State, and common partnership with the U.S., would also lead to a partial normalisation of relations between the Rojova and many of the Islamist militant groups fighting under the Free Syrian Army – although this was a truce of circumstantial necessity which was not expected to last.

The Rojova and its YPG militias proved to be the only major effective fighting force in Syria which was neither oriented towards radical jihadism nor aligned with the Syrian government. Despite Turkish objections and an ongoing Turkish commitment to the jihadist insurgency, which increasingly included embedding Turkish officers with Islamist militant units, the U.S. would increase support for the Rojova and deploy special forces to the Kurdish-held territory.[95] The YPG, however, had limited manpower for operations beyond the Kurdish territories, which conflicted with the Western imperative of occupying large parts of Syrian territory after pushing back Islamic State in order to deny them to the Syrian government. This and the U.S.' need to develop a more ethnically diverse force which could be presented as an alternative to the Syrian government led America to oversee the creation of the Syrian Democratic Forces (SDF) on October 11, 2015. This included both the Rojova's YPG militias and various Western sponsored Islamist non-Kurdish militias under a fighting force which was promised American material and support and was backed on the ground by U.S. special forces units. Unlike the Rojova, the SDF was openly hostile to Damascus.

While the SDF began as a predominantly Kurdish force, over 90% of new recruits were of Arab origin which resulted in a slow erosion of the Kurdish majority.[96] Western-backed Islamist and non-Kurdish groups joined the alliance at a considerable rate in 2016, including multiple former Free Syrian Army factions. Groups joining in the first quarter of 2016 alone included the Martyrs of Dam Brigade, the Martyr Qasim Areef Battalion, the Soldiers of the Two Holy Mosques Brigade – a former part of the Army of Mujaheddeen, and the Jihad in the Path of God Brigade. There was little hiding their strongly Islamist orientation, as the militant groups' names reflected. The Islamist contingent would continue to grow, and under the umbrella of the Syrian Democratic Forces, the U.S. had an effective cover to press into Syrian territory. The forceful conscription of local men in captured areas by the SDF as it expanded its territory would only further reduce the force's Kurdish composition.[97] Syrian Democratic Forces conscription efforts would include recruitment of children from both genders, including those as young as 13 who were forced into active duty, according to United Nations reports.[98]

The distinction between the Islamist and Kurdish elements which made up the SDF was significant, with the YPG holding no particular animosity towards the Syrian government or towards Russia, and at times cooperating with them. Islamist elements by contrast were firmly committed to the Syrian state's overthrow and creation of an Islamic state, and sought to capitalise on Western support to achieve this. During the Northern Aleppo Offensive in February 2016 the YPG had notably cooperated with the SAA and Russian forces against Turkish backed jihadist groups, with Syrian officers flying into the Rojova by helicopter in January 2016 to coordinate an offensive. For the YPG, which had repeatedly clashed with Turkish forces and Turkish-backed jihadists in recent months, the possibility that the SAA could open a land corridor from Aleppo to northern Syria was appealing and meant that Kurdish forces would no longer be surrounded by Islamist groups. Russian Il-76 and Iranian C-130 aircraft subsequently dropped supplies by parachute into the Rojova as a sign of good will. Cooperation with Russian and Syrian forces allowed the YPG to seize territory from Turkish backed militants and unify the Kurdish enclaves along the Turkish border, and played a key role in that phase of the northern Aleppo offensive.[99]

Despite the YPG's cooperation with the Syrian government, which continued even after the formation of the Syrian Democratic Forces, the SDF would increasingly become a threat to Syrian sovereignty. This was due to both the SDF's growing Islamist composition and to the growing Western influence over it, with U.S. and European forces increasingly deployed to northern Syria and embedded in SDF frontline units. From early 2017, in the aftermath of the SAA's capture of Aleppo and amid its rapid push into Homs to take Palmyra, the U.S. began to support efforts by the SDF to expand its territory by rapidly seizing ground from Islamic State. IS' self-proclaimed capital, Raqqa, and its extensive oil fields in Deir ez-Zor, were the U.S.' primary targets.

In February 2017 the head of the U.S. Central Command, General Joseph Votel, flew into SDF controlled territory around 100km north of Raqqa and met with senior alliance commanders to discuss the next phase of the offensive. He inspected militiamen in training and stated that a larger deployment of American personnel may be necessary, with U.S. cargo aircraft beginning major new arms deliveries shortly afterwards.[100] By creating the SDF and cultivating relations with Rojova, the U.S. had effectively given itself a major foothold on Syrian soil. This was key to facilitating its further efforts to shape the country's future, to retaining a large sphere of influence, and to potentially carrying out a Kosovo-style partitioning of the north of the country to indefinitely deny Damascus full control of its territory.

Even as General Votel was holding meetings, the SDF and U.S. special forces units backed by American aircraft were rapidly pressing further into Syrian territory, capturing 60 villages and 1762 square kilometres of land in a week-long offensive.[101] American special forces played a key role acting as forward air controllers, allowing aircraft to more precisely strike their targets, with this air support relied on very heavily by the SDF which lacked any substantial armour or artillery. By the end of the month the joint SDF-U.S. force was poised to cut the last route from Raqqa to Iraq, thus isolating the IS capital and potentially placing a major Syrian city under its control.

U.S. personnel deployed to Syria included not only special forces, but also engineering experts and medical and psychological warfare teams who were all supplied through a network of small airstrips set up on Syrian soil which received MC-130 and CV-22 transports. Psy-ops were supported by EC-130J aircraft which were tasked with broadcasting propaganda. As of February 2017, an estimated 500 U.S. personnel were operating alongside the SDF, although the significance of this medium sized contingent was much greater than its numbers implied.[102] The ability to embed small numbers of American personnel with SDF units was a major force multiplier, and gave the impression of a local effort rather than a U.S. invasion while also ensuring that less sensitive 'grunt work' would not need to be done by Americans. Furthermore, forces deployed were largely drawn from elite units including the Army Special Forces and the Navy SEALs, which were trained to operate in much smaller numbers than regular soldiers or marines. Added to this was the massive support from the air, from both a vast network of bases in Jordan, the UAE, Qatar and other countries, as well as from carrier groups boasting hundreds of cruise missiles and dozens of F-18E fighters which were ready and on call. The U.S. was in effect invading Syria to seize a portion of its territory and was doing so in a much more subtle and cost-free way than prior operations in Iraq, Afghanistan, Grenada, Panama or other target states. The new approach required far fewer boots on the ground.

The advance on Raqqa maintained high momentum into March, with the SDF and U.S. special forces capturing the strategically located Tabqa Airbase near the city and trapping several IS fighters in the process. On March 9 it was announced that 400 new personnel, including Army Rangers and a U.S. Marine artillery unit, would be dispatched alongside 155mm artillery guns and AH-64 Apache attack helicopters to further expand the American military presence.[103] A further 2,500 paratroopers were deployed to Kuwait to be ready for operations in Syria or Iraq upon request.[104] U.S. officials from this time increasingly began to indicate that there would be a purpose for American forces in Syria beyond combatting the Islamic State – the official pretext for their presence – which was widely interpreted to be alluding to limiting the gains of the Syrian government. Former special adviser to the Obama administration on Syria, Fred Hof, alluded to this most directly and stated regarding the goal of denying the Syrian government access to Syrian territory: "there needs to be an executable plan for post-conflict governance that keeps the Assad regime – the main reason for violent extremism in Syria – out of areas liberated from ISIS [IS]."[105]

## Notes

1   Nordeen, Lon O., *Air Warfare in the Missile Age*, Washington D.C., Smithsonian Books, 2010 (p. 167).
    'Afghans harass Soviets despite inferior weapons,' *Christian Science Monitor,* May 28, 1980.
2   Ripley, Tim, *Operation Aleppo: Russia's War in Syria*, Lancaster, Telic-Herrick Publications, 2018 (p. 39).
3   Ibid (pp. 41–42, 70–71).
4   'Russia is expanding its military options in Syria,' *Oxford Analytica*, April 25, 2016.
    'TOS-1A Heavy Flamethrower – Russia's Unique and Devastating Weapon,' *Military Watch Magazine,* January 29, 2018.
    Swearngen, Jake, 'This Russian Tank-Mounted Rocket Launcher Can Incinerate 8 City Blocks,' *Popular Mechanics,* September 14, 2015.

5    'Saudi Ready To Send Ground Troops To Syria,' *Sky News*, February 4, 2016.
     'UAE says it is ready to send ground troops to Syria,' *Al Jazeera*, February 7, 2016.
6    Merat, Arron, '"The Saudis couldn't do it without us": the UK's true role in Yemen's deadly war,' *The Guardian*, June 18, 2019.
     Wintour, Patrick, '"Serious" questions over SAS involvement in Yemen war,' *The Guardian*, March 27, 2019.
     Sampathkumar, Mythili, 'US special forces secretly deployed to assist Saudi Arabia in Yemen conflict,' *The Independent*, May 3, 2018.
     'French special forces on the ground in Yemen: Le Figaro,' *Reuters*, June 16, 2018.
7    Snyder, Stephen, 'Who's winning the war in Yemen?,' *PRI*, July 3, 2015.
     Baron, Adam, 'Everyone Is Losing Yemen's War,' *Foreign Policy*, April 28, 2015.
8    McDowall, Angus and Stewart, Phil and Rohde, David, 'Yemen's guerrilla war tests military ambitions of big-spending Saudis,' *Reuters*, April 19, 2016.
     Griffing, Alexander, 'Why Saudi Arabia and "Little Sparta" Still Can't Defeat Iran in Yemen,' *Haaretz*, July 22, 2018.
     Murkin, George, 'Saudi Arabia gets little bang for its buck for investing in its armed forces – but that may be about to change,' *The Policy Institute at King's*, March 5, 2018.
9    'Syria says any foreign troops would "return in coffins",' *Al Jazeera*, February 6, 2016.
10   'Syrian Army, Hezbollah, Russian Air Force Coordinating for Aleppo Liberation Operation,' *Fars News Agency*, October 14, 2015.
11   Stephens, Bret, 'The Man Who Humbled Qassim Suleimani,' *New York Times*, January 11, 2019.
12   Ripley, Tim, *Operation Aleppo: Russia's War in Syria*, Lancaster, Telic-Herrick Publications, 2018 (p. 36).
13   Perry, Tom and Al-Khalidi, Suleiman, 'Syrian rebels say they receive more weapons for Aleppo battle,' *Reuters*, October 19, 2015.
14   'Syrian army advances against Islamic State east of Aleppo: Syria state TV,' *Reuters*, November 28, 2015.
15   'Syrian army seizes Aleppo, takes aim at ISIL in Raqqa,' *Al Jazeera*, February 21, 2016.
16   Karam, Zeina, 'AP Explains: Why Syria's M5 is Assad's highway to victory,' *Associated Press*, February 14, 2020.
17   Lund, Aron, 'Evaluating the Russian Intervention in Syria,' *Carnegie Middle East Center*, December 7, 2015.
18   Toumaj, Amir and Peck, Max, 'The IRGC's involvement in the battle for Aleppo,' *Long War Journal*, February 13, 2016.
19   'Syrian army, allies break rebel siege of Nubl, Zahraa,' *The Daily Star*, February 4, 2016.
     'Syria conflict: Government "cuts Aleppo rebel supply route",' *BBC News*, February 3, 2016.

20 International Institute for Strategic Studies, *The Military Balance*, Volume 120, 2020, Chapter Eight: East Asia and Australasia (p. 377).

21 'Syrian government forces in north choke opposition supply lines,' *The Guardian*, February 5, 2016.
McDowall, Angus and Tsvetkova, Maria, 'Syrian army closes in on last Aleppo rebels,' *Reuters*, December 20, 2016.

22 Ripley, Tim, *Operation Aleppo: Russia's War in Syria*, Lancaster, Telic-Herrick Publications, 2018 (p. 66).

23 Corbeil, Alexander, 'Russia is Learning About Hezbollah,' *Carnegie Endowment for International Peace*, January 11, 2017.

24 Ripley, Tim, *Operation Aleppo: Russia's War in Syria*, Lancaster, Telic-Herrick Publications, 2018 (p. 105).

25 Grove, Thomas, 'Russian Special Forces Seen as Key to Aleppo Victory,' *Wall Street Journal*, December 16, 2016.

26 Ripley, Tim, *Operation Aleppo: Russia's War in Syria*, Lancaster, Telic-Herrick Publications, 2018 (pp. 13–14, 129).

27 Cenciotti, David, 'Russia has just deployed its most advanced spyplane to Syria,' *The Aviationist*, February 15, 2016.
'Аналитики обнаружили в Сирии секретный российский самолет-разведчик' [Analysts find secret Russian spy plane in Syria], *NewsRu*, February 16, 2016.

28 'Syria rebels reach evacuation deal with government,' *Al Jazeera*, December 14, 2016.

29 'Aleppo evacuation is complete, Red Cross says,' *Reuters*, December 23, 2016.

30 Steele, Jonathan, 'A no-fly zone for Aleppo risks a war that could engulf us all,' *The Guardian*, October 12, 2016.

31 'Syrian rebels' Aleppo offensive could amount to war crimes, UN envoy warns,' *The Guardian*, October 31, 2016.

32 'East Aleppo civilians "shot at" by rebels to prevent them leaving during truce,' *The Independent*, Occtober 21, 2016.
Ripley, Tim, *Operation Aleppo: Russia's War in Syria*, Lancaster, Telic-Herrick Publications, 2018 (p. 115).

33 Ibid (p. 15, 127).

34 Ibid (pp. 14–15, 126, 128).

35 Solomon, Feliz, 'U.S. Says it Will End Syria Talks with Russia Unless Bombing of Aleppo Stops,' *Time*, September 29, 2016.
'Syria war: Russia rejects US calls to halt bombing eastern Aleppo,' *BBC News*, September 29, 2016.

36 Marcus, Jonathan, 'Aleppo: Is a no-fly zone the answer?,' *BBC News*, October 11, 2016.
Wintour, Patrick, 'May questions Syria no-fly zone proposal,' *The Guardian*, October 12, 2016.

37 Borger, Julian, 'Russia vetoes UN resolution to stop bombing of Aleppo,' *The Guardian*, October 8, 2016.

38 Corbeil, Alexander, 'Russia is Learning About Hezbollah,' *Carnegie Endowment for International Peace*, January 11, 2017.

39  Ripley, Tim, *Operation Aleppo: Russia's War in Syria*, Lancaster, Telic-Herrick Publications, 2018 (pp. 68–69).
40  Binnie, Jeremy, 'Iskander missile launcher spotted in Syria,' *IHS Jane's 360*, March 31, 2016.
41  'Russian Tu-22M3 "Backfire" long-range bombers strike ISIS from Iran's Hamadan airfield,' *RT*, August 16, 2016.
42  'Sukhoi Su-34 plane nicknamed "Duckling": Russian Aerospace Force's best bomber,' *TASS*, August 23, 2016.
43  Hennigan, W. J. and Wilkinson, Tracy, 'Russian use of Iranian air base shows Moscow's renewed military might,' *Los Angeles Times*, August 18, 2016.
44  Khalaj, Monavar and Hille, Kathrin, 'Tehran halts Russian raids on Syria from Iran,' *Financial Times*, August 22, 2016.
    Khalaji, Mehdi and Nadimi, Farzin, 'Russia Uses an Iranian Air Base: Two Essays,' *Washington Institute*, August 17, 2016.
45  'The Legacy of the Soviet Union's Ambitious Aircraft Carrier Program – Part One,' *Military Watch Magazine*, October 18, 2018.
46  Rogoway, Tyler, 'Russia's Carrier Was Designed To Be Heavily Armed Even Without Its Air Wing,' *The Drive*, October 25, 2016.
    'Should the Admiral Kuznetsov Re-Emphasise its Original Role as a Missile Cruiser? Zicron Hypersonic Cruise Missiles Could Make Russia's Carrier a Lethal Ship Killer,' *Military Watch Magazine*, February 17, 2020.
47  Huard, Richard, 'Meet the Ulyanovsk: Russia's 85,000 Ton Monster Aircraft Carrier,' *National Interest*, September 28, 2019.
48  'How powerful are catapults of aircraft carriers? Well, very powerful,' *Technology.org*, June 3. 2019.
    Crenshaw Jr., Lewis W., 'EMALS technology on Ford carriers will help the US Navy accomplish its mission,' *Defense News*, September 14, 2020.
49  Ripley, Tim, *Operation Aleppo: Russia's War in Syria*, Lancaster, Telic-Herrick Publications, 2018 (p. 117).
50  'Russian MIG-29 Crashes in Med After Takeoff From Aircraft Carrier,' *Sputnik*, November 14, 2016.
51  'Kremlin on Su-33 Accident in Mediterranean: "Main Thing is the Pilot is Alive",' *Sputnik*, December 5, 2016.
52  'Admiral Kuznetsov aircraft carrier's experience in Syria including in training programs,' *TASS*, October 30, 2017.
53  'Russia's Tupolev-95MSM bomber delivers first-ever strike on mission to Syria,' *TASS*, November 17, 2016.
54  Ripley, Tim, *Operation Aleppo: Russia's War in Syria*, Lancaster, Telic-Herrick Publications, 2018 (p. 122).
55  'Syria war: Almost 500,000 refugees return in 2017 – UN,' *BBC News*, June 30, 2017.
56  Ripley, Tim, *Operation Aleppo: Russia's War in Syria*, Lancaster, Telic-Herrick Publications, 2018 (p. 130).
57  'Shoygu Says Russia Daily Delivers 2,000 Tons Cargo to Syria,' *Military Today*, November 3, 2016.
58  'Documentary on Russian Military Police in Syria,' *ANNA News*, 2017.
59  Ibid.

60 Ripley, Tim, *Operation Aleppo: Russia's War in Syria*, Lancaster, Telic-Herrick Publications, 2018 (p. 86).

61 Koparan, Omer and Temizer, Selen, 'NW Syria returns to normal after Turkish operation,' *Andalou News Agency*, August 22, 2018.

62 Gurcan, Metin, 'Assessing the Post–July 15 Turkish Military Operations Euphrates Shield and Olive Branch,' Policy Note 59, *Washington Institute*, 2019 (p. 15).

63 'US-Led Coalition Used 4 Planes, 1 Drone in Deir ez-Zor Strike – Russian MoD,' *Sputnik*, September 16, 2016.

64 Malsin, Jared, 'How a Mistaken U.S.-Led Air Attack Could End the Syria Cease-Fire,' *Time*, September 18, 2016.

65 El Deeb, Sarah, 'U.S. says it might have struck Syrian troops while targeting ISIS,' *Chicago Sun Times*, September 17, 2016.
'Syria conflict: US air strikes "kill dozens of government troops",' *BBC News*, September 18, 2016.

66 'Source Discloses Coordination between US, ISIL in Attacking Syrian Army in Deir Ezzur,' *Fars News Agency*, September 18, 2016.

67 Ripley, Tim, *Operation Aleppo: Russia's War in Syria*, Lancaster, Telic-Herrick Publications, 2018 (p. 108).

68 'Statement from Pentagon Spokesman Capt. Jeff Davis on U.S. strike in Syria,' *U.S. Department of Defense*, April 6, 2017.
Risk, Robert, 'US air strikes in Syria: Why America really attacked pro-Assad militia convoy,' *The Independent*, May 19, 2017.
Browne, Ryan, 'New details on US shoot down of Syrian jet,' *CNN*, June 22, 2017.

69 'ISIL "recaptures" Palmyra from Syrian forces,' *Al Jazeera*, December 11, 2016.

70 'How "Wagner" came to Syria,' *The Economist*, November 2, 2017.
Tsvetkova, Maria, 'Russia underplayed losses in recapture of Syria's Palmyra,' *Reuters*, March 22, 2017.

71 'Syrian army forms volunteer corps to fight militants,' *Reuters*, November 22, 2016.

72 Mitzer, Stijn, 'Replenishing the Stocks: Russian deliveries of T-62Ms and BMP-1s reach Syria,' *ORYX*, February 17, 2017.

73 'Russian general hit by roadside bomb in Syria loses both legs,' *RT*, March 6, 2017.

74 'Russia's General Staff reveals details of Palmyra operation,' *TASS*, March 3, 2017.
Dearden, Lizzie, 'Isis driven out of ancient Syrian city of Palmyra for second time,' *The Independent*, March 2, 2017.

75 'Six Russian Tu-22 Long-Range Bombers Strike Daesh Targets in Syrian Deir ez-Zor,' *Sputnik*, January 23, 2017.

76 'Syria: Tupolev "Bear" bombers destroy IS bases in Raqqa Province – MoD,' *Ruptly*, February 17, 2017.

77 Tomlinson, Lucas, 'Russia sends Syria its largest missile delivery to date, US officials say,' *Fox News*, February 8, 2017.

78 'Damascus water supply cut after rebels pollute it: authority,' *Reuters*, December 23, 2016.

79   'Syria: Clashes erupt after regime negotiator killed near Damascus,' *Al Araby,* January 5, 2017.

80   Bishku, Michael B., 'Israel and the Kurds: A Pragmatic Relationship in Middle Eastern Politics,' *Journal of South Asian and Middle Eastern Studies*, vol. 41, no. 2, Winter 2018 (pp. 52–72).
     Razoux, Pierre, *The Iran-Iraq War,* Cambridge, MA, Harvard University Press, 2015 (pp. 492–493).
     Menachem Begin on the Israel Home Service, September 29, 1980, BBC Summary of World Broadcasts, ME/6537, October 1, 1980.

81   Van Bruinessen, Martin, 'The Kurds between Iran and Iraq,' *Middle East Research and Information Project,* no. 141, July-August 1986 (pp. 14–27).

82   Bishku, Michael B., 'Israel and the Kurds: A Pragmatic Relationship in Middle Eastern Politics,' *Journal of South Asian and Middle Eastern Studies*, vol. 41, no. 2, Winter 2018 (p. 62).

83   Kingsley, Patrick, 'The World Condemns Erdoğan's War on Kurds. But Turkey Applauds,' *New York Times,* October 16, 2019.

84   'Flight of Icarus? The PYD's Precarious Rise in Syria,' *International Crisis Group,* May 8, 2014.

85   Walcott, John and Hennigan, W. J., 'U.S. Spies Say Turkish-Backed Militias Are Killing Civilians as They Clear Kurdish Areas in Syria,' *Time*, October 28, 2019.

86   Stein, Aaron and Foley, Michelle, 'The YPG-PKK connection,' *Atlantic Council,* January 26, 2016.
     Ünal, Ali, 'PM Davutoğlu: PYD will get same response as PKK if it poses threat to Turkey,' *Daily Sabah,* October 14, 2015.

87   Stein, Aaron and Foley, Michelle, 'The YPG-PKK connection,' *Atlantic Council,* January 26, 2016.

88   Azizi, Bradost, 'Islamists Fighting Kurds in Syria Admit to Turkish Military Support,' *Rudaw,* February 6, 2013.

89   Bulos, Nabih and Hennigan, W.J. and Bennett, Brian, 'In Syria, militias armed by the Pentagon fight those armed by the CIA,' *Los Angeles Times,* March 27, 2016.

90   'Stop Arming Terrorists,' *Website of Congresswoman Tulsi Gabbard* (https://gabbard.house.gov/news/StopArmingTerrorists).

91   'We finally know what Hillary Clinton knew all along – U.S. allies Saudi Arabia and Qatar are funding Isis,' *The Independent*, October 14, 2016.

92   Barnes, Julian E., 'B-1 Pilots Describe Bombing Campaign Against ISIS in Kobani,' *The Wall Street Journal*, February 18, 2015.
     Grant, Rebecca, 'The Siege of Kobani,' *Air Force Magazine,* August 29, 2018.
     'Islamic State crisis: US intensifies airs strikes in Kobane,' *BBC News,* October 15, 2014.

93   'U.S. says Kobani shows how to beat Islamic State; key city of Mosul may require new tactics,' *Japan Times*, January 27, 2015.

94   'Kurdish forces storm last stronghold of ISIS in Kobane's countryside,' *ARA News*, March 20, 2015.

95   Ackerman, Spencer, 'US military special forces pictured aiding Kurdish fighters in Syria,' *The Guardian*, May 26, 2016.

96   'Syrian-Kurdish SDF successfully absorbing non-Kurdish groups, says US,' *Rudaw,* March 9, 2016.
     'Anyone for Raqqa?,' *The Economist,* November 10, 2016.
     'Talal Silo: our major aim founding SDF was uniting military factions,' *Hawar News Agency*, October 10, 2016.

97   'Residents of Manbij protest against conscription in Kurdish militias,' *Zaman Al Wasl,* November 5, 2017.
     'Manbij residents face off against SDF over conscription policy,' *Al Monitor,* November 24, 2017.
     'Tension and resentment in Manbij due to tens of arrests of young men by the military police for the "self-defense duty",' *SOHR,* November 7, 2017.

98   'UN: US-backed SDF recruits children,' *Al Jazeera,* March 7, 2018.
     'Syrian Democratic Forces arrested a girl for conscription in Aleppo city on May 23,' *SNHR,* May 29, 2020.

99   Ripley, Tim, 'Aleppo evacuation deal marks end of resistance in key city,' *IHS Jane's Defence Weekly*, December 21, 2016 (p. 65).
     Andresen, Pascal, 'Friends or Foes? A Closer Look on Relations Between YPG and the Regime,' *Bellingcat,* September 12, 2016.

100  Gordon, Michael R., 'More U.S. Troops May Be Needed Against ISIS in Syria, a Top General Says,' *New York Times,* February 22, 2017.

101  Arafat, Hisham, 'Kurdish-led, US-backed Syrian alliance reaches Euphrates,' *Kurdistan 24,* February 28, 2017.

102  Gordon, Michael R., 'More U.S. Troops May Be Needed Against ISIS in Syria, a Top General Says,' *New York Times,* February 22, 2017.

103  Kennedy, Merrit, 'U.S. Is Sending About 400 Marines To Syria,' *NPR,* March 9, 2017.

104  Panzino, Charlsy and deGrandpre, Andrew, 'The U.S. is sending 2,500 troops to Kuwait, ready to step up the fight in Syria and Iraq,' *Army Times,* March 9, 2017.

105  Malsin, Jared, 'The U.S. Troop Presence in Syria Is at Its Highest Ever. But How Long Are They on the Ground for and Why?,' *Time*, March 12, 2017.

# Chapter 7

# Land Grabs: The West Moves In

## A Race for Territory

Following the capture of Palmyra, the Syrian Arab Army allocated the bulk of its forces to pursuing a further push into Islamic State–held territory, with Homs, Deir ez-Zor, and the jihadist group's capital, Raqqa, being the primary targets for multiple simultaneous offensives. Time was of the essence, as the longer it took for Syrian forces to reclaim IS territory the more of it would fall under the control of the U.S. Military and the militias of the Syrian Democratic Forces operating under its sponsorship and protection. Land occupied by the U.S. would be extremely difficult to recapture, as America would throw the full weight of its military behind the SDF and the hundreds of U.S. personnel dispersed among them, which made it imperative for the SAA to ensure that as little territory as possible fell under their control.

Russia was heavily invested in a Syrian success and deployed its own assets to help the SAA reach and capture the Raqqa governate as quickly as possible, directly involving its forces in widespread offensive operations to an unprecedented extent. It deployed more Su-34 strike fighters, special forces teams and advisors, Su-25SM attack jets and new Russian-manned heavy artillery units.[1] These deployments were complemented by a massive expansion of the Russian communications network, in particular satellite communications, specifically for the operation.[2] Russia also increased the flight rates of its A-50 airborne early warning and control aircraft over central Syria to expand sensor coverage, ensured that several bombers in Russia itself were always ready to provide long-range fire support, and placed the Black Sea Fleet on a rota to ensure that ships with Kalibr cruise missiles were constantly on station within range of the theatre. These moves were taken with potential threats from the U.S. strongly in mind.[3]

With Russian special forces fighting shoulder to shoulder with the SAA on the ground, and its aircraft continuing to provide massive fire support and key intelligence, it also dispatched mine warfare and military police units to demine and ensure stability in towns and villages that IS forces had withdrawn from.[4] Quds Force trained militias and Iranian drone units also played an important supporting role in the offensive, while Hezbollah focused on assisting parallel SAA offensives in the country's far east against Islamic State in Deir ez-Zor.

The U.S. appeared to have given up on groups such as the Al Nusra Front and other jihadist forces which had first comprised the Free Syrian Army, with the new Syrian Democratic Forces proving more effective since they were built up around an American 'boots on the ground' support structure and could cooperate closely with U.S. forces in the field. Turkey, however, had remained heavily committed to the old insurgency. This largely stemmed from its very close cooperation with these jihadist groups, many of which were partially based in Turkey and which had had Turkish special forces embedded among their ranks since the earliest days of the war. Turkish hostility towards the YPG, which formed a significant part of the U.S.-backed Democratic Forces' fighting strength, was another major factor. Turkey thus also moved to expand the area under the control of its proxies by pushing into IS-held territory, largely at the expense of the U.S.-backed Democratic Forces which it sought to deny as much territory as possible particularly near the Turkish border regions. With Islamic State's defeat appearing inevitable, there were effectively three rival sides trying to acquire as much Syrian land as possible – although only one had any legal claim to it.

Pressing into Syrian territory in the final weeks of 2016 and into the new year, the Turkish Army deployed large numbers of modern German-supplied Leopard II tanks. These were widely considered in the West to be the most capable tanks in the world but would repeatedly face humiliating losses in combat.[5] While IS anti-tank weapons were far from state of the art, the heavy losses

Turkish armour suffered would tarnish the reputation of Europe's finest tank indefinitely – with similar losses again incurred the following year. British media reported that the Leopard showed "numerous faults exposed in lethal fashion,"[6] with America's *Stars and Stripes* assessing that the tank's reputation "has taken a pounding in battles with Islamic State militants"[7] and the *National Interest* highlighting that its combat performance "shockingly illustrated" that they were "not so good armour after all."[8] German media similarly stressed the devastating blow the engagements had done to what was arguably the most prolific export product of the country's defence sector.[9] *Military Watch Magazine* highlighted that armour losses likely accelerated Turkey's shift to rely on South Korean tanks in future, despite their considerable cost, due to their superior capabilities.[10] Turkish military leaders described their armour's early engagements with IS as "trauma" – a testament to the success the jihadist group was having against one of NATO's largest armies.[11]

Adding further complexity to the conflict was the apparent Russian and American competition for influence in the Kurdish YPG, with Moscow well aware that weakening Kurdish support for the U.S. and encouraging closer ties with both itself and with Damascus would undermine the American hold over northern Syria, particularly after Islamic State was defeated. With Turkey and the YPG clashing in the border regions in early March, Russia capitalised on the opportunity by holding secret talks with the Kurdish leadership and agreeing to send Russian and Syrian troops to form a buffer zone at the border to prevent further Turkish attacks. Russian forces were on the move within hours of the agreement being made, which provided them with a key foothold in northern Syria, seriously hindered American efforts to control the area, and also presented Moscow as a protector of the Kurds against Turkey and its jihadist affiliates. The U.S. responded quickly by applying pressure on the YPG leadership to be allowed to take this role for itself, but with the Kurds' deal with Russia already made, both U.S. and Russian troops would patrol the border area. The area was thus left contested but under the control of neither party, and came to be known as the 'joint security zone.'[12]

The SAA began an offensive drive into IS held territory in the first week of May, aimed at capturing its main strongholds of Raqqa and Deir ez-Zor, with the Tiger Forces spearheading the advance. Morale among the jihadists remained low, with their forces consistently prone to making early retreats while leaving behind snipers, improvised bombs and suicide bombers to delay the Syrian advance. These rearguard forces often included dozens and at times hundreds of heavily armoured pick-up trucks laden with explosives advancing at full speed towards SAA lines, which usually required heavy weapons to stop. Despite this, SAA advances were still rapid with over 6,000 square kilometres of IS territory captured by the end of the month[13] and every major town in the Aleppo governate, as well as the Jirrah Airbase, entirely secured. This allowed the Tiger Forces to move from Aleppo into the Raqqa governate before the first of June, and by the 10th the government had seized 20,000 square kilometres of ground.[14]

The move into Raqqa placed the Tiger Force-led SAA contingent in direct competition with the Syrian Democratic Forces in the race to capture Islamic State territory, with Syrian troops bypassing the SDF by moving through the desert and subsequently capturing the strategically located town of Resafa. With the Islamic State failing to put up any organised resistance, the SAA reached the Euphrates river in early July and successfully blocked the SDF and the Americans embedded within their ranks from advancing further south. While Russian assistance on the ground was limited, with the elite composition of the Tiger Force meaning this was not a requirement as it was for other units such as those in the 5th Corps, Russia did provide significant assistance in attempting to win the support of tribal militias in Raqqa. The United States and Russia were both placed in fierce competition in this regard, with many of these militias having previously fought with the Islamic State but ultimately having no ideological affiliations beyond loyalty to the interests of their tribe. These were interests both sides pledged to be able to satisfy, but with the rapid and apparently unanticipated arrival of the Syrian Arab Army in the area seriously disrupting American plans, Russia was able to win over significant numbers of tribal fighters.[15]

With only limited deconfliction mechanisms between the SAA and U.S. backed forces, and with both sides in fierce competition for territory and the Tiger Forces having apparently ended American plans to place the large majority of the Raqqa governate under its influence, there remained significant tensions. On June 18, the day of the capture of Resafa, a Syrian Su-22 strike fighter was shot down after threatening the SDF. U.S. forces had called in an F-18E carrier-based fighter, which fired a state-of-the-art new AIM-9X missile at the Syrian aircraft. This was widely considered the most advanced heat seeking missile in the Western world. The missile notably missed its target, and despite its age the Cold War era strike fighter's countermeasures proved capable of deflecting the attack. This forced the American pilot to deploy an AIM-120 radar-guided missile, which was built for much longer range engagements and was far from ideal for a short-range fight, but succeeded in striking the slow and unmanoeuvrable jet which had no anti-aircraft capabilities of its own to retaliate. The AIM-9's failure at very close range and against a countermeasures suite over 30 years older than it, described as "disturbing" by *Popular Mechanics* given how heavily NATO relied on the missile, would be assessed dozens of times by defence analysts.[16] More significantly for Damascus and its partners, however, was the fact that the U.S. was now enforcing a no-fly zone within Syria's own borders – one which would expand significantly if the SDF was allowed to occupy more territory.

In parallel to its advance into Raqqa, the SAA was also pushing southward against Western backed insurgents holding territory in the Jordanian border regions, with Western special forces from Britain, Norway and the United States deployed to support the militants. Serving as direct auxiliaries to the Western forces in the south, much as the SDF was to the north, were a grouping of insurgent militias calling themselves the New Syrian Army (NSyA), which was one of the several groups receiving Western sponsorship in the area. The area under NSyA control notably also bordered Islamic State held territory, and the Western backed militias would begin an offensive against IS early in 2017. Much like the U.S.-backed SDF to the north, the goal of this campaign was to expand the territory under Western control at the expense of both IS and the Syrian government. The support of both American airstrikes and of Western special forces within its ranks effectively shielded the NSyA from direct attack by the SAA or Russia.

The SAA would respond to the rapid expansion of territory in the south under Western control by seeking to cut off the NSyA, deploying multiple armoured units which approached the insurgent stronghold of Al Tanf in early June. The U.S. responded by declaring that all Syrian territory within 50 kilometres of Al Tanf was a deconfliction zone, and that any party that approached would come under attack. The U.S. was thus effectively again denying the Syrian military access to its own territory. When government-aligned militias tested the outskirts of this deconfliction zone, they were bombed by American aircraft on May 6 and again on May 18. The second attack saw the militias fire on the American jets, forcing them to attack from high altitude, with the aircraft causing an estimated 31 casualties including six deaths.[17] In this case, however, the SAA would not be deterred and would continue to advance towards the NSyA.

The SAA advance was supported by Iranian Quds Force militias and their advisors, and Iran's Shahed 129 strike drones flew overhead to attack NSyA units on June 8 – with the missile it fired exploding just a few metres from a U.S. special forces truck. This was the first time any country had attacked American troops from the air since the North Koreans and Chinese had done so in the Korean War in 1953, and Russian Su-30 and Su-35 jets circled overhead as an apparent warning against retaliation. The U.S. dispatched an F-15 fighter to shoot down the Iranian drone but did not retaliate against SAA or militia forces likely due to the presence of the Russian jets. One June 10 the SAA reached the Iraqi border to the east of Al Tanf – thus completely cutting off the Western forces and the NSyA from further expansion into IS-held territory in that region. Footage was soon afterwards released by the Syrian Defence Ministry showing columns of SAA units, including modern T-90 tanks and anti-tank missile systems, manning this cut-off line and boxing in and isolating Al Tanf.[18] Although the Western forces and the NSyA remained on Syrian soil, they were effectively contained.

## Political Theatre and More Western Attacks

While the campaign to capture Raqqa was ongoing, tensions between the U.S. and Syria and its partners would escalate sharply in April. This followed allegations by the White Helmets organisation that the Syrian government had carried out a chemical weapons attack in the town of Khan Shaykhun in the Idlib governate on April 4. The governments of the United States, Britain, France, Turkey, Saudi Arabia and Israel would subsequently quickly claim that the Syrian government was responsible.[19] Russia and Syria denied the allegations, stating that the attack was staged by the White Helmets, with the incentive for such a fabrication being to provide the Western powers with a pretext to launch a further military attack on Syrian government positions. Such attacks would be illegal, insofar as they would be carried out without authorisation from the United Nations Security Council, unilaterally, and without provocation.[20]

It was not until the following year that U.S. Defence Secretary James Mattis would admit what Damascus, Moscow and several independent journalists and analysts had been stressing from the outset – that there had been no evidence of a Syrian chemical attack. "We have other reports from the battlefield from people who claim it's been used [but] we do not have evidence of it," Mattis stated, meaning the White Helmets had essentially been taken at their word as a pretext for military action. "We're looking for evidence of it," Mattis concluded, but a year later there was still nothing to implicate the Syrian government.[21] Given the level of intelligence sharing between NATO allies, Mattis' statement directly contradicted a French claim from a year prior that Paris had undeniable proof of SAA culpability. This proof either did not exist or was deemed insufficient by the U.S.[22]

The White Helmets organisation, responsible for the claims of an attack Mattis had mentioned, had played a growing role in the war since 2014. It was the centre of much controversy, with Russia, Iran and Syria all considering it a terrorist organisation while the Western powers hailed it as a humanitarian group. The nature of this organisation received extremely polarised coverage in global media, with major Western outlets issuing sharp rebukes to even slight criticisms of the White Helmets.[23] Non-Western outlets and so-called 'alternative media' meanwhile repeatedly published images of White Helmets and Al Qaeda affiliated jihadists standing side by side, alongside verified quotes from jihadist groups praising the organisation's members as comrades in arms against the Syrian government.[24] The White Helmets' ties with jihadist groups led it to being banned from operating in both Kurdish and government controlled areas of Syria.[25] Former British Army officer James Le Mesurier, also a former member of the Olive Group private security firm which would later merge with America's Blackwater, was the leading co-founder of the White Helmets organisation which received funding from many of the same parties which were sponsoring the insurgency itself. The Russian Foreign Ministry claimed Le Mesurier was also a former MI6 agent, which was not uncommon for retired officers involved such activities.[26]

Journalists and observers in Syria would consistently issue harsh criticisms of the White Helmets, slamming it as a tool for propaganda which was being exploited by the West and exacerbating the population's suffering. Canadian journalist Eva Bartlett, who reported from the frontlines in Syria, presented considerable evidence that the White Helmets frequently staged videos for propaganda purposes,[27] although such claims were roundly dismissed across major Western news outlets. Australian journalist John Pilger similarly referred to the White Helmets as a "complete propaganda construct" of the Al Qaeda affiliated Al Nusra Front.[28] British journalist Vanessa Beeley, who observed the Syrian conflict for several weeks on the ground and conducted multiple recorded interviews with locals,[29] similarly showed that the White Helmets had "ties to private security firms and to deep state in both U.S. and UK," was being used to fabricate atrocities and provide pretexts for Western military intervention, and was comprised of members of Al Qaeda linked terror groups.[30] Delegations from the British parliament's House of Lords and from the Church of England who visited Syria as observers in 2018 fully verified the claims made by Bartlettt, Beeley, Pilger and others.[31] Claims regarding the White Helmets' nature as a propaganda group were supported by later footage of a White Helmets film set in Syria showing an SAA chemical attack being staged, with actors appearing in multiple scenes playing roles of both victims and paramedics.[32] Footage of White Helmets not only posing with members of UN-recognised terrorist groups, but also assisting jihadist militants in disposing of the bodies of beheaded Syrian soldiers, gave much credibility to the claim that the group was indeed linked to jihadist terror operations in the country.[33]

While the Organisation for Prohibition of Chemical Weapons (OPCW) claimed to have confirmed in mid-April that Sarin nerve gas had been used in Syria, the claim that the SAA had carried out the attack was extremely dubious. Not only was there no proof as to who the perpetrator of the attacks was, with aforementioned evidence showing that insurgents had a chemical weapons capability (see Chapter 4), but the evidence of any Sarin use at all was questionable. Former UN weapons inspector Scott Ritter notably criticised the OPCW investigation on the grounds that it relied almost solely on chemical samples provided by the White Helmets and groups with ties to the insurgency. This gave these actors, which had much to gain from a Western attack on Syria, considerable room to fabricate evidence.[34] Britain's ambassador to the United Nations announced that samples had also been provided to British scientists and "tested positive for Sarin or a Sarin-like substance," although when journalist Tim Ripley from *Jane's Defence Weekly* sought to access the scientific reports through a Freedom of Information Act, the Foreign Office refused to "confirm or deny" whether they actually existed. This indicated that these tests may never have even taken place.[35] The argument for Syrian complicity, or that any kind of Sarin attack had occurred, was very far from watertight.

Washington quickly pledged to take military action against Damascus, although it had no legal pretext for doing so, not only because the attack was unproven but also because use of chemical weapons did not equate to a green light for Western attacks against a UN member state under any international law. The Syrian Air Force's Shayrat Airbase near Palmyra was chosen as the target for an American attack, as it was claimed that the alleged SAA chemical attack had been launched from the facility. The Pentagon later highlighted that approximately 100 Russian personnel were conducting operations from the facility, and while this facilitated a portrayal in the West of Russia as complicit in the alleged chemical attack, it also complicated potential operations to target the airbase.[36] In the late evening of April 6, Russian forces at Khmeimim Airbase were contacted by the U.S. Military with a warning that Shayrat Airbase was soon to be targeted by over 50 Tomahawk cruise missiles launched from American destroyers. Much as Syrian and Russian forces were wary of hitting the SDF due to the embedding of American personnel among them, the U.S. similarly sought to ensure that any Russian personnel could be evacuated from the airbase. In doing so, however, the U.S. also effectively provided the SAA with a warning of the attack – which would inevitably be conveyed through the Russians. This allowed Syrian forces to ensure that aircraft and other valuable war materials were stored in hardened bunkers and gave personnel time to take cover, with the slow subsonic Tomahawk missiles having neither the speed nor the penetrative capabilities required to threaten targets sheltered by fortifications.

After being struck by 59 cruise missiles the airbase appeared to be only partially damaged, with Su-22 strike fighters conducting sorties against insurgents within hours. As U.S. analysts at *The Drive* noted "unless you count old concrete as a weapon system or enemy, last night's strikes did no substantial damage to Assad's war fighting capability.... The strike did not even take out the base's runway or taxiways temporarily, meaning more missions can be flown from Shayrat in the near term. Even the base's air defences were left intact." They highlighted, as many analysts did at the time, that the attack was a purely political gesture with the early warning ensuring that it achieved very little militarily.[37] Moscow nevertheless slammed the attack as "an act of aggression against a sovereign country violating the norms of international law under a trumped-up pretext," claiming that it was an attempt to distract attention from growing reports of the high civilian casualties caused by American operations in Iraq.[38] This was likely a reference to the ongoing battle at Mosul, which saw a particularly high death toll among non-combatants and multiple allegations of serious U.S. war crimes.[39]

It appeared that the illegal strike, therefore, was intended more for appearance's sake rather than to actually erode the SAA's capabilities. The first reason for this was the considerable demand in the Western world for some kind of military action against the Syrian government. This stemmed from the West's centuries-old view of itself as the possessor of the world's supreme moral and humanitarian values, and as a global policeman to enforce these values with universal jurisdiction. In Western eyes, this placed it effectively above international law when pertaining to undertaking attacks on UN member states. The second reason was that an attack on Syria was seen to benefit the American position in Northeast Asia, the primary foreign policy focus of both the Trump and Obama administrations, as a show of force directed at both North Korea and China at a particularly sensitive time.

U.S. tensions with North Korea were rising fast in early 2017, with the East Asian state on the verge of developing viable nuclear missile deterrent capable of striking the American mainland which it proceeded to demonstrate later that year.[40] The U.S. had come to rely heavily on imposing secondary sanctions on parties trading with North Korea and threatening its major economic partners, China in particular, in order to increase pressure on Pyongyang.[41] With Beijing effectively closing the only legal avenue for Western strikes on either North Korea or Syria by vetoing or threatening to veto any Western-drafted resolutions authorizing use of force at the United Nations Security Council, it was highly notable that the American missile strike was launched as President Donald Trump was hosting his Chinese counterpart Xi Jinping for dinner. Syria was a close economic and defence partner of both China and North Korea, and the illegal attack sent an unmistakable message – American military action could not be constrained by international law, the UN Charter or the Security Council. President Trump was demonstrating his willingness to launch attacks on Chinese defense partners without UNSC approval and as a brazen crime of aggression – an action which had serious implications for the Korean Peninsula where American attentions were already focused. Trump reportedly leaned over to Xi mid-meal and informed him that a strike which he had ordered was currently underway.[42] Although Xi succeeded over the following days in convincing Trump that China was not in a position to influence Pyongyang,[43] the American attack on Syria arguably had far greater significance for Northeast Asia than it did for Syria itself.[44]

North Korea, for its part, cited this kind of illegal Western military action, which it termed "a clear and unforgivable act of aggression against a sovereign state," as precisely the reason why it was pursuing a nuclear deterrent in the first place.[45] With the U.S. launching further attacks on Syrian forces in May[46] and June,[47] Russia would offer stern warnings against such behavior and would be joined by China in carrying out unprecedented joint naval exercises in the Mediterranean in July. The two thereby presented a joint front in defence of Syria against the West, much as they had at the UNSC.[48] China stated its support for Russia's position, with Defense Minister Wei Fenghe pledging at the Moscow Conference on International Security: "the Chinese side has come to show Americans the close ties between the armed forces of China and Russia, especially in this situation. We have come to support you."[49] A week later on April 12, China announced large-scale live fire naval drills in the Taiwan Strait, which were interpreted by a number of military analysts as being intentionally scheduled to coincide with Western threats against Russia and Syria and a buildup of Western military forces near the latter. By doing so China ensured that the Western Bloc was pressed on multiple fronts, in solidarity with its embattled partners Damascus and Moscow.[50]

## Taking Deir ez-Zor

The Syrian Arab Army initiated an assault on one of Islamic State's final strongholds in mid-September, pressing into Deir ez-Zor with extensive support from Quds Force trained militias as well as from Russia. The degree of Russian participation in the operation was unprecedented, and with the SAA stretched across multiple other fronts the burden on militia groups was also unusually high. The Russian Air Force notably forward deployed Su-25 attack jets and Mi-24 attack helicopters to Tiyas Airbase in central Syria, placing them much closer to Deir ez-Zor than deployments from Khmeimim Airbase had and allowing them to conduct dozens of strikes per day. At the higher end of the Russian inventory, strike fighters and surveillance drones would maintain a strong presence over Deir ez-Zor, and were supported by daily sorties by the A-50 'flying radar' which helped coordinate the campaign and provide an early warning against potential threats.

In mid-August SAA units began to use Mi-17 transport helicopters to redeploy behind Islamic State lines, receiving support from Russian Ka-52 attack helicopters and, in the planning stages, from Russian military advisors. These airborne assaults allowed it to capture territory far more quickly. The first of these operations was conducted in the Raqqa governate on the night of August 11–12 and advanced SAA lines to just 120km west of Deir ez-Zor.[51] The final vestiges of the Islamic State would subsequently be cleared out of the area, with the insurgents losing ground rapidly to the SAA across the country and lacking the momentum or firepower to conduct any meaningful counteroffensives. The speed of the SAA's advances ensured that the opportunities for Western powers to capture territory in Syria were greatly reduced, with gains continuing to be made into the following months as IS territory was whittled down to almost nothing.

The SAA and allied forces built up their assets in both eastern Raqqa and in eastern Homs from mid-August in preparation for an assault on Deir ez-Zor, with the two forces expected to link up during the operation. Spearheading the assault were the Tiger Forces, the Republican Guard 800th regiment and the new 5th

Corps, which advanced into the governate from late August with little opposition. The primary target was the base of the SAA's 137th Brigade, which despite a major Western airstrike the year before and repeated Islamic State attempts to capture it, had held out under siege since 2013. The SAA came within 50km of Deir ez-Zor city by August 31 and came within three kilometres of the besieged military base on September 4, with remaining IS forces and a large minefield lying between them. The siege was broken the following day at around 14:00, with the Russian Navy firing three Kalibr cruise missiles to support the advance. Relieving Tiger Force units subsequently met with the members of the 137th Brigade, embraced them and posed together for photos. While it is disputed whether Deir ez-Zor was besieged from July 2014 when Islamic State took over the area, or from a year earlier when Al Qaeda linked militants had also besieged the local garrison before IS displaced them, the latter interpretation would make Deir ez-Zor one of the ten longest known sieges in world history – exceeding any other in the 20th or 21st centuries.

The 137th Brigade, led by their charismatic Druze commander the 'Lion of the Republican Guard,' General Issam Zahreddine, had endured massive and sustained pressure from Islamic State against considerable odds. The Russian military intervention had done much to relieve the burden on the garrison, with a vastly expanded logistical capacity facilitating more supply drops from the air. The aforementioned Russian strikes launched in November 2015, allegedly in response to the downing of an airliner over Sinai by IS, saw over 50 aircraft attack jihadist positions in Deir ez-Zor and take a heavy toll on its forces. The Russian Defence Ministry claimed 600 militants were killed by its cruise missile attacks alone.[52] In January 2016, when a large scale IS offensive overran key parts of the 137th Brigade's defence line, Tu-22M bombers were dispatched from bases in Russia itself to launch missile strikes on IS positions, with some of the aircraft also carpet bombing jihadist units with massive quantities of unguided munitions. With over 1,300 targets reportedly destroyed, this had ensured that IS would not turn its advances into a complete victory.[53]

After relieving the siege, the SAA's Tiger Force began operations alongside Hezbollah units to break through IS positions
to Deir ez-Zor Airbase, which had been isolated from the 137th
Brigade base since IS had made gains earlier in the year. Supported
by Russian Su-25 attack jets, there was relatively light resistance
and the siege on the base was lifted on September 9.[54] SAA units
from the Tiger Force and 5th Corps were also deployed to the north
for operations to secure territory up to the bank of the Euphrates
river, with the bulk of operations concluding by the September 24
and much of IS' forces having crossed north over the river. The
Russian Foreign Ministry had announced on September 15 that
some SAA units had crossed the river,[55] causing tensions with the
SDF which that day pledged to prevent a government advance
and saw the Euphrates as a dividing line between them.[56] The two
sides would race to secure the oil and gas fields held by Islamic
State,[57] which if placed under U.S. control would deny Damascus
key revenues for post-war reconstruction (see Chapter 8).

Following the announcement of an SAA river crossing, the
Pentagon claimed the Russian Air Force had bombed SDF forces
on September 16, with tensions continuing to rise in the aftermath.[58]
Amphibious vehicles, ferries and specialised Soviet-era bridging
equipment were used to rapidly expand the SAA contingent across
the river, providing it with vehicles including battle tanks and
APCs. Multiple amphibious operations allowed the SAA to seize
several villages across the Euphrates, with a bridgehead rapidly
built up and personally overseen by Russian Lieutenant General
Valery Asapov – the 5th Corps' senior advisor. Like the Syrian
Democratic Forces, Islamic State also realised both the danger
of allowing the SAA to cross the Euphrates, and the opportunity
SAA crossings presented for striking vulnerable units over the
river. Accordingly, IS launched drone strikes on and attempted to
surround SAA bridging sites. Russia responded to the urgency of
the situation by dispatching a Russian Army bridging unit which
used much more modern equipment including PMM-2M amphibious bridging ferries.[59] The Russian engineers quickly had a 210
meter long MARM road bridge working over the Euphrates that
was able to accommodate all kinds of vehicles including heavy

tanks – a target against which IS forces then launched multiple further drone strikes albeit to little effect.[60] Islamic State forces in Deir ez-Zor would persistently launch attacks on the SAA, at times with some success, with a drone unit causing a chain of massive explosions after striking a major arms depot at the Deir ez-Zor city sports stadium on October 8.[61] IS units on the ground increasingly emphasized mobility, which allowed them to better carry out hit-and-run raids that undermined SAA control of the governate and caused significant losses. Despite the damage caused and the effectiveness of their tactics, the remaining militants were ultimately quelled by overwhelming force.

Russian forces continued to play a major role in the campaign in eastern Syria, with the close proximity in which the SAA was operating to U.S.-backed forces making a Russian presence valuable as a deterrent to U.S. attacks. Russia quickly set up a forward base inside Deir ez-Zor city's former police academy and dispatched a sizeable de-mining team of 175 personnel to the area. After neutralising remaining IS positions outside the governate's capital, including the smaller cities of Mayadin and Abu Kamal,[62] the final target in Deir ez-Zor was the T-2 oil pumping station. This was one of the most prized targets in the area, and was taken by Hezbollah, Tiger Force and Fatemiyoun Brigade units with significant air support from Iranian drones. Russian air support[63] and missile strikes from Kilo Class submarines in the Mediterranean[64] played a key role in many of these engagements throughout October and into November. With very limited resources and manpower by this stage in the conflict, there was little IS could do to turn the tide and its forces would ultimately face defeat in Deir ez-Zor by early December.

## A New Kind of War

The defeat of the Islamic State in Deir ez-Zor marked the beginning of the end of major clashes between the Syrian Arab Army and Islamist insurgent groups as the primary focus of the Syrian War. The SAA moved on to capture jihadist held territories across the country, culminating in the capture of Daraa city – the

Jordanian border settlement where the war had first begun – six months later in July 2018. Upon the defeat of the insurgents in Daraa, *Foreign Policy* proclaimed in the title of a prominent article 'The Syrian War Is Over, and America Lost.' It highlighted that the Western objective of toppling the Syrian government had decidedly failed, and that America's inability to apply its power to reshape the country, as it had reshaped Iraq and Libya before, had shaken regional allies' faith in its dominance over the Middle East.[65] The UN special envoy for the Syrian conflict, Staffan de Mistura, had ten months prior similarly announced that the Western-backed opposition to the Syrian government had lost the war, and that this needed to be accepted as a reality.[66] Hezbollah's General Secretary Hassan Nasrallah had declared a government victory in the Syrian War in September 2017, five days after Mistura had,[67] and was followed by Israeli Defence Minister Avigdor Lieberman in November[68] and by Russian President Vladimir Putin in December who both declared the same.[69] While the Western goal of imposing a change in government had decisively been thwarted, efforts by the U.S. and its allies to effectively deny Syria a return to pre-war normalcy and a final conclusion to the conflict would continue. This ensured that what would have been a six-year war could extend for over twice that length or even indefinitely.

While insurgents operating independently were effectively neutralised by the SAA, significant parts of Syrian territory in the north and northeast were still occupied by the U.S. and Turkey respectively. Each of these areas hosted Islamist insurgent groups under the protection of the NATO states, with the Turks protecting the Al Nusra front and various affiliated jihadist groups which previously fought under the Free Syrian Army, while the Americans offered protection to the aforementioned jihadist groups it had allowed to join the Syrian Democratic Forces. The unwillingness of the Syrian Arab Army or its partners to go head to head with foreign powers such as the U.S., France and Norway, which deployed large numbers of their own forces to the occupied Syrian territories and demonstrated a readiness to defend their occupation with major air strikes, meant that the occupations would continue indefinitely. Deployment of NATO troops to Syrian soil would be paired with Western economic warfare efforts to weaken the Syrian state to the greatest extent possible.

The joint campaign of the U.S. Military and the Syrian Democratic Forces in Raqqa in late 2017 played a key role in the new strategy to undermine Syrian sovereignty. Their seizure of the governate's capital, Raqqa city, provided them with control over a major population centre and was a major boon to their control over northern Syria. The city was encircled in June and SDF forces began to penetrate it in July. The U.S. Department of Defence reported that by mid-October the SDF had taken over 1,300 casualties despite considerable American support, with the Islamic State putting up a staunch defence of its capital.[70] The city centre around the Al Naim roundabout area was dubbed the Circle of Hell due to the strength of IS defences there, with the jihadists using a similar tactic to that Al Nusra and other Al Qaeda-linked groups had used against the SAA – namely using hospitals packed with human shields as headquarters and as staging grounds for attacks.[71] Although there were only a few hundred IS fighters left in Raqqa city by mid-October, who were occupying around 10 percent of the centre, rooting them out from their heavily forti-fied positions was expected to take the lives of hundreds more SDF personnel. This led the two sides to come to an agreement, similar to that the SAA had made with Al Qaeda linked groups in Aleppo, to allow 250 of the remaining IS fighters and over 3000 of their family members, supporters, and hostages to be granted safe passage and transported to IS frontline positions. This included around 400 people who were taken by force as human shields.[72]

The campaign to seize Raqqa was extremely destructive, drawing limited criticism even from within Western media. As early as mid-June UN war crimes investigators reported: "We note in particular that the intensification of air strikes, which have paved the ground for an SDF advance in Raqqa, has resulted not only in staggering loss of civilian life, but has also led to 160,000 civilians fleeing their homes and becoming internally displaced."[73] The situation only worsened in the following weeks, with U.S.-led coalition airstrikes at times killing over 100 civilians in a day.[74]

While the West had roundly criticised the Russian air campaign against militants Aleppo a few months prior, the contrast between the two campaigns in terms of the precautions taken to avoid killing civilians was stark.[75] This could be partly explained by Russia's greater emphasis on a 'hearts and minds' approach, but also by the fact that the U.S. was at this stage doing its utmost to ensure that territorial gains could be made as quickly as possible in order to deny more territory to the Syrian government. Precautions to avoid civilian casualties tended to prolong operations considerably.

Both Damascus and Moscow had shown growing concerns regarding the nature of the American bombing campaign, and in particular what appeared to be the intentional destruction of vital and very costly infrastructure which, unlike the Syrian Air Force and its partners, the U.S. made little effort to avoid damaging. The Russian envoy to the UN office in Geneva, Alexei Borodavkin, had stated in October 2016 regarding the conduct of the U.S.-led air campaign: "the U.S.-led coalition has been systematically destroying infrastructure in government-controlled areas, delivering crushing strikes to civilians and the Syrian Army."[76] The Russian Defence Ministry had drawn attention to the same ongoing issue in April 2017, stating: "long before the start of the Russian campaign, the [overwhelmingly Western anti-IS] international coalition has been systematically destroying Syria's economic infrastructure to weaken the legitimate government as much as possible, heedless of burdens for civilians resulting in millions of refugees."[77]

While damage to Syrian infrastructure from the American bombing campaign was devastating, other aspects of the campaign were more serious still. In February 2017 the U.S. used one of the most toxic weapons in the world against civilian areas in Syria – depleted uranium shells.[78] These had previously been used in civilian areas in Iraq[79] and Yugoslavia[80] with often horrifying long lasting effects for the local populations including drastic rises in cancer rates and birth defects for the local populations. This contamination would last millions of years due to the element's very long radioactive half-life.[81] It is unclear if this was the only

American attack using such a weapon, possibly to combat test a new kind of depleted uranium round, or if there were further incidents throughout the campaign.

Alongside depleted uranium, in early September the U.S. Air Force was also reported to have used white phosphorus munitions in the town of Hajin in Deir ez-Zor. Exposure to burning phosphorus caused deep burns which were extremely difficult to heal, and its fumes were highly toxic, with the strike on Hajin reportedly causing large fires.[82] Although these weapons were banned under the Geneva Convention, the U.S. kept white phosphorous munitions in its inventory under the pretext of using them for smoke screens rather than against living targets. Considering that the very presence of the U.S. Military in Syria was already in direct violation of international law, it was hardly difficult to conceive that it would carry out further violations by using illegal weapons – ones also used by Turkey[83] and Israel[84] against civilian areas. Syrian state media also claimed that the U.S. had employed cluster munitions against civilian population centres in Deir ez-Zor, where civilian casualties from U.S. bombing were notably very high.[85]

After seizing Raqqa city in mid-October the primary objective of the U.S. and SDF advance was the capture of the Al Omar oil field, which was the largest in Syria and had the capacity to produce 75,000 barrels per day.[86] The field had been seized by IS in July 2014, and its capture by the SDF on October 23, 2017, which marked the end of the Raqqa campaign, allowed the U.S. to illegally extract and export Syrian oil to fund its operations in the country. More importantly, denying this key resource to Damascus would seriously undermine Syria's post-war reconstruction efforts and strongly complement escalating Western economic warfare efforts against the country (see Chapter 8). Al Omar was hardly the only major fossil fuel reservoir the SDF succeeded in taking, with its capture of the large Conoco gas field in late September also considered a major loss for the Syrian government.[87]

Syrian Arab Army and Syrian Democratic Forces units saw one of their few major direct military engagements in February 2017. While the circumstances of the clash remain uncertain, with the U.S. claiming the Syrian government was responsible, the

American response sent a strong signal that attacks on its forces and its proxies occupying Syrian soil would not be tolerated and would be countered with overwhelming force. On February 7 American troops stationed at the Conoco gas field called in large scale air strikes, including B-52H heavy bombers, AC-130 gun-ships, AH-64E Apache attack helicopters and both F-15E and F-22 heavy fighter jets to attack an SAA contingent in the vicinity.[88] The Americans alleged that Syrian forces had been advancing on the gas field, with some sources also claiming Russian forces were involved, although the Syrian government claimed the incident was an unprovoked "massacre."[89]

An investigative report by Germany's *Der Spiegel* claimed that while there were around 250 personnel from the SAA and various militias advancing towards Kasham, where U.S. and SDF forces were based, Russian forces were not among the advancing formations. Between ten and twenty Russian contractors were nevertheless killed in these American airstrikes, as they were stationed in the nearby town of Al Tabiyeh which was also hit by the U.S. attacks. Militiamen involved included both members of the local Bekara and Albo Hamad tribes as well as Quds Force trained foreign militiamen. The dead, according to the German report, included 80 Syrian soldiers, around 100 militiamen and around 70 tribal fighters.[90] U.S. Secretary of Defence James Mattis notably played down the possibility of Russian government involvement in the clash, stating in response to such reports that: "It makes no sense, it does not appear to be anything coordinated by the Russians."[91]

Western claims that Russian forces had joined an assault on the Conoco gas field, rather than being "in the wrong place at the wrong time" as the *Spiegel* account put it, are somewhat dubious given Russia's modus operandi in Syria. A notable example was the aforementioned assault on Al Tanf by the SAA on June 8, which had been held by Western special forces and affiliated militias. The assault had seen Russian Su-30 and Su-35 jets circle overhead to ensure than when the U.S. Air Force retaliated, it did not strike SAA positions themselves and instead only targeted an Iranian drone overhead. This was one of the few cases where

Syrian forces had attacked Western forces on the ground directly, and they had received extensive Russian support in the form of fighter jets flying overhead as a deterrent to escalation. It would be highly unusual, therefore, for an SAA offensive to take place which would not be provided similar support from the Russian Air Force particularly as Russian personnel were nearby. The exact course of events is unlikely to be fully verified in the near future. The U.S. show of strength, however, whether it was self-defence or indeed a massacre, demonstrated that it was willing to deploy massive firepower to ensure that the illegal occupation of much of Syrian territory remained unchallenged. It was also a demonstration of the extent of force the U.S. Military could bring to bear, despite the relatively small contingent deployed on the ground, due to the presence of airbases across the length and breadth of the Middle East hosting all manner of combat aircraft which could quickly lay down fire support.[i]

In late March, with the SAA continuing to make gains across the country against remaining jihadist outposts, the insurgency suffered another major blow as President Donald Trump announced that the U.S. would be withdrawing its forces from Syria in the near future.[92] The reasons for announcing such a move, which was met with dismay across much of the Western world particularly among the American left and in Europe, were manifold. They ranged from the strongly non-interventionist and anti-war orientation of much of Trump's support base[93] to the imperative of reducing costs and rebalancing away from the Middle East. The president's move in this direction was harshly criticised throughout the Western media as irresponsible, with widespread demands for the illegal occupation to continue under the pretexts of holding a tough line against the Syrian government and protecting Kurdish forces from neighbouring Turkey.[94]

---

i   The incident was followed three days later on February 10 by a successful U.S. drone strike on a Syrian T-72 tank, allegedly in self-defence after it had fired on American positions. Clashes between SAA and U.S. forces were otherwise infrequent, however. (Pawlyk, Oriana, 'US MQ-9 Reaper Drone Takes Out Russian T-72 Tank in Syria,' *Military.com*, February 13, 2018.)

In contrast to the Trump administration, which was just over a year old and had run on a platform of reconciliation with Syria and Russia and a withdrawal from the Middle East, the new administration in France would surpass even its predecessor in hawkishness and a strong tendency towards interventionism. French foreign policy had often been far more aggressive than that of the United States especially in the post-Cold War years. France had, alongside Germany, led calls for an illegal NATO military attack on Yugoslavia in the 1990s, while the United States was much more reluctant to do so.[95] In 2011 France had been the first country to launch airstrikes on Libya, a war which the U.S. had again been more hesitant to join, with leaked emails from State Secretary Hillary Clinton later revealing that a prime motivation for Paris was to prevent Tripoli's implementation of the African Gold Dinar gold backed currency.[96] This program would have seriously threatened France's neo-colonial sphere of influence in much of Africa, which the French economy was heavily dependent on retaining privileged access to.[97] In East Asia, too, France took the lead among European powers in deploying military force as part of a containment effort against China, and led calls for a greater European commitment to maintaining a large military presence in the region.[98] In 2013, while the political establishments in Britain and the U.S. had both hesitated regarding the possibility of attacking Syria, France had appeared the most eager to launch such an illegal military intervention and refrained only due to the lack of U.S. backing.[99]

In line with this long trend, France's newly elected President Emanuel Macron committed on March 29 to sending French military personnel to support the illegal occupation of northern Syria and bolster the SDF. Macron met with SDF leaders to assure them of Paris' support to this end, and while France had already provided extensive training to these militias, and its special forces already had strong presence in the area, French involvement would only escalate going forward.[100] With the U.S. showing growing hesitancy regarding its commitment to the campaign against the Syrian state, France would play a growing role in contributing to the broader Western war effort against the country.

## Douma and Another Highly Publicised Western Attack

On April 7, 2018, an estimated 40 to 50 people were reported killed in an alleged chemical weapons attack in the city of Douma, which was one of the insurgency's few remaining strongholds. Claiming to have proof of Damascus' culpability, France led the Western powers in attributing blame to the Syrian government and in calling for military action against Syria in response, with Britain and the United States closely following.[101] Russia and Syria both claimed that the alleged chemical attack was staged, with the Syrian Foreign Ministry referring to Western claims of such attacks as having become an "unconvincing stereotype" fabricated to undermine the country.[102] A number of international analysts supported the assessment that the attack was indeed staged, on the basis of both available evidence that the White Helmets had staged such incidents in the past, and that the Syrian government, having almost neutralised the insurgency in that part of the country, had no incentive to carry out chemical attacks. The Russian Military had notably issued statements in mid-March citing "reliable intelligence" that the White Helmets and militants were planning to stage and film a chemical weapons attack on civilians as a means of gaining Western military support.[103]

At the United Nations Security Council the three Western permanent members would veto a Russian-proposed resolution to investigate the chemical attack, with Russia reciprocating by vetoing a Western-proposed resolution which could have legalised an attack on the Syrian government. On April 14 France, Britain and the U.S. again bypassed the United Nations to launch another attack on Syrian government positions, and like their attack in April 2017 it constituted a crime of aggression without provocation or UN authorisation.[104] This move was supported by both the European Union[105] and NATO,[106] although even Britain's BBC highlighted that the justification for the attack "would return the world to the era before the advent of the UN Charter" – which had outlawed crimes of aggression and stripped states of the right to unilaterally attack others.[107] It was notable that no evidence of Syrian culpability had been presented, with the attack carried out just hours before inspectors from the Organisation for the Prohibition of Chemical Weapons arrived in the country.[108]

Sites targeted included a scientific research centre in Damascus, an equipment storage facility and command post near Homs, and multiple alleged chemical weapons storage facilities.[109] American B-1B heavy bombers deploying from Qatar fired nineteen JASSM-A cruise missiles, which were supplemented by sixty Tomahawk missiles fired by a Ticonderoga Class cruiser and two Arleigh Burke Class destroyers from the Red Sea and the Persian Gulf. This was disputed by an anonymous official from the U.S. Department of Defence who informed the *Washington Post* that 100 Tomahawk missiles had been launched – with the discrepancy potentially covering for the fact that several missiles had been intercepted.[110] A Virginia Class nuclear powered attack submarine launched six more Tomahawks from the Mediterranean. The attack was supported by four F-22, twelve F-15 and twelve F-16 fighters and EA-6B and E-11A-electronic warfare jets, which all deployed as a precaution against Syrian retaliation. Britain and France also contributed to the offensive and respectively deployed four Tornado and five Rafale fighter jets launching eight and nine Storm Shadow and Scalp cruise missiles. A French Aquitaine Class frigate further launched three MdCN cruise missiles. This contingent was supported by extensive aerial refuelling, airborne early warning and reconnaissance aircraft from the U.S. and France.

While the forces arrayed against Syria by the U.S. and France in particular were considerable, the attack was widely criticised by analysts in the West, Turkey and Israel as ineffective political theatre. Much like strikes of the previous year, their limited scope had a negligible effect on the tide of the war.[111] Speaking anonymously, an Israeli official directly contradicted Western claims that the operation had significantly influenced the Syrian conflict and countered: "The statement of 'Mission Accomplished' and [the assertion] that Assad's ability to use chemical weapons has been fatally hit has no basis." [112] A senior Israeli military official separately stated: "If President Trump had ordered the strike only to show that the U.S. responded to Assad's use of chemical weapons, then that goal has been achieved. But if there was another objective – such as paralyzing the ability to launch chemical weapons or deterring Assad from using it again – it's doubtful any of these objectives have been met."[113] Israel had been pressing for the United States to be "more active in the Syrian arena," with Defence Minister Avigdor Lieberman highlighting that due to unfavourable power trajectories in Syria and a looming government victory late in 2017, "the more the United States will be active, the better it will be for the State of Israel."[114] The underwhelming nature of the much-hyped subsequent U.S.-led military strike, therefore, was met with widespread disappointment in Israel as well as among the West's Gulf allies.

As had been the case in 2017, the Western powers were deterred from launching anything more than a token attack. Furthermore, the damage from the strike may well have been significantly less than intended if unverified Syrian and Russian reports were correct in contending that the bulk of the missiles launched had been intercepted by Syrian air defences.[115] Considering that the Western missiles used in the attack were all subsonic designs with low manoeuvrability, and the capabilities of Syria's air defence network had been improved with Russian and Korean assistance, this was highly possible. While it could not be confirmed how many Western missiles were shot down, Syrian defences had just two months prior downed an Israeli F-16I with advanced electronic warfare capabilities,[116] and had had a long time to prepare for more Tomahawk missile strikes with some prior knowledge of what their targets would be.

Not only was the attack underwhelming, but the blowback against Western interests was also considerable. Two American cruise missiles landed far from their targets, intact and unexploded in the Syrian desert, leading to widespread speculation that they had been brought down by Russian electronic warfare systems deployed to the country. The missiles – either Tomahawk or JASSM designs – were subsequently recovered and sent to Russia by plane on April 18, with the information gained likely to be shared to allow Western adversaries to better counter them.[117] Russian air defences including S-400s and A-50 aircraft, were notably active and scanning Syrian airspace throughout the attack, which provided a valuable opportunity to analyse NATO's latest cruise missiles in flight.

In response to the Western attack, Chief of the Main Operational Directorate of the Russian General Staff Colonel General Sergey Rudskoy highlighted that Moscow was willing to consider plans to equip Syria, and potentially "other states," with advanced air defence systems such as the S-300. This would be done to provide a more effective defence and deter potential future American or European offensive actions.[118] First deputy chairman of the Russian parliament's lower house defence committee, Alexander Sherin, further specified: "It is necessary to consider not only deliveries of missile defence systems, but also deliveries accompanied by those people who can train the personnel of these countries, so that Syria, Iran and North Korea could deploy these systems, if they wanted."[119] While Russia's need to remain on good terms with Israel led it to decide against providing S-300s to Syria in May,[120] it would continue to provide upgrades to the S-300s already in Iranian service.[121] North Korea had already developed its own analogue to the S-300, the Pyongae-5,[122] although it would over the next two years begin to field more advanced successors to this system which were speculated to have benefitted from transfers of Russian S-400 technologies.[123]

While the Russian military presence, and to a lesser extent Syria's own strategic deterrent, had been key to deterring anything more than a token Western attack, reports in the U.S. indicating a desire for strikes which were more aggressive still in nature highlighted why it was imperative that Western ambitions be reined in. Western analysts had widely questioned why Syria's government could not be brought down completely with military attacks, as the governments of Iraq, Panama, Libya, Grenada and many more before them had. A notable example was an article published by *The Conversation* titled: 'Why Can't Trump Just Take Out Assad?.' This point was raised on the dual basis that not only did the West have an inherent right as the self-proclaimed moral leader of the world to act above international law and determine which governments could stay and which needed to be brought down, but also that the West had near unrestricted power to do so in the post-Cold War world. While the former remains a key ideological basis for the predominant worldviews in the Western world, the latter was no longer the case.

U.S. President Donald Trump later recalled in 2020 that he had supported taking military action to kill the Syrian president in April 2018 but had been talked out of taking such action by Defence Secretary James Mattis. It was unclear whether President Trump was being honest or simply trying to appear tough, which was often popular with voters in an election year, with Trump having stated in September 2018 that the assassination of President Assad was "never ever discussed." This was in response to claims by journalist Bob Woodward that he had advocated an assassination.[124] The U.S. president would strongly criticise Russia for supporting "Animal Assad,"[125] whom he otherwise referred to as "a Gas Killing Animal who kills his people and enjoys it."[126] Nevertheless, with Russia's air defences and fighters on standby, and its warships and bombers beyond Syria well within a few minutes' range of it, the U.S. was forced to refrain from its tendency to launch strikes on the capitals of third world nations and assassinate their leaders.[ii]

The OPCW released its findings on the alleged Douma chemical weapons attack in December 2019. Its report notably sparked considerable controversy due to both the methodology used and the leaks issued by whistle blowers from within the organisation highlighting misconduct in the investigation. While the report alleged that the Syrian government was responsible for a chemical attack, leaked documents and emails showed that a significant number of the inspectors raised the issue that the final report "did not reflect the views of the team members that deployed to Douma." The documents revealed that the OPCW had

---

ii  A notable precedent for an attempted assassination through air strike was the Reagan administration's attempt to kill Libyan leader Muammar Gaddafi in 1986. (Hersh, Seymour M., 'Target Qaddafi,' *New York Times,* February 22, 1987.)

For a list of several dozen third world leaders the U.S. has sought to assassinate, see: Blum, William, *Killing Hope: U.S. Military and C.I.A. Interventions Since World War II,* London, Zed Books, 2003 (Appendix III).

omitted evidence which had strongly contradicted the claim that Syria had been responsible.

Regarding how the report reached its conclusions, British OPCW engineer & ballistics expert Ian Henderson, who had been on the ground in Douma at the site of the alleged attack as part of the investigation team, noted:

My concern which is shared by a number of other inspectors relates to the subsequent [OPCW] management lockdown and the practices in the later analysis and compilation of the final report. There were two teams deployed, one team, which I joined shortly after the start of field deployments, was to Douma in Syria. The other team deployed to country X. The main concern relates to the announcement, in July 2018, of a new concept, the so-called FFM [Fact-Finding Mission] core team which essentially resulted in the dismissal of all of the inspectors who had been on the team deployed to locations in Douma and had been following up with their findings and analysis. The findings in the final FFM report were contradictory, were a complete turnaround with what the team had understood collectively during and after the Douma deployments and by the time of release of the interim report, in July 2018, our understanding was that we had serious misgivings that any chemical attack had occurred.

What the final FFM report does not make clear and thus does not reflect the views of the team members who deployed to Douma, in which case I can only really speak for myself at this stage. The report did not make clear what new findings, facts, information, data or analysis in the fields of witness testimony, toxicology studies, chemical analysis and engineering and or ballistic studies, had resulted in a complete turnaround in the situation from what was understood by the majority of the team and the entire Douma team in July 2018. In my case, I had followed up with a further six months of engineering and ballistics studies into the cylinders, the result of which had provided further support for the view there had not been a chemical attack.[127]

Essentially, the conclusions of the team on the ground were discarded and the conclusions of a second team based outside Syria, which were contradictory, were chosen instead.[128] Several of Henderson's colleagues came forward with similar reports regarding the nature of the OPCW's investigation, with significant documentation released through Wikileaks to support these claims and highlight the deliberate omission of evidence and misrepresentation of the team's findings on the ground in Syria.[129]

Former Director of Britain's special forces, Major General John Holmes, who had headed a panel of nine to hear whistleblower testimony from a senior OPCW scientist in Brussels, said the case for a lack of OPCW transparency in the Douma investigation was "very convincing" and that perhaps "the issued report did not reflect the findings on the ground."[130] The whistleblower, reporting anonymously as 'Alex,' had stated that "most of the Douma team felt the two reports on the incident, the interim and final reports, were procedurally irregular and possibly fraudulent."[131] Holmes highlighted that "Alex" "stood there for four five hours and he had proof of all his allegations," and that he was "extremely well qualified" for his position and highly convincing. All the documents in the whistleblower report, according to Holmes, contained strong indicators that the OPCW report did not reflect the findings on the ground, citing as an example the positions of the alleged gas canisters which showed that they could not have been dropped from the air by SAA aircraft as the White Helmets and the final OPCW report had claimed. Holmes highlighted that biases and external influences on the OPCW's procedures could lead to the organisation losing credibility, and that it was essential for the OPCW to prevent such recurrences or else the world would lose a vital institution.[132]

Former Chief of Staff to United States Secretary of State Colin Powell and retired Army Colonel, Lawrence Wilkerson, similarly stressed that the conduct of the OPCW in Douma needed to be corrected for the sake of the organisation's future credibility and viability. The investigation, he stated, was "a very convoluted process which produced a good report [the first report exonerated Damascus] and then produced a report that was more politically influenced than it was a report on the facts." He described it as a "tragic mistake," an "egregious situation" and "an attempt to subvert an otherwise pretty sound organisation." Wilkerson noted regarding the OPCW report that it came as part of a broader trend under which the U.S. placed immense pressure on international organisations to reflect its own interests – something he witnessed first-hand. He highlighted as an example the efforts leading up to the 2003 invasion of Iraq to press the International Atomic Energy Agency to fall in line with allegations that Iraq was developing nuclear weapons, which was the central pretext for the illegal U.S.-led invasion but went against available evidence. Another example was the extensive efforts to ensure that from its foundation, the International Criminal Court would not prosecute Americans for war crimes despite these being committed widely and across much of the world. Beyond these two examples, Wilkerson stated: "we brought undue pressure on other international organisations to more or less influence them to make decisions that were in line with our policy preferences and in line with our security preferences."[133]

Comparisons between the alleged Douma chemical attack and Iraq's alleged weapons of mass destruction were made widely, including by former UN Assistant Secretary-General and UN Humanitarian Coordinator for Iraq Hans von Sponeck.[134] Criticising sensational reporting on the Douma chemical attacks, Wilkerson stated:

> I saw that some of the claims were preposterous, simply preposterous. When you see a man standing beside a crater, for example, and alleged VX or Sarin was used, you know its preposterous. The man would be dead. I know how effective these kinds of chemical weapons are. And I know also what kind of weapons Syria had in stockpile. We had a dossier on that... Count me very

sceptical on even any use of chemical weapons by the Syrian government in Syria, that's the start point.[135]

Former British ambassador to Syria Peter Ford noted regarding the danger to the Western position posed by revelations that the chemical weapons allegations were false:

> It's an embarrassing development for the three powers [U.S., UK and France] which used the pretext of the Douma incident to bomb Syria in 2018. The whole narrative for the war of Syria would come apart at the seams. It would call into question not only the Douma incident but all the other many incidents that had been cited to allegedly prove that Assad is a butcher who is gassing his people. And the thing about Douma is that it was the one and only occasion when independent international experts were able to go to the alleged site of the alleged incident and actually find out what went on or what didn't go on in this case... The evidence pointed away from Assad being responsible. It's clear from the latest leaks that the people, the experts who actually went to the site were very unhappy about the way their findings were doctored by other officials of the OPCW, some of whom were working from Turkey and working hand-in-glove with the Western powers.[136]

Ford referred to claims of Syrian Arab Army chemical weapons attacks on civilians as "the crux of the anti-Syria narrative" in the West. He stressed that these allegations were vital to prevent the Syrian government from being seen as the 'good side' in the war whenever evidence emerged that the anti-government insurgency was overwhelmingly comprised of Al Qaeda type militant groups.[137] Much as was the case with coverage of the White Helmets, Western media outlets would harshly criticise those journalists, experts and investigators who highlighted the considerable inconsistencies in the allegations being made against the Syrian state.

# Notes

1   'Dozen of Russian Su-25 Attack Aircraft Passed Through Iran to Syria,' *Defense 24,* January 12, 2017.
2   'Russian tech experts set up land satellite network in Syria,' *TASS,* August 25, 2017.
3   Ripley, Tim, *Operation Aleppo: Russia's War in Syria,* Lancaster, Telic-Herrick Publications, 2018 (pp. 163–165).
4   'Russia says 4 military police battalions deployed to Syria,' *Military Times,* July 26, 2017.
5   'Islamic State: We captured Turkish tanks in Syria battle,' *Middle East Eye,* December 22, 2016.
6   Davies, Gareth, 'The £4million German tank dubbed "one of the best in the world" is shown up in Syria: Leopard 2 bought by Turkey to fight British-backed Kurds has numerous faults exposed in lethal fashion,' *Daily Mail,* January 31, 2018.
7   Lekic, Slobodan, 'Germany's Leopard tanks prove vulnerable in Islamic State fight,' *Stars and Stripes,* January 17, 2017.
8   Roblin, Sebastien, 'Turkey's Leopard 2 Tanks Are Getting Crushed in Syria,' *National Interest,* November 9, 2019.
9   'Er galt als unzerstörbar: In Syrien wird ein Panzer-Mythos zerstört' [It was considered indestructible: a tank myth is being destroyed in Syria], *Focus,* January 12, 2017.
    Hegmann, Gerhard, 'Syrien: Leopard-2-Verluste kratzen am deutschen Panzer-Mythos' [IS fighters destroy the German tank myth], *Die Welt,* January 12, 2017.
10  'Turkey's European Made Tanks Continue to Prove Highly Vulnerable Against Lightly Armed Insurgent Groups, Ankara looks to South Korea for Alternatives,' *Military Watch Magazine,* January 22, 2018.
    'Turkey's Elite Korean Battle Tanks; How the Ambitious Atlay Program Based on the K2 Black Panther Reflects Ankara's Aspirations,' *Military Watch Magazine,* July 16, 2018.
    'South Korea Puts World's Best Battle Tank Back in Production; Manufacture of Elite K2 Black Panthers Resumes,' *Military Watch Magazine,* June 1, 2019.
11  Gebauer, Matthias and Schult, Christoph, 'Berlin Weighs Tank Deal with Turkey to Free Journalist,' *Spiegel,* January 22, 2018.
12  Ripley, Tim, *Operation Aleppo: Russia's War in Syria,* Lancaster, Telic-Herrick Publications, 2018 (p. 160).
13  'Syrian army, allied militia gain ground against IS,' *AP News,* May 27, 2017.
14  'Çöl taarruzu: Suriye ordusu, +20.000 kilometrekare alanı kontrol altına aldı' [Desert offensive: Syrian army took control over 20,000 square kilometers], *Al Masdar News,* June 10, 2017.
15  Ripley, Tim, *Operation Aleppo: Russia's War in Syria,* Lancaster, Telic-Herrick Publications, 2018 (pp. 166–167).
16  'How Did a 30 Year-Old Su-22 Defeat a Modern AIM-9X?,' *Key Aero,* June 23, 2017.

Mizokami, Kyle, 'How Did a 30-Year-Old Jet Dodge the Pentagon's Latest Missile?,' *Popular Mechanics,* June 26, 2017.

17  Fisk, Robert, 'US air strikes in Syria: Why America really attacked pro-Assad militia convoy,' *The Independent,* May 19, 2017.

18  Ripley, Tim, *Operation Aleppo: Russia's War in Syria,* Lancaster, Telic-Herrick Publications, 2018 (pp. 168–170).

19  Schleifer, Theodore and Merica, Dan, 'Trump: "I now have responsibility" when it comes to Syria,' *CNN,* April 6, 2017.

20  Bellingeer III, John B., 'Legal Questions Loom Over Syria Strikes,' *Council on Foreign Relations,* April 15, 2018.

21  Burns, Robert, 'US has no evidence of Syrian use of sarin gas, Mattis says,' *Associated Press,* February 2, 2018.

22  Smith-Spark, Laura, 'France "has proof" Assad regime was behind Syria chemical weapon attack,' *CNN,* April 26, 2017.

23  Solon, Olivia, 'How Syria's White Helmets became victims of an online propaganda machine,' *The Guardian,* December 18, 2017.

24  Blumenthal, Max and Norton, Ben, 'Yet another video shows U.S.-funded white helmets assisting public-held executions in rebel-held Syria,' *Salon,* May 25, 2017.
Tuberville, Brandon, 'Al-Qaeda Leader Praises White Helmets As "Hidden Soldiers Of The Revolution",' *Mint Press News,* May 9, 2017.

25  van Wilgenburg, Wladimir, 'Kurds say White Helmets not welcome to help fight fires in northeast Syria,' *Kurdistan 24,* June 14, 2019.

26  Sanchez, Raf and Cheeseman, Abbie and Oliphant, Roland and Yuksekkas, Burhan and Mendick, Robert, 'James Le Mesurier, British ex-army officer who trained Syria's White Helmets, found dead in Istanbul,' *The Telegraph,* November 11, 2019.

27  Almasian, Kevork, 'Eva Bartlett Debunks Syrian War & Exposes White Helmets,' *Syriana,* May 30, 2018.
Bartlett, Eva, 'Decision to bring White Helmets to Canada dangerous and criminal,' *RT,* August 10, 2018.

28  'How the World May End – John Pilger on Venezuela, Trump & Russia' [Interview with John Pilger], *Going Underground – RT,* May 25, 2017.

29  'Eastern Ghouta – White Helmets Embedded with Terrorist Groups,' *Youtube Channel of Vanessa Beeley,* May 6, 2018.
'White Helmets Working With Al Qaeda: Bab Al Nairab, Aleppo,' *Youtube Channel of Vanessa Beeley,* May 2, 2017.

30  Beeley, Vanessa, 'John Pilger: The White Helmets Are A "Complete Propaganda Construct",' *Mintpressnews,* May 26, 2017.

31  Kennedy, Dominic, 'White Helmets left Omran Daqneesh in pain to harm Assad, claims Rev Andrew Ashdown",' *The Times,* June 5, 2018.
Kennedy, Dominic, 'Syria trips by clergy and peers "undermine UK",' *The Times,* October 27, 2018.

32  'White Helmets making staged video of Idlib chemical attack – SANA,' *TASS,* September 22, 2018.

33  'Syria's White Helmets suspend members caught on camera during rebel execution,' *RT,* May 19, 2017.

'White Helmets member caught on camera disposing of Syrian soldiers' mutilated bodies,' *RT,* June 23, 2017.

34    Ritter, Scott, 'Ex-Weapons Inspector: Trump's Sarin Claims Built On "Lie",' *The American Conservative,* June 29, 2017.

35    Ripley, Tim, *Operation Aleppo: Russia's War in Syria,* Lancaster, Telic-Herrick Publications, 2018 (p. 162).

36    Vanden Brook, Tom and Onyanga-Omara, Jane and Korte, Gregory, 'Pentagon says Russia could have stopped Syrian chemical weapons attack,' *USA Today,* April 7, 2017.

37    Rogoway, Tyler, 'America's Tomahawk Missile Attack on Syria's Shayrat Air Base Was a Sham,' *The Drive,* April 7, 2017.
      Read, Zen, 'Syrians Say Air Base Operational Just One Day After U.S. Cruise Missile Strikes,' *Haaretz,* April 8, 2017.

38    'Putin calls US strikes against Syria "aggression against sovereign country",' *TASS*, April 7, 2017.

39    Malsin, Jared, 'Civilian Casualties From American Airstrikes in the War Against ISIS Are at an All-Time High,' *Time,* March 26, 2017.
      George, Susannah, 'Mosul is a graveyard: Final IS battle kills 9,000 civilians,' *Associated Press,* December 21, 2017.
      Hall, Richard, 'Were high civilian casualties in Mosul unavoidable?,' *The World,* July 13, 2017.

40    Abrams, A. B., *Immovable Object: North Korea's 70 Years At War with American Power,* Atlanta, Clarity Press, 2020 (Chapter 14: Introducing Mutual Vulnerability: Implications of North Korea Attaining a Nuclear-Tipped ICBM).
      Warrick, Joby and Nakashima, Ellen and Fifield, Anna, 'North Korea now making missile-ready nuclear weapons, U.S. analysts say,' *Washington Post,* August 8, 2017.
      Dominguez, Gabriel, 'USFK confirms North Korea's Hwaseong-15 ICBM can target all of US mainland,' *Janes,* July 11, 2019.

41    Mullen, Mike and Nunn, Sam and Mount, Adam, *A Sharper Choice on North Korea: Engaging China for a Stable Northeast Asia,* Council on Foreign Relations, Independent Task Force Report No. 74, September 2016.
      *Background Briefing by Senior Administration Officials on the Visit of President Xi Jinping of the People's Republic of China,* Washington D.C., April 4, 2017.
      Baker, Gerard and Lee, Carol and Bender, Michael, 'Trump Says He Offered China Better Trade Terms in Exchange for Help on North Korea,' *Wall Street Journal,* April 22, 2017.
      Lee, Dong Hyuk, 'Analysis: What Trump Inherited from Obama,' *VOA,* June 7, 2018.

42    Alexander, Harriet and Boyle, Danny and Henderson, Barney, 'US Launches Strike on Syria – How it Unfolded,' *The Telegraph,* April 7, 2017.

43    Baker, Gerard and Lee, Carol and Bender, Michael, 'Trump Says He Offered China Better Trade Terms in Exchange for Help on North Korea,' *Wall Street Journal,* April 22, 2017.

44   Abrams, A. B., *Immovable Object: North Korea's 70 Years At War with American Power*, Atlanta, Clarity Press, 2020 (Chapter 20: Economic Warfare).

45   Park, Ju-min and Kim, Jack, 'North Korea calls U.S. strikes on Syria "unforgivable",' *Reuters,* April 8, 2017.

46   Risk, Robert, 'US air strikes in Syria: Why America really attacked pro-Assad militia convoy,' *The Independent*, May 19, 2017.

47   Browne, Ryan, 'New details on US shoot down of Syrian jet,' *CNN*, June 22, 2017.

48   Gady, Franz-Stefan, 'Chinese Navy Conducts Live-Fire Drill in Mediterranean,' *The Diplomat*, July 13, 2017.

49   Tiezzi, Shannon, 'China, Russia, "Show Americans" Their Close Relationship,' *The Diplomat*, April 10, 2018.

50   'China to mount navy drills in Taiwan Strait "to support Russia",' *South China Morning Post*, April 12, 2018.

51   'Russian KA-52 Helicopters, Syrian MRBLs Work in Tandem To Attack Islamic State Positions,' *Defense World,* August 14, 2017.
     'Russian Defense Ministry appreciates Army's air drop operation behind ISIS lines,' *Syrian Arab News Agency,* August 14, 2017.
     'Syrian army for first time liberates town from Islamic State in airborne operation,' *TASS,* August 14, 2017.

52   'Over 600 IS terrorists killed by cruise missiles in Deir ez-Zor – Russian defense minister,' *TASS,* November 20, 2015.

53   'Russian Warplanes Destroy Over 1,300 Terrorist Targets in Syria in One Week,' *Sputnik,* January 2, 2016.

54   'Syrian army breaks ISIL siege in Deir Az Zor airbase,' *Al Jazeera,* September 9, 2017.

55   'Russia: Syria government forces now on east bank of Euphrates river,' *Reuters,* September 15, 2017.

56   Perry, Tom and Dadouch, Sarah, 'U.S.-backed Syrian fighters say will not let government forces cross Euphrates,' *Reuters,* September 15, 2017.

57   Osseiran, Hashem and Oilver, Nawar, 'The Battle for Deir Ezzor Continues,' *Atlantic Council,* October 6, 2017.

58   'Russia accused of striking US-backed forces in Syria,' *Deutsche Welle,* September 15, 2017.

59   'Russia has deployed PMM-2M amphibious bridging ferry in Syria,' *Army Recognition,* September 27, 2017.

60   'Russian Army Erects Bridge in Syria Amidst Shelling by Terrorists,' *Defense World,* September 26, 2017.
     'Russian army puts up bridge in record time to deploy heavy arms, aid across Euphrates,' *TASS,* September 26, 2017.

61   'Syria: Footage shows Islamic State drone blowing up stadium ammo dump,' *ABC News,* October 25, 2017.

62   'Syria army, allies retake Albu Kamal from IS: military source,' *Yahoo News,* November 19, 2017.

63   'Russian strategic bombers strike IS terrorists in Syria,' *Xinhua,* November 18, 2017.

'Russian Tu-22M3 long-range bombers conducts airstrikes in Syria,' *DefPost,* November 23, 2017.

64 'Two Russian Project 636.3 Submarines Launched Cruise Missile Against IS Targets in Syria,' *Naval Recognition,* October 6, 2017.
'Russian Sub Launches Strike With Cruise Missiles on Daesh in Deir ez-Zor,' *Sputnik,* October 31, 2017.
'Russia targets ISIS with Kalibr cruise missiles,' *CSIS Missile Threat,* November 3, 2017.

65 Cook, Steven A., 'The Syrian War Is Over, and America Lost,' *Foreign Policy,* July 23, 2018.

66 'Syrian conflict: Opposition must face reality it lost war against Assad, UN says,' *ABC News,* September 6, 2017.

67 Perry, Tom and Golubkova, Katya, 'Hezbollah declares Syria victory, Russia says much of country won back,' *Reuters,* September 12, 2017.

68 'Israel's defense minister says Syria's Assad has won the civil war,' *Times of Israel,* October 3, 2017.

69 Isachenkov, Vladimir, 'Putin declares victory on visit to air base in Syria,' *AP News,* December 11, 2017.

70 'Department of Defense Press Briefing by General Jarrard via teleconference from Baghdad, Iraq,' *U.S. Department of Defense,* October 31, 2017.

71 'Islamic State fighters using human shields in Raqqa pockets as U.S.-backed forces take most of city,' *Japan Times,* September 22, 2017.
Davison, John, 'Islamic State hostages, strongholds stand between U.S.-backed forces and Raqqa's capture,' *Reuters*, October 2, 2017.
Sim, David, 'Battle for Raqqa photos: Isis confined to hospital and stadium, with hostages and snipers in both,' *International Business Times,* October 3, 2017.

72 Somerville, Quentin and Dalati, Riam, 'Raqqa's dirty secret,' *BBC News,* November 13, 2017.
Gayle, Damien, 'Last Isis fighters in Raqqa broker deal to leave Syrian city – local official,' *The Guardian,* October 14, 2017.

73 'Raqqa battle: "Staggering" civilian toll in strikes on IS,' *BBC News,* June 14, 2017.

74 '"Coalition strikes kill 106 civilians" in Al Mayadeen,' *Al Jazeera,* May 26, 2017.

75 Ripley, Tim, *Operation Aleppo: Russia's War in Syria,* Lancaster, Telic-Herrick Publications, 2018 (pp. 127–128).

76 'US-Led Coalition Destroys Infrastructure in Syria, Attacks Civilians – Envoy,' *Sputnik,* October 21, 2016.

77 'US Coalition Has Been Destroying Syrian Infrastructure Since 2012 - Russian MoD,' *Sputnik,* April 4, 2017.

78 Oakford, Samuel, 'The United States Used Depleted Uranium in Syria,' *Foreign Policy,* February 14, 2017.

79 Edwards, Rob, 'U.S. fired depleted uranium at civilian areas in 2003 Iraq war, report finds,' *The Guardian,* June 19, 2014.

80 '"Up to 15 tons of depleted uranium used in 1999 Serbia bombing" – lead lawyer in suit against NATO,' *RT,* June 13, 2017.

81    Hindin, Rita and Brugge, Doug and Panikkar, Bindu, 'Teratogenicity of depleted uranium aerosols: A review from an epidemiological perspective,' *Environmental Health,* vol. 4, no. 17, August 26, 2005.

Doyle, P. and MacOnochie, N. and Davies, G. and MacOnochie, I. and Pelerin, M. and Prior, S. and Lewis, S., 'Miscarriage, stillbirth and congenital malformation in the offspring of UK veterans of the first Gulf war,' *International Journal of Epidemiology,* vol. 33, no. 1, 2004 (pp. 74–86).

Sen Gupta, Amit, 'Lethal Dust: Effects of Depleted Uranium Ammunition,' *Economic and Political Weekly,* vol. 36, no. 5/6, February 2001 (pp. 454–456).

82    'US jets strike Syrian town with banned white phosphorus bombs – Russian Defense Ministry,' *RT,* September 9, 2018.

83    Trew, Bel, 'Turkey faces scrutiny over alleged use of white phosphorus on children in northern Syria,' *The Independent,* October 19, 2019.

84    McCarthy, Rory, 'Israel accused of indiscriminate phosphorus use in Gaza,' *The Guardian,* March 25, 2009.

'Long-Burning Fires: White Phosphorous on Sheikh Rajleen,' *In Gaza,* 2009 (https://ingaza.wordpress.com/2009/01/16/long-burning-fires-white-phosphorous-on-sheikh-rajleen/).

85    'US-led coalition uses banned cluster bombs in Deir Ezzor,' *Syrian Arab News Agency,* November 14, 2018.

'Syria war: "Cluster bombs" dropped on IS-held village,' *BBC News,* June 28, 2017.

86    Masters, James, 'Syria's largest oil field captured by US-backed forces,' *CNN,* October 23, 2017.

87    Al-Khalidi, Suleiman, 'U.S.-backed forces capture big gas field in Syria's Deir al-Zor: senior commander,' *Reuters,* September 23, 2017.

88    Gibbons-Neff, Thomas, 'How a 4-Hour Battle Between Russian Mercenaries and U.S. Commandos Unfolded in Syria,' *New York Times,* May 24, 2018.

89    'Syria war: Assad's government accuses US of massacre,' *BBC News,* February 8, 2018.

90    Reuter, Von Christoph, 'The Truth About the Russian Deaths in Syria,' *Der Spiegel*, March 2, 2018.

91    'Media Availability with Secretary Mattis En Route to Brussels,' *U.S. Department of Defense,* February 13, 2018.

92    Browne, Ryan and Starr, Barbara, 'Trump says US will withdraw from Syria "very soon",' *CNN,* March 29, 2018.

93    Hemmer, Nicole, 'After the Syria strikes, right-wing non-interventionists are back in the wilderness,' *Vox,* April 15, 2017.

Steinhauer, Jennifer, 'Trump's Opposition to "Endless Wars" Appeals to Those Who Fought Them,' *New York Times,* November 1, 2019.

Thomsen, Jacqueline, 'Trump supporters slam decision to launch strikes against Syria,' *The Hill,* April 14, 2018.

94    Hanoush, Feras, 'The Dangers of a US Withdrawal from Syria,' *Atlantic Council,* April 8, 2018.

Alaaldin, Ranj, 'How withdrawing from Syria would embolden Russia and Iran,' *Brookings Institute,* April 5, 2018.

95   Macleod, Alex, 'French Policy toward the War in the Former Yugoslavia: A Bid for International Leadership,' *International Journal*, vol. 52, no. 2, Spring, 1997 (pp. 243–264).

96   Asher-Schapiro, Avi, 'Libyan Oil, Gold, and Qaddafi: The Strange Email Sidney Blumenthal Sent Hillary Clinton In 2011,' *Vice News*, January 12, 2016.

97   'Just Business: China Encroaches on Former French Colonies in Africa,' *Sputnik*, May 20, 2015.
'France's Colonial Tax Still Enforced for Africa, "Bleeding Africa and Feeding France",' *Centre for Research of Globalization*, January 14, 2015.
Marchesin, Philippe, *Mitterand l'Africain*, Universite de Paris (http://www. politique-africaine.com/numeros/pdf/058005.pdf).

98   Panda, Ankit, 'French Defence Minister to Urge EU South China Sea Patrols,' *The Diplomat*, June 6, 2016.
Paskal, Cleo, 'A French Pivot to Asia,' *The Diplomat*, May 1, 2017.
Kelly, Tim and Kubo, Nobuhiro, 'French carrier to lead joint amphibious Pacific drill in show of force aimed at China,' *Reuters*, March 17, 2017.
Kubo, Nobuhiro, 'French amphibious carrier visits Japan ahead of Pacific show of power,' *Reuters*, April 29, 2017.

99   Bremer, Catherine and Irish, John, 'France says ready to act over Syria, despite British refusal,' *Reuters*, August 30, 2013.

100  Irish, John and Pennetier, Marine, 'France's Macron vows support for northern Syrians, Kurdish militia,' *Reuters*, March 29, 2018.

101  'Syria "chemical attack": France's President Macron "has proof",' *BBC News*, April 12, 2018.

102  'Foreign Ministry: Allegations of using chemical weapons unconvincing stereotype,' *Syrian Arab News Agency*, April 8, 2018.

103  'Russia says U.S. plans to strike Damascus, pledges military response,' *Reuters*, March 13, 2018.

104  Bellingeer III, John B., 'Legal Questions Loom Over Syria Strikes,' *Council on Foreign Relations*, April 15, 2018.
'Syria strikes violated international law – are the rules of foreign intervention changing?,' *The Conversation*, April 18, 2018.

105  'Mogherini says EU backs strikes on Syria, reiterates political solution,' *Xinhua*, April 14, 2018.
Oroschakoff, Kalina, 'Broad support from EU leaders for Syria strikes,' *Politico*, April 14, 2018.

106  'Statement by the NATO Secretary General on the actions against the Syrian regime's chemical weapons facilities and capabilities,' *NATO Press Release*, April 14, 2018.

107  Weller, Marc, 'Syria air strikes: Were they legal?,' *BBC News*, April 14, 2018.

108  Burns, Robert and Colvin, Jill and Miller, Zeke, 'Trump: US, allied strikes aimed at Syria's chemical weapons,' *AP News*, April 14, 2018.

109  Rocha, Veronica and Wills, Amanda and Ries, Brian, 'US, UK and France strike Syria,' *CNN*, April 13, 2018.
'Syria air strikes: UK confident strikes were successful, says PM,' *BBC News*, April 14, 2018.

110  Gearan, Anne and Ryan, Missy, 'U.S. launches missile strikes in Syria,' *Washington Post*, April 13, 2018.

111  Derbyshire, Jonathan, 'Opinion today: Syria strikes accomplish little,' *Financial Times*, April 17, 2018.
McCausland, Phil and  Talmazan, Yuliya, 'Trump's U.S.-led airstrike on Syria won't stop Assad's chemical capabilities, experts say,' *NBC News*, April 15, 2018.
Mason, Paul, 'Futile air strikes on Syria won't defeat Assad and Putin,' *New Statesman*, April 11, 2018.
Al-Marashi, Ibrahim, 'Trump's strike didn't stop Assad last year and won't stop him now,' *Al Jazeera*, April 14, 2018.

112  Bergman, Ronen, 'Israeli intelligence: Objectives of Western strike in Syria not achieved,' *Ynet News*, April 17, 2018.

113  Ibid.

114  'Israel sees Assad winning Syria war, urges more U.S. involvement,' *Reuters*, October 3, 2017.

115  Beaumont, Peter and Roth, Andrew, 'Russia claims Syria air defences shot down 71 of 103 missiles,' *The Guardian*, April 14, 2018.

116  'Syria shoots down Israeli warplane as conflict escalates,' *BBC News*, February 10, 2018.

117  'Blowback from Western Strikes Intensifies; Syria Recovers Two Unexploded U.S. Cruise Missiles, Sends to Russia for Analysis,' *Military Watch Magazine*, April 23, 2018.
'Syria hands over two unexploded cruise missiles to Russia found after US strike – source,' *TASS*, April 19, 2018.

118  'Russia Considers Providing Syria with More Modern Air Defences; Other Defence Partners to Follow,' *Military Watch Magazine*, April 15, 2018.
'Trump's Syria Missile Strike May Set Back Israel's Strategic Position,' *Astute News*, April 22, 2018.

119  'Russia Considers Providing Syria with More Modern Air Defences; Other Defence Partners to Follow,' *Military Watch Magazine*, April 15, 2018.

120  'Russia Cancels S-300 Sale to Damascus at Israel's Request; How Moscow's Support for Syria Has Waned Since the USSR's Fall,' *Military Watch Magazine*, May 13, 2018.

121  'Deterring the West: Russia Bolsters Iranian Air Defences With New Missiles for S-300 Systems – Reports,' *Military Watch Magazine*, July 18, 2020.

122  'North Korean Air Defence Systems Take Centre Stage - Ballistic Missiles Conspicuous by their Absence; What the Latest Military Parade Signifies Regarding Pyongyang's Evolving Strategy,' *Military Watch Magazine*, September 10, 2018.
'KN-06 (Pon'gae-5),' Missile Threat, *CSIS Missile Defense Project*, June 15, 2018.

123  'North Korea Now Has Its Own Version of the S-400 Long Range Air Defence System - What Capabilities to Expect,' *Military Watch Magazine*, October 11, 2018.

124 Woodward, Alex, "'I had shot to take out Assad": Trump claims he was close to killing Syrian leader but Mattis stopped him,' *The Independent*, September 15, 2020.
Samuels, Brett, 'Trump says he wanted to take out Syria's Assad but Mattis opposed it,' *The Hill*, September 15, 2020.

125 Nussbaum, Matthew, 'Trump blames Putin for backing "Animal Assad",' *Politico*, April 4, 2018.

126 Sullivan, Eileen and Shear, Michael D., 'Trump Promises Strike on Syria and Warns Russia Against Backing Assad,' *New York Times*, April 11, 2018.

127 'Douma false "chemical weapon" narrative: Ian Henderson speaks to UN about OPCW report,' *Youtube Channel of Vanessa Beeley*, January 20, 2020.

128 Ibid.

129 'OPCW Douma Docs,' *Wikileaks* (https://wikileaks.org/opcw-douma/document/).
'OPCW Douma Docs, Omission_of_ppb_levels_in_Interim_R_on_6-July,' *Wikileaks* (https://wikileaks.org/opcw-douma/document/Omission_of_ppb_levels_in_Interim_R_on_6-July/).
'OPCW Douma Docs, DG-memo1,' *Wikileaks* (https://wikileaks.org/opcw-douma/document/DG-memo1/).

130 'Ex-British Special Forces Director- OPCW Could Lose All Credibility Over Syria Douma Leaks!,' *Going Underground, RT*, January 27, 2020 (Episode 836).

131 ONeill, James, 'Emerging Evidence on Continuing Allied Lies About the War in Syria,' *New Eastern Outlook*, February 19, 2020.

132 'Ex-British Special Forces Director- OPCW Could Lose All Credibility Over Syria Douma Leaks!,' *Going Underground, RT*, January 27, 2020 (Episode 836).

133 Lawrence Wilkerson Speaking at the Arria-Formula Meeting of the United Nations Security Council, April 16, 2021.

134 Hans von Sponeck Speaking at the Arria-Formula Meeting of the United Nations Security Council, April 16, 2021.
Aaron Maté, 'Did Trump Bomb Syria on False Grounds?,' *Nation*, July 24, 2020.

135 Lawrence Wilkerson Speaking at the Arria-Formula Meeting of the United Nations Security Council, April 16, 2021.

136 Becker, Brian and Kirakou, John, 'Loud and Clear News of the Day – With Peter Ford,' *Sputnik*, December 17, 2019.
'Western Narrative of Syrian Chemical Attacks "Comes Apart at Seams" Amid OPCW Leaks,' *Sputnik*, December 18, 2019.

137 Becker, Brian and Kirakou, John, 'Loud and Clear News of the Day – With Peter Ford,' *Sputnik*, December 17, 2019.
'Western Narrative of Syrian Chemical Attacks "Comes Apart at Seams" Amid OPCW Leaks,' *Sputnik*, December 18, 2019.

# Chapter 8

# Ending the Syrian War

## The End of the War

By the end of 2018 it was evident that the Syrian War was drawing to a close, with U.S. Director of National Intelligence Dan Coats concluding at the beginning of the following year that the insurgency had been defeated.[1] In the first week of December, UN special Syria envoy Staffan de Mistura said there was "no major military territorial conflict" at present, with almost all territory which had not been captured by the SAA being under the control of parties Syrian forces dared not attack – namely the militaries of the United States and Turkey.[2] On December 11, 2018, the Syrian Arab Army ordered the demobilization of a portion of its conscript and reserve personnel, which was an unprecedented step reflecting falling manpower requirements as control of the large majority of the country's territory continued to stabilise.[3] Seven months later in July 2019, as part of the same trend, Hezbollah announced that it was withdrawing a portion of its forces from Syria as the SAA was now capable of managing security without their support.[4]

On December 19, following on from his pledge to do so in March,[5] U.S. President Donald Trump declared that the Islamic State had been decisively defeated and that the U.S. forces in Syria, which numbered well over 2000 personnel at that point, were to be withdrawn within 60–100 days.[6] The move was described across much of Western media as a "shock" to American allies and was very widely and harshly criticised in the West,[7] both for reducing pressure on the Syrian government and its allies and for "abandoning" the SDF. One of the few things which unified American lawmakers across both major parties at this point was support for military action and opposition to non-interventionism, with many in the West believing the SDF under U.S. protection should form

the basis of a Kosovo-type separate government artificially partitioned from Syria.

Trump's withdrawal pledge was followed by signs of a
crack in the hardline position taken by the Gulf States against
Syria, with the United Arab Emirates reopening its embassy in
Damascus on December 28[8] and Bahrain following suit on the
29.[9] This amounted to an effective recognition that the Syrian government had prevailed in the conflict. It was also interpreted as an
attempt to further undermine Qatar and Turkey, the two regional
powers which had been most hostile to Damascus and most sup-
portive of the insurgency, due to the major rift between them and
the remainder of the Gulf States that had begun in 2017. Signs
of rapprochement between the Gulf States and Syria were seen
with much apprehension in the West, which went to considerable
lengths to discourage any improvements in relations.[10]

In the face of a prospective U.S. withdrawal, Kurdish forces in
the SDF requested that the Syrian Arab Army return to the Manbij
countryside in northern Aleppo near Turkish positions, with some
reports indicating that an SAA contingent was deployed in the
final week of December.[11] Kurdish groups expressed a strong
willingness to see a return of Syrian government rule, particularly
given the possibility of attempts by Turkish backed jihadist groups
to impose their own authority alongside the Turkish military.[12]
Ankara claimed the Kurds had no authority to make such a decision – somewhat ironically since it was the Turkish military presence in Syria and its support for Al Qaeda linked militants which
were illegal – as opposed to the restoration of Syrian government
control over Syrian territory which the Kurds had every legal right
to request.[13] It was confirmed in early January that Russian military police were tasked with patrolling the area between Kurdish
and Turkish held parts of Syria as peacekeepers.[14] The Syrian
Foreign Ministry had notably stated that it was open to granting
Kurdish regions of Syria greater autonomy after the war,[15] which
bore a very stark contrast to the expected conduct of Turkey and
its jihadist affiliates which were known among other things for
ethnic cleansing of Kurdish held areas.[16]

The Trump administration's withdrawal decision was almost unanimously opposed across the Western world, with the imperative of a continued Western occupation of northern Syria[17] highlighted by a wide range of figures. These ranged from French President Macron, who pledged to keep French occupation forces in northern Syria even if the Americans left,[18] to the head of the New York based International Rescue Committee, David Miliband, who coined the term 'Westlessness' to claim insufficient Western interventionism was a leading problem facing Syria.[19] Britain and France notably drafted plans to fully replace the American occupation force by surging their own military presences in northern Syria,[20] with Germany entering secret talks to send aircraft to patrol the area.[21] This was to ensure that even with U.S. forces gone, and the Kurds requesting a return of the Syrian military, the territory could still be forcibly denied to the Syrian government and kept under Western control by the more hawkish European states.

Britain ultimately pulled back from committing to replace the American occupation force, as it notably lacked the air power needed to enforce its presence without U.S. support.[22] Its special forces would nevertheless continue to operate extensively on Syrian soil[23] alongside those of other Western states such as Norway[24] and Denmark.[25] France continued to take the lead in holding to a hard line position against Syria, having threatened not only to attack the Syrian state whenever needed, but also to remake the country in the image of the West.[26] "I have a broader message, a simple message: You can count on us. We will be there not only for today's wars but also for those of tomorrow," the French Armed Forces Minister Florence Parly pledged regarding prospective future attacks against the Syrian forces.[27]

No Western forces had authorisation from either Damascus or the United Nations to be in Syria, which meant that all Western military activities on Syrian soil were still entirely illegal. Despite the initial European panic, the Trump administration was prevented from seeing through plans for a full withdrawal[28] due largely to immense domestic pressure[29] in the U.S. from both political parties,[30] the State Department and the intelligence

services. Outgoing U.S. special representative for Syria engagement, James Jeffrey, would publicly admit in November 2020 that
defence officials were intentionally deceiving the administration
regarding the scale of military operations in Syria due to their
disagreement with the policy of withdrawal, with the number
of occupation troops remaining in the country far exceeding the
numbers President Trump had agreed to. This highlighted the
limits of the president's power when going against the consensus
view of the foreign policy establishment.[31]

Although a full-scale withdrawal did not materialise, following the partial U.S. withdrawal in October 2019 Kurdish forces
quickly moved to further strengthen ties with the Syrian government and with Russia. This facilitated the deployment of Russian
peacekeepers and the Syrian Arab Army to strategic positions in
northern Syria where American special forces had formerly been
deployed – a major gain for the Syrian government.[32] The partial
withdrawal was thus not only rebuked across the Western media,
but was also widely described as a "gift to Assad and Putin."[33] As
highlighted by the director of the Middle East and North Africa
programme at the European Council on Foreign Relations, Julien
Barnes-Dacey, as a result of its agreement to effectively protect
the Kurds "Damascus is looking stronger than ever."[34] The purpose of these Syrian and Russian deployments was to prevent
expansion by Turkey and Turkish-backed militants into parts of
northern Syria with a predominantly Kurdish demography, with
the Kurdish YPG militias unable to hold back such forces without
support. Facing mounting Western criticism for the new partnership, SDF commander in chief and YPG leader Mazloum Abdi
stated that the choice between partnership with the Syrian government and Russia and occupation by Turkish forces and affiliated
jihadist groups was a choice "between compromises and the genocide of our people."[35] Considering the prior conduct of Turkish
backed jihadist groups, which Turkish special forces operated
closely alongside, this may not have been much of exaggeration.
Russia's stern criticism of a Turkish invasion of northern Syria as
"unacceptable" did much to gain the Kurds' favour,[36] and as the
predominant Kurdish groups sought only greater autonomy, not

outright separation or a change in the Syrian government, there was much room for cooperation.

The Syrian government now had a foothold in northern Syria and was on the way to reassimilating Kurdish areas, albeit with more autonomy than before the war. This left only two major barriers to bringing the war to a complete end. These were the Western occupation of some remaining areas of northern Syria, in particular the centres of the country's oil and gas industries, as well as the ongoing jihadist occupation of the Idlib governate on the Turkish border under Ankara's protection.

## Economic Warfare and the West's Ongoing Campaign Against Syria

While fighting across the large majority of Syrian territory drew to a close, the Western powers which had played the leading role in organising the insurgency were going to considerable lengths to exacerbate Syrian losses, prolong its state of economic ruin and thereby prevent the country's re-emergence as a major independent player in the Middle East. This strategy had two major facets, which were the employment of primary and secondary economic sanctions to hinder post-war reconstruction and the illegal appropriation of Syrian natural resources to deny revenues to the state needed for reconstruction.

*Foreign Policy* gave one of the most astute assessments of the nature of both the intentions of the Western powers towards post-war Syria and of their sanctions regime, stating in July 2020:

> When James Jeffrey, U.S. special envoy for Syria, said on May 12 that his job was to make Syria "a quagmire for the Russians," the remark went largely unnoticed. Jeffrey's words were not merely, it turns out, intended to convey a general sense of opposition to Russian designs in Syria. They headlined a series of measures intended to prevent the return of normality to regime-controlled Syria, to foment renewed crisis, and thus to turn Syria from an asset to a burden for both Moscow and Tehran.

The main method for achieving these goals has been the strangling of the Syrian economy.[37]

Wartime damage to Syrian infrastructure had been considerable, with the United Nations estimating the cost of reconstruction at approximately $250 billion – four times the country's pre-war GDP. Although this was on the high side, and could likely be considerably lower if non-Western parties were contracted for infrastructure development, the amount was still considerable.[38] Sectors affected ranged from power generation to water and sanitation, with over 50% of social infrastructure out of operation.[39] In the past the Soviet Union and the Warsaw Pact countries such as East Germany and Czechoslovakia had provided major assistance to third world countries for both post-war reconstruction and economic modernisation. The most significant instances were China from 1949 after its civil war[40] and North Korea from 1953 after the Korean War,[41] both of which had suffered much more severe damage than Syria but successfully recovered relatively quickly due to Soviet Bloc assistance. In the post-Soviet world, however, third world states were in a much weaker position to pursue post-war recovery, meaning Syria would suffer for lack of support from a superpower sponsor with the USSR now gone.

Syria's economy had quickly deteriorated during the war, and by 2013 several of the country's oilfields and much of its agricultural land had fallen under insurgent control. This forced the Syrian government to import both oil and food for the first time. Syria imported 1.5 million tonnes of wheat in 2014, and by early 2015 was importing 60,000 barrels per day of oil.[42] Iran stepped in as a leading source of economic support from this point, providing $1 billion in loans for food imports and to support depleted foreign reserves, and $3.6 billion for oil. Iraq, too, provided oil at 50% below market price which did much to reduce the burden on the Syrian government.[43] Syria's debt grew in the war's first three years from 29% of GDP in 2010 to 59% in 2013, much of it owed to Iran, and this would continue to rise quickly.[44] Iran was able to entrench itself as a central player in the Syrian economy during the war, with bilateral trade growing from $300 million in

2010 to $1 billion in 2014 despite an overall contraction of the Syrian economy. Iran quickly emerged as Syria's largest trading partner with a free trade agreement having been implemented in 2012.[45] Although Iranian assistance had been invaluable during the war, the country was in a poor position to assist with post-war reconstruction. Renewed American economic sanctions on Tehran under the Donald Trump administration from 2018 and a collapse in the price of oil meant infrastructure in parts of Iran itself fell into a poor state, and so long as Syria remained stable it was far from a priority for Iran to stimulate Syrian growth. Nevertheless, some investments from Iranian firms including agreements to build a power plant, an oil refinery[46] and housing units in Damascus[47] were made.

Although it had lost its superpower status in 1991, and its economy had contracted very sharply in the aftermath and had yet to recover,[48] Russia also promised assistance to the Syrian recovery effort from an early stage.[49] While Moscow controlled an economy which was far weaker and less dynamic than it had been the Cold War years when the Soviet economy had been the second largest in the world[50] and consistently one of the two fastest growing, Russia could still provide some limited support and was expected to have first choice for major contracts particularly in the oil and gas sectors.[51] Development of the Tartus port and of Syria's railway infrastructure, with a view of linking the Mediterranean coast to the Persian Gulf by rail, was another project in which Russia had shown considerable interest.[52]

While Russian and Iranian support were limited, North Korea[53] and China[54] were well known for robust, fast and highly cost-effective infrastructure development as seen in their own countries. Both were expected to play leading roles in reconstruction efforts with both having extensive experience in carrying out overseas infrastructure projects across the world.[55] North Korea had made significant contributions to Syria's health sector during the war, as was frequently reported by Syrian state media,[56] and the two had signed trade agreements and expanded trade considerably in that time.[57] Syria showed a particular interest in commissioning Korean companies for reconstruction in 2019, with agreements signed for new free trade zones that year.[58] The two began discussions on post-war reconstruction no later than 2017.[59] The very high purchasing power foreign currencies had in the Korean economy, particularly relative to Russia and Iran, meant that this may well have presented the most cost effective option. It was notable that Syrian products also had a growing presence at Pyongyang's international trade fairs, possibly indicating an expanding volume of trade between the two countries, with the size of their presence being wholly disproportionate to the size of the Syrian economy.

China, too, was a leading provider of economic assistance which would allow Syria to further withstand Western pressure, and like North Korea it shared much more in common with Syria ideologically than Russia or Iran did.[60] Aside from potential investment, China's position as the world's largest economy[61] and by far the largest industrial producer largely undermined the effects of Western and allied embargoes – as almost any goods, from heavy industrial machinery to consumer products, were made readily available. The shift in the global economy away from the West, fuelled primarily by China's rise, was thus a major asset to countries being targeted by Western economic warfare across the world from Venezuela and Zimbabwe to Myanmar and Iran. By mid-2018 China had pledged to invest $2 billion in Syrian industry, centred on a plan to construct an industrial estate that could house up to 150 companies.[62] Chinese firms subsequently took centre stage at the 60th Damascus International Fair in 2018, which was the first since the war started, with more than 200 in attendance.[63] At the fair considerable assistance for the Syrian economy was promised including the construction of car manufacturing facilities, steel and power plants, and hospital development.[64] Assistance from the Chinese state has been considerable, with one example being the donation of 800 electrical power generators which were delivered at a ceremony at the port in Latakia in October 2018.[65] Multiple further donations, ranging from 100 new busses provided to help rebuild the country's public transport system in June 2019,[66] to medical supplies[67] and COVID-19 test kits[68] in 2020, gave much needed support to Syria's post-war economy.

China's Huawei, the world's largest telecommunications equipment firm, signed agreements in late 2015 committing to rebuild Syria's entire telecommunications system, with China offering $6 billion worth of investments in addition to $10 billion worth of existing contracts that year.[69] Perhaps most significantly, several analysts highlighted that China could link Syria into the China-Central Asia-West Asia economic corridor as part of its Belt and Road Initiative. This had the potential to fuel growth and provide far greater opportunities for the Syrian economy than those that had existed before the war.[70] Construction of a railway network from Syria's Homs governate to ports in Lebanon could be a key part of this.[71] China was Syria's largest trading partner preceding the war, with its firms having a major role in the Syrian oil industry, and while this relationship would have almost certainly ended had a Western, Gulf or Turkish appointed successor to the Ba'ath Party taken power, the fact that the Syrian state prevailed provided significant grounds for maintaining and expanding positive ties.[72] China quickly restored its position as the country's leading trading partner, and by 2017 80% of Syrian exports were going to the East Asian country.[73]

The U.S. and Europe, for their part, sought to obstruct and deter Chinese investment by preventing businesses in Syria from using dollars or euros for trade. America also threatened to impose secondary economic sanctions on Chinese firms operating in Syria, which would limit their access to the Western-centred global financial system and to any business opportunities with Western firms.[74] Based on prior cases of Chinese investment in countries similarly targeted by the West, such as North Korea and Venezuela, this was expected to cause only a partial reduction in Chinese interest in Syria – with Chinese firms highly adept in and at times receiving state support to evade Western sanctions. With many major Chinese firms and banks already heavily sanctioned for doing business with Western target states,[75] they are likely to be more averse to Western threats when considering investment in Syria.

The Arab Gulf States, with the notable exception of Qatar, emerged as a key potential source of funds for Syrian reconstruction efforts due largely to their eagerness to counter Iranian influence in Syria and to take a stand against Turkish expansionism.[76] These states had all cut or downgraded relations with Syria after the outbreak of the war and overseen its expulsion from the Arab League, but by balancing them against Iran and against Turkey in particular, or at least appearing to do so, Damascus could potentially gain considerable investment or even aid for its war-torn economy. Signs of improving relations between Damascus and the Saudi-led bloc of Gulf States began to emerge from late 2018, first with the unexpected embrace of the Syrian and Bahraini foreign ministers at the UN General Assembly in September.[77] This was followed by a revelation to Kuwait's *Al Sahed* newspaper by President Assad that Syria had reached a "major understanding" with unnamed Arab states after years of hostility.[78] In late October Jordan, a state heavily dependent on Gulf patronage and locked closely into the Gulf States' sphere of influence, reopened the Nassib-Jaber border crossing with Syria which, as the *Financial Times* reported, was "worth billions of dollars... marking a step towards reintegrating Syria into the regional economy."[79]

In December the visit to Damascus by Sudanese president Omar Al Bashir, a longstanding Western adversary who had nevertheless maintained close relations with the Gulf States, was widely interpreted as the beginning of a normalisation process between Syria and the Gulf. Sudan, a significant arms supplier to Syria, was expected serve as an intermediary.[80] Bashir was the first Arab leader to visit Syria since the war began, and led one of a minority of Arab governments which maintained close ties to Damascus. He had previously voiced support for Syria and the Russian military intervention there, stating: "Peace isn't possible without Assad... What's happening in Syria is the result of American intervention there. Instability in the region is a direct result of U.S. intervention."[81] The overthrow of his 30-year administration in a Western-backed coup four months later and installation of a staunchly pro-Western government, which oversaw a near total economic collapse in Sudan within 18 months,[82] eliminated the possibility of a Sudanese role in the peace process.[83] Nevertheless, the reopening of the UAE and Bahraini embassies in Damascus by the end of December 2018 signalled a significant geopolitical shift regarding Syria's position,[i] and with the insurgency defeated Syria was increasingly being seen as a potential asset to the Gulf States' ambitions rather than a target.[84] Tunisia, a small Arab state closely aligned with both the Gulf and the West, simultaneously announced that it was resuming direct flights to Damascus on December 27.[85]

The Western powers went to considerable lengths to prevent a potential rapprochement between Damascus and the Western client states in the Arab world, with the passing of the Caesar Act in the United States in 2020 threatening secondary sanctions on any foreign company which participated in reconstruction efforts in Syria. Deterring Gulf investment in or rapprochement with Syria, and ensuring that Western client states continued to conduct policy in line with the West's hard line against the Syrian government, were repeatedly highlighted by analysts as key reasons for passing the Caesar Act. As an assessment from the *Brookings Institute* stated on June 19, 2020, two days after the act came into force, its implementation "throws serious obstacles in the path of the Gulf regimes, including the United Arab Emirates, which have begun to normalize their ties with the Assad regime, abandoning their support of Syria's opposition over the past decade." The paper acknowledged that sanctions would bring suffering "to Syrians already reeling from 10 years of violent conflict and economic deprivation," but highlighted that Western economic warfare efforts would be sustained "to move the regime toward a meaningful political transition."[86]

---

i    Saudi Arabia notably backed away from reconciliation with Damascus following the controversy over its alleged role in killing the journalist Jamal Khashoggi in October 2018, which led it to fall back into line with the Western powers against Syria as part of a broader effort to improve its image in the Western world. In May 2021 signs re-emerged of a potential thaw in relations when the head of the Saudi General Intelligence Directorate, General Khalid Humaidan, led a delegation to Damascus. "Events have shifted regionally and that provided the opening," a Saudi official commented on the meetings, which he said had been planned for a long time. (Maracon, Joe, 'The Muted Arab Attempt to Restore Influence in Syria,' *Arab Center Washington DC,* March 18, 2020.) (Chulov, Martin, 'Meeting between Saudi and Syrian intelligence chiefs hints at détente,' *The Guardian,* May 4, 2021.)

Since the outset of the war, "political transition" in Western rhetoric had consistently meant nothing less than the stepping down of the Syrian president,[87] and most often the removal from power of the Ba'ath Party as well. This and the imposition of Western-style political reforms were a key prerequisite for the Western powers to deescalate their economic warfare efforts.[88] Not only were the countries of the Western Bloc unilaterally waging economic warfare until their extreme conditions were met, but they would also exert a strong influence on the United Nations to support these efforts. Leaked internal documents revealed that the UN had directives to provide no humanitarian aid to Syria until there was a "political transition." This directive was initially denied by UN officials[89] before being confirmed by whistle blowers inside the organisation, and had notably led UNESCO to deny Russian requests to help restore partially destroyed World Heritage sites in Syria. This effectively made the UN complicit[ii] in the Western effort to impose a change of government in Syria by impeding its post-war recovery and placing downward pressure on living standards.[90]

What the West had failed to achieve by a proxy war it was now trying to achieve through economic warfare, namely the toppling of the political organisation which had presented the oldest and at times the staunchest opposition to Western hegemony over the Middle East for over half a century – the Syrian Ba'ath Party. Turkey, for its part, would if anything support a much harder line against Syria, as indicated by a prominent publication by the director of the Security and Defence Research Program at the leading Istanbul-based think tank EDAM, Can Kasapoğlu. Titled 'Time

ii  Syrian government sources had repeatedly alleged that there was a strong bias at the UN towards the Western agenda for the removal of the Syrian government. Cited among other things were statements favouring a removal of Bashar Al Assad as president by UN Special Envoy to Syria, Lakhdar Brahimi, discrimination towards Syria's UN ambassador including cutting feeds during speeches, intentional provision of poor translators, and exclusion by officials from important sessions addressing the Syrian conflict. (Foreign Ministry: Brahimi Statements Deviate from the Essence of his Mission, *Syrian Arab News Agency*, January 10, 2013.) (Bartlett, Eva, 'Scoundrels & gangsters at UN: Silencing the Syrian narrative, *RT*, February 4, 2015.)

to Put "Maximum Pressure" on Syrian Baath Regime,' it high-lighted, among other things, that the Syrian government's close ties to both North Korea and Hezbollah meant it needed to be targeted for intensive pressure – presumably until it cut ties with all NATO adversaries and adopted a pro-Western foreign policy stance.[91] The paper reflected the general trend of Turkish hostility towards Syria and its willingness, more so than any other Middle Eastern state, to support a hard line and back Western economic warfare efforts.

Western efforts to cripple the Syrian economy since 2011 were consistently undermined by an inability to impose sanctions through the United Nations Security Council, with such resolutions having been vetoed by the Council's two non-Western per-meant members China and Russia. Both countries also harshly condemned Western unilateral sanctions aimed at preventing post-war reconstruction in Syria, with the Chinese representative referring to such efforts as "simply inhumane" and repeatedly calling for their cessation.[92] The two non-Western states' use of the veto at the Security Council to prevent the Western powers from targeting Syria notably fueled Western calls for a reform of the Council to annul the veto system and facilitate easier passage of Western drafted resolutions in future.[93] Insofar as the Western world was positioned at the heart of the global financial system, however, even unilateral sanctions could harm the Syrian econ-omy. Nevertheless, the shift in the centre of global economy away from the West and towards East Asia, combined with the West's very extensive use of unilateral sanctions against states which opposed its will, meant the impact on Syria was somewhat weaker than expected.[94] Not only were many firms now more willing to risk being sanctioned by the West, but the means of sanctions eva-sion had also increased considerably as a growing community of countries were targeted and as many more still, from Indonesia[95] to India[96] to Egypt[97] among several others, were threatened with targeting.

Alongside sanctions, the economic crises in Iran from 2019 due primarily to Western sanctions and low oil prices,[98] and even more severely in neighbouring Lebanon in 2020 due largely to the high level of corruption in the country,[99] served to seriously undermine the Syrian economy. The Lebanese crisis in particular contributed to a period of hyperinflation as the Syrian lira went into free fall. In April 2020 the United Nations World Food Programme estimated that the cost of a basket of basic goods such as flour and oil had increased by 111 percent in just twelve months,[100] leaving many families with serious food shortages.[101] The COVID-19 health crisis that year would only further exacerbate this, with soaring prices causing unprecedented hardship[102] in previously stable government strongholds.[103] It was notable that other Western targets such as North Korea had managed to keep prices[104] and exchange rates[105] stable and maintain respectable growth rates[106] despite enduring much harsher sanctions. Syria, however, was not only less developed from the outset and less self-reliant, but the severe damage done to the economy by the war meant the country was in no position to endure concerted Western economic warfare efforts or provide for its population.

The combination of war followed by intense sanctions to prevent reconstruction had previously been used by the Western powers to target Iraq in the 1990s. There sanctions had followed the devastation of Iraqi infrastructure by Western air attacks which left the population without power, medicine or clean water[107] and on a below starvation level calorie intake.[108] It was estimated that over 500,000 children died as a direct result.[109] The Syrian situation was less severe, in part because the West had failed to pass UNSC sanctions resolutions against it where they had succeeded against Iraq. Furthermore, due largely to Russian intervention, they had been unable to launch an unrestricted Iraq-style bombing campaign which would have further destroyed the country's infrastructure. The situation was still serious, however, and as in Iraq Syria's access to medicines was hindered by the sanctions regime. This was particularly dangerous considering the already devastating impact of the war on public health.[110] The fallout from U.S. and EU sanctions was observed long before their escalation in 2020, with award winning Middle East correspondent for the *Financial Times* and *The Independent,* Patrick Cockburn, stating in 2016 that they were "imposing an economic siege on Syria as a whole." Strongly implying that they could be considered war crimes, he stressed that Western sanctions could be killing more civilians than major military sieges were – raising death rates considerably by blocking supplies of medicine and spare parts for medical equipment among other means.[111] The West appeared to be doing everything possible to exacerbate the crisis and prevent a recovery, which in turn ensured that the Syrian population would know no post-war respite. The desolation of war with Western-backed jihadist militants was thus replaced by the suffering of a largely Western imposed destitution.

While the defeat of the Western-backed insurgency was a foregone conclusion, prolonging both the economic and the security crises in the country was pursued by the Western powers with the intent of spoiling the Syrian government's victory. This was attested to in March 2020 by the State Department's special envoy for Syria James Jeffrey, who stated that while the SAA "are out to get a military victory in all of Syria… our goal is to make it very difficult for them to do that by a variety of diplomatic, military, and other actions." Jeffrey highlighted that the continued presence of U.S. personnel in the country was "a complication" for Damascus' efforts to restore the pre-war status quo, as was the U.S. and EU "ban on any reconstruction assistance to put this country back together again." He further pledged that the U.S. would respond "in a very savage military way" should the SAA use chemical weapons again, meaning offensive military options were still on the table.[112] Beyond this, the U.S. had pledged to "disrupt" any oil shipments to government owned ports in Syria to further undermine economic recovery.[113] Britain acted on this in 2019 and deployed the Royal Marines to seize an Iranian tanker heading for Syria,[114] which it agreed to release under significant Iranian pressure but only on the condition that the oil onboard was not delivered to the Syrian government.[115]

Israel, too, was reported in March 2021 to have carried out several dozen attacks on Iranian shipping to Syria in international waters over the past year, with a particular focus on attacking ships carrying oil. *Haaretz* described it as part of an "all out effort" by the Israeli Navy for which a wide range of weapons, including submarines and mines, were used against civilian shipping.[116] These attacks, combined with Western and Turkish control of many of Syria's oil facilities, were credited with causing shortages in Syria and thereby placing further pressure on its economy. The chief executive of the Foundation for Defense of Democracies think tank, Mark Dubowitz, described the Israeli attacks as "keeping with a broader economic warfare campaign" after "Israel stepped up the game beyond sanctions to sabotage." Attacking civilian shipping in international waters was a serious crime and was done with tacit U.S. support.[117] Israel was also suspected by a number of analysts of attacking maritime pipelines within Syria itself, which had been destroyed with explosive charges in 2019 and caused major oil spills.[118]

Complementing the West's unilaterally imposed sanctions regime, and other forms of pressure, the U.S. also took action to illegally appropriate Syrian oil and gas to deny substantial revenues to the government. While U.S. forces began a withdrawal from much of northern Syria late in 2019, relinquishing around 75% of territory previously occupied,[119] the U.S. Military would not only maintain but also heavily reinforce its hold over oil and gas producing areas.[120] President Donald Trump summed up the purpose[iii] of America's limited but very focused military presence at a press briefing as follows: "We have troops guarding the oil, other than that we're out of Syria,"[121] a point he reiterated on multiple occasions.[122] Such actions were equated by some analysts with pillaging – a war crime.[123] Sending one's military to occupy a UN member state's oil fields, forcefully appropriate its oil and

---

iii  Beyond the theft of oil, Syrian government sources alleged that U.S. forces used incendiary weapons to burn crop fields in government-controlled areas. If confirmed this would closely mirror tactics previously used in Vietnam and appeared to be aimed at exacerbating Syria's already serious food insecurity to complement other economic warfare efforts. Beginning in 2019, anti-government militants also began to more widely turn to the targeting of staple crops such as wheat and barley aimed at denying food to the Syrian population living in government-controlled areas, which by then represented the overwhelming majority of the population. ('Thermal balloons dropped by US plane set fire to wheat crops in Hasaka countryside,' SANA, May 17, 2020.) ('Syrian fighters burning crops, using food as "weapon of war": U.N.,' Reuters, June 4, 2019.)

keep its revenues represented yet another serious and brazen Western violation of international law made at Syria's expense.

Defence Secretary Mark Esper attempted to portray operations to control oil facilities as efforts to "deny ISIS access to oil revenue," although this did nothing to explain either the ongoing extraction and sale of oil or why the facilities were not returned to Syrian custody. President Trump was much more blunt, stating: "In the old days, you know, when you had a war, to the victor belong the spoils. You go in. You win the war and you take it."[124] According the Senator Lindsey Graham, a leading advocate of this policy, its intention was to specifically to deny funds from oil extraction to the Syrian government, as well as appropriating funds for American coffers "to pay for our military commitment in Syria."[125] This closely resembled a common colonial era practice where Western powers would rely on resource extraction from non-Western states where they had imposed their military presences to effectively pay for their forced occupations. A deal to expand work on oil extraction in U.S.-occupied areas of Syria by contracting the American firm Delta Crescent Energy LLC began to be implemented near the end of 2020, after the firm received a license from the U.S. Treasury to support these operations.[126] The amount of Syrian oil under U.S. control was considerable, and combined with a smaller quantity under Turkish control, it was reported by Syria's Oil Minister Bassam Touma to account for a full 90% of the country's production capacity.[127]

On October 26, 2020, the Russian Defence Ministry issued the following statement regarding illegal U.S. oil extraction: "Tank trucks guarded by U.S. military servicemen and private military companies smuggle oil from fields in eastern Syria to other countries. In the event of any attack on such a convoy, U.S. special operations forces and combat aviation are immediately used to protect it... Revenues from smuggling Syrian oil arrive at numbered bank accounts of U.S. private military companies and intelligence services through brokerage firms that interact with it." It highlighted that the American military presence and its oil extraction operations were set to continue indefinitely. "The space intelligence images show that Syrian oil was actively extracted and transported on a mass scale by tank trunks for processing outside Syria under the reliable protection of U.S. troops both before and after the defeat of the Islamic State... What Washington is doing now, that is, capturing and holding oil fields in eastern Syria under its control, is, putting it bluntly, international state-sponsored gangsterism," the Ministry statement concluded.[128]

The European Union had notably also endorsed the appropriation of Syrian oil by parties other than the Syrian government since the war's early stages and made an exception to its oil trade embargo on Syria to allow imports of crude oil and petroleum products from insurgent-held areas only. A key pretext for this was to provide economic support to the insurgents to further strengthen them against the government.[129] American lawmakers indicated in late October, 2019, that efforts would be made to increase oil production in order to extract greater revenues – effectively accelerating the rate at which Syrian resources were being illegally appropriated.[130] Following this, in mid-November the U.S. Army transferred M1 Abrams battle tanks to Syria to ensure control of oil facilities could be better maintained, with two military bases also constructed in the area[131] and heavy rocket artillery systems already deployed.[132] In September 2020 these assets were reinforced with an order to deploy M2 Bradley heavy infantry fighting vehicles,[133] which according to a later statement by the chief of the Central Command, Frank McKenzie, was intended specifically to "show teeth" to the Russians.[134] A larger presence allowed the U.S. Military to push back against efforts to restrict its access to Syrian territory, a notable example being when an SAA checkpoint attempted to prevent American forces from passing in August 2020. U.S. forces quickly responded with a strike by attack helicopters which caused three Syrian casualties, and thus served as a warning against future efforts to restrict its assets' freedom of movement.[135]

Russia's General Staff and Defense Ministry separately accused the U.S. of using its occupation of Syrian territory to provide safe haven to remaining jihadist insurgents other than those in the SDF for operations against Russian forces,[136] alleging that the U.S. was hosting training camps in Syria for Islamist militants under its protection.[137] According to the Defense Ministry and other Russian military sources America had at times supported Islamic State remnants, with the close proximity in which IS and U.S. forces were regularly operating in without fighting one another frequently cited.[138] Indeed, UN reports indicated that IS had been given "breathing space" in areas under U.S. control, in stark contrast to the areas where the SAA and its partners were able to operate.[139]

Russian allegations[iv] of U.S. support for these militants[v] were corroborated by all major non-Western parties on the ground, including the Syrian government,[140] Iran[141] and even NATO ally Turkey,[142] as well as by lawmakers within the U.S. itself. U.S. Congresswoman Tulsi Gabbard, for one, accused President Donald Trump in September 2018 of "standing up to protect the 20,000 to 40,000 Al Qaeda and other jihadist forces in Syria, and threatening Russia, Syria and Iran with military force if they dare attack these terrorists." The Congresswoman, a U.S. Army veteran, referred to the president as acting "as the protective big brother of Al Qaeda and other jihadists."[143] In 2017 she had put forward the Stop Arming Terrorist Act (H.R. 608) alongside fourteen co-sponsors in an attempt to prevent the Obama administration from using federal agency funds to assist the Islamic State, Al Qaeda, or any of their affiliates.[144] A complementary act was put forward in the Senate six weeks later, the Stop Arming Terrorists Act (S. 532),

---

iv  The Russian Defence Ministry alleged in 2018 that a U.S. P-8 Poseidon aircraft had coordinated large scale drone attacks by Al Qaeda linked insurgents on Russian positions, and separately that America was providing IS with key intelligence using its surveillance assets to launch more precise attacks against Russian forces. ('Drones used by Syrian terrorists "require advanced training" – Russian MoD in response to US,' *Sputnik*, January 9, 2018.) ('Inquiry Into Death of Russian Lt. Gen. Asapov Shows Data Leaks to Daesh – Source,' *Sputnik*, September 26, 2017.)

v   Such allegations of U.S. support for IS were tacitly backed by leaked emails from U.S. Secretary of State Hillary Clinton, which revealed that the U.S. had turned a blind eye to its allies, Saudi Arabia and Qatar, "providing clandestine financial and logistic support to ISIS and other radical groups in the region." ('We finally know what Hillary Clinton knew all along – US allies Saudi Arabia and Qatar are funding Isis,' *The Independent*, October 14, 2016.)

on the basis of the same allegations.[145] While these allegations all followed on from a very long history of strong American support for jihadists against enemy states, an international consensus on the issue has yet to be reached.[vi]

The fact that it was not in the U.S. interest to see Islamic State or Al Qaeda defeated in Syria, however, was widely attested to by influential figures in the country's foreign policy establishment. John Bolton, the U.S. ambassador to the United Nations and later National Security Advisor to President Donald Trump, insisted in an article for the *New York Times* that "defeating the Islamic State" was "neither feasible nor desirable" so long as the Syrian government remained in power.[146] Senators John McCain and Lindsey Graham, writing for the *Wall Street Journal*, similarly stressed that "defeating Islamic State also requires defeating Bashar Assad" – arguing strongly against attempting to do the former without first or simultaneously seeing through the latter.[147] Career Ambassador James Jeffrey, who until five months prior had served as the U.S. Special Representative for Syria, in a similar vein in April 2021 described Al Qaeda linked militant groups in Syria's Idlib governate as an "asset" and "the least bad option of the various options on Idlib." This meant that if the alternative was restoration of Damascus' rule, it was favourable for U.S. interests for terrorist elements to persist.[148] The statements made by officials appeared to effectively describe the thinking behind U.S. policy towards Syria.

The American military presence in Syria would not go completely unchallenged, with Russian forces conducting harassment operations starting in 2018, including flying helicopters near U.S. troops[149] and using electronic warfare to jam their drones[150] and other key weapons systems.[151] In response, U.S. Marines conducted live fire exercises on Syrian soil as a show of force,[152] the first of

---

vi  America's considerable power and demonstrated willingness to act against parties which investigated or voiced allegations regarding its misconduct overseas effectively deterred most parties from doing so. This placed it effectively above reproach, and meant that the international response to signs of its support for terror groups on the ground differed greatly from what it would have been if another country had been responsible for the same actions.

which closely coincided with a massive show of force by Russian Marine special forces backed by air and naval units where assault capabilities were demonstrated.[153] The growing presence of the Syrian Arab Army on the ground in proximity to U.S. forces was seen as "troubling," and placed further pressure on the occupation force particularly from late 2019.[vii] In January 2020 a non-lethal clash between U.S. and Russian forces near an American occupied oil field saw U.S. forces block an attempted Russian effort to reach a strategic location, and was reportedly one of several such engagements taking place.[154] In August four Americans were lightly injured in a vehicle collision during another harassment operation.[155] With these operations continuing, the quarterly report to Congress by the Pentagon, the State Department and the U.S. Agency for International Development published in May 2021 stressed that Russia's objective was to "harass and constrain U.S. forces, with the ultimate goal of compelling U.S. forces to withdraw from northeastern Syria."[156]

In February 2020 the U.S. Defence Department reported that locals had attacked American forces with stones and dirt, with some civilians attempting to light American military vehicles on fire. Multiple protests against the American military presence were staged by locals, some peaceful and others using force.[157] Arab tribes in the oil-rich areas under U.S. occupation accused Western-backed militias of assassinating their tribal sheikhs in August 2020, giving them one month to withdraw or they would attack the "American occupiers" and the affiliated militants.[158] Local militiamen had notably briefly exchanged fire with American forces on February 12 after attempting to block a U.S. military convoy.[159] Similar harassment operations were reportedly also conducted by Russian fighters against American military aircraft,[160] which alongside interceptions of Israeli[161] and Turkish[162]

---

vii While U.S. ground forces were not numerous enough to conduct similar harassment operations, American combat aircraft would do so, notably making a dangerous approach to an Iranian civilian airliner over Syria in July 2020 which forced the pilots to take evasive manoeuvres and injured multiple passengers. ('Passengers injured as US fighter jet comes close to Iranian plane,' *Al Jazeera*, July 24, 2020.)

attacks on Syrian forces demonstrated that Russia perceived itself to now be in a stronger position and could make a greater commitment to Syria's defence. Damascus itself sent a strong signal regarding its growing options for action, and in March 2021 launched a precise ballistic missile strike on an oil facility that was operated by insurgents under Turkish protection. The facility had been sending Syrian oil across the Turkish border. This was interpreted by analysts as a signal to both Turkey and the United States over their oil appropriation activities.[163]

## Turkey's War

By 2019 Turkey had assumed the role of the leading supporter of jihadist groups, including Al Qaeda affiliates such as Al Nusra, on the ground in Syria. Where the West was shifting to a greater focus on economic warfare against Syria, Israel was relying heavily on its own forces to directly secure its objectives, and the Gulf States with the exception of Qatar had distanced themselves from supporting the insurgency,[164] Turkey's position had remained relatively consistent. Turkish relations with both the Western Bloc and with Russia had nevertheless shifted significantly over the course of the war, and contrasted strongly with its position in 2015 when it shot down a Russian Su-24 aircraft. Key causes of this shift were an attempted coup in Turkey in mid-July 2016 and growing Western support for Kurdish YPG militias in Syria.

Turkish media outlets widely claimed that the United Arab Emirates, which alongside Qatar was one of the Western Bloc's leading defence partners in the gulf region, had supported the failed July coup attempt and funnelled $3 billion to the conspirators – citing leaked emails from the UAE ambassador as evidence.[165] Turkish sources also widely alleged that the CIA was involved, with authorities issuing an arrest warrant for former Director of the Middle East Program of the Woodrow Wilson International Center for Scholars, Henri J. Barkey, on the basis that he was a CIA agent and a key organiser of the attempted coup.[166] A warrant for the arrest of the vice-chair of the United States National Intelligence Council, a former CIA employee, was subsequently issued on the basis that he had also helped to engineer the coup attempt.[167] The country also took steps to apprehend U.S. State Department officials working in Turkey on terrorism charges, while detaining 50,000 people domestically and dismissing a further 150,000 from work over suspicions of improper loyalties.[168]

American involvement was something large segments of Turkish society agreed on, with polls indicating that 69% of Turks believed the CIA was behind the unpopular coup attempt. The *New York Times* reported shortly afterwards: "Turkey may be a deeply polarized country, but one thing Turks across all segments of society – Islamists, secular people, liberals, nationalists – seem to have come together on is that the United States was somehow wrapped up in the failed coup."[169] The lack of an early NATO response to protect or openly side with the Turkish government was also perceived negatively in Ankara, with many Turkish analysts taking it as a sign of Western complicity. The coup attempt thus precipitated an unprecedented rift in U.S.-Turkish relations, although the extent of the damage to their relationship was often exaggerated, and also affected the country's relations with Russia and the dynamics of the Syrian conflict. By causing frictions between Ankara and Washington, shaking the Turkish state and its military and intelligence establishments, and leading to the arrest or dismissal of large numbers of highly trained Turkish personnel, the coup attempt was seen to have considerably undermined Turkey's ability to project power into Syria.[170]

Although Turkey's Islamist-leaning leadership shared the West's animosity towards Russia, Syria and Iran, the country was also emerging as an increasingly independent pole in global politics that could, in the long term, challenge Western hegemonic ambitions in a way that client states dependant on Western protection such as Israel or the Gulf States could not.[171] An ideologically westernised military government aligned with the fiercely pro-Western Fethullah Gülen movement was thus likely to be favourable to Western interests. While it is unlikely that the UAE acted alone in Turkey, Western involvement in the coup attempt is unlikely to ever be fully confirmed.

Suffering harsh Western criticism for its post-coup crack-down, and with its economy also under serious pressure from ongoing Russian economic sanctions imposed after the Su-24 shootdown incident the year before, Ankara moved to accelerate the mending of relations with Russia which had already begun to take shape. Turkish President Erdoğan announced that the two Turkish pilots who had shot down the Russian aircraft were arrested on suspicion of links to the Gülen movement.[172] The mil-itant Alparslan Çelik was also arrested, as per an earlier Russian request, due to his responsibility for downing the Russian rescue helicopter sent to save the Su-24's crew. Russia, for its part, also sought to capitalise on the coup's fallout, with President Putin being the first world leader to call President Erdoğan and congrat-ulate him for prevailing.[173] Multiple reports notably indicated that Russian intelligence had received warning of the coup attempt and provided Erdoğan's government with advanced notice – although this could not be confirmed.[174]

Turkey quickly thanked Russia for its "unconditional sup-port" during the coup attempt, bearing stark contrast to the harsh reprimand directed towards the United States.[175] Renewal of rela-tions with Turkey, followed by a lifting of sanctions on Ankara,[176] placed Russia in the difficult but potentially rewarding position of carrying out a detente and forming the beginnings of a strategic partnership with the country – while also being unofficially at war with it by directly combatting Turkish-backed insurgents in Syria and supporting Syrian Arab Army efforts to do the same. A fast growing Turkish dependence on Russia, however, allowed Moscow to press for both Turkish non-intervention in the final stages of the Aleppo campaign that year,[177] and later to end the con-flict in Idlib in March 2020 on terms more favourable to Russian and Syrian interests.[178] By the end of 2016 Turkey had announced plans to purchase the Russian S-400 surface-to-air missile system under a $2.5 billion contract, choosing it over competing Western and Chinese designs, which would cause further frictions with the West. The S-400 purchase led Washington to evict Turkey from the F-35 fighter program, in which it had been not only a client but an integral member, and Ankara would subsequently be threatened repeatedly with American economic sanctions if it did not either destroy or return the S-400 missile system.[179]

While Turkish F-35s were set to be downgraded by the U.S., due primarily to an Israeli request to ensure it preserved a qualitative advantage with its own F-35s,[180] eviction from the program was still a major loss. Although other aircraft could replace the American jet in Turkey's modernisation plans, the country had made considerable investments in manufacturing over 900 F-35 components as a partner in the wider program.[181] Ankara nevertheless persisted with its plans to acquire S-400 systems,[182] due in part to the loss of trust in Western NATO members, with the Russian-made system diversifying its arsenal away from and if necessary allowing it to counter Western hardware.[183] Indeed, the Turkish state news agency *Anadolu* highlighted that the S-400 could benefit Turkish security precisely because it could be used to shoot down American stealth aircraft.[184] Furthermore, with Turkey repeatedly indicating that it could make major further purchases of Russian arms beyond the S-400, including very high end fighter aircraft such as the Su-57[185] and S-500 air defence systems,[186] it provided something of a deterrent to the U.S. imposing sanctions. More U.S. pressure would only drive Turkey into further cooperation with Russia and provide a greater economic boost to the Russian defence sector, which Ankara used as leverage against Washington.

Turkey would increasingly emerge as a rogue actor in Syria. It was at once in conflict with Russia, the Syrian government and Iran due to its support for jihadist insurgents in the Idlib governate, and also on bad terms with the West for its frequent attacks on Western backed Kurdish forces in the north. Turkey's hostility to the U.S. military presence was perhaps most clearly shown by its bracketing of American special forces with heavy artillery fire in October 2019 as a means of intimidation.[187] More significant, however, were ongoing tensions with Damascus over Turkish intervention to prevent Syrian forces from recapturing the Idlib governate, and protection of Al Qaeda linked groups based there. By 2018 Idlib represented the final stronghold of the Al Nusra Front and many of its affiliates, and a staging ground for jihadist factions to launch offensives and harassment operations against Syrian and Russian forces across the country. Turkish intervention and support was key to ensuring that, while Islamist militants across almost all the remainder of Syria had been successfully routed, Idlib remained under the control of Al Qaeda linked insurgents. An assessment by leading U.S. terrorism expert Professor Robert Rabil, which was published by the *National Interest* in 2019, highlighted that "Idlib is virtually an Islamic state ruled by the most hardcore of Salafi-jihadis," and that it "has the largest concentration of hardened and most unyielding Salafi-jihadis. Estimates of their number vary with the median ranges between sixty thousand and ninety thousand."[188] To put this figure in perspective, the number of militants in Idlib under Turkish protection was larger than the size of most countries' standing armies.

Syrian and Russian forces bombarded jihadist positions in Idlib throughout much of 2017, and intensified their attacks in February 2018[189] after Turkish-backed militants shot down a low-flying Russian Su-25 jet,[190] and again in March 2019[191] as the SAA made gradual advances in the area. Bombardment included precision strikes using Russia's now thoroughly tested Su-34 strike fighters, neutralising vital targets such as arms factories to soften the defences of the jihadist forces in the area.[192] In response to Syrian advances in August 2019, Turkish F-16 fighters entered the country's airspace and attempted to attack SAA forces to cover the retreat of jihadist militants on the ground. They were intercepted and turned back, however, by Russian Su-35s. Turkey was seeing its offensives thwarted by the advanced Russian fighters while at the same time holding negotiations with Russia to purchase Su-35s for its own air force – a highly peculiar situation reflecting its pursuit of both war and rapprochement separately but simultaneously.[193]

Had Turkey not placed the last major bastion of jihadist forces in Syria under its protection, it is likely that the Syrian War would have ended in 2018 with Idlib recaptured alongside the country's other thirteen governates. Islamist insurgents, including militants from across the Middle East, Russia, Chinese Xinjiang, Central Asia, Europe and North Africa, were so concentrated in Idlib that the United States envoy to the coalition fighting the Islamic State, Brett H. McGurk, emphasized in 2017 that "Idlib Province is the largest Al Qaeda safe haven since 9/11."[194] Turkish protection was the only thing keeping it that way and preventing the SAA and its partners from rooting terrorist elements out. British media reports notably also highlighted that Turkey was recruiting former fighters from the Islamic State terror group to further strengthen its defences in Idlib, and with IS defeated many of its former members found common cause with the Al Qaeda affiliates in the jihadist-run governate.[195]

The Turkish military presence in Idlib, and diplomatic efforts by Russia, led to temporary agreements to postpone a full-scale ground offensive into the governate in 2018[196] and 2019.[197] This effectively collapsed in January 2020, however, with Damascus alleging that militants in Idlib were persistently shelling settlements in Aleppo and quickly responding with an offensive to neutralise their positions.[198] The claim of unprovoked shelling of civilians in Aleppo was later confirmed by Russian observers.[199] On January 26 the Syrian Arab Army initiated a renewed offensive which saw it press deep into jihadist-held territory to quickly capture several towns and villages and much of the M5 highway. Turkey was quick to respond with large redeployments of personnel and armaments across the border into Idlib from January 31. On February 3 it was reported that Turkish and Syrian forces had begun to clash directly and on a significant scale, with both sides taking losses.[200] As jihadist militias alone were failing to hold the line, Turkish F-16s and rocket artillery units were deployed to provide significant fire support to slow the Syrian offensive.[201] The SAA nevertheless continued to take ground, and on February 3 state media announced the uncovering of a massive underground Al Nusra Front headquarters spanning two-storeys and approximately 1,000 square metres built from reinforced concrete under the Maarat Al Numan museum.[202] The strategically located town had been captured on January 28,[203] and the complex gave an indication of how well dug in jihadist forces were – with positions further into Idlib being even more heavily fortified.[204]

Militants from the Turkistan Islamic Party,[viii] a jihadist group comprised of fighters from China's Xinjiang province which was responsible for terror attacks on civilians across the Chinese mainland, played a major role in early clashes with the SAA in Idlib. These militants were highly effective in combat, using drones and car bombs to take a significant toll on the Syrian Army,[205] and were considered to have exerted a disproportionate influence over Idlib and been a major force multiplier for jihadists based there due to their unmatched ferocity.[206] Turkey had long been the leading supporter of Islamist groups in western China, and an estimated 5000 fighters in Syria had been recruited from there[207] – although some estimates were considerably higher.[208] According to reporters on the ground and civilians interviewed, these militants committed particularly severe atrocities against the local population.[209] Their bastion in Idlib, a staging ground for attacks on China itself,[210] had been of considerable concern in Beijing.[ix] This fueled greater Chinese interest in the Syrian conflict and closer cooperation with the Syrian government[211] including extensive intelligence sharing[212] and other support for the Idlib campaign – the exact nature of which was not confirmed.[213]

Turkish attacks on the Syrian Army would further intensify, with a Turkish Air Force F-16 shooting down a Syrian Mi-17 transport helicopter operating over Idlib on February 12. Unlike the Russian Su-24 shootdown incident in 2015, Turkey was no longer claiming the aircraft were anywhere near Turkish airspace – but

---

viii Despite being a major Al Qaeda affiliate, and having committed multiple widely recognised atrocities against civilians, the Turkistan Islamic Party's designation as a terrorist organisation was notably rescinded by the U.S. in 2020. This paved the way for more open support as part of a broader campaign targeting China and Syria. (Liu, Zhen, 'China accuses US of double standards as it drops ETIM from terrorism list,' *South China Morning Post*, November 6, 2020.)

ix As one Chinese jihadist in Syria told the Associated Press: "We didn't care how the fighting went or who Assad was. We just wanted to learn how to use the weapons and then go back to China." (Shih, Gerry, 'Uighurs fighting in Syria take aim at China,' *AP News*, December 23, 2017.)

was brazenly shooting down Syrian aircraft over Syrian territory.[214] Russia responded the following week by supporting the Syrian air campaign, and while not providing protection against Turkish attacks directly, it would launch extensive airstrikes on jihadist targets in Idlib using Su-24M strike fighters.[215] On February 27 the Russian Defence Ministry announced that, complementing growing logistical and training support and provision of advanced munitions, Turkey had increased fire support for jihadists on the ground. That day the militants would claim their first major victory since the beginning of the offensive, recapturing the strategically located town of Saraqeb which lay at the intersection of the M5 and M4 highways, the loss of which hindered SAA logistical efforts.[216] With Turkish special forces and other personnel increasingly interspersed with the Islamist militants in Idlib,[217] casualties among Turkish forces from the bombardment of militant positions began to steadily increase. On February 27 alone Turkey reportedly lost 33 personnel in Idlib, which Russia stated had been intermingled with jihadists on the ground and were not targeted intentionally.[218]

Russia itself escalated with deployment of Su-34 jets for renewed strike missions from February 28, with the aircraft carrying more firepower and striking more precisely. The deployment of the Su-34, a more survivable aircraft, was also seen as a response to the growing air defence capabilities demonstrated by jihadist militants on the ground. Turkey was not only providing jihadists with advanced handheld anti-aircraft missile launchers in significant quantities, but also deploying its own specialists to support militants and fire on Syrian and Russian aircraft.[219] The Su-34s were reportedly tasked specifically with neutralising air defences to allow older aircraft, such as the Su-24M and Syrian MiG-23BN jets,[220] to conduct strikes more safely.[221] The beginnings of direct Russian involvement in the Idlib campaign not only provided new capabilities, particularly in the air, but also served as a deterrent to further escalation of the Turkish intervention.

Syrian forces continued to press their offensive through late February and into March, with NATO expressing full solidarity with Turkey's attacks on SAA positions[222] and the U.S.[x] offering to supply ammunition.[223] Ongoing Turkish operations against the Syrian Arab Army notably received support from across Syria's south-western border, with Israeli attack helicopters making an unusual incursion into Syrian territory on February 27 to attack SAA positions across the settlements of Al Qahtaniyah, Al Hurria and Al Qunaitra.[224] This led to speculation that Turkey and Israel – historical military partners[225] which were both benefactors of the Al Nusra Front – were coordinating to prevent a Syrian recapture of Idlib and to stretch the SAA between two fronts, or else that Israel was of its own accord supporting Turkish actions by pressing the SAA on the southern front.[226]

Despite support from Russian airstrikes the SAA began to see its rapid early gains reversed by jihadist forces, which were operating with Turkish air and artillery support and often with embedded Turkish special forces. Hezbollah units assisting the Syrian advance reportedly took significant losses to Turkish forces in late February,[227] while the Turkish Defence Ministry reported on March 1 it had shot down two Syrian-operated Su-24M strike fighters in Syrian airspace. This came as part of a much broader Turkish assault into Syrian territory, which included air strikes against Syria's Al Nayrab military airport.[228] These were the largest most direct sustained attacks against Syria by a state actor since the war had begun, with Turkey effectively enforcing an occupation by the Al Qaeda linked groups it was sponsoring with a major military intervention.[229]

With the SAA having no comparable air support and having yet to begin operating its newly delivered S-300PMU-2 air defence systems (See Annex I), the army was forced to quickly

---

x   The U.S. subsequently attempted to leverage Turkey's need for assistance in Idlib by offering support in exchange for a dropping of the Turkish contract to acquire Russian S-400 air defence systems. Ankara, which appeared to be going to great lengths to maintain positive relations with Moscow despite the situation in Idlib, and had avoided criticising Russia, would refuse. ('US Envoy to NATO Floats Idlib Aid 'Package' to Turkey in Exchange for Dropping Russia's S-400s,' *Sputnik*, April 4, 2020.)

cut its losses and ensure that the ground taken at the start of the campaign would not be lost. Russia provided assistance to achieve this objective, deploying two modern Admiral Grigorovich Class frigates armed with Kailbr cruise missiles to the Mediterranean Sea in what was widely seen as a show of force aimed at Turkey.[230] Russia subsequently deployed its military police forces to recently captured areas of Idlib near the frontlines.[231] In order to avoid direct clashes with Russian forces Turkey did not directly support jihadist offensives into areas held by Russian military police, which included the strategically located city of Saraqeb where Russian units were deployed just one day after it was recaptured by the SAA. These deployments ensured that the SAA's Idlib offensive of early 2020 was not completely fruitless, and the Syrian state could retain much of the territory it had initially been able to recapture.[232]

An intensive series of aircraft shootdowns occurred in the first few days of March, and on March 1 the Syrian Arab Army destroyed six Turkish drones in just 24 hours.[233] Drones such as the Anka-S were relied on heavily to provide air support to Islamist militias on the ground, and continued to take heavy losses with at least three more shot down in the next three days.[234] Turkish F-16s shot down a Syrian L-39 light attack jet over Idlib on March 3, with one of the pilots parachuting into an area controlled by Turkish-backed jihadists. Taken prisoner, he was quickly killed and his body grotesquely mutilated.[235] Turkish fighters' control of the air was unchallenged with the Syrian Air Force sending no air superiority aircraft of its own. After a ceasefire was agreed on March 5, and came into effect the following day, it was expected that, should diplomacy fail, Syria would attempt a further push into Idlib once post-war recovery of both the economy and the military had placed it in a stronger position to do so. This could potentially be assisted by S-300PMU-2 batteries and new MiG-29SMT fighters, both of which would make it difficult for Turkish F-16s to operate, particularly given its Air Force's serious shortage of trained pilots and officers after the 2016 purges.[236]

Ankara subsequently moved to cement its control over Idlib and prepare for a new SAA offensive, creating a unified command centre in August to oversee future military operations in the occupied governate.[237] Damascus accused it of pursuing the "Turkification and displacement of inhabitants" in the Syrian governate, which included efforts to impose the use of Turkish currency, renaming squares and streets after Ottoman figures, and "trying to change legal, demographic, economic and financial character of the occupied territories." In line with this trend, several jihadist groups operating alongside Turkish forces named themselves in honour of the Ottoman Empire such as the Sultan Muhammad Al Fateh Brigade and the aforementioned Sultan Murad Brigade.[238] Many of these militant units were largely comprised of ethnically and culturally Turkic fighters. The fact that the 500 years of Ottoman imperial rule over Syria was widely seen by Syrians to have been a particularly dark period in the country's history, due in large part to the brutal nature Turkish conduct towards its Arab, Armenian and Jewish subjects which all made up significant parts of Syria's demography, made this a particularly sensitive issue.[239]

Turkey's close partnership with and extensive support for jihadists in Idlib, including multiple Al Qaeda linked groups and many former Islamic State fighters, would have implications well beyond the Syrian theatre. It supported a largely ideologically driven foreign policy referred to by many analysts as 'Neo-Ottomanism.' Turkey deployed jihadist militants from December 2019 to support the Libyan Government of National Accord (GNA),[240] an Islamist-leaning and Muslim Brotherhood backed[241] contender for rule of the country which had been placed in power after the NATO military intervention in 2011. The GNA received extensive Turkish support in its war with the Egyptian and UAE backed Libyan National Army, with the army supported by the large majority of loyalists to the government of Libya which had existed before the Western intervention. Jihadists sent from Idlib, backed by Turkish drones,[242] played a major role in supporting the GNA and furthering Turkish foreign policy objectives. With Syria supporting the Libyan National Army,[243] which relied heavily on Russian supplied arms[244] and military contractors,[245] the battle lines in Libya mirrored those in Syria itself. This notably led Israeli paper *Haaretz* to frame an argument that "the war in Syria is moving to Libya."[246] Crucially however, unlike in Syria, neither of Libya's warring parties were considered hostile to Western interests in the region meaning the Western Bloc was open to working with both sides.

In lieu of Turkish ground forces, jihadists from Idlib began to be used as something resembling a Turkish foreign legion, and were deployed to secure Turkey's interests not only in Syria and Libya but also in Azerbaijan. Militants were stationed there from September 2020 to assist a push by Azerbaijan's armed forces to seize the disputed Nagaro-Karabakh region from Armenia.[247] The deployment of Al Qaeda linked militants to the frontlines was cause for serious concern for Iran[248] and Russia[249] which both bordered Azerbaijan, with Syria throwing its full support behind Armenia to counter Turkish encroachments. Armenia had similarly supported Syria against Turkish-backed militants, having sent a team of 83 mine warfare experts, medical personnel and security officers to assist Russian operations in post-war Aleppo in 2019.[250] Aside from Qatar, Azerbaijan was one of very few countries which could be considered a close Turkish strategic partner after Ankara's provocations towards its neighbours and against both Russia and the West. The fact that Azerbaijan had an overwhelming Shiite majority, but was nevertheless a close partner of Turkey, Israel and the West and saw Sunni jihadist militants fighting alongside its own forces, notably did much to undermine the narrative that conflict in the Middle East and Central Asia was predominantly sectarian based.

The Al Nusra Front in Idlib increasingly showed signs of trying to improve its image in the West, with its commander-in-chief Abu Mohammad Al Julani conducting his first interview with U.S. media in February 2021 in which he stressed that Idlib "is not a staging ground for executing foreign jihad."[251] Julani was listed as a Specially Designated Global Terrorist by the U.S. State Department,[252] and had similar terror designations from several other countries as well as from the United Nations itself.[253] Nevertheless, Western support for Turkey's moves to protect his organisation's territory in Idlib, and a statement in early March by former U.S. Syria Envoy James Jeffrey describing Julani's forces as an "asset" to American goals in the country, appeared to provide an opening for cooperation.[254] Appearing in a Western-style suit, which was unprecedented for an Al Qaeda affiliated leader, the core of Julani's argument was that the small jihadist 'state' which Turkey was sustaining in Idlib was not a threat to or an enemy of the West, and should be viewed as the 'good side' in the struggle against Damascus.[255]

There may have been a possibility for some kind of Western recognition of Idlib as a separate entity from Syria with the goal of an eventual Kosovo-style partitioning, which would allow Turkey and jihadists on the ground to further formalise the governate's separation. An assessment published by Chatham House described Turkey as having provided Julani's militants with "political cover both regionally and internationally to protect it from being targeted as a terrorist group," as well as "legitimation and protection."[256] Turkish involvement in Julani's public relations offensive[xi] was highly likely, with the country remaining in a strong position to press for an improvement in ties between its proxies on the ground and its NATO allies. Executive director of the Middle East Center for Reporting and Analysis, Jerusalem-based journalist Seth J. Frantzman, observed following Julani's interview: "Julani and his extremists are selling themselves to the West now... these kinds of groups have a long history of trying to get Western support for their local, religious-extremist genocidal activities." Frantzman described the militants in Idlib as forces which "spend their time attacking local people and killing minorities," observing that "religious minorities have all been removed

---

xi   Russian diplomatic sources reported in May 2021 that a representative of Britain's MI6, Jonathan Powell, suggested Julani "should announce plans to abandon subversive activities against Western countries and build close cooperation with them," and had recommended an interview with American press "in order to create a positive image for the alliance that he heads and rehabilitate it in the future. There are plans to engage some of the UK's allies, primarily the U.S., in efforts aimed at rebranding the Al Nusra group." A meeting between Powell and Julani reportedly took place in Idlib near the Turkish border, with Western intelligence agencies seeking stronger ties with Al Nusra with the goal of its eventual removal from terrorism listings. ('British intelligence suggests al-Nusra start cooperating with West – diplomatic source,' *TASS,* May 31, 2021.)

from an area that was once diverse" – an aspect which the large majority of Western reports overlooked when covering Idlib. The possibility of more overt Western support for a more formal partitioning of Idlib under jihadist rule remained significant.[257]

Turkey's occupation of Idlib appears set to remain indefinitely, and according to some analysts is part of a long-term effort by Ankara to restart the Syrian insurgency and eventually overthrow the Syrian government and install an Islamist proxy in its place. This is an objective the Erdoğan administration has strong ideological as well as strategic motives to pursue. Turkey's former Foreign Minister Yasar Yakis stated to this effect in early 2020: "Turkey initially did not intend to fight in Syria against Syrian soldiers but became too active in Idlib, where it defended armed Salafi jihadist groups. However, now Turkey has no intention of abandoning them, and continues to protect them." Its end goal, he stated, was the imposition of political change on its neighbour and the removal of Bashar Al Assad as president of Syria, for which control Idlib would provide valuable leverage.[258] Affirming this five months later in July, President Erdoğan stated that Turkey would not recognise the results of Syria's ongoing parliamentary elections, and that it would maintain its illegal military occupation of Idlib until there was political change. "Until the Syrian people are free, peaceful and safe, we will remain in this country," he stated, using rhetoric more commonly associated with his NATO allies in the West. The irony of the statement was not lost on the many analysts who highlighted that Idlib was at that time under the rule of Al Qaeda affiliated terror groups. The goal of the Idlib occupation was to eventually allow Turkey to reshape all of Syria in line with its interests and ideology – an end which also strongly aligned with the interests of Ankara's NATO allies.[259]

## Notes

1   Jones, Susan, 'DNI Coats Says Syria's Assad Will "Seek to Avoid Conflict With Israel and Turkey",' *CNS News*, January 29, 2019.

2   'Syrian army demobilises some conscripted, reservist officers,' *Reuters*, December 10, 2018.

3   Ibid.

4   'Hezbollah cut down its forces in Syria: Nasrallah,' *Reuters*, July 12, 2019.

5    Browne, Ryan and Starr, Barbara, 'Trump says US will withdraw from Syria "very soon",' *CNN*, March 29, 2018.
6    Ali, Idrees and Stewart, Phil, 'Trump starts withdrawal of U.S. forces from Syria, claims victory,' *Reuters*, December 19, 2018.
7    Chulov, Martin, 'Trump shocks allies and advisers with plan to pull US troops out of Syria,' *The Guardian*, December 19, 2018.
     Feaver, Peter and Inboden, Will, 'The Realists Are Wrong About Syria,' *Foreign Policy*, November 4, 2019.
     Bowman, Bradley, 'Trump Syria withdrawal decision immoral and short-sighted,' *Military Times*, October 8, 2019.
     Keel, Rachel, 'Five unintended consequences of Trump's Syria withdrawal,' *The Hill*, October 16, 2019.
     '"Shocking": Trump Is Criticized For Pulling Troops From Syrian Border,' *NPR*, October 7, 2019.
     Sevastopulo, Demetri and Williams, Aime and Fedor, Lauren, 'House condemns Donald Trump for Syria withdrawal,' *Financial Times*, October 16, 2019.
     O'Toole, Gavin, 'Trump's Syria policy dismays Europe as Turkey launches campaign,' *Al Jazeera*, October 10, 2019.
8    'UAE reopens Syria embassy in boost for Assad,' *Reuters*, December 27, 2018.
9    Yahya, Marwa, 'Spotlight: Reopening of UAE, Bahrain embassies in Damascus signals mending of Syrian-Arab relations,' *Xinhua*, December 29, 2018.
10   Toms, Lauren, 'Bipartisan duo of lawmakers urge Trump to oppose international efforts to restore ties with Syria,' *Washington Times*, October 27, 2020.
     Eydemann, Steve, 'The Caesar Act and a pathway out of conflict in Syria,' *Brookings Institute*, June 19, 2020.
     Ghantous, Ghaida and Georgy, Michael, 'U.S. pressing Gulf states to keep Syria isolated: sources,' *Reuters*, February 18, 2019.
11   McKernan, Bethan, 'Syrian troops mass at edge of Kurdish town threatened by Turkey,' *The Guardian*, December 28, 2011.
12   'Syrian army declares entering Manbij city, following withdrawal of Kurdish militia,' *Xinhua*, December 28, 2018.
     Trevithick, Joseph, 'Syrian Standoff: Kurds Ask Assad For Help Fighting Turkish Forces As Americans Leave,' *The Drive*, December 28, 2018.
13   'Russian military police in Syria begin patrols near Turkish border,' *TASS*, January 8, 2019.
     'Conflicting reports on Syrian entry into key Kurdish town of Manbij,' *CBS News*, December 28, 2018.
14   'Russian military police in Syria begin patrols near Turkish border,' *TASS*, January 8, 2019.
15   'Syria to consider granting Kurds greater autonomy,' *Reuters*, September 26, 2017.
16   Walcott, John and Hennigan, W. J., 'U.S. Spies Say Turkish-Backed Militias Are Killing Civilians as They Clear Kurdish Areas in Syria,' *Time*, October 28, 2019.

Carlin, Maya, 'As ISIS Recedes, Yazidis Face Persecution From Turkish Militias,' *National Interest,* February 17, 2021.

17    Friedersdorf, Conor, 'How the Press Sustains the Forever War,' *The Atlantic,* December 21, 2018.

18    Dönmez, Beyza Binnur, 'France to maintain troops in Syria,' *Andalou News Agency,* January 17, 2019.
      'Syria conflict: Macron criticises Trump's withdrawal decision,' *BBC News,* December 23, 2018.

19    Miliband, David, 'Syria's Tragedy, Our Lessons,' *CSIS,* March 2, 2020.

20    'UK, France Wanted to Send Their Own Troops to Syria After Trump Ordered Withdrawal – Report,' *Sputnik,* November 28, 2019.

21    Huggler, Justin, 'Germany "in secret talks to send aircraft to patrol Syrian safe zone",' *The Telegraph,* May 30, 2019.

22    'UK, France Wanted to Send Their Own Troops to Syria After Trump Ordered Withdrawal – Report,' *Sputnik,* November 28, 2019.

23    Greenfield, Patrick, 'Two British special forces soldiers injured by Isis in Syria,' *The Guardian,* January 6, 2019.
      Sommerville, Quentin, 'UK special forces pictured on the ground in Syria,' *BBC News,* August 8, 2016.
      'British special forces "operating alongside rebels in Syria",' *Middle East Eye,* June 7, 2016.

24    Murphy, Jack, 'Details Emerge About Special Forces Base in Syria Nearly Overrun By ISIS, Medals For Valor to be Awarded,' *SOFREP,* April 14, 2017.

25    'Denmark says deploying special forces to Syria against Islamic State,' *Reuters,* January 20, 2017.
      'Danish Special Forces assigned with new tasks in the Coalition's fight against Da'esh,' *Ministry of Foreign Affairs of Denmark* (https://um.dk/en/news/newsdisplaypage/?newsid=00c6dc7d-1d35-4d7c-be95-df08e5d850a7).

26    'US, France & allies should not leave, must build "new Syria after war" – Macron,' *RT,* April 22, 2019.

27    'French Defence Chief: "We Will Strike Assad Again if Necessary",' *Sputnik,* March 21, 2019.

28    Ali, Idrees and Stewart, Phil, 'No pressure to withdraw from Syria by specific date: U.S. general,' *Reuters,* March 7, 2019.
      'About 200 U.S. peacekeepers are to remain in Syria,' *CBS News,* February 21, 2019.
      Schmitt, Eric and Haberman, Maggie, 'Trump Said to Favor Leaving a Few Hundred Troops in Eastern Syria ,' *New York Times,* October 20, 2019.

29    '"Shocking": Trump Is Criticized For Pulling Troops From Syrian Border,' *NPR,* October 7, 2019.
      Sevastopulo, Demetri and Williams, Aime and Fedor, Lauren, 'House condemns Donald Trump for Syria withdrawal,' *Financial Times,* October 16, 2019.

30    Feaver, Peter, 'The Realists Are Wrong About Syria,' *Foreign Policy,* November 4, 2019.

31   Bowden, Ebony, 'Retiring diplomat says defense officials misled Trump on troop count in Syria,' *New York Post,* November 13, 2020.

32   Fahim, Kareem and Dadouch, Sarah and Englund, Will, 'Russia patrolling between Turkish and Syrian forces after U.S. troops withdraw,' *The Washington Post,* October 15, 2019.

33   Paton Walsh, Nick, 'Trump's betrayal of the Kurds is a gift to Putin and Assad,' *CNN,* October 8, 2019.
     'Donald Trump's tricky Syria "gift" to Vladimir Putin,' *Deutsche Welle,* October 15, 2019.

34   Crowcroft, Orlando, '"Damascus is looking stronger than ever": What next for Syria as Kurds join forces with Assad?,' *Euronews,* October 15, 2019.

35   Abdi, Mazloum, 'If We Have to Choose Between Compromise and Genocide, We Will Choose Our People,' *Foreign Policy,* October 13, 2019.

36   Sevastopulo, Demetri and Williams, Aime and Pitel, Laura and Foy, Henry, 'US delegation to press Turkey for Syrian ceasefire,' *Financial Times,* October 16, 2019.

37   Spyer, Jonathan, 'Trump's Syria Policy Is Working,' *Foreign Policy,* July 1, 2020.

38   Calamur, Krishnadev, 'No One Wants to Help Bashar al-Assad Rebuild Syria,' *The Atlantic,* March 15, 2019.

39   Basic Infrastructure & Service Rehabilitation, Syria, United Nations Development Program (https://www.sy.undp.org/content/syria/en/home/development-impact/in-depth.html) (accessed November 4, 2020).

40   'Economic Relations of Communist China with the USSR Since 1950,' Economic Intelligence Report, *Office of Research and reports at the Central Intelligence Agency,* May 1959.
     Zhang, Baichun and Zhang, Jiuchun and Fang, Yao, 'Technology Transfer from the Soviet Union to the People's Republic of China: 1949–1966,' *Comparative Technology Transfer and Society,* vol. 4, no. 2, August 2006 (pp.105–71).

41   Armstrong, Charles K., '"Fraternal Socialism": The International Reconstruction of North Korea, 1953–62,' *Cold War History,* vol. 5, 2005 (pp. 161–187).
     Fendler, Karoly, 'Economic Assistance and Loans from Socialist Countries to North Korea in the Postwar Years 1953–1963,' *Asien,* vol. 42, January 1992 (pp. 39–51).
     Frank, Rüdiger, *Die DDR und Nordkorea: Der Wiederaufbau der Stadt Hamhung von 1954–1962* [GDR and North Korea: The reconstruction of the city of Hamhung from 1954–1962], Aachen, Shaker, 1996.
     'Soviets to help rebuild war–damaged North Korea – archive, 1953,' *Manchester Guardian,* September 21, 1953.

42   Butter, David, 'Syria's Economy Picking up the Pieces,' *Chatham House Research Paper,* June 2015.

43   'Syria: the view from Iraq,' *European Council on Foreign Relations,* June 24, 2013.

44   'Syria,' *CIA World Factbook* (https://www.cia.gov/library/publications/the-world-factbook/geos/sy.html/).
     Phillips, Christopher, *The Battle For Syria: International Rivalry in the New Middle East,* New Haven, Yale University Press, 2016 (p. 164).

45    al-Saadi, Salam, 'Iran's stake in Syria's economy,' *Carnegie Endowment*, June 2, 2015.

46    'Tehran prepares for postwar Syria,' *AEI Critical Threats Project*, March 29, 2019.
      Ahronheim, Anna, 'Iran to lease part of Latakia port,' *Jerusalem Post*, April 8, 2019.

47    Behravesh, Maysam, 'Iran's ambitious postwar reconstruction in Syria,' *Al-Monitor*, March 5, 2019.

48    Menshikov, S., 'Russian Capitalism Today,' *Monthly Review*, vol. 51. no. 3, 1999 (pp. 82–86).

49    'North Korea wants to help Syria rebuild,' *Washington Post*, May 1, 2019.

50    Walt, Stephen M., 'Yesterday's Cold War Shows How to Beat China Today,' *Foreign Policy*, July 29, 2019.
      Parker, Richard, 'Inside the Collapsing Soviet Economy,' *The Atlantic,* June 1990.

51    Matveev, Igor, 'Russia weighs two reconstruction strategies for Syria,' *Al Monitor*, December 23, 2019.
      'Russia Plans To Help Syria Rebuild Devastated Oil, Power Industries," *RFERL*, February 14, 2018.

52    'Russia eyes major commercial projects in Syria,' *AP News*, December 17, 2019.

53    Feron, Henri, 'Pyongyang's Construction Boom: Is North Korea Beating Sanctions?,' *NK News,* July 18, 2017.
      MacDonald, Hamish, 'Rapid progress made on construction site near Ryomyong Street,' *NK News*, February 22, 2018.
      Zwirko, Colin, 'Photos: North Korea's new-age apartments join a greater wave of modern design,' *NK News,* November 11, 2020.
      Petricic, Sasa, 'Why Pyongyang is using gleaming skyscrapers to show "potential of socialist Korea",' *CBC News,* April 13, 2017.
      Williams, Martyn, 'North Korea's Post-Typhoon House-Building Boom,' *38 North*, November 18, 2020.
      Williams, Martyn, 'Thousands of New Dwellings Declared Complete in Samjiyon,' *38 North*, November 19, 2020.

54    Weller, Chris and Johnson, Robert and Giang, Vivian, '30 giant Chinese infrastructure projects that are reshaping the world,' *Business Insider,* June 20, 2016.
      Zhou, Cissy, 'China's top 10 infrastructure projects for 2020 and beyond will help boost its slowing economy,' *South China Morning Post*, January 28, 2020.

55    Schifrin, Nick and Sagalyn, Dan, 'China's massive Belt and Road initiative builds global infrastructure – and influence,' *PBS,* September 27, 2019.
      Seiff, Kevin, 'North Korea's surprising, lucrative relationship with Africa,' *Washington Post*, July 10, 2017.
      Holloway, Beetle, '9 Spectacular African Monuments Built By North Korea,' *Culture Trip*, July 17, 2018.

56    'DPRK Ambassador affirms his country's readiness to support health sector in Syria,' *Syrian Arab News Agency*, July 25, 2016.

57    'North Korea scales up trade with Syria,' *Enab Baladi,* February 15, 2019.

58   Rebuilding Syria on Twitter, December 12, 2019 (https://twitter.com/ SyriaRebuilt/status/1205149675747205120).

59   'Syria, North Korea Discuss Cooperation in Reconstruction,' *The Syrian Observer*, November 23, 2017.

60   O'Connor, Tom, 'China May Be the Biggest Winner of All If Assad Takes Over Syria,' *News Week*, January 19, 2018.
     Calabrese, John, 'China and Syria: In War and Reconstruction,' *Middle East Institute*, July 9, 2019.

61   Allison, Graham, 'China Is Now the World's Largest Economy. We Shouldn't Be Shocked,' *National Interest*, October 15, 2020.

62   Burton, Guy, 'China and the Reconstruction of Syria,' *The Diplomat*, July 28, 2018.
     Liu, Zhen, 'US withdrawal from Syria leaves China's plans for investment up in the air, analysts say,' *South China Morning Post*, December 29, 2018.
     Lyall, Nicholas, 'China in Postwar Syria,' *The Diplomat*, March 11, 2019.

63   Zhou, Laura, 'Syria courts China for rebuilding push after fall of Islamic State's strongholds,' *South China Morning Post*, November 25, 2017.
     Pauley, Logan, 'Why an end to the war in Syria gives China an opportunity to extend its influence,' *South China Morning Post*, October 14, 2018.

64   Lyall, Nicholas, 'China in Postwar Syria,' *The Diplomat*, March 11, 2019.
     Pauley, Logan, 'China stakes out a role for itself in post-war Syria,' *Asia Times*, October 3, 2018.

65   '800 electrical power transformers arrived in Lattakia as a grant from China,' *Syrian Arab News Agency*, October 10, 2018.

66   'China donates 100 buses to support public transportation in Syria,' *Xinhua*, June 20, 2019.

67   'China donates new medical supplies to Syria to help fight COVID-19 pandemic,' *Xinhua*, September 24, 2020.

68   'China donates COVID-19 test kits to Syria,' *Global Times*, April 16, 2020.

69   Akulov, Andrei, 'China Joins Russia in Syria: Shaping New Anti-Terrorist Alliance,' *Strategic Culture Foundation*, September 22, 2016.

70   Pauley, Logan, 'Why an end to the war in Syria gives China an opportunity to extend its influence,' *South China Morning Post*, October 14, 2018.

71   Lin, Christina, 'The Belt and Road and China's Long-term Visions in the Middle East,' *ISPSW Strategy Series: Focus on Defense and International Security*, no. 512, October 2017.
     Anderson, Finbar, 'China looks to invest in North Lebanon,' *Daily Star*, July 12, 2018.

72   'Factbox – Syria's energy sector,' *Reuters*, September 5, 2011.

73   '中国驻叙利亚大使：中国坚持和平解决叙利亚问题'    [Chinese Ambassador to Syria: China insists on the peaceful settlement of the Syrian issue], *CCTV*, March 16, 2017.

74   Hemenway, Dan, 'Chinese strategic engagement with Assad's Syria,' *Atlantic Council*, December 21, 2018.

75   'US hits Chinese firms as it boosts North Korea sanctions,' *Financial Times*, November 21, 2017.
     'US imposes sanctions on Chinese companies for helping North Korea,' *Al Jazeera*, March 22, 2019.

'Three Chinese banks hit by US probe into North Korea links,' *Financial Times,* June 25, 2019.

'U.S. appeals court upholds ruling against Chinese banks in North Korea sanctions probe,' *Reuters,* July 31, 2019.

'U.S. Steps Up Pressure on China Over North Korean Coal Exports,' *Wall Street Journal,* December 8, 2020.

76  Taylor Luck, 'Postwar Syria? Arab world moving to bring Damascus back into the fold,' *Christian Science Monitor*, January 19, 2019.

77  'Bahrain, Syria regime foreign ministers hug, kiss at UN,' *The New Arab,* October 1, 2018.

78  'Syria's Assad Reaches "Understanding" With Arab States,' *Voice of Asia,* October 3, 2018.

79  Chloe, Cornish, 'Reopening of Syrian-Jordan border revives regional trade,' *Financial Times,* October 30, 2018.

80  'Spotlight: Sudanese president's visit prelude for restoring Syria, Arab relations,' *Xinhua*, December 17, 2018.

81  Abdelrahim, Adel, 'Sudanese president's Damascus visit raises eyebrows,' *Andalou News Agency,* December 18, 2018.

82  'Sudan pound continues decline, experts warn of economic collapse,' *Xinhua*, August 21, 2020.

'Sudan declares state of economic emergency after sharp fall in currency,' *Reuters,* September 10, 2020.

83  'Deepening Crisis: Sudan Marks One Year Since Coup Ejected Popular Strongman From Power,' *Military Watch Magazine*, April 11, 2020.

84  Yahya, Marwa, 'Spotlight: Reopening of UAE, Bahrain embassies in Damascus signals mending of Syrian-Arab relations,' *Xinhua,* December 29, 2018.

'UAE reopens Syria embassy in boost for Assad,' *Reuters,* December 27, 2018.

85  'Tunisia resumes direct flights with Syria as UAE reopens Damascus embassy,' *Middle East Monitor,* December 27, 2018.

86  Eydemann, Steve, 'The Caesar Act and a pathway out of conflict in Syria,' *Brookings Institute*, June 19, 2020.

87  Stearns, Scott, 'Clinton: Russia Needs to Back Syrian Transition to Remove Assad,' *Voice of Asia,* June 3, 2012.

88  McDowall, Angus, 'Long reach of U.S. sanctions hits Syria reconstruction,' *Reuters*, September 2, 2018.

Website of the U.S. Department of State, Under Secretary for Economic Growth, Energy, and the Environment, Bureau of Economic and Business Affairs, Counter Threat Finance and Sanctions, Economic Sanctions Policy and Implementation, Syria Sanctions (https://2009-2017.state.gov/e/eb/tfs/spi/syria/index.htm).

89  'В ООН заявили об отсутствии "секретной директивы" по Сирии' [UN says no "secret directive" on Syria], *TASS*, August 22, 2018.

90  'Leaked secret directive shows UN won't help to rebuild Syria until there's "political transition",' *RT,* September 2, 2018.

Parameters and Principles of UN assistance in Syria, October 2017 (https://www.kommersant.ru/docs/2018/UN-Assistane-in-Syria-2017.pdf).

'Реконструкция только после политических реформ' [Reconstruction only after political reforms], *Kommersant,* September 2, 2018.

91  Kasapoğlu, Can, 'Time to Put "Maximum Pressure" on Syrian Baath Regime,' *Andalou News Agency,* June 4, 2020.

92  Nichols, Michelle, 'U.S. to impose sanctions aimed at blocking Syria military victory,' *Reuters,* June 16, 2020.

'China's UN envoy urges U.S. to immediately lift unilateral sanctions on Syria,' *CGTN,* November 26, 2020.

'Speech at the Meeting of leaders of Russia, Iran and Turkey on Syrian settlement by President of Russia Vladimir Putin,' *The Kremlin,* July 1, 2020.

93  Sheeran, Scott, 'The U.N. Security Council veto is literally killing people,' *Washington Post*, August 11, 2014.

'The Security Council's sine qua non: The Veto Power,' *Rutgers Global Policy Roundtable,* Occasional Paper Eight, 2018.

Akin, David, 'In bid for UN Security Council seat, Canada's position on reform could be a barrier: analyst,' *Global News*, January 3, 2020.

94  'Despite fiery rhetoric, Caesar's Syria sanctions fizzle,' *Financial Times,* June 23, 2020.

95  Greenlees, Donald, 'Russia sanctions putting strain on US relationship with Indonesia,' *Asia Link* (https://asialink.unimelb.edu.au/asialink-dialogues-and-applied-research/commentary-and-analysis/russia-sanctions-putting-strain-on-us-relationship-with-indonesia).

96  'Sanctions on India over S-400 missile deal? A possibility, says US envoy,' *Business Standard,* May 21, 2020.

Gady, Franz-Stefan, 'US Warns India Over S-400 Air Defense System Deal With Russia,' *The Diplomat*, June 17, 2019.

97  Cornwell, Alexander, 'Egypt risks U.S. sanctions over Russian fighter jet deal: U.S. official,' *Reuters*, November 18, 2019.

98  Hafezi, Parisa and Barbuscia, Davide, 'Currency crisis impoverishes Iranians, strains economic defenses,' *Reuters*, July 7, 2020.

'Six charts that show how hard US sanctions have hit Iran,' *BBC News*, December 9, 2019.

Ebadi, Ebad, 'Oil price drop brings more economic challenges for Iran,' *Atlantic Council*, May 18, 2020.

99  'Assad says billions of dollars of Syrian deposits trapped in Lebanon,' *Middle East Eye,* November 5, 2020.

Hall, Richard, 'Corruption brought Lebanon to its knees. The explosion was a coup de grace,' *The Independent,* August 5, 2020.

100  World Food Program Syria, Country Brief, April 2020 (https://reliefweb.int/sites/reliefweb.int/files/resources/2020%2004%20Syria%20Country%20Brief.pdf).

101  'Syria faces severe bread shortages as US sanctions worsen economy,' *Al Jazeera,* July 10, 2020.

102  Tsurkov, Elizabeth and al-Ghazi, Suhail, '"People can't even afford to buy bulgur": Discontent is on the rise as Syria's economic crisis worsens,' *Middle East Institute*, February 28, 2020.

103 'Syria's children "go to bed hungry" as prices soar,' *Financial Times,* May 24, 2020.
104 Pearson, James and Park, Ju-Min, 'Despite sanctions, North Korea prices steady as Kim leaves markets alone,' *Reuters*, August 8, 2016.
Kim, Christine and Chung, Jane, 'North Korea 2016 economic growth at 17-year high despite sanctions: South Korea,' *Reuters*, July 21, 2017.
105 'North Korea's Stable Exchange Rates Confound Economists,' *Associated Press*, November 16, 2018.
106 Kim, Christine and Chung, Jane, 'North Korea 2016 economic growth at 17-year high despite sanctions: South Korea,' *Reuters*, July 21, 2017.
Lankov, Andrei, 'Sanctions working? Not yet ...,' *Korea Times*, May 29, 2016.
Pearson, James and Park, Ju-Min, 'Despite sanctions, North Korea prices steady as Kim leaves markets alone,' *Reuters*, August 8, 2016.
Maresca, Thomas, 'Report: North Korea economy developing dramatically despite sanctions,' *UPI,* December 4, 2019.
107 Gellman, Barton, 'Allied Air War Struck Broadly in Iraq,' *Washington Post*, June 23, 1991.
108 Joy, Gordon, *Invisible War: The United States and the Iraq Sanctions,* Cambridge, MA, Harvard University Press, 2010 (p. 25).
Woertz, Eckart, 'Iraq under UN Embargo, 1990–2003, Food Security, Agriculture, and Regime Survival,' *The Middle East Journal,* vol. 73, no. 1, Spring 2019 (p. 101).
Blaydes, Lisa, *State of Repression: Iraq under Saddam Hussein,* Princeton, NJ, Princeton University Press, 2018 (pp. 122–124).
109 'Sanctions Blamed for Deaths of Children,' *Lewiston Morning Tribune*, December 2, 1995.
Stahl, Lesley, 'Interview with Madeline Albright,' *60 Minutes*, May 12, 1996.
110 Ghisn, Ziad, 'How economic sanctions negatively affect the health sector in Syria: a case study of the pharmaceutical industry,' *LSE Blogs*, April 16, 2020.
'Damascus: medicine crisis ahead of US "Caesar" sanctions,' *Zaman Al Wasl*, June 6, 2020.
'Why Economic Sanctions on Syria Must Stop,' *Relief Web*, August 1, 2020.
McDowall, Angus, 'Long reach of U.S. sanctions hits Syria reconstruction,' *Reuters*, September 2, 2018.
111 Cockburn, Patrick, *War in the Age of Trump: The Defeat of ISIS, the Fall of the Kurds, the Conflict with Iran,* New York, OR Books, 2020 (p. 148).
112 'Special Briefing With Ambassador James Jeffrey and Ambassador David Satterfield,' *U.S. Department of State,* March 10, 2020.
113 'US promises to "disrupt" oil shipments to Syria, sanctions Russian & Iranian companies,' *RT*, November 20, 2018.
114 Mikelionis, Lukas, 'Britain seizes Iranian oil tanker headed to Syria, furious Tehran summons British ambassador over "destructive" action,' *Fox News*, July 5, 2019.

115 'UK to facilitate release of Iranian tanker if it gets Syria guarantees – Hunt,' *Reuters*, July 13, 2019.

116 Harel, Amos, 'A Deep Dive Into Israeli-Iranian Naval War,' *Haaretz*, March 19, 2021.

117 Lubold, Gordon and Faucon, Benoit and Schwartz, Felicia, 'Israeli Strikes Target Iranian Oil Bound for Syria,' *Wall Street Journal*, March 11, 2021.

118 Trevithick, Joseph, 'Israel Has Been Launching Clandestine Attacks On Iranian Shipping: Report,' *The Drive*, March 11, 2021.

Joffre, Tzvi,, 'Underwater oil pipelines sabotaged near Syria,' *Jerusalem Post*, June 24, 2019.

119 Brett Mcgurk on Twitter, 'We have American soldiers with an ill-defined mission in Syria ("protect the oil") after abandoning 3/4 of once stable territory on Trump's orders, now forced to navigate roads controlled by Russian and Syrian regime forces. Too much to ask of our brave warriors. This was today,' February 12, 2020.

Schmiitt, Eric, 'Russians Pressure U.S. Forces in Northeast Syria,' *New York Times*, February 14, 2020.

120 Cooper, Helene and Schmitt, Eric, 'U.S. to Deploy Hundreds of Troops to Guard Oil Fields in Syria, Pentagon Officials Say,' *New York Times*, October 25, 2019.

121 'Remarks by President Trump in Press Briefing,' *The White House*, September 18, 2020.

122 Crowley, Michael, '"Keep the Oil": Trump Revives Charged Slogan for New Syria Troop Mission,' *New York Times*, October 26, 2019.

123 Finnegan, Conor, '"We're keeping the oil" in Syria, Trump says, but it's considered a war crime,' *ABC News*, October 29, 2019.

124 Crowley, Michael, '"Keep the Oil": Trump Revives Charged Slogan for New Syria Troop Mission,' *New York Times*, October 26, 2019.

125 Ibid.

126 Seligman, Lara and Lefebvre, Ben, 'Little-known U.S. firm secures deal for Syrian oil,' *Politico*, August 3, 2020.

127 Ilya Tsukanov, 'Syrian Minister Reveals What Percentage of Country's Oil is Stolen by US and Its Allies,' *Sputnik*, March 19, 2021.

128 'US smuggles Syrian oil to other countries – Russian Defense Ministry,' *TASS*, October 26, 2019.

129 'EU eases Syria oil embargo to help opposition,' *BBC News*, April 22, 2013.

130 'Graham Statement on Syria,' *Website of U.S. Senator Lindsey Graham*, October 23, 2019 (https://www.lgraham.senate.gov/public/index.cfm/2019/10/graham-statement-on-syria).

131 'U.S. Reinforces Control Over Syrian Oil with New Armour From Bases in Iraq,' *Military Watch Magazine*, November 14, 2019.

132 Browne, Ryan, 'Exclusive: US deploys long-range artillery system to southern Syria for first time,' *CNN*, June 13, 2017.

133 'U.S. Deploys Bradley Fighting Vehicles to Guard Occupied Oil Fields in Northern Syria,' *Military Watch Magazine*, September 22, 2020.

134 'US Backed Troops in Syria With Armor to "Show Teeth" to Russians, CENTCOM Chief Says,' *Sputnik*, December 10, 2020.

135 'Two U.S. helicopters attack Syrian army checkpoint in northeast Syria: state media,' *Reuters*, August 17, 2020.

136 'Syrian regime forces enter buffer zone surrounding US base,' *CNN*, October 4, 2017.

137 'US lets militants train, mount attacks from its Syrian bases – chief of Russian General Staff,' *RT*, December 27, 2017.
'All Syrian Terrorist Groups Receive Weapons, Tasks From Abroad – Russian MoD,' *Sputnik*, March 24, 2018.

138 'US special ops forces & hardware spotted at ISIS positions north of Deir ez-Zor – Russian MoD,' *RT*, September 24, 2017.
'US Support for Terrorists in Syria Main Obstacle of Defeating Them – Russian MoD,' *Sputnik*, October 4, 2017.

139 'ISIS given "breathing space" in parts of Syria under US-backed forces' control,' *RT*, August 18, 2018.

140 'No role for West and allies in Syria until they cut support to terrorists – Assad,' *RT*, August 21, 2017.

141 'Iran accuses US of alliance with ISIS, claims to have proof,' *RT*, June 11, 2017.

142 'West's shadow behind all terrorist groups, including Daesh – Erdoğan,' *Sputnik*, October 8, 2017.
'I have confirmed evidence Turkey's President Recep Tayyip Erdoğan claims US-led coalition forces have supported ISIS,' *The Sun*, October 8, 2017.

143 U.S. Congresswoman Tulsi Gabbard Speaks on House Floor, September 13, 2018.

144 *H.R. 6504 – To prohibit the use of United States Government funds to provide assistance to Al Qaeda, Jabhat Fateh al-Sham, and the Islamic State of Iraq and the Levant (ISIL) and to countries supporting those organizations, and for other purposes*, 114th Congress, U.S. Congress, 2015–2016.
Carden, James, 'Why Does the US Continue to Arm Terrorists in Syria?' *The Nation*, March 3, 2017.

145 'Dr. Rand Paul Introduces the Stop Arming Terrorists Act,' *Official Website of Senator Rand Paul*, March 2017.

146 Bolton, John, 'John Bolton: To Defeat ISIS, Create a Sunni State,' *Wall Street Journal*, November 24, 2015.

147 McCain, John and Graham, Lindsey, 'To Defeat Islamic State, Remove Assad,' *Wall Street Journal*, October 6, 2014.

148 Frantzman, Seth J., 'Did former US officials support extremists in Syria as an "asset"?,' *The Jerusalem Post*, April 6, 2021.

149 Schmiitt, Eric, 'Russians Pressure U.S. Forces in Northeast Syria,' *New York Times*, February 14, 2020.

150 Trevithick, Joseph, 'The Russians Are Jamming US Drones in Syria Because They Have Every Reason To Be,' *The Drive*, April 10, 2018.

151 Seligman, Lara, 'Russian Jamming Poses a Growing Threat to U.S. Troops in Syria,' *Foreign Policy*, July 30, 2018.

152 Al-Khalidi, Suleiman, 'U.S. marines conduct big drills with rebels in southern Syria,' *Reuters*, September 13, 2018.

Pickrell, Ryan, 'This was the Marine exercise in Syria to deter Russian attacks,' *We Are The Mighty,* September 12, 2019.

153 'Russian marines land on Syrian shores in massive Mediterranean drills,' *RT,* September 8, 2018.

154 Wolfgang, Ben, 'U.S.-Russia "engagements" underscore danger of oil mission in Syria,' *Washington Times,* January 22, 2020.
Wolfgang, Ben, 'Standoff: U.S. troops block Russian forces from capturing Syrian oil field,' *Washington Times,* January 21, 2020.

155 Baldor, Lolita and Burns, Robert, 'Vehicle collision with Russians injures 4 US troops in Syria,' *Military Times,* August 26, 2020.

156 Cole, Brendan, 'Russia Tells U.S. Only Their Troops Are Welcome in Syria,' *Newsweek,* May 6, 2021.

157 'Russian Forces Increase Pressure on U.S. Troops in Syria as Local Civilians Turn on the U.S. Military,' *Military Watch Magazine,* February 16, 2020.

158 'Local Arab Tribes Challenge Western Occupation of Northern Syria,' *Military Watch Magazine,* August 22, 2020.

159 'Syria: US troops open fire on locals in northeast, killing 1,' *NBC News,* February 12, 2020.

160 'U.S. Navy Says Syria-Based Russian Su-35 Made Unsafe Approach While Intercepting P-8 Submarine Hunter,' *Military Watch Magazine,* April 16, 2020.

161 'Su-35 in Action: Russian Air Force's Elite Intercept Israeli Jets Over Syria,' *Military Watch Magazine,* December 10, 2019.

162 'Russian Su-35s Intercept Turkish F-16s Over Syria's Idlib – Reports,' *Military Watch Magazine,* August 20, 2019.

163 'Strong Signal to Turkey: Syrian Army Destroys Jihadist Oil Facility in Major Ballistic Missile Strike,' *Military Watch Magazine,* March 8, 2021.

164 Chulov, Martin, 'Victory for Assad looks increasingly likely as world loses interest in Syria,' *The Guardian,* August 31, 2017.

165 Paksoy, Yunus, 'UAE allegedly funneled $3B to topple Erdoğan, Turkish government,' *Daily Sabah,* June 13, 2017.

166 'Turkey seeks arrest of ex-CIA officer over suspected coup links: Hurriyet,' *Reuters,* December 1, 2017.
Barkey, Henri J., 'Why Is Turkey Accusing Me of Plotting a Coup?,' *New York Times,* September 1, 2016.

167 'Turkey seeks arrest of ex-CIA officer over suspected coup links: Hurriyet,' *Reuters,* December 1, 2017.

168 Edelman, Eric, 'Fight for these State Department workers detained in Turkey,' *Washington Post,* July 30, 2018.
Karadeniz, Tulay and Solaker, Gulsen, 'U.S. still seeking explanation for arrest of staff in Turkey: ambassador,' *Reuters,* October 11, 2017.

169 Arango, Tim and Yeginsu, Ceylan, 'Turks Can Agree on One Thing: U.S. Was Behind Failed Coup,' *New York Times,* August 2, 2016.

170 Lund, Aaron, 'How Will the Failed Coup in Turkey Affect Syria?,' *Carnegie Middle East Center,* July 28, 2016.
McLeary, Paul, 'Failed Coup Could Upend Turkish Military,' *Foreign Policy,* July 16, 2016.

'Erdoğan's counter-coup weakens the Syrian rebels,' *The Economist*, June 24, 2016.

171 Bayar, Gozde and Aksut, Fahri, 'Turkey to never recognize US Mideast plan: Erdoğan,' *Andalou News Agency*, January 31, 2020.
Torchia, Christopher, 'Tension with Washington helps fuel Turkey-Venezuela alliance,' *Washington Post*, August 18, 2020.
Kingsley, Patrick, 'The World Condemns Erdoğan's War on Kurds. But Turkey Applauds,' *New York Times*, October 16, 2019.

172 'Turkish pilots who downed Russian jet detained: Erdoğan,' *Hurriyet Daily*, July 21, 2016.

173 'Erdoğan says glad to receive Putin's call after Turkey coup attempt,' *TASS*, August 9, 2016.
'One on One: Alexandr Dugin, special representative of the Russian president,' *TRT World*, December 1, 2016.

174 'Russia warned Turkey of imminent army coup, says Iran's FNA,' *TASS*, July 21, 2016.

175 'Turkey Thanks Russia for Support During Coup,' *Moscow Times*, July 25, 2016.

176 Hille, Kathrin, 'Russia lifts most sanctions imposed on Turkey after downing of jet,' *Financial Times*, May 31, 2017.
'Russia lifts sanctions on Turkish food in diplomatic thaw,' *BBC News*, June 2, 2017.

177 Jones, Seth G., 'Moscow's War in Syria,' *CSIS*, May 2020 (p. 61).
Sayigh, Yezid, 'Where Next?,' *Carnegie Middle East Center*, December 19, 2016.

178 Candar, Cengiz, 'Erdoğan's dance with Putin: Humiliating, but face-saving,' *Al-Monitor*, March 6, 2020.
Taspinar, Omer, 'As Erdoğan licks wounds over Idlib, Putin wins again,' *Asia Times*, March 5, 2020.
'Erdoğan's pivot to Putin has left Turkey weaker,' *Financial Times*, March 4, 2020.
'Of course it's coincidence: Kremlin spokesman denies trolling Erdoğan with bronzework of Russo-Turkish war,' *RT*, March 6, 2020.
Baydar, Yavuz, 'Erdoğan's pyrrhic victory cannot hide the fact he has come home empty-handed,' *Ahval*, March 9, 2020.

179 Pamuk, Humeyra, 'Turkey needs to "get rid of" Russian S-400 system to overcome impasse with U.S. – U.S. official,' *Reuters*, November 21, 2019.
Coskun, Orhan, 'Turkey preparing for possible U.S. sanctions over S-400s: minister,' *Reuters*, May 22, 2019.

180 'Downgraded Version for Turkey? Israel and U.S. Hold Talks on Withholding Vital F-35 Software From Ankara,' *Military Watch Magazine*, May 29, 2018.

181 'Turkey to continue manufacturing F-35 components through 2022, Pentagon says,' *Daily Sabah*, June 30, 2020.
Toksabay, Ece and Gumrukcu, Tuvan, 'Turkish defense firms set to lose billions after F-35 removal,' *Reuters*, July 18, 2019.

182 'Erdoğan: No step back from S-400 deal with Russia,' *Al Jazeera*, June 4, 2019.

183 Karako, Tom, 'Coup-proofing? Making Sense of Turkey's S-400 Decision,' *CSIS*, July 15, 2019.

184 Snow, Shawn, 'Turkish state media boasts about new missile, ability to shoot down US aircraft,' *Military Times*, September 20, 2017.

185 '"We're Going to Buy This One"? Turkish President Inspects Russia's New Su-57 Fighter Ahead of Possible Acquisition,' *Military Watch Magazine*, August 27, 2019.
'Turkish Military Reviewing Russia's Su-35 for its Next Generation Fighter Requirements,' *Military Watch Magazine*, August 27, 2019.

186 'Turkey and Russia to Begin Discussions for Joint Production of S-500 Missile System – President Erdoğan,' *Military Watch Magazine*, May 19, 2019.
'Turkey Takes Official Steps Towards Potential S-500 Acquisition; Could Ankara Deploy the Prometheus Air Defence System Alongside its Soon to Be Delivered S-400?,' *Military Watch Magazine*, June 26, 2018.

187 Lamothe, Dan, 'U.S. forces say Turkey was deliberately "bracketing" American troops with artillery fire in Syria,' *Washington Post*, October 13, 2019.

188 Rabil, Robert G., 'Defeating the Islamic State of Idlib,' *National Interest*, June 13, 2019.

189 'Russia intensifies bombing of Syria's Idlib after rebels down jet, killing pilot,' *Reuters*, February 5, 2018.

190 Rogoway, Tyler, 'Russian Su-25 Frogfoot Attack Jet Shot Down In Syria,' *The Drive*, February 3, 2018.

191 Al-Khalidi, Suleiman, 'Russian and Syrian air strikes intensify on last rebel bastion,' *Reuters*, March 13, 2019.

192 'Russian Strike Jets Pound Al Qaeda Targets with Precision Strikes in Syria; The Su-34's Role in the Idlib Offensive,' *Military Watch Magazine*, September 6, 2018.
'Russian Su-34 Jets Destroy Drone-factory of Pro-West Terrorists in Syria's Idlib,' *Defence World*, September 5, 2018.

193 'Russian Su-35s Intercept Turkish F-16s Over Syria's Idlib – Reports,' *Military Watch Magazine*, August 20, 2019.

194 'Assessing the Trump Administration's Counterterrorism Policy,' *Middle East Institute*, July 27, 2017.
Hubbard, Ben, 'In a Syria Refuge, Extremists Exert Greater Control,' *New York Times*, August 13, 2017.

195 Cockburn, Patrick, 'Turkey accused of recruiting ex-Isis fighters in their thousands to attack Kurds in Syria,' *The Independent*, February 7, 2018.

196 'Idlib assault on hold as Russia, Turkey agree on buffer zone,' *Al Jazeera*, September 17, 2018.

197 'Russia declares "ceasefire" as Syrians try to storm border post,' *Al Jazeera*, August 30, 2019.

198 'Militants continue to shell outskirts of Aleppo – Syrian Arab Army,' *TASS*, January 13, 2020.

199 'Eight people killed as militants shell Aleppo suburbs, says Russian reconciliation center,' *TASS*, January 21, 2020.

200 'Turkish soldiers killed in Syrian army shelling in Idlib,' *BBC News,* February 3, 2020.

201 'Turkish and Syrian Forces Clash as Damascus Moves to Recapture Idlib: Artillery and F-16s Provide Cover for Jihadist Militants,' *Military Watch Magazine,* February 3, 2020.

202 'Army discovers underground headquarters for terrorists in Idleb countryside,' *Syrian Arab News Agency,* February 3, 2020.

203 'Pro-government forces enter key Syrian rebel town of Maaret al-Numan,' *Middle East Eye,* January 28, 2020.

204 'Syrian Army Uncovers Secret Underground Al Qaeda Operations Headquarters Amid Northward Counterterrorism Operations,' *Military Watch Magazine,* February 4, 2020.

205 'Up to 450 militants attack Syrian forces in Idlib,' *TASS,* January 23, 2020.

206 Al-Ghadhawi, Abdullah, 'Uighur Jihadists in Syria,' *Center For Global Policy,* March 18, 2020.

207 Blanchard, Ben, 'Syria says up to 5,000 Chinese Uighurs fighting in militant groups,' *Reuters,* May 11, 2017.

208 Vagneur-Jones, Antoine, 'War and opportunity: the Turkistan Islamic Party and the Syrian conflict,' *Fondation pour la recherche stratégique,* no. 7, March 2, 2017.

209 Vltchek, Andre, 'March of the Uyghurs,' *New Eastern Outlook,* July 21, 2019.

210 Lin, Christina, 'Idlib militants eye China, Central Asia as next targets,' *Asia Times,* August 13, 2018.
Shih, Gerry, 'Uighurs fighting in Syria take aim at China,' *AP News,* December 23, 2017.
Wu, Wendy, 'Rising tide of jihadists stopped trying to return to China, Chinese advisers say,' *South China Morning Post,* January 8, 2017.
Martina, Michael and Blanchard, Ben, 'Uighur IS fighters vow blood will "flow in rivers" in China,' *Reuters,* March 1, 2017.

211 'China boosts Syria support,' *Global Times,* August 18, 2016.
Pauley, Logan and Marks, Jesse, 'Is China Increasing Its Military Presence in Syria?,' *The Diplomat,* August 20, 2018.
Zhou, Lara, 'China's role in Syria's endless civil war,' *South China Morning Post,* April 7, 2017.

212 Lin, Meilian, 'Xinjiang terrorists finding training, support in Syria, Turkey,' *Global Times,* July 1, 2013.

213 'Chinese Ambassador To Syria: We Are Willing To Participate "In Some Way" In The Battle For Idlib Alongside The Assad Army,' *The Middle East Media Research Institute,* August 1, 2018.
Neriah, Jacques, 'Chinese Troops Arrive in Syria to Fight Uyghur Rebels,' *Jerusalem Center for Public Affairs,* December 20, 2017 (unconfirmed).

214 'Turkish F-16 Downed Syrian Mi-17 Helicopter Over Idlib – Reports,' *Military Watch Magazine,* February 12, 2020.

215 'Escalation in Idlib: Russian Strike Fighters Pound Turkish Backed Jihadists to Cover Syrian Allies,' *Military Watch Magazine,* February 20, 2020.

216 'Fighting Escalates in Syria's Idlib: Turkey Intervenes More Actively to Support Jihadist Militants – Loses Nine Soldiers,' *Military Watch Magazine,* February 27, 2020.

217 al-Aswad, Harun and Soylu, Ragip, 'Two Turkish soldiers killed as Syrian rebels stage assault on Idlib's Neirab,' *Middle East Eye,* February 20, 2020.

218 'Syria war: Alarm after 33 Turkish soldiers killed in attack in Idlib,' *BBC News,* February 28, 2020.

219 'Turkish military firing at Russian, Syrian military planes in Idlib: Military source,' *Press TV,* February 27, 2020.

220 'Су-34 ВКС России и МиГ-23 ВВС Сирии в небе над Идлибом!' [Su-34 of the Russian Aerospace Forces and the MiG-23 of the Syrian Air Force in the skies over Idlib!], *Insider – Youtube Channel,* February 26, 2020 (https://www.youtube.com/watch?v=7sRHKgPxHtU&feature=emb_logo).

221 'Russia Deploys Elite "Hellduck" Bombers for Strikes on Jihadists as Clashes in Idlib Escalate,' *Military Watch Magazine,* February 28, 2020.

222 McKernan, Bethan and Sabbagh, Dan, 'Nato expresses "full solidarity" with Turkey over Syria airstrikes,' *The Guardian,* February 28, 2020.

223 'US Intends to Support Turkey's Actions in Syria's Idlib by Supplying Ammunition – Report,' *Sputnik,* March 3, 2020.

224 'Israeli Helicopters Attack Syrian Army Positions in Quneitra Province, Syrian State Media Reports,' *Sputnik,* February 27, 2020.

225 'Turkey-Israel Defence Agreement,' *Strategic Comments,* vol. 2, issue 6, 1996 (pp. 1–2).
Ozbek, Togla, 'Turkey accepts first Aselsan-modified F-4E Phantom,' *Flight Global,* March 9, 2010.

226 'Israel and Turkey Coordinating Attacks? Syrian Army Engaged on Two Fronts as Ankara and Tel Aviv Organise Strikes From North and South,' *Military Watch Magazine,* February 27, 2020.

227 'Turkish strike in Syria kills nine Hezbollah members, wounds 30: source,' *Reuters,* February 29, 2020.

228 'Turkish military strikes airport in Syria's Aleppo: Anadolu,' *Reuters,* March 1, 2020.

229 'Turkey shoots down two Syrian fighter jets over Idlib,' *Reuters,* March 1, 2020.
Cencciotti, David, 'The Turkish Air Force shot down two Syrian Su-24 Fencers today. A Turkish Anka-S drone drone was also downed,' *The Aviationist,* March 1, 2020.

230 Archus, Dorian, 'Russia sends 2 frigates to East Mediterranean as tension rises at Syria,' *Naval News,* February 28, 2020.
'Russia Dispatches Warships with Modern Kalibr Cruise Missiles as Tensions with Turkey Heat Up Over Idlib Clashes,' *Military Watch Magazine,* February 29, 2020.

231 'Russian military police deployed to Syria's Saraqib,' *TASS,* March 2, 2020.

232 'Russia Deploys Military Police to Block Turkish Backed Jihadists' Offensive into Syria,' *Military Watch Magazine,* March 5, 2020.

233 'Syria Destroys 6 Turkish Combat Drones, Turkish F-16s Down 2 Syrian Su-24 Jets,' *Defense World,* March 2, 2020.

234 'Wreckage of Turkish combat drone uncovered In southeast Idlib,' *Defence Point,* March 19, 2020.

'Images of one of the Turkish drones shot down by Syrian Arab Army units in Idleb,' *Syrian Arab News Agency*, March 4, 2020.

'Two Turkish Air Force Drones Reportedly Shot Down By Syrian Air Defence Over Idlib,' *Fighter Jets World*, March 3, 2020.

235 'Syrian Pilot Killed As Turkey Downs Warplane: Monitor,' *International Business Times*, March 3, 2020.

236 Gurcan, Metin, 'Turkish military purges decimate career officer, pilot ranks,' *Al Monitor*, May 29, 2018.

Stein, Aaron, 'Turkey's fighter pilot problems,' *Atlantic Council*, September 8, 2017.

'Turkey's purge of its own F-16 pilots severely crippled military capabilities – analyst,' *Ahval*, July 7, 2020.

Krever, Mick and Shubert, Atika, 'Turkish purges leave armed forces weak, dismissed officer warns,' *CNN*, February 1, 2017.

Bozkurt, Abdullah, 'Turkish Air Force crippled after mass purge of pilots by Erdoğan government,' *Nordic Monitor*, January 8, 2020.

237 'New Turkish Command Center Covering Idlib Cements Illegal Occupation of Northern Syria,' *Military Watch Magazine*, August 17, 2020.

238 'Statement by Syria's Representative to the UN Dr. Bashar Ja'afari during a Security Council session on situation in Syria,' *Permanent Mission of the Syrian Arab Republic to the United Nations*, August 19, 2020.

239 Angold, Michael, *Christianity: Eastern Christianity*, London, Cambridge University Press, 2006 (p. 512).

Lutsky, Vladminir Borisovich, *Modern History of the Arab Countries*, Moscow, Progress Publishers, 1969 (Chapter XXVII).

Li, Daisy, 'Social Stratification in Ethno-Religious Conflict: Divide in the Pre- and Post-Ottoman Empire,' *Yale Historical Review*, Spring 2017 (pp. 88–113).

240 Debre, Isabel, 'Pentagon report: Turkey sent up to 3,800 fighters to Libya,' *AP News*, July 18, 2020.

Trew, Bel, 'Syrian rebels reportedly part of Turkish contingent to be sent to defend Libya's government in Tripoli,' *The Independent*, December 27, 2019.

241 Vohra, Anchal, 'It's Syrian vs. Syrian in Libya,' *Foreign Policy*, May 5, 2020.

242 Gatopoulos, Alex, '"Largest drone war in the world": How airpower saved Tripoli,' *Al Jazeera*, May 28, 2020.

243 'Syria's Assad announces support for Haftar and Sisi in Libya,' *Middle East Monitor*, June 24, 2020.

244 'Libya's First MiG-29s: Is Russia Delivering New Fighters to Back the LNA's War Effort?,' *Military Watch Magazine*, May 23, 2020.

'MiG-29 in Action Over Libya: Newly Delivered Russian Fighter Seen Over Besieged City,' *Military Watch Magazine*, July 12, 2020.

'Haftar's Pantsir System Shoots Down Libyan Army's Bayraktar TB2 Drone,' *Defense World*, May 25, 2020.

Katz, Brian and Bermuudez Jr., Joseph S., 'Moscow's Next Front: Russia's Expanding Military Footprint in Libya,' *CSIS*, June 17, 2020.

245 Katz, Brian and Bermuudez Jr., Joseph S., 'Moscow's Next Front: Russia's Expanding Military Footprint in Libya,' *CSIS*, June 17, 2020.

Nichols, Michelle, 'Up to 1,200 deployed in Libya by Russian military group: U.N. report,' *Reuters*, May 6, 2020.

246 Bar'el, Zvi, 'The War in Syria Is Moving to Libya, With New Players and Shuffled Alliances,' *Haaretz*, July 25, 2020.

247 Abdulrahim, Raja, 'Turkish-Backed Syrian Fighters Join Armenian-Azeri Conflict,' *Wall Street Journal*, October 14, 2020.
Irish, John and Rose, Michel, 'France accuses Turkey of sending Syrian jihadists to Nagorno-Karabakh,' *Reuters*, October 1, 2020.
'Azerbaijan Bolstered By Turkish Trained Jihadist Militants in Fight Against Armenia – Reports,' *Military Watch Magazine*, September 28, 2020.

248 'Russia, Iran concerned about Syrian and Libyan fighters in Nagorno-Karabakh: Moscow,' *Al Arabiya*, October 3, 2020.
'Iran expresses concern over presence of terrorists and Turkey's involvement in Karabakh conflict,' *News.am*, October 6, 2020.

249 'Russia warns that Nagorno-Karabakh could become Islamist militant stronghold,' *Reuters*, October 6, 2020.
'Russian Foreign Intelligence Service Concerned as Turkey Transfers Al Qaeda-Linked Militants to Azerbaijan,' *Military Watch Magazine*, October 7, 2020.

250 'Armenia sends mine-clearing experts, doctors to Syria,' *Fox News*, February 9, 2019.

251 Boghani, Priyanka, 'Syrian Militant and Former Al Qaeda Leader Seeks Wider Acceptance in First Interview With U.S. Journalist,' *Frontline*, April 2, 2021.

252 'Terrorist Designation of Al-Nusrah Front Leader Muhammad Al-Jawlani,' *U.S. Department of State*, May 16, 2013.

253 Abu Mohammed Al-Jawlani, QDi.317, United Nations Security Council, official website of the United Nations (https://www.un.org/securitycouncil/sanctions/1267/aq_sanctions_list/summaries/individual/abu-mohammed-al-jawlani).

254 Boghani, Priyanka, 'Syrian Militant and Former Al Qaeda Leader Seeks Wider Acceptance in First Interview With U.S. Journalist,' *Frontline*, April 2, 2021.
Frantzman, Seth J., 'Did former US officials support extremists in Syria as an "asset"?,' *Jerusalem Post*, April 6, 2021.

255 Boghani, Priyanka, 'Syrian Militant and Former Al Qaeda Leader Seeks Wider Acceptance in First Interview With U.S. Journalist,' *Frontline*, April 2, 2021.
'Al-Jolani: "Hayat Tahrir Al-Sham" Poses No Threat to US,' *Al Mayadeen*, April 5, 2021.

256 Al Kanj, Sultan, 'Reviewing the Turkey–HTS Relationship,' *Chatham House*, May 2019.

257 Frantzman, Seth J., 'Did former US officials support extremists in Syria as an "asset"?,' *Jerusalem Post*, April 6, 2021.

258 'Turkey Wants Bashar Assad's Resignation – Ex-Turkish FM,' *Sputnik*, February 28, 2020.

259 'Erdoğan says Turkey will remain in Syria "until Syrian people are free",' *Reuters*, July 21, 2020.

# CONCLUSION

# Who Won in Syria?

For decades preceding the Syrian War, and throughout its duration, there was a stark clash in worldviews underlying the conflict between Damascus and the Western world. This pertained to their contrasting perceptions of the nature of international relations, world order and states' right to self-determination. Syria, which had won its independence in the aftermath of the Second World War, expressed a belief in global and regional orders comprised of nation states equal in their rights to sovereignty, including self-defence and self-determination and prohibiting forced external interference into their domestic affairs. This was the same order enshrined in the United Nations Charter, with importance attributed to sovereignty and self-determination drawing on Syria's historical memory of hundreds of years of brutal occupation under both Turkey and France and years of subsequent resistance against attempted U.S. manipulation of its domestic policies.

This contrasted strongly with the framework of international relations the Western Bloc sought for decades to universalise, under which both the world and regional orders were centred on Western dominance. Such a framework would allow the U.S. and Europe to influence the affairs of all other states, maintain unrestricted freedom for military intervention, and retain indefinite dominion globally. Former Assistant Secretary to the U.S. Treasury under Ronald Reagan, associate editor at the *Wall Street Journal* and holder of the William E. Simon chair in economics at CSIS, Paul Craig Roberts, noted to this effect: "The United States has an ideology of world hegemony and does not accept any prospect of any country being sovereign or acting on its own. You have to be an American vassal state." According to Roberts the U.S., influenced by its own extreme ideological position, intended to destroy those states seeking to retain genuine sovereignty.[1] This essential clash of visions for the nature of the international system has been the primary point of contention between Syria and the West and the underlying cause of conflict, with each intent on and unyielding in maintaining its position and certain of the virtue of its cause.

The Western paradigm was exemplified by a February 2021 interview with former U.S. Naval Intelligence Officer and Commander in the U.S. Navy John Jordan, a prominent national security analyst. When asked why the U.S. should have a right to build military facilities on the territory of a UN member state without its government's permission, which was widely considered an illegal act of aggression and a violation of Syrian sovereignty, Jordan justified it as follows: "First of all the government of Syria is not freely elected. There's a lot of people in Syria that don't think the Assad regime is legitimate." When told that the U.S. was never invited by the Syrian government to build military bases or deploy its troops, Jordan countered: "The Syrian government itself isn't elected and its own legitimacy is seriously in question. It is *not a democratically elected government*. Therefore it doesn't have the same legitimacy as, say, a Western government does." He concluded: "An invitation from the Assad regime doesn't legitimacy create."[2]

While the Damascus government was the UN recognised representative of Syria and had been recognised as such by the overwhelming majority of non-Western countries across the world, elections and a Western-style liberal democratic political system by contrast had no association with a government's legitimacy under the United Nations Charter or any kind of international law. These were purely a Western conception for how governments should be selected – and the fact that the West did not approve of whether or how Syrian elections were held or who was in power meant nothing in terms of international law. Nor was there any doubt under the Syrian constitution as to whether or not the Damascus government was legitimate.

The notion that any country could be forced to accept the presence of a Western military on its soil and have its government deemed illegitimate if it did not accept Western political values and adopt a Western style political system, as demonstrated in Syria, is an extremely dangerous one.[i] A world order premised on such precedents would effectively allow the West free rein to disregard the established norms of international law and invade, occupy and plunder any country under the pretext that it had not sufficiently Westernised its political system. This kind of international system would mirror that of the colonial era where, instead of a lack of Western political values, an alleged lack of civilisation in a targeted country had commonly been used as a pretext for Western military intervention. The 'civilising mission' has been replaced by the 'democratising mission' – and where the West had once presented itself as the judge of what proper civilisation was for the whole world, it now presented itself as the judge of what proper political values must be adopted. Imposing political Westernisation replaced imposing cultural Westernisation as the new pretext for Western aggression, but the crusade for assertion of Western dominance globally continued much the same. By using political ideology as a pretext to violate both state sovereignty and international laws against crimes of aggression – the most serious of all international crimes – the Western powers used a

---

i    The use of Syria's lack of Western style liberal democracy as a pretext to delegitimise and attack the state, not only by the Western powers but also by Western-aligned states in the Middle East, was seen by many as at least somewhat ironic. An example was Syria's UN envoy, Bashar Jaafari, who stated regarding Qatari calls for the Syrian government's overthrow in 2012 on the basis of its lack of a Westernised liberal democratic political system: "It is really strange these days...that some oligarchic states cosponsor draft resolutions promoting the alternation of power, the freedom of assembly, the promotion of democracy, and the protection and promotion of human rights...those very states don't even have a constitution, let alone a genuine electoral system." While neither Syria nor Qatar had Westernised political systems, the latter aligned its foreign policy closely with Western interests, provided favourable terms to Western firms for investment, and condoned the indefinite presence of Western military personnel on its soil. Had Damascus done the same, its lack of a Westernised system of government would likely have been overlooked. (Lynch, Colum, 'The Killing Machine vs. Al Jazeera,' *Foreign Policy,* February 2012.)

new iteration of the 'civilising mission' as a pretext for aggression and plunder. In doing so, they threatened the very foundations of the post-Second World War world order and directly contravened the principles of the United Nations Charter.

Support for Damascus from Russia, Iran, North Korea and China among others, and Russian efforts to deny the Western powers the ability to control Syrian airspace and forcefully topple its internationally recognised government, were largely consequences of these states' shared paradigm with Syria for viewing international relations. Preserving Syrian sovereignty was particularly vital considering the extent to which those states outside the Western sphere of influence had become a minority in the post-Cold War world. The result was a global Western military presence and profound Western political and economic influence over states across the world – referred to by scholars as "a historically unprecedented system of semi sovereign states."[3] The United States maintained over 800 military bases overseas, which according to *The Nation* amounted to "more bases in foreign lands than any other people, nation, or empire in history."[4] It accounted for 95 percent of foreign military installations globally with the majority of the remaining 5 percent belonging to allied Western military powers. Deployments of U.S. special forces were even more widespread. In 2016 they were deployed to 138 countries,[5] and have been increasingly relied on as a tool "to maintain global dominance" – a scalpel where heretofore direct colonial rule was the hammer.[6]

The prevalence of U.S. and Western military units overseas is a key pillar of the Western world's ability to project power globally against those parties which challenge or otherwise undermine the Western-led order. Rather than state sovereignty and global consensus, the presence of Western soldiers in the vast majority of countries strongly indicates an order premised on total Western hegemony. In this context, the Syrian War has represented a pivotal moment determining whether the country would remain independent, or whether it would be forcefully placed under Western control as dozens before it – from Japan[7] and the Philippines[8] to Grenada,[9] Iraq[10] and Afghanistan[11] – had been. Had Syria been defeated, damage to resistance in the wider Middle East and beyond would also have been significant. As senior Iranian cleric Mehdi Taeb had stressed regarding the importance of protecting the country: "If the enemy attacks us and wants to take either Syria or [the outlying Iranian province of] Khuzestan, the priority is to keep Syria... If we keep Syria, we can get Khuzestan back too, but if we lose Syria, we cannot keep Tehran."[12] Had Damascus fallen, Iran and Hezbollah may have quickly followed.

The extent to which media and information warfare played vital roles in the Syrian War was unprecedented for a Middle Eastern conflict, both in fuelling early support for the insurgency and in gaining popular support in the West and the Islamic world for the isolation and pressurising of Syria. An important aspect of this was the consistent portrayal of the war through the paradigm of a greater Shiite-Sunni sectarian conflict by Western and Gulf media. This allowed them to alienate the predominantly Shiite 'Axis of Resistance' – the only significant barrier to complete Western hegemony in the Middle East – from the bulk of the region's populations who were Sunnis. Doing so not only undermined potential pan-Arab solidarity with Syria, but also undercut the previously considerable support Hezbollah had enjoyed both in the Arab world and more broadly among Muslims following its 2006 victory over Israel.

The narrative of a sectarian Shiite-Sunni war had serious inconsistencies, the most notable being the diversity of the Syrian state and the Ba'ath Party leadership which strongly represented all minorities but was predominantly Sunni. This included a Sunni Prime Minister, Religious Minister, Foreign Minister, Interior Minister, presidential National Security Advisor and First Lady among other important figures, with ideological and political affiliations rather than religious or ethnic backgrounds being prized by the Syrian state. Sunnis were better represented in government than any other religious group, which reflected their majority status as well as the lack of sectarian division or institutional religious discrimination in Syria. The sectarian paradigm was also seriously contradicted by the status of President Assad's Alawite sect, which was very distinct from both mainstream Sunni and Shiite sects, and by the positions taken by Muslim states such as Egypt, Sudan, Algeria[13] and Azerbaijan. The former three were Sunni but supported Syria, while the latter was Shiite but aligned closely with Turkey and Israel.[14] Nevertheless, the effort to demonise the Syrian state as somehow being a tool of Shiite nationalism against the Sunni world was largely successful due to the dominance the Western world and its partners had over the media landscape.

The Syrian War was considerably longer than any Middle Eastern war in the Cold War era or since, and could well retain the title of the region's longest hot war in the 21st century. The conflict was prolonged considerably by a succession of direct interventions by external parties, the most notable being Al Qaeda from 2011, Hezbollah from 2013, the Islamic State from 2014, Russia the following year and the U.S. and Turkey soon afterwards, with both government and insurgent forces receiving continuous flows of arms and support. The Western powers and Turkey remain unlikely to yield the territory they have occupied or to allow for a normalisation of Syria's international relations for the foreseeable future. As a result, the standoff between Damascus and the NATO powers forcefully occupying Idlib and northern Syria is expected to last for several years more and potentially into the second half of the 2020s. This will likely depend on the extent to which the SAA and its partners can afford to impose continuous costs on occupying forces while deterring them from pursuing more radical forms of escalatory retaliation. The March 2021 Syrian ballistic missile strike on an insurgent oil facility operating under Turkish protection and delivering fuel into Turkey, and simultaneous strengthening of Syrian air defences, were interpreted by some as steps in this direction.[15]

The end of the Donald Trump administration in January 2021 portended a much harder line from Washington against Syria, including a redoubling of economic warfare efforts and a cementing of the American commitment to maintaining the occupation of the northern regions. The Joe Biden administration showed several early signs of a harder line against Damascus, including sending a military convoy into the country in its first week in office[16] and conducting airstrikes against Quds Force

backed militias in its sixth week.[17] Even more so than its predecessors, however, the Biden administration has placed East
Asia and particularly China at the centre of its foreign policy and
security priorities.[18] The growing strain on the U.S. military from
fast expanding Chinese and North Korean military capabilities,
which have led Washington to prioritise diverting forces to East
Asia where possible,[19] is likely to influence how long America
remains committed to its occupation in Syria. The outcome of the
economic, technological and strategic competition between China
and the U.S., in turn, will very heavily influence the balance of
power in the Middle East and could well determine whether or not
the Syrian state will survive in the long term.

 While Syria's war has been long and often brutal, by the standards of major wars both globally and in the Arab world the damage and the death toll has been far from exceptional considering
its length. With a death toll estimated at between approximately
380,000 and 580,000 on the war's tenth anniversary in early 2021,
the numbers killed were just a fraction of those of the Iran-Iraq
War (1980–88: between 600,000 and 1.07 million killed)[20] or the
Algerian war of independence (1954–62: between 960,000 and
over 1.5 million killed).[21] The preceding major conflicts of the
Cold War beyond the Middle East had been far more intense and
brutal still, such as the Korean War (1950–53: 5 million or more
killed)[22] and the Vietnam War (1965–1974: 3.1 million or more
killed).[23] The death toll of the Indonesian military's Cold War
purge of leftist party members and their families, largely orchestrated by the Western powers and aided by Islamists, killed far
more in a single year than the death toll of ten years of war in
Syria, with estimates ranging from 500,000 to over 3 million.[24]
Operation Desert Storm, launched against Ba'athist Iraq by a
U.S.-led coalition in January 1991 and lasting just 44 days, caused
over 100,000 Iraqi military casualties[25] (the BBC claimed up to
200,000)[26] and thousands more civilians dead. Over 500,000 children died from the fallout of the Western bombing campaign and
subsequent economic sanctions on Iraq in the following years.[27]
While these comparisons do not detract from the Syrian War's
importance or the extent of its tragedy, they do offer important

context to understanding the conflict in perspective, and to avoiding exaggerations regarding its extremity.

Perhaps much more significantly than material damage, the
Syrian War had potentially very serious global repercussions due
to the way Western powers sought to use their military intervention
against Damascus to claim that an international legal precedent
had been set. The West's inability to violate Syria's sovereignty
with warplanes and cruise missiles without also violating international law led a growing number of Western scholars to claim
that, by going ahead and striking Syrian territory illegally which
the U.S. and its allies did from 2015, customary international law
itself had been changed. In the West the attacks on Syrian government targets in 2017 and 2018 were often described as 'Grotian
moments' – events which marked "a fundamental change in the
existing international system" which many Western scholars
claimed sparked a major reformation of customary international
law when pertaining to crimes of aggression. This argument was
based on the premise that, since the Western powers had taken
alleged humanitarian abuses in the form of chemical attacks as
pretexts to strike Syria, attacking countries on similar grounds
should from then on be considered legal.[28] This was effectively
a tenuous attempt to use military action, which directly violated
both the UN charter [Article 2 (4)] (the *jus cogens* prohibition on
the use of force) as well as existing customary international law,
to set a legal precedent. Since customary law was based on consistent state conduct across the international community of nations,
the argument that illegal attacks by Western powers effectively in
isolation from the norms of the wider world could change it was
far from strong.

Although the radical premise that the West could so fundamentally alter international law unilaterally was entirely contrary
to international law itself, this had considerable support across the
Western world. The idea that when the Western powers committed
a crime, that action became the international norm and therefore
a new part of customary law, in many ways recalled a 1972 statement by U.S. President Nixon who had claimed following the
Watergate scandal and the exposure of his illegal actions: "Well,

when the president does it that means that it is not illegal."[29] In this context the West was "the president" and the rest of the world were the subjects. Thus the narrative was advanced that if Western actions were illegal, it could only be because customary international law needed to be reformed to make them legal. The West itself, like "the president," could not be in the wrong – an argument which reflected an ideology of Western supremacism and exceptionalism.[30]

The rest of the world would be forced to accept on this basis not only that the Europeans and Americans were the ones who set the rules, but also that the West now had every legal right to attack them if it could claim a moral pretext to do so. This had potentially highly destabilising consequences for global order, and by discarding the post–Second World War legal prohibition against crimes of aggression the West was returning the world to a chaotic order that resembled that of the colonial era. As seen in Korea,[31] Iraq (in both 1991[32] and 2003[33]), Libya,[34] Yugoslavia[35] and elsewhere, when the West saw an opportunity for aggression to expand its global hegemony it was always able fabricate a terrible atrocity to provide a pretext. It was now trying to rewrite international law, or at least claim it interpreted the law as having been rewritten by its own illegal actions, to legitimise this practice of aggression with humanitarian pretexts. If aggression was legal, then only might made right and countries outside the Western sphere of influence would enjoy no legal protections from attack – leaving only those protections their militaries could provide.

Regarding the war's outcome, whether either side can claim to have "won" in Syria remains debatable. While Damascus prevailed, avoiding the fates of other Western target states such as Afghanistan, the cost to it and its allies in blood and treasure has been considerable. The outcome saw no territorial or strategic gains by Syria, but significant and possibly indefinite territorial losses to NATO occupation forces in Idlib, Hasakah, Raqqa, and Deir ez-Zor. Although the Western powers and their regional allies failed to destroy the Syrian Ba'ath Party and apply an Afghan or Libyan model for the subjugation of the country, Western interests were furthered considerably and at a relatively negligible cost.

Not only was Syria effectively neutralised as a capable independent actor in the Middle East, one which is unlikely to recover fully for many years to come, but the commitment of large numbers of Western or even allied soldiers to the battlefront was not necessary. The war against Syria, while largely organised by the West, from training and logistics for insurgents to the information warfare campaign, was overwhelmingly funded by the Arab Gulf States,[36] with the manpower coming from Muslim populations across the world – from Saudi convicts to Chechen and Xinjiang Islamists. Saudi funding for insurgent groups alone was estimated in 2016 as approximately $700 million per year – or around 40% of the Syrian state's pre-war defence budget. This combined with contributions from Qatar, Kuwait, Turkey and others meant there was little need for direct Western financial support.[37]

Even though Syria prevailed, the West was able to achieve its destruction at very little cost to itself, much as had been the case in Afghanistan before it, meaning the final outcome of the war still represents a strengthening of the Western position at Damascus' expense. As NATO Secretary General Wesley Clark testified, citing a memo from the Office of the U.S. Secretary of Defence in 2001, Washington had planned to "attack and destroy the governments in seven countries in five years," starting with Iraq and subsequently targeting "Syria, Lebanon, Libya, Somalia, Sudan and Iran."[38] Iran was the final target, but the goal was ultimately the complete subjugation of the Middle East and North Africa to Western interests, as had been the status quo before the Cold War. As of 2021, with Ba'athist Iraq toppled, Lebanon on the verge of collapse, Hezbollah militarily stretched and the Chinese- and Russian-friendly governments of Libya and Sudan violently overthrown with Western backing, this strategy has largely succeeded. Although Iran benefitted from considerable support from China, North Korea and Russia, which have respectively focused on economic backing, technology and arms transfers and strategic support, Western efforts to re-arrange the entire Middle East and Arab world against the Islamic Republic have shown growing signs of success. Iran is thus expected to face fast growing pressure in the coming years. The neutering of Syria, which though still governed by the Ba'ath Party has been made into more of a burden on its Iranian and Russian partners than an asset and is in too weak a position to seriously affect regional affairs beyond its borders, played a key role in bringing about Iran's isolation.

## Notes

1  'The U.S. govt bent on world hegemony, Russia stands in its way – Reagan economic ex-advisor,' *RT*, December 4, 2014.

2  'US secretly building airport in Syria near oil field,' *The News With Rick Sanchez, RT America*, February 15, 2021.

3  Stone, I. F., *Hidden History of the Korean War*, Amazon Media, 2014 (Foreword by Bruce Cumings).

4  Vine, David, 'The United States Probably Has More Foreign Military Bases Than Any Other People, Nation or Empire in History,' *The Nation*, September 14, 2015.

5  Durden, Tyler, 'U.S. Special Forces Deployed To 70 Percent of The World In 2016,' *Ron Paul Institute for Peace and Prosperity*, February 11, 2017.
Turse, Nick, 'Special Ops, Shadow Wars, and the Golden Age of the Grey Zone,' *Tom Dispatch*, January 5, 2017.

6  Philips, Michael M., 'New ways the U.S. projects power around the globe: Commandoes,' *Wall Street Journal*, April 24, 2015.

7  Abrams, A. B. *Power and Primacy: A History of Western Intervention in the Asia-Pacific*, Oxford, Peter Lang, 2019 (Chapters One and Two).

8  Ibid (Chapter 5: America in the Philippines: How the United States Established a Colony and Later Neo-Colony in the Pacific).

9  Chayes, Abram, 'Grenada Was Illegally Invaded,' *New York Times*, November 15, 1983.

10  MacAskill, Ewen and Borger, Julian, 'Iraq war was illegal and breached UN charter, says Annan,' *The Guardian*, September 16, 2004.
Higham, Scott and Stephens, Joe, 'New Details of Prison Abuse Emerge,' *Washington Post*, May 21, 2004 (p. A01).
Sealey, Geraldine, 'Hersh: Children sodomized at Abu Ghraib, on tape,' *Salon*, July 15, 2004.

11  Weiner, Tim, 'History to Trump: CIA was aiding Afghan rebels before the Soviets invaded in '79,' *Washington Post*, January 7, 2019.
Coll, Steve, 'CIA in Afghanistan: In CIA's Covert War, Where to Draw the Line Was Key,' *Washington Post*, July 20, 1992.

12  Blanford, Nicholas, 'Why Iran is standing by its weakened, and expensive, ally Syria,' *Christian Science Monitor*, April 27, 2015.

13  'Severe message from Algeria: "Syria must rejoin the Arab League",' *Middle East Monitor*, March 3, 2020.
'Algerian Ambassador: We stand by Syria in combating all forms of terrorism,' *Syrian Arab News Agency*, November 2, 2017.

14   Gut, Arye, 'Why did Israel choose Azerbaijan?,' *Jerusalem Post,* September 7, 2017.
     Gut, Arye, 'Israel, Azerbaijan strengthen and expand strategic partnership,' *Jerusalem Post,* January 21, 2018.
     Fraser, Suzan, 'AP Explains: What lies behind Turkish support for Azerbaijan,' *AP News,* October 2, 2020.
15   'Strong Signal to Turkey: Syrian Army Destroys Jihadist Oil Facility in Major Ballistic Missile Strike,' *Military Watch Magazine,* March 8, 2021.
16   'US military convoy enters northeast Syria: report,' *i24 News,* January 22, 2021.
     Rogin, Josh, 'Opinion: Biden must fix Obama's biggest foreign policy failure,' *Washington Post,* September 4, 2020.
17   Trevithick, Joseph, 'Biden Strikes Back: What We Know About The Bombing Raid On Iran's Militias,' *The Drive,* February 25, 2021.
18   Stashwick, Steven, 'The Asia-Pacific is Biden's Top Security Priority,' *The Diplomat,* February 23, 2021.
     Bertrand, Natasha and Seligman, Lara, 'Biden deprioritizes the Middle East,' *Politico,* February 22, 2021.
19   'Background Press Call by a Senior Administration Official on the Official Working Visit of Japan,' *The White House,* April 15, 2021.
     McLeary, Paul, 'Marines Downgrade Russia Threat To Focus on China,' *Breaking Defense,* March 2, 2021.
     Carey, Glen, 'U.S. Pentagon Chief Wants to Reallocate Forces to Indo-Pacific,' *Bloomberg,* December 8, 2019.
     Cunningham, Finian, 'Biden Drops Afghan Mess to Target China, Russia,' *Sputnik,* April 15, 2021.
20   Pelletiere, Stephen C. and Johnson, Douglas V., *Lessons Learned: Iran–Iraq War,* Washington, D.C., Fleet Marine Force Reference Publication, December 1990 (pp. 117–119).
21   'France admits torture during Algeria's war of independence,' *Al Jazeera,* September 13, 2018.
     'Millions of dead later, Algeria's War of Independence never ended,' *TRT World,* July 5, 2020.
22   'Korean War,' *History.com.*
23   Shenon, Philip, '20 Years After Victory, Vietnamese Communists Ponder How to Celebrate,' *New York Times,* April 23, 1995.
24   'Looking into the massacres of Indonesia's past,' *BBC News,* June 2, 2016.
     'Indonesia's killing fields,' *Al Jazeera,* December 21, 2012.
25   Cooper, Patrick, 'Coalition deaths fewer than in 1991,' *CNN,* June 25, 2003.
26   'Flashback: 1991 Gulf War,' *BBC News,* March 20, 2003.
27   'Sanctions Blamed for Deaths of Children,' Lewiston Morning Tribune, December 2, 1995.
     Stahl, Lesley, 'Interview with Madeline Albright,' 60 Minutes, May 12, 1996.
     'Iraq conflict has killed a million Iraqis,' Reuters, January 30, 2008.
28   P. Scharf, Michael and Sterio, Milena and Williams, Paul R., *The Syrian Conflict's Impact on International Law,* Cambridge, Cambridge University Press, 2020.

Scharf, Michael P., 'Striking a Grotian Moment: How the Syria Airstrikes Changed International Law Relating to Humanitarian Interventions,' *Case Western Reserve University, Faculty Publications,* 2019.

Sterio, Milena, 'Humanitarian Intervention Post-Syria: A Grotian Moment,' *Cleveland-Marshall College of Law, Law Faculty Articles and Essays,* vol. 20, no. 2, 2014 (pp. 343–356).

'Syria strikes violated international law – are the rules of foreign intervention changing?,' *The Conversation,* April 18, 2018.

'The Syrian War's Forcing Effect on International Law,' SOHR, May 13, 2020.

29    Dewar, Helen, 'President Isn't Above the Law, Nixon Insists,' *Washington Post,* June 5, 1977.

30    P. Scharf, Michael and Sterio, Milena and Williams, Paul R., *The Syrian Conflict's Impact on International Law,* Cambridge, Cambridge University Press, 2020.

Scharf, Michael P., 'Striking a Grotian Moment: How the Syria Airstrikes Changed International Law Relating to Humanitarian Interventions,' *Case Western Reserve University, Faculty Publications,* 2019.

'Syria strikes violated international law – are the rules of foreign intervention changing?,' *The Conversation,* April 18, 2018.

31    Stone, I. F., *Hidden History of the Korean War,* Amazon Media, 2014 (Chapter 45: Atrocities to the Rescue).

Abrams, A. B., *Immovable Object: North Korea's 70 Years At War with American Power,* Atlanta, Clarity Press, 2020 (pp. 84–85).

Cumings, Bruce, *The Korean War: A History,* Modern Library Edition, 2010 (p. 177).

Shaines, Robert A., *Command Influence: A story of Korea and the politics of injustice,* Denver, CO, Outskirts Press, 2010 (p. 54).

32    'Deception on Capitol Hill,' *New York Times,* January 15, 1992.

Walton, Douglas, 'Appeal to pity: A case study of the argumentum ad misericordiam,' *Argumentation,* Albany, State University of New York Press, 1997 (pp. 136–137).

Krauss, Clifford, 'Congressman Says Girl Was Credible,' *New York Times,* January 12, 1992.

Rowse, Aruther E., 'Teary Testimony to Push America Toward War,' *The San Francisco Chronicle,* October 18, 1992 (p. 9/Z1).

Rowse, Arthur E., 'How to build support for war,' *Columbia Journalism Review,* September–October 1992.

Sriramesh, Krishnamurthy, *The global public relations handbook: theory, research, and practice,* Abingdon, Taylor & Francis, 2009 (p. 864).

33    O'Neill, Brendan, 'Not a shred of evidence,' *Spectator,* February 21, 2004.

34    Bosco, David, 'Was there going to be a Benghazi massacre?,' *Foreign Policy,* April 7, 2011.

Kuperman, Alan, 'Lessons from Libya: How Not to Intervene,' *Harvard Kennedy School Belfer Center,* September 2013.

Bosco, David, 'A Model Humanitarian Intervention? Reassessing NATO's Libya Campaign,' Harvard *Kennedy School Belfer Center,* Summer 2013.

Pedde, Nicola, 'The Libyan conflict and its controversial roots,' *European View,* vol. 16, 2017 (pp. 93–102).

'5 things the U.S. should consider in Libya,' *USA Today,* March 22, 2011.

35   Parenti, Michael, *To Kill a Nation: The Attack on Yugoslavia,* London, Verso, 2000 (pp. 83–86).

Pilger, John, 'Calling the humanitarian bombers to account,' *Counterpunch,* December 11–12, 2004.

36   Mazzetti, Mark and Apuzzo, Matt, 'U.S. Relies Heavily on Saudi Money to Support Syrian Rebels,' *New York Times,* January 23, 2016.

Khalaf, Roula and Fielding Smith, Abigail, 'Qatar bankrolls Syrian revolt with cash and arms,' *Financial Times,* May 16, 2013.

37   Hersh, Seymour, 'Military to Military,' *London Review of Books,* vol. 38, no. 1, January 2016 (pp. 11–14).

38   Greenwald, Glen, 'Wes Clark and the neocon dream,' *Salon,* November 26, 2011.

# ANNEX

# Israel's War

## Israel Versus Iran and Hezbollah in Syria

Not long after its outbreak the Syrian War quickly became a battleground for multiple external parties with pre-existing hostilities to combat one another by making military contributions to opposing sides. Examples of preceding conflicts included, inter alia, that which both Russia and North Korea had with the United States, that between Chechen military units loyal to the Russian Federation[1] and anti-Russian Chechen jihadists, and that between the Afghan Shiite militias and the former affiliates of the Mujahideen in Afghanistan. Those parties which had traditionally been aligned with or supported by the West, the latter parties in the examples given above,[2] generally aligned themselves against Damascus, while those which perceived themselves as resistance to Western global hegemony aligned themselves with the Syrian government. So it was that Iran and Hezbollah's conflict with Israel would come to overshadow the later stages of the Syrian War.

While Hezbollah and Iranian Quds Force involvement in support of the Syrian government has already been elaborated, as has major Israeli support for jihadist groups to weaken Syria and its partners,[3] the conflict between them became more direct as the tide of the war shifted decisively against the Islamist insurgency from 2016. This was largely due to Israeli concerns that Iran in particular would exploit Damascus' newfound reliance on its military support to entrench itself in Syria and deploy new Quds Force trained militia groups near the Israeli border – much as it had earlier helped entrench Hezbollah on Israel's Lebanese border. Should new Iranian-aligned militias establish a presence near the Israeli-held Golan Heights unimpeded, they were expected to take a similar course to Hezbollah. This would include building up local public support and establishing deep and complex tunnel and bunker networks to allow them to operate relatively freely despite Israel's control of the air. Such a development would present Israel with the possibility of a two-front war in the event of renewed conflict with Hezbollah – a potential game changer.

Also concerning for Israel was a growth in the number Shiite Muslims from abroad, including from Afghanistan, Iraq and Iran itself, settling permanently in southern Damascus near the Sayyeda Zeynab shrine. Some speculated that this new community would form the basis of a Shia stronghold, similar to the Dahieh region of Beirut, which could in turn form the basis for a new Hezbollah-type organisation[4] – referred to with much apprehension in the West as a 'Syrian Hezbollah.'[5] While new militias were Shiite-led, they often recruited Sunni tribesmen to serve in their ranks and worked closely with pro-government Sunni and other non-Shiite militia groups, undermining the narrative of a sectarian ideology motivating their activities.[6] Alongside the buildup of local militia groups with Quds Force assistance, Lebanese Hezbollah had also deployed up to 8,000 fighters to Syria armed with a range of rocket artillery systems – many of which were likely to stay even after the war concluded. It also trained and advised several newer militia groups in partnership with the Quds Force.[7] Israeli Defence Minister Avigdor Lieberman highlighted the need for swift Israeli action against these forces, stating in May 2018: "I know one thing for certain. We will not allow the Iranians to base themselves in Syria and there will be a price for that. We have no other choice. To agree to an Iranian presence in Syria, it's agreeing to the fact that the Iranians will put a noose around your neck."[8]

Tel Aviv had a strong interest in seeing the overthrow of the Syrian government, much as its partners in the West and the Gulf did, which would represent the final death of the Arab nationalist threat that had overhung the Jewish state since the early 1950s. Such an outcome would also facilitate much greater freedom of action for the Israeli Defence Forces in the region, with Syrian ballistic missiles, chemical weapons and air defences all having for decades been directed primarily at restraining Israel's military power. Israeli interest in the war in Syria, however, was much more influenced by Damascus' value to and partnership with Iran and Hezbollah, rather than animosity towards the Syrian state itself – as great as that was. This was primarily due to the unexpected defeat the Israeli military had suffered to Hezbollah in 2006, which had shaken the country and made neutralising the group a vital priority.[9]

Attesting to the depth of Israel's animosity towards Iran and Hezbollah and the extent to which combatting these actors was prioritised, Israeli Defence Minister Moshe Ya'alon stated that it was more favourable to have jihadists rule over Syria, including if necessary the Islamic State, rather than allowing Iran to gain a foothold in the country. "In Syria, if the choice is between Iran and the Islamic State, I choose the Islamic State.... Our greatest enemy is the Iranian regime that has declared war on us," he said in January 2016.[10] Ya'alon also expressed concern that "Iran tried to open a terror front against us on the Golan Heights,"[11] in reference to the growing presence of Quds Force affiliated militias near the Israeli border. This did a great deal to explain the later-revealed Israeli policy of arming Al Qaeda linked militants in the area,[12] which although dangerous were much more hostile towards Iran than they were towards Israel. According to Ya'alon, Islamic State had apologised for the sole incident where its forces did target Israel, indicating that the terror group did not see the country as a target. Both Tel Aviv and Islamic State were primarily focused on targeting their mutual enemies, namely the Syrian government, Hezbollah, the Iranian Quds Force, and their affiliates.[13]

It is notable that while Israel undoubtedly saw Iran and its regional partners as its primary adversaries in the post-Arab nationalist Middle East, at least since the fall of Ba'athist Iraq in 2003, Tehran had from the earliest days of its Islamic Revolution confined Israel to the status of a secondary adversary. Israel was accordingly termed the 'Smaller Satan,' relative to the revolution's primary adversary, the United States, which was termed the 'Great Satan.'[14] Iran's primary objective in Syria was not defined as countering Israel, but rather as supporting the only remaining state in the Arab Middle East outside the Western sphere of influence to defend its sovereignty – thereby putting Western expansionism in check. Supporting Damascus was seen as imperative despite the very stark ideological discrepancy between Syria's secular Ba'athist party state and Iran's Islamic Republic, with both united primarily by their opposition to Western regional hegemony. Iran's buildup of local militia forces was only pursued later in the war in response to the Syrian Arab Army's failure to combat the jihadist insurgency unsupported, and with the immediate objective of securing Syria against militants who were backed primarily by the West, Turkey and the Gulf. Building up a force against Israel was a secondary and longer-term goal for Iran which only began to materialise once the tide of the war had decisively turned in Damascus' favour, leading to a considerable increase in Iranian-Israeli tensions in Syria from 2017.

In parallel to the growth in Iranian involvement, Hezbollah gained greater operational flexibility in Syria and highly valuable combat experience, which was repeatedly highlighted by both Western and Israeli analysts as a major threat to Israeli and allied interests.[15] As a senior Israeli military officer quoted by the *New York Times* stated, involvement in the Syrian war had been "a major burden for Hezbollah but also a major advantage... I have no doubt that Hezbollah gained much more self-confidence because of the Syrian experience." Regarding the militia's modernisation efforts, he warned: "A Hezbollah with modern surface-to-air systems, with modern U.A.V.'s, with modern cyber capabilities, well, this is a different Hezbollah."[16] Gabi Siboni, director of the military and strategic affairs program at the Institute for National Security Studies at Tel Aviv University, stated to similar effect regarding Hezbollah's battle hardening in Syria: "This kind of experience cannot be bought... It is an additional factor that we will have to deal with. There is no replacement for experience, and it is not to be scoffed at."[17] This contrasted with earlier assessments by figures such as Yoram Schweitzer, an expert at Israel's Institute for National Security Studies, who described the war in Syria as Hezbollah's "Vietnam, Afghanistan or Iraq." He argued that although Hezbollah was gaining valuable combat experience, "the price it is paying is greater than the gain."[18] Such

early assessments did much to explain why Israel was supporting
Al Qaeda linked groups in Syria, namely to prolong the war and
wear down Hezbollah units sent to support Damascus much as the
U.S. had done to wear down the Soviet armed forces sent to assist
Kabul three decades prior.

Although Israel's conflict with Iran and Hezbollah escalated
significantly in 2017, after the SAA's capture of Aleppo and amid
growing signs of an imminent defeat for the jihadist insurgency,
there were significant clashes between them on Syrian soil in
the preceding four years. Israel began strikes on Syrian territory
under the pretext of attacking Hezbollah in 2013, with attacks
carried out on January 30, May 3 and 5, July 5 and October 31
of that year, and three further rounds of similar strikes initiated
the following year. Iranian sources alleged a further strike had
been carried out on February 12, 2013, as a targeted assassination
of Iranian Major General Hassan Shateri. The general was at the
time the highest-ranking Quds Force officer ever killed abroad.[19]
Many Israeli strikes reportedly targeted the Syrian Arab Army
rather than Hezbollah but were reported by Israel as attacks on
Hezbollah in order to avoid openly involving itself in the campaign against Syria. Doing so would have risked fostering sympathy for Damascus' position in the Muslim world on the basis of
widespread anti-Israeli sentiments.

Israel achieved its greatest successes in this phase of the
campaign with the targeted killing of Hezbollah commander
Mohamad Issa and Iranian Quds Force Brigadier General
Mohammad Ali Allahdadi in an air strike in January 2015.[20]
Hezbollah was quick to retaliate, causing nine Israeli military
casualties in a small symbolic attack launched from Lebanon.[21]
Eight more rounds of Israeli airstrikes on SAA and Hezbollah
positions were reported in 2015, escalating near the end of the
year, and occurring on April 25, July 25, October 31, November
11, 23 and 28, and December 19 and 26. Targets ranged from
weapons facilities to military bases. These were followed by two
more rounds of attacks in November and December 2016. The
former reportedly struck a military compound in Damascus and
a Hezbollah weapons convoy, while the latter struck Mezzeh

Airbase near Damascus including its runway, command centre and an SAA divisional operations centre. May 2016 also saw the killing of one of Hezbollah's most senior military commanders, Mustapha Badreddine, whom Lebanon's Hezbollah-aligned Al Mayadeen TV reported had been killed in an Israeli airstrike. The cause of his death was never fully confirmed.[22]

Alongside an escalation of the Israeli intervention in Syria, the year 2017 also saw Israel's Defence Ministry begin to openly press the United States to become more active in the conflict, citing the looming defeat of the jihadist insurgency which seriously undermined Israeli and Western interests.[23] Israel's Chief of Staff, Gadi Eisenkot, referred to a "significant change in Iran's strategy" at around this time, stating: "Their vision was to have significant influence in Syria by building a force of up to 100,000 Shiite fighters from Pakistan, Afghanistan and Iraq. They built intelligence bases and an air force base within each Syrian air base."[24] This claim was indirectly supported by a statement by Hassan Nasrallah in June 2017, when he pledged that "thousands, even hundreds of thousands of fighters from Iraq, Yemen, Iran, Afghanistan and Pakistan" would join the fight against Israel – presumably to be on call for the next possible conflict.[25] Iraq's Harakat Hezbollah Al Nujaba militia notably formed a "Golan Liberation Brigade" at around this time, which was a strong indicator of its long term intention to target Israel and end its occupation of the Syrian Golan Heights.[26] Chief of Staff Eisenkot gained government approval for a shift in the Israeli strategy for intervention in Syria in January 2017 – a major turning point in the conflict with Iran and its allies – which facilitated a sharp expansion of the scope of attacks.[27]

On January 12, 2017, Israeli aircraft struck Mezzeh Airbase in rural Damascus. The strike reportedly caused a massive explosion, and was followed by an attack on an alleged Hezbollah weapons shipment near the capital on February 22. On March 17 Israel again struck under the pretext of targeting Hezbollah's weapons. The Syrian Arab Army claimed to have shot down an Israeli fighter and damaged another during this incident – a claim Israel denied.[28] Syrian S-200 long range air defence systems are thought to have been responsible for the alleged shootdown. The incident was followed by a strike on Damascus International Airport on April 27. On September 7 the Israeli Air Force bombed a target near the city of Masyaf in the Hama governate, which Israeli sources claimed was a chemical weapons site, killing at least two Syrian soldiers.[29] A further strike on a Hezbollah weapons depot near Damascus was reported on September 22.[30] On October 16, 2017, Israel struck Syrian S-200 defence systems near Damascus after they reportedly fired on Israeli reconnaissance planes flying over Lebanon.[31] Further strikes, reportedly against Syrian military facilities, were conducted on November 1 and December 2 and 7.

Israel conducted further airstrikes in February 2018, with Syria using its S-200 air defence systems to shoot down an Israeli F-16I fighter – the country's most modern class of fully operational[32] combat jet. Israel only confirmed the downing after independent footage was released showing the aircraft being neutralised. An Israeli F-15 was also reportedly damaged, but managed to return to base and made an emergency landing – one of several reported cases of Israeli jets suffering damage to Syrian air defences but not being shot down.[33] Israel retaliated with further strikes on Syrian air defences, and used long range air-to-surface missiles launched from beyond Syrian airspace to avoid having to engage Syrian defences from a close distance. Arguably more significantly than the F-16 shootdown, Iran's Shahed 171 radar evading reconnaissance drone made its combat debut in February, penetrating Israeli airspace and proving very difficult for Israeli defences to neutralise. The drone's performance made a strong impression on Israeli officials, and demonstrated Iran's ability to launch drone attacks on Israeli targets. Israel's Patriot missile batteries, the most advanced Western ground based anti-aircraft missile systems available, notably proved unable to neutralise the Iranian Shahed 171 and consequentially the drone had to eventually be neutralised at short range by an attack helicopter. Former head of Mossad Danny Yatom stated regarding the incident: "It was a sophisticated operation. The UAV was almost an exact replica of the U.S. drone that fell in their territory [RQ-170]. If it had exploded somewhere in Israel, it may not have been possible to identify it as an Iranian manufactured drone."[34] This was hardly the first time Iranian drones had tested Israeli defences, with a much less advanced non-stealthy Ayoub drone having penetrated airspace near Israel's nuclear complex at Dimona in 2012 and sent back live images of military exercises and bases before eventually being detected and shot down by an Israeli fighter.[35]

Iran made extensive use of drones in the Syrian theatre, and Iranian media reported in October 2018 that 700 drone strikes had been carried out against Islamic State targets on Syrian soil by that point in the war.[36] Hundreds of further strikes targeted other jihadist groups such as Al Nusra as well as IS positions in Iraq. The Quds Force gained extensive experience operating drones in combat – primarily the Shahed 129 which resembled and was roughly equivalent to the American Predator and the Chinese Wing Loong designs. As tensions with Israel further escalated, however, Iran introduced more sophisticated drones into the theatre. These had advanced radar-evading capabilities and had benefitted from technologies reverse engineered from the American RQ-170 stealth drone brought down over Iran in 2011.[37] The Saeqeh and Shahed 171, 181 and 191 designs used a similar airframe design closely based on the RQ-170, which the Iranians claimed had been improved with stronger and lighter materials and which analysts widely suspected Iran had developed with Chinese support.[38] The Shahed series were configured for precision strikes, and the Saeqeh for reconnaissance.

In September 2018, in response to an Islamic State terror attack in the Iranian city of Ahvaz which caused over 95 casualties,[39] Iran carried out a major strike on IS positions in Syria. The strike used both Zolfaqar and Qiam ballistic missiles and stealth drones armed with precision guided bombs.[40] The IS militants targeted had been based within three miles of U.S. positions in Syria, and the strike took American forces totally by surprise and was seen as a major show of force against the United States.[41] This not only demonstrated that Iran could seriously threaten U.S. forces with its stealth aircraft and missiles, but also highlighted how close Islamic State positions were to American forces – a peculiarity many analysts drew attention to since the U.S. had begun to occupy parts of Syria.[42] The implications of this strike for

Israeli security were also significant, insofar as the growing Quds Force presence in Syria was likely to be supported by a sizeable and highly sophisticated drone fleet and a wide array of missiles which could precisely engage targets across Israel if required.

Israel continued to escalate attacks in 2018, striking a military facility near Palmyra in March and attacking Tiyas Airbase in Homs – a major Iranian supply hub – on April 9. On May 6 a mysterious explosion killed eight members of the Syrian Air Force's 150th Air Defence Division, the unit responsible for downing the Israeli F-16 three months prior, with Israel subsequently blamed. On May 7 an Israeli airstrike reportedly neutralised depots and rocket launchers suspected of belonging to the Quds Force in Al Kiswah city, 13 kilometres from Damascus, killing nine people.[43] This was followed by four airstrikes on Quds Force positions before the end of the month, one of which reportedly struck an Iranian long ranged air defence system. Six further strikes were conducted over the next two months. In an apparent attempt to restore its image after the very public loss of an F-16I, the Israeli Air Force claimed to have deployed newly commissioned F-35 fighters for combat missions in May, which made it the first to ever use these aircraft in combat.[44] The deployment appeared to be much more for appearance's sake than anything else, however, with the aircraft still far from ready for high or medium intensity combat.[45] The jets were fitted with reflective lenses which prevented nearby Russian air defence systems from studying them, but which also totally nullified their stealth capabilities.[46]

The perceived danger from Iranian precision strike capabilities was only further exacerbated by an attack on the Abqaiq oil refinery and Khurais oil field in Saudi Arabia in September 2019, which was carried out by Iranian drones and cruise missiles deployed either by Yemeni Ansarullah Coalition insurgent forces or by Iranian units directly. The drones and missiles managed to evade Saudi Arabia's state-of-the-art air defences with little difficulty and strike with a very high degree of accuracy, which had significant implications for Israeli security. Defence systems in place included American Patriot and European Crotale and Skyguard batteries, none of which managed to neutralise a single drone or missile.[47] Furthermore, in April 2021 a missile launched from Syria into Israel evaded the country's multi-layered air defence network and struck near its Dimona nuclear facility. The strike came a few days after an Israeli cyber-attack on an Iranian nuclear facility, leading to widespread speculation that it may have been a warning shot using a short-range ballistic missile to deter further attacks on Iran's nuclear program. Israeli sources claimed that the strike was accidental and was not conducted by a ballistic missile but rather a Syrian surface to air missile which had gone far off course. Sources on both sides emphasized that the incident showed how fallible Israeli air defences could be and how vulnerable core targets in Israel really were even to relatively basic attacks.[48]

Israel suffered a series of incidents affecting several facilities of strategic importance in April and early May, which were widely speculated to have been attacks involving Iran or its affiliates in retaliation against Israeli attacks on Iranian assets in Syria, at sea and in Iran itself. These included an explosion at an Israeli rocket factory,[49] a major fire at an oil refinery in Haifa,[50] a reported attack on a Mossad safehouse in Iraq,[51] and a string of cyberattacks targeting Israeli firms – alongside the missile strike near Dimona. Iranian Major General Hossein Salami claimed in early May that these incidents were a sign that Israel's "national security bubble has burst," and underlined how vulnerable the country was.[52] The implications for Syrian security were significant, as a more vulnerable Israel could potentially be more easily deterred it from striking Syrian territory.

## Containment of Israel

Arguably the most significant event in the Israeli air campaign against Syria occurred in September 2018 when, following reports that a Russian Il-20 surveillance aircraft operating from Khmeimim Airbase had disappeared, it emerged that the aircraft had been shot down during an Israeli attack. According to the Russian Defence Ministry, Israel had provided only a minute's warning that an attack was taking place, when considerably longer warnings were usually given to prevent potential clashes.[i] Furthermore, Israel had warned that targets would be struck in northern Syria, but subsequently attacked targets in the west of the country near Russian military facilities. "The misleading information provided by the Israeli officer about the area of strikes did not allow the Russian Il-20 airplane to move timely to a safe area," the Defence Ministry concluded in an official statement.[53] Worse still, the Israeli fighter aircraft reportedly used the slow and bulky Il-20 as cover against Syrian air defences, leading to the Russian aircraft being destroyed by an S-200 battery.[54] Israel was subsequently seriously rebuked for its actions, which would have a long lasting effect on the Russo-Israeli relationship, with the Russian Defence Ministry quickly issuing the following statement: "We consider these provocative actions by Israel as hostile. Fifteen Russian military service members have died because of the irresponsible actions of the Israeli military. This is absolutely contrary to the spirit of the Russo-Israeli partnership."[55]

While Israel waged war against Hezbollah and Iran in Syria, Russia's stance was non-interference in a conflict between regional powers. This contrasted with its sterner defence of Iranian and Syrian interests in the face of threats from extra-regional actors – namely the Western powers. Russia reportedly jammed U.S. fighters approaching Iranian airspace,[56] provided Iran with assistance in tracking American F-35 stealth aircraft,[57] and was willing at least under Vladimir Putin's administrations to supply Iran with advanced weapons to counter potential Western attacks.[58] It provided no similar protection against Israeli threats, however. Where Russia provided significant protection for Syria against Western threats including preventing the creation of no-fly zones or safe zones on Syrian territory, stopping multiple Western attacks, and strongly rebuking attacks when they did take place, this was far from the case for Israeli strikes. Although Israel's

---

i    The Russian military curiously detected a missile launch from a French warship operating in the area coinciding with the incident – the target of which was never revealed. (Neumann, Scott, 'Russian Surveillance Plane Accidentally Shot Down By Syrian Forces, Moscow Says,' *NPR,* September 18, 2018.)

close alignment with the West made it difficult for the two states to cooperate closely, Moscow and Tel Aviv maintained a special relationship[ii] – with President Putin referring to Israel as a "Russian speaking country" due to its high population of Soviet migrants which resulted in close familial ties between the two populations.[59] Furthermore, Israel had refrained from adopting the West's hard line stance against Russia, refusing to vote with the vast majority of Western client states at the United Nations on the Crimean crisis,[60] and maintaining limited military cooperation with the former superpower.[61] Israel's UN voting pattern on Russia-related issues would shift away from this stance by the end of 2018.[62]

The Russian Defence Ministry issued a further statement five days later, more harshly condemning Israeli actions, stating that the Israeli Air Force's operations:

> either lacked professionalism or were an act of criminal negligence to say the least. Therefore, we believe that the blame for the tragedy with the Russian Ilyushin Il-20 aircraft lies entirely with the Israeli air forces and those who made the decision to carry out such actions… the Israeli jets created a direct threat to any passenger or transport aircraft that could have been there at that time and could have become victims of the adventurism of the Israeli military.

The ministry highlighted that it would take "steps everyone will notice" to improve the security of Russian forces in Syria in light of this.[63] Frants Klintsevich, a member of the Russian parliament's upper house's defence committee, warned that day that Russia had the option of escalating to totally deny Israel access to Syrian airspace, stating: "The essence and meaning

---

ii   This relationship notably allowed Russia to play a role in mediating between Syria and Israel in securing the release of Syrian spy Sidqi Al Maqt in January 2020 from an Israeli prison, which Israel agreed to, to help secure the release of Israeli traveller Naama Issachar, who was arrested in Russia for possession of illegal drugs. ('Israel releases Syrian spy, Golan ambulance attacker, in goodwill gesture,' *Times of Israel*, January 10, 2020.)

of our response is to completely eliminate the possibility of such incidents in the future. We, for example, have all the necessary resources to completely close the Syrian airspace for Israel, and this is only one of the options."[64]

There was an apparent rift between the Russian Defence Ministry and the civilian government regarding the kind of response favoured. The former advocated a hard line against Israel and issued the large majority of criticisms over the Il-20 incident, while the latter, mindful of the importance of the Russo-Israeli relationship, sought a more moderate response. Israeli Prime Minister Benjamin Netanyahu notably called President Putin within hours to express his condolences, and reportedly persuaded him not to take a hard line on the issue.[65] The tone of the conversation contrasted strongly with that between Russian Defence Minister Sergei Shoigu and his Israeli counterpart Avigdor Lieberman, in which Shoigu warned that "the Israeli side bears full responsibility" for the plane's downing and that Russia "reserves the right to retaliate."[66] On September 24, Minister Shoigu announced that S-300 surface to air missile systems would be delivered to the Syrian military within two weeks[67] – a move seen with much apprehension both in Israel and in the West[68] and met with threats from both to destroy the system after it was delivered.[69]

The S-300 variant delivered was not one of the more modern S-300V4 or VM variants, previously sold to Egypt and Venezuela respectively, but was the older S-300PMU-2 system which had served in the Russian military since 1997. Although less sophisticated, it still posed a very serious threat to Israeli aircraft at long ranges and was prized for its high mobility, its powerful sensors and electronic warfare countermeasures, and its ability to engage up to 32 targets simultaneously.[70] The S-300PMU-2 was designed to engage high end stealth aircraft such as American F-22 Raptors, and it was well positioned to deny Israel's fleet of much older non-stealthy F-15 and F-16s jets access to Syrian airspace.[71] As the S-300PMU-2 was an older design no longer in production, it was reportedly delivered second hand and free of charge from a Russian air defence unit which received S-400s to replace it.[72] Compared to the S-200, a design which dated back to the mid-1960s, the S-300PMU-2 represented a revolutionary boost to Syrian capabilities and threatened to put a major check on Israeli operations.

American analysts at *The Drive* had warned that with delivery of the S-300 "you have what amounts to a total change in the aerial equation over Syria" – one which "will greatly increase the complexity and danger" of Western operations and "will also make future attacks on Assad's military capabilities far more perilous." They highlighted that many Western military aircraft were effectively "defenceless against radar-guided surface-to-air missiles" such as those the S-300 employed.[73] Israeli aircraft initially gave Syrian airspace a wide berth, with Ksenia Svetlova from the Israeli parliament's defence committee confirming in early November that "the S-300 has changed the balance of power in the region" and that Israeli fighters had not entered Syrian airspace ever since its delivery.[74] It would soon emerge, however, that the S-300s delivered to Syria had remained under the control of Russian officers, meaning that when Israeli attacks did resume the SAA was not permitted to respond.[75] Conversely, however, so long as Russian officers were present at the Syrian S-300 sites, Israel would be unable to target them.

On January 20, 2019, Israeli aircraft struck military targets in Syria in response to an alleged Quds Force rocket attack near its borders.[76] While the S-300 was not activated, other Syrian air defences systems were ready to neutralise the threat. Although they lacked the range needed to strike far away Israeli fighters they could still shoot down the subsonic missiles being fired into Syria.[iii] From January 2019 reports consistently indicated that Syria was having unprecedented successes in blunting Israeli attacks using its air defences. Although not used in combat, the S-300 could potentially still help by providing targeting data to other lower-end systems such as the Pantsir-S1 and Tor-M1 which

---

iii The fact that Israeli aircraft were increasingly forced to attack Syria from outside its airspace notably limited offensive options, restricting them to using standoff missiles rather than short ranged guided bombs, with the latter being the only means to strike fortified targets such as bunkers and underground fortifications.

were fully under Syrian control.[77] Alongside providing the S-300, Russia also equipped the Syrian Air Defence Forces' command posts with automated control systems to better facilitate centralised control, which likely played a significant role in improving its defensive capabilities.[78]

On January 23, 2019, the Russian Foreign Ministry issued a lightly worded warning against further Israeli attacks on Syria, stating: "The practice of arbitrary strikes on the territory of a sovereign state – in this case, we are talking about Syria – should be ruled out... We should never allow Syria, which has suffered years of armed conflict, to be turned into an arena where geopolitical scores are settled."[79] It remained uncertain whether this unusual criticism of Israeli strikes was issued on the basis of intelligence that further attacks were planned, or whether it had any impact on Israeli behaviour, but by voicing disapproval Russia could potentially follow up with action should Israeli strikes on Syria escalate. By having maintained control of Syria's S-300PMU-2 system and holding back letting the SAA employ it in the face of Israeli strikes, Russia had kept a powerful card to play to block Israeli access to Syrian airspace without needing to directly intervene with its own assets. The deed could be done at any time by simply giving the Syrians control of their own system, without requirements to train new personnel or ship in new hardware. Russia's leverage was thus considerable, but it was unwilling to expend it at this time to protect the Quds Force, Hezbollah or the SAA from generally minor losses to sporadic air attacks. The threat of using this leverage may also have served to deter an increase in Israeli strikes at a time when Tel Aviv saw the situation on the ground fast deteriorating.

Israel continued low level strikes against Syria with what was still only a relatively loose check on its operations by Russia, although as the situation increasingly stabilised on the ground Russia was able to take a harder line and unprecedentedly would intercept several Israeli attacks using its own advanced fighter aircraft. Five such incidents reportedly took place on August 24,[80] September 10[81] and 19,[82] November 12,[83] and December 7, 2019,[84] all of which saw Russia's elite Su-35 fighters intercept

Israeli combat aircraft attempting to attack Syrian targets. An earlier incident in May 2018 had seen an interception carried out by Su-34 strike fighters over Lebanon.[85] Furthermore, in August 2019 Israeli media reported that a Russian Navy submarine was found to be conducting operations in Israeli waters, which was interpreted by several analysts as a show of force intended to send a strong signal regarding the Syrian conflict.[86] In May 2020 Russia supplied Syria with its first post-Soviet class of fighter jet, the MiG-29SMT, which was considered more capable in air-to-air combat than Israel's F-16s,[87] although it was acquired in very small numbers and was not intended for combat in anything short of a full scale war.[88] Syria had also commissioned Belarusian assistance to enhance its older MiG-29A fighters with new electronic warfare systems a few months prior.[89]

The MiG-29 and S-300 sales likely marked the beginning of a years' long effort to rebuild Syrian air defences, in parallel to the rebuilding of the post-insurgency economy, to allow it to eventually be able to protect its own airspace. The Il-20 incident would not be the last time Israel faced harsh Russian criticism for using large foreign aircraft as shields for its fighters, with the Israeli Air Force's repeated practice of using civilian air traffic at Damascus International Airport to prevent Syrian air defences from firing on them being harshly reprimanded.[90] Another notable extreme measure Israeli jets took to evade improving Syrian defences was to attack through Jordanian and Iraqi airspace using high endurance F-15 fighters, and copying the transponder codes of American F-15s which flew over the two countries frequently in order to disguise their presence.[91]

Despite the frequency of Israeli low-level airstrikes the expansion of Iranian military power on the ground continued, with Israeli attacks only slowing but not reversing this trend. As the *Jerusalem Post* noted in November 2020, the lack of decisive results from the attacks meant that they may need to continue indefinitely, and despite airstrikes having gone on for several years: "the reality in Syria is that Iran's role and its entrenchment have not diminished."[92] As Iran notably continued to expand its presence and those of its affiliates in Syria, Iranian drone capabilities emerged as another area of serious concern for Israel. In March 2019 a large formation of 50 Iranian drones conducted a major exercise dubbed 'Way to Jerusalem' – a clear show of force aimed at Israel – with most of the drones being advanced stealth designs. The exercise marked the first time so many Iranian drones simulated offensive operations simultaneously, and they did so at distances of more than 1,000 km away from one another while demonstrating their ability to use precision guided weapons.[93] The growing use of artificial intelligence in the Iranian drone program played a key role in facilitating such large and coordinated assaults,[94] and showed that Iran had increased its capability to threaten Israeli targets with precision strikes without needing to escalate to the use of ballistic missiles. With Iranian drones having previously not only penetrated but loitered at length in Israeli airspace, it could potentially carry out similar operations in future using unmanned strike aircraft to retaliate against Israeli attacks as its foothold in Syria grew more established.

On July 8, 2020, Iran's Defence Ministry finalised an agreement to upgrade Syria's air defences. This reportedly entailed deployment of indigenous weapons systems manned by Iranian personnel. Iran was thereby effectively placing its own forces on the frontlines against Israel, in a way the Soviet Union[95] and North Korea[96] had during the Cold War, but which post-Soviet Russia had proven unwilling to do. A report from the Washington Institute was among several which highlighted that this development threatened to disrupt operations by Damascus' adversaries over Syrian airspace,[97] and while less advanced than their latest Russian counterparts, Iranian long range air defence systems were still considered far more capable than those used by the Syrian Military.[98] The deployment also provided Iran with an opportunity to combat test its new sensor and missile technologies against Western and Israeli hardware.

The vast majority of Israeli airstrikes throughout the Syrian War notably engaged targets forming a triangle between the Lebanese border, Damascus, and the Israeli border – a relatively small part of Syrian territory which reflected Israel's primary interest in neutralising targets deployed near its territory.[99] Almost all Israeli strikes on Syria were illegal and unprovoked, but unlike those conducted by Western powers, the Israeli attacks had the pretext of protecting the country's immediate security interests near its borders. This a least made them somewhat more legitimate than offensive interventions from Western nations thousands of miles overseas. Where Western powers attempted to use humanitarian pretexts to justify attacks on Syria, and even an outright military occupation of northern Syria and appropriation and sale of its resources, Israel was generally more transparent regarding the nature of its objectives. The intensity of clashes between Israel and both Hezbollah and Iranian forces in Syria could best be described as a limited war which all sides knew, due to the sheer destructive capabilities of their arsenals, should not be escalated beyond the Syrian theatre. It was commonly referred to in Israel itself as the "campaign between wars" on this basis – reflecting a constant Israeli effort to degrade enemy capabilities which would improve the country's chances of winning an all-out war with the Axis of Resistance should it later occur.[100]

# Notes

1    Osborn, Andrew, 'Putin ally says Chechen spies infiltrate Islamic State in Syria,' *Reuters*, February 8, 2016.
     Walker, Shaun, 'Putin should unleash Chechen troops on Isis, says region's president,' *The Guardian,* October 2, 2015.

2    Afghanistan:
     Rashid, Ahmed, *Taliban: Militant Islam, Oil and Fundamentalism in Central Asia*, New Haven, CT, Yale University Press, 2001 (pp. 128–129).
     Cook, Robin, 'The struggle against terrorism cannot be won by military means,' *The Guardian*, June 8, 2005.
     'Al Qaeda's Origins and Links,' *BBC News*, July 20, 2004.
     Chechnya:
     'Putin accuses U.S. of directly supporting Chechen militants,' *Press TV*, April 26, 2015.
     'American political scientist: Western Intelligence used Azerbaijan to export terrorism into Russia,' *Panorama*, May 30, 2015.
     Congressional Record, Volume 151, Part 17, 109th Congress, 1st Session, October 7 to 26, 2005, U.S. Congress.

3    Tsurkov, Elizabeth, 'Inside Israel's Secret Program to Back Syrian Rebels,' *Foreign Policy,* September 6, 2018.

Gross, Judah Ari, 'IDF chief finally acknowledges that Israel supplied weapons to Syrian rebels,' *Times of Israel,* January 14, 2019.

Levi, Daneil J., 'Israel Just Admitted Arming anti-Assad Syrian Rebels. Big Mistake,' *Haaretz,* February 3, 2019.

Ravid, Barak, 'UN Reveals Israeli Links With Syrian Rebels,' *Haaretz,* April 10, 2018.

Tsurkov, Elizabeth, 'Israel's Deepening Involvement with Syria's Rebels,' *War on the Rocks,* February 14, 2018.

4    Phillips, Christopher, *The Battle For Syria: International Rivalry in the New Middle East,* New Haven, Yale University Press, 2016 (p. 164).

5    Smyth, Philip, 'How Iran Is Building Its Syrian Hezbollah,' *The Washington Institute,* March 8, 2016.

6    Smyth, Philip, 'Iran Is Outpacing Assad for Control of Syria's Shia Militias,' *The Washington Institute,* April 12, 2016.

7    Uskowi, Nader, *Temperature Rising: Iran's Revolutionary Guards and Wars in the Middle East,* Lanham, MD, Rowman & Littlefield, 2018 (p. 82).

8    Liebermann, Oren, 'Iran and Israel Draw Closer to War Than Ever,' *CNN,* May 1, 2018.

9    Mahanaimi, Uzi, 'Humbling Of The Supertroops Shatters Israeli Army Morale,' *The Sunday Times,* August 27, 2006.

Heller, Aron, 'Lebanon Offensive Criticised in Israel,' *Washington Post,* July 26, 2006.

Salem, Paul, 'The Aftereffects of the Israeli-Hizbollah War,' *Contemporary Arab Affairs,* vol. 1, no. 1, 2008 (pp. 15–24).

Matthews, Matt M., *We Were Caught Unprepared: The 2006 Hezbollah-Israeli War,* Fort Leavenworth, U.S. Army Combined Arms Center Combat Studies Institute Press, 2008.

10   Ari Gross, Judah, 'Ya'alon: I would prefer Islamic State to Iran in Syria,' *Times of Israel,* January 19, 2016.

11   Ibid.

12   Ari Gross, Judah, 'IDF chief finally acknowledges that Israel supplied weapons to Syrian rebels,' *Times of Israel,* January 14, 2019.

Tsurkov, Elizabeth, 'Inside Israel's Secret Program to Back Syrian Rebels,' *Foreign Policy,* September 6, 2018.

Levi, Daneil J., 'Israel Just Admitted Arming anti-Assad Syrian Rebels. Big Mistake,' *Haaretz,* February 3, 2019.

'UN Peacekeepers Observe IDF Interacting with Al Nusra in Golan,' *UN Tribune,* December 4, 2014.

13   Ari Gross, Judah, 'Ex-defense minister says IS "apologized" to Israel for November clash,' *Times of Israel,* April 24, 2017.

14   Khomeini, Ruhollah. *American plots against Iran* (Speech), Qum, November 5, 1979.

Farnaz Fassihi, 'The U.S. Is Still Iran's Great Satan,' *Wall Street Journal,* July 17, 2015.

'Netanyahu: For Iran's mullahs "Israel is the small Satan and American is the great Satan",' *Jerusalem Post,* September 1, 2015.

15   Katz, Muni and Pollak, Nadav, 'Hezbollah's Russian Military Education in Syria,' *Washington Institute,* December 24, 2015.

Zitun, Yoav, 'Top IDF Officer: Hezbollah Marked Our Artillery Guns,' *Ynet News*, August 7, 2013.

Blanford, Nicholas, 'The Battle for Qusayr: How the Syrian Regime and Hizb Allah Tipped the Balance,' *Combatting Terrorism Center at West Point*, vol. 6, issue 8, 2013.

16   Kershner, Isabel, 'Israel Watches Warily as Hezbollah Gains Battle Skills in Syria,' *New York Times*, March 10, 2014.

17   Ibid.

18   Ibid.

19   Filkins, Dexter, 'The Shadow Commander,' *The New Yorker*, September 23, 2013.

20   Casey, Nicholas, 'Two Israeli Soldiers Killed in Attack Claimed by Lebanon's Hezbollah,' *Wall Street Journal*, January 29, 2015.

21   'Israel admits its fire killed Spanish UN peacekeeper,' *BBC News*, April 7, 2015.

22   'Hezbollah commander Badreddine killed in Syria,' *BBC News*, May 13, 2015.

23   'Israel sees Assad winning Syria war, urges more U.S. involvement,' *Reuters*, October 3, 2017.

24   Stephens, Bret, 'The Man Who Humbled Qassim Suleimani,' *New York Times*, January 11, 2019.

25   Khatib, Dania Koleilat, *The Syrian Crisis: Effects on the Regional and International Relations*, Singapore, Springer, 2020 (p. 76).

26   Daoud, David, 'How Hezbollah Will Use Foreign Fighters to Conquer Lebanon,' *Haaretz*, April 27, 2018.

27   Stephens, Bret, 'The Man Who Humbled Qassim Suleimani,' *New York Times*, January 11, 2019.

28   Wang, Mingyan, 'Syria claims to have shot down Israeli plane after raids near Palmyra,' *CGTN*, March 17, 2017.

29   Winer, Stuart, 'Israeli jets said to hit chemical weapons, missile site in Syria,' *Times of Israel*, September 7, 2017.

30   'Israeli jets reportedly strike weapons depot outside Damascus,' *Times of Israel*, September 22, 2017.

31   'Israeli jets attack anti-aircraft battery in Syria,' *Al Jazeera*, October 16, 2017.

32   Grazier, Dan, 'Why the F-35 Isn't Ready for War,' *National Interest*, March 20, 2019.

33   Rogoway, Tyler, 'Flurry Of Aircraft Shoot-Downs And Counter-Strikes Erupt Across Israel And Syria,' *The Drive*, February 10, 2018.

Trevithick, Joseph, 'Syria Finally Gets Its S-300 SAM System, But It's A Token Capability At Best,' *The Drive*, October 2, 2018.

34   'Former Mossad chief: We must take the Iranian threats very seriously,' *Jerusalem Post*, April 15, 2018.

'Tehran's Stealth Drones; Full Implications of Iran's Acquisition of the U.S. RQ-170 in the Middle East and Beyond,' *Military Watch Magazine*, February 1, 2020.

35   'Hezbollah drone photographed secret IDF bases,' *Jerusalem Post*, October 14, 2012.

'The UAV lesson,' *Jerusalem Post,* October 13, 2012.

36   'Iran says it has carried out 700 drone attacks in Syria,' *i24 News,* October 16, 2018.

37   'Tehran's Stealth Drones; Full Implications of Iran's Acquisition of the U.S. RQ-170 in the Middle East and Beyond,' *Military Watch Magazine,* February 1, 2020.
'Iran builds attack drone similar to captured US model, local media say,' *The Guardian,* October 1, 2016.

38   'China's New Sharp Sword Attack Drone; An Unmanned Bomber in All But Name,' *Military Watch Magazine,* May 25, 2018.
'Tehran's Stealth Drones; Full Implications of Iran's Acquisition of the U.S. RQ-170 in the Middle East and Beyond,' *Military Watch Magazine,* February 1, 2020.

39   'Iran uses drones and missiles in cross border attack on enemies in Syria,' *Army Recognition,* October 4, 2018.
'Iran fires missiles at militants in Syria over Ahvaz attack,' *BBC News,* October 1, 2018.

40   Trevithick, Joseph, 'Iran Claims Their RQ-170-Shaped Drones And Missiles Hit Targets In Syria Near U.S. Forces,' *The Drive,* October 1, 2018.

41   Starr, Barbara and Feingold, Spencer and Bozorgmehr, Shirzad and Cullinane, Susannah, 'Iran missiles in Syria land "within three miles" of US troops,' *CNN,* October 1, 2018.

42   'ISIS given "breathing space" in parts of Syria under US-backed forces' control,' *RT,* August 18, 2018.
'"It's Interesting How Daesh and US Forces are so Close to Each Other" – Prof,' *Sputnik,* October 4, 2018.

43   Karam, Zeina, 'Syrian media report Israeli attack near capital Damascus,' *AP News,* May 9, 2018.

44   Ahronheim, Anna, 'IAF commander: Israel first to use F-35 jet in combat,' *Jerusalem Post,* May 22, 2018.

45   Grazier, Dan, 'Why the F-35 Isn't Ready for War,' *National Interest,* March 20, 2019.
Trevithick, Joseph, 'Today's F-35As Not Worth Including In High-End War Games According To Air Force General,' *The Drive,* April 12, 2021.
'Air Force General Warns F-35 Still Far From Ready For War: Problematic Jets Not Worth Including in War Plans,' *Military Watch Magazine,* April 15, 2021.

46   Cenciotti, David, 'Image Of Israeli F-35 Flying Off Beirut (With Radar Reflectors) As Well As More Details About The Adir's First Strikes Emerge,' *The Aviationist,* May 24, 2018.

47   Hellyer, Marcus and Millar, David and Ruser, Nathan, 'What the strike on Saudi Arabia's oil facilities teaches us,' *Australian Strategic Policy Institute,* September 18, 2019.
Frantzman, Seth J., 'Are air defense systems ready to confront drone swarms?,' *Defense News,* September 26, 2019.

48   'بازتاب سقوط موشک در نزدیکی «دیمونا»| آیا اسرائیل هم به سرنوشت سعودی‌ها گرفتار خواهد شد؟‹

[Reflecting on a rocket crash near Dimona: Will Israel also suffer the fate of the Saudis?], *Tasnim News,* April 22, 2021.

Frantzman, Seth J., 'Aiming at Dimona: Did the Syrian regime purposely target Israel?,' *Jerusalem Post,* April 22, 2020.

Babak Taghvaee on Twitter: 'Update: #IRGC Backed #Syrian #Hezbollah launched a ballistic missile (Probably Tashrin or Fateh-110) from North of #Syria at #ShimonPerez Nuclear site of #Israel at #Dimona. #Israel Air Defense Command fired a MIM-104D via Patriot PAC-2/GEM+ at the missile,' April 22, 2021.

'Iranian general appears to take responsibility for rocket attack targeting Israeli nuclear site,' *The New Arab,* April 22, 2021.

'فاتح ١١٠» أو «تشرين».. حادثة ديمونة «رسالة إيرانية» أم «سقوط عرضي»؟'

[Fateh 110 or Tishreen ... the Dimona incident, an "Iranian message" or an "accidental downfall"?], *Al Araby,* April 22, 2021.

'Israël: le "fatal" coup à "Fateh-110"...' [Israel: the "fatal" blow to "Fateh-110" ...], *Pars Today,* April 24, 2021.

49  Lovell, MariTi Blaise, 'Explosion at Israeli Rocket Factory Part of Deliberate, "Controlled" Trial, State Contractor Say,' *Sputnik,* April 21, 2021.

50  'Video: Oil Refinery on Northern Israeli City of Haifa Catches Fire – Reports,' *Sputnik,* April 30, 2021.

51  Artyukhina, Morgan, '"Unknown Resistance Forces" Attack Iraq Office of Israel's Mossad Spy Agency – Reports,' *Sputnik,* April 14, 2021.

52  'Israel's Security Bubble Burst; Be Ready for the Last Blow, Threatens IRGC Commander,' *International Business Times,* May 8, 2021.

53  'Russian MoD: Israel Violated Agreement With Russia to Prevent Incidents in Syria,' *Sputnik,* September 23, 2018.

54  'Russian MoD: S-400 data shows Israeli F-16 hid behind Russian Il-20 to avoid Syrian missile,' *RT,* September 24, 2018.

55  'First Shot of an Israeli-Russian Conflict? Moscow Threatens Response After Downing of Il-20 Surveillance Plane Over Syria,' *Military Watch Magazine,* September 18, 2018.

'Russia Blames Israel After Military Plane Shot Down Off Syria,' *BBC News,* September 18, 2018.

56  Axe, Davd, 'Surprise! When U.S. Fighters Approach Iran, Russia Jams Their Signal,' *National Interest,* December 30, 2019.

57  Suciu, Percy, 'Is Russia Helping Iran Track F-35 Stealth Fighters?,' *National Interest,* August 29, 2020.

58  Roblin, Sebastien, 'Iran Has Lots of Ways to Kill An Air Force (Thanks to Russia and China),' *National Interest,* October 5, 2019.

'Russian ambassador says "no problem" selling S-400 to Iran when arms ban expires,' *Times of Israel,* October 4, 2020.

'Iran gets first missile shipment for S-300 system,' *Times of Israel,* July 18, 2016.

59  'Putin says he considers Israel a Russian-speaking country,' *Times of Israel,* September 19, 2019.

60  Charbonneau, Louis and Donath, Mirjam, 'U.N. General Assembly declares Crimea secession vote invalid,' *Reuters,* March 27, 2014.

61  'Russia Deploys Forpost Reconnaissance Drones In Crimea,' *Defense World,* August 16, 2019.

62  Keinon, Herb, 'In rare move, Israel casts vote against Russia at U.N.,' *Jerusalem Post,* December 18, 2018.

63  'Russian MoD: Israel Violated Agreement With Russia to Prevent Incidents in Syria,' *Sputnik,* September 23, 2018.

64  'Russia Capable of Denying Israel Access to Syrian Airspace – Senior Russian MP,' *Sputnik,* September 23, 2018.

65  Isachenkov, Vladimir, 'Putin seeks to defuse downing of Russian plane off Syria,' *AP News,* September 19, 2018.

66  Ibid.

67  'Syria Will Deploy the S-300 Within Two Weeks; Russian Defence Ministry Takes Response to Israeli Actions Into Its Own Hands,' *Military Watch Magazine,* September 24, 2018.

68  '"Who Will Control Them?" US "Very Concerned" About S-300s in Syria – Envoy,' *Sputnik,* November 7, 2018.
    Mason, Jeff, 'Russia missile sale to Syria is "significant escalation"– U.S.' Bolton,' *Reuters,* September 24, 2018.

69  Winer, Stuart, 'Minister: Israel might destroy Syrian S-300s, even if manned by Russians,' *Times of Israel,* November 6, 2018.
    'Israel to destroy Syria's S-300 defence system, US general says,' *Middle East Monitor,* October 18, 2018.
    'IDF General Vows to "Remove Threat" of Syrian S-300s if Used on Israeli Jets,' *Sputnik,* April 19, 2019.
    'US May Scramble F-22 Fighters in Response to S-300 Missiles in Syria – Reports,' *Sputnik,* October 4, 2018.

70  'S-300PMU-2 vs. S-400; How Capable is Syria's New Air Defence Platform Compared to the Russian Military's Own?,' *Military Watch Magazine,* September 29, 2018.

71  'S-300s in Syria Will Be Able to "See" America's 5th-Gen Jets,' *Sputnik,* October 8, 2018.

72  'В Кремле не стали комментировать условия поставки С-300 Сирии' [The Kremlin did not comment on the terms of delivery of the S-300 Syria], *TASS,* October 9, 2018.

73  Rogoway, Tyler, 'America's Tomahawk Missile Attack on Syria's Shayrat Air Base Was a Sham,' *The Drive,* April 7, 2017.

74  'Effective Deterrence? Israeli Jets Give Syrian Targets a Wide Berth Following S-300 Delivery,' *Military Watch Magazine,* November 7, 2018.

75  Nadimi, Farzin, 'Iran-Syria Air Defense Pact Could Disrupt Allied Operations,' *Washington Institute,* July 24, 2020.

76  Kershner, Isabel, 'Israel Confirms Another Attack on Iranian Targets in Syria,' *New York Times,* January 20, 2018.

77  'Syrian Defences Intercept Israeli Missile Strike on Damascus; Balance of Power in the Sky Continues to Shift,' *Military Watch Magazine,* January 21, 2019.

78  'Russia to Supply S-300 Air Defense System, Command Posts to Syria,' *Defense World,* September 24, 2018.

79   Keinon, Herb and Hoffman, Gil, 'Russia to Israel: Stop "arbitrary" attacks in Syria,' *Jerusalem Post*, January 23, 2019.

80   Leone Dario, 'Report: Russian Su-35s Allegedly Forced Israeli Aircraft Out of Syrian Airspace,' *National Interest*, August 29, 2019.

81   'Russian Su-35s Intercept Israeli Warplanes Over Syria: Media reports,' *Defense World*, September 13, 2019.

82   'Российские истребители заблокировали новую атаку Израиля на Сирию' [Russian fighters block new Israeli attack on Syria], *Avia Pro*, September 20, 2011.

83   'Российские Су-35 вновь перехватили израильские самолёты над Сирией' [Russian Su-35s again intercepted Israeli planes over Syria], *Avia Pro*, November 13, 2011.

84   'Su-35 in Action: Russian Air Force's Elite Intercept Israeli Jets Over Syria,' *Military Watch Magazine*, December 10, 2019.

85   'In rare face-off, Russian jets reportedly intercept Israeli planes over Lebanon,' *Times of Israel*, May 28, 2018.

86   Blumenthal, Itai, 'Russian submarine spotted in Israeli territorial waters,' *Ynet News*, November 11, 2019.

87   Hughes, David, 'Luftwaffe Mig Pilots Effective with Archer,' *Aviation Week and Space Technology*, December 23–20, 1996 (p. 83).
'How Capable is Syria's MiG-29 Fighter Fleet? Upgrades and Newly Delivered Airframes Improve Air Defences,' *Military Watch Magazine*, February 24, 2021.
'Syria Finally Receives Modern Fighter Jets From Russia: MiG-29SMTs to Bolster Damascus,' *Military Watch Magazine*, June 1, 2020.
Fitchett, Joseph, 'German Pilots Test Former Foes' Best : Aboard MiG-29, a Glimpse Into the Other Side,' *New York Times*, August 22, 1997.

88   'Syria Finally Receives Modern Fighter Jets From Russia: MiG-29SMTs to Bolster Damascus,' *Military Watch Magazine*, June 1, 2020.

89   'Фотофакт: Белоруссия оснастила сирийские МиГ-29 мощными системами РЭБ' [Belarus has equipped the Syrian MiG-29 with powerful electronic warfare systems], *Avia Pro*, August 23, 2019.

90   'Russia Slams Israel's Use of Civilian Airliner as Cover for Strikes on Syria,' *Military Watch Magazine*, February 7, 2020.
Cunningham, Erin, 'Israeli airstrikes near Syria's capital endangered civilian airliners, Russia says,' *Washington Post*, December 26, 2018.

91   'Israel's F-15I Strike Fighters Mimic U.S. Jets, Use Complex Manoeuvres to Target Blind Spot in Syrian Air Defences,' *Military Watch Magazine*, May 12, 2018.
Trevithick, Joseph, 'Let's Talk About This Rumor That Israeli F-15s Mimicked US Jets To Strike At Iran In Syria,' *The Drive*, May 1, 2018.

92   Frantzmann, Seth J., 'Pompeo says Iran isolated but Israel's Syria airstrikes show otherwise,' *Jerusalem Post*, November 19, 2020.

93   Frantzman, Seth J., '50 Iranian drones conduct massive "way to Jerusalem" exercise – report,' *Jerusalem Post*, March 14, 2019.

94   Rubin, Michael, 'Iran's Military Is Making Strides Into Twenty-First Century Technology,' *National Interest*, August 8, 2019.

95  Popov, V. I., 'Desantnye korabli osvaivayut Sredizemnoye more' [Landing ships are mastering the Mediterranean Sea], *Taifun,* February 2002 (p. 45).

Gordon, Yefim, *MiG-25 "Foxbat" and MiG-31 "Foxhound": Russia's Defensive Front Line,* Leciester, Aeropax, 1997 (pp. 46–51).

Ginor, Isabella and Remez, Gideon, *Foxbats over Dimona: The Soviets' Nuclear Gamble in the Six-Day War,* New Haven, Yale University Press, 2007 (p. 214).

Aderet, Ofer, 'The Secret Israel-Soviet Union War Nobody Knew About,' *Haaretz,* January 11, 2020.

96  El-Shazly, Saad, *The Crossing of the Suez,* American Mideast Research, 2003 (p. 81–83).

Berger, Andrea, *Target Markets, North Korea's Military Customers in the Sanctions Era,* Abingdon, Routledge, 2017 (pp. 64–65).

Leone, Dario, 'An unknown story from the Yom Kippur war: Israeli F-4s vs North Korean MiG-21s,' *The Aviationist,* June 24, 2013.

Bechtol, Bruce and Maxwell, David, 'North Korean Military Proliferation in the Middle East and Africa: A Book Launch,' Presentation at the Korea Economic Institute of America, September 25, 2018.

McCarthy, David, *The Sword of David: The Israeli Air Force at War,* New York, Skyhorse, 2014 (p. 9).

97  Nadimi, Farzin, 'Iran-Syria Air Defense Pact Could Disrupt Allied Operation,' *Washington Institute,* July 24, 2020.

98  'Could Iran's Pledge to Reinforce Syria's Air Defences Be a Game Changer? Bavar-373 and Khordad 15 May Soon Guard Damascus,' *Military Watch Magazine,* July 14, 2020.

99  Jones, Seth G. and Harrington, Nicholas and Bermudez Jr., Joseph S., 'Dangerous Liaisons: Russian Cooperation with Iran in Syria,' *Center for Strategic and International Studies,* July 16, 2019.

100 Stephens, Bret, 'The Man Who Humbled Qassim Suleimani,' *New York Times,* January 11, 2019.

Melman, Yossi, 'Why Syria Isn't Firing Its S-300 Missiles at Israeli Jets,' *Haaretz,* May 15, 2020.

# INDEX